THE HOME RULE CRISIS

1912-14

Edited by
Gabriel Doherty

MERCIER PRESS

IRISH PUBLISHER – IRISH STORY

In memory of my parents
Seán Doherty 1931–85 and
Lena Doherty (née Kenny) 1929–2014

MERCIER PRESS

Cork

www.mercierpress.ie

© The individual contributors, 2014

ISBN: 978 1 78117 245 2

10 9 8 7 6 5 4 3 2 1

A CIP record for this title is available from the British Library

Printed and bound in the EU.

Contents

Cork studies in the Irish revolution

This is the first of a series of books that will appear over the coming decade. It contains, as will future volumes, the selected proceedings of conferences organised within University College Cork on the subject of the major events and developments that marked the 'revolutionary decade' in modern Irish history, 1912–23. Each volume will bring together young, up-and-coming scholars, senior figures within the Irish historical profession, and individuals outside that profession with valued perspectives on the period, with a view to conveying to the broader public the most up-to-date research on the event, events or theme covered by the volume.

The second volume in the series, on the 1913 Dublin Lockout and the more general cause of labour during the revolutionary decade, is scheduled to appear next, with the third, on Ireland and the First World War, to follow shortly thereafter. Further volumes – including (amongst others topics) examinations of the 1916 Rising, the international dimensions to the revolutionary decade, the War of Independence, partition and the Irish Civil War – will follow at approximately yearly intervals.

Acknowledgements

The editor wishes to thank the following individuals for their assistance either in the preparations for the original conference in University College Cork, or in the production of this volume:

University College Cork: President Michael Murphy, Vice-President & Registrar Paul Giller, Maria Carroll, Dara O'Shea, Louise Tobin, Ruth McDonnell, Sonya Kiely, the General Service operatives, Professor Caroline Fennell, Anne Marie Cooney, Charlotte Holland, Deirdre O'Sullivan, Geraldine McAllister, Maeve Barry, Sheila Cunneen, Dr Donal Ó Drisceoil, Dr John Borgonovo and Dr Andy Bielenberg.

Mercier Press: Mary Feehan, Sharon O'Donovan, Niamh Hatton, Patrick Dunphy, Sarah O'Flaherty and Wendy Logue.

Department of the Taoiseach: Jerry Kelleher.

Department of Foreign Affairs and Trade: Jennifer Whelan.

Department of Arts, Heritage and the Gaeltacht: John Kennedy, Sabina O'Donnell and Stephen Brophy.

The original conference was organised with the support of a grant from the Reconciliation/Anti-sectarianism fund of the Department of Foreign Affairs and Trade, and this volume has been produced with the support of a grant from the Department of Arts, Heritage and the Gaeltacht. The editor wishes to express his thanks to the ministers in question.

List of Contributors

JONATHAN BARDON was born and educated in Dublin but has spent almost all of his adult life in Belfast, retiring from Queen's University in 2008. His most recent book is *The Plantation of Ulster* (2011). His other publications include: *Belfast: an illustrated history* (1982); *Dublin: a thousand years of Wood Quay* (1984); *A History of Ulster* (1992, updated 2001); and *A History of Ireland in 250 Episodes* (2008). He has written historical documentaries for Channel 4 and the BBC, including 48 twenty-minute and 360 five-minute dramatised programmes on the history of Ireland for BBC Radio Ulster.

TOM BARTLETT is professor of Irish history at the University of Aberdeen. He formerly worked at University College Dublin where he was professor of modern Irish history, and in the National University of Ireland, Galway. His most recent publication is *Ireland: a history* (Cambridge, 2010).

EUGENIO BIAGINI is an alumnus of the Scuola Normale Superiore di Pisa and is currently professor of modern and contemporary history at the University of Cambridge and a college fellow of Sidney Sussex College. He first came to Sidney in 1985–6 as a visiting scholar, before becoming a junior research fellow at Churchill College, Cambridge, in 1987. Having spent two years in the Department of History of Newcastle University, he became an assistant professor of modern British history at Princeton. He came back to Cambridge, to Robinson College, in 1996, becoming a university lecturer in 1998, a reader in 2000 and a professor in 2011. He returned to Sidney in 2008. He has written on Gladstonian liberalism, the Italian Risorgimento and anti-fascism in the 1940s. His current research interests include various aspects of Irish and British history since the 1910s, with particular reference to democracy, civil rights and religious minorities.

TIM BOWMAN was born and raised in Bangor, County Down. He took his first degree from Queen's University, Belfast in 1995 and completed his PhD in 1999, in the now sadly defunct Department of History at the University of Luton (now Bedfordshire) under the supervision of Professor Ian F. W. Beckett. He held lecturing posts at Queen's University, Belfast, the University of Durham and King's College London (based at the Joint Services Command and Staff College) before going to Kent in 2005. To date his research has considered aspects of the British Army in the Great War and the Ulster Volunteer Force of 1910–22. He is currently completing a co-authored book (with Professor Mark Connelly) concerning the Edwardian British Army and will then turn his attention to a co-authored work (with Professors Ian Beckett and Mark Connelly) concerning the British Army in the Great War. His next major research project will concern the Irish soldier in the British Army c. 1793–1968.

KURT BULLOCK is an associate professor of English at Grand Valley State University, an institution of 25,000 students located in south-west Michigan. He teaches contemporary literature and theory, including undergraduate and graduate courses on Irish literature. His articles have appeared in *New Hibernia Review* and *American Drama*, among other journals.

IAN CAWOOD is head of history at Newman University College in Birmingham. He leads Newman's undergraduate modules on modern British history as well as a fieldwork module focusing on the English cathedral. His research interests include the identity, culture and political structure of Liberal Unionism, 1886–1912, and regional history, including (but not exclusively) that of the English West Midlands. He is the author of *The Liberal Unionist Party: a history* (Ibtauris, 2012).

DOMINICK CHILCOTT went to school at St Joseph's College, Ipswich (De La Salle brothers), spent a year in the Royal Navy as a midshipman, and read philosophy and theology in Oxford University. He is a career diplomat who joined the Foreign and Commonwealth Office thirty years ago. He has served as high commissioner to Sri Lanka and Maldives (2006–7), deputy ambassador to the United States (2008–11), ambassador to Iran (for six weeks only in late 2011 – the posting was ended by the attack on the embassy), and is now ambassador to Ireland. In addition to those postings, Dominick has served in Ankara (1985–8), Lisbon (1993–5) and at the UK's mission to the European Union in Brussels (1998–2002). Between overseas assignments, he has worked in the Foreign and Commonwealth Office in London on European, African and Middle Eastern affairs. He has been a private secretary to two foreign secretaries, Sir Malcolm Rifkind and the late Robin Cook. He was director of the Iran Policy Unit in 2003 and director for bilateral relations with European countries from 2003 to 2006.

PAULINE COLLOMBIER-LAKEMAN was awarded her PhD on the topic of *Le discours des leaders du nationalisme constitutionnel irlandais sur l'autonomie de l'Irlande: utopies politiques et mythes identitaires* from the Université Paris 3 – Sorbonne Nouvelle in 2007. Her current research work is focused on the relationship between Ireland and the British Empire. She has taught nineteenth- and twentieth-century history of the British Isles as well as English language at the following universities: Paris 3, Le Mans, Nantes and lately Strasbourg, where she was appointed *maître de conférences* (lecturer) in 2009. Recent publications include 'Ireland and the empire: the ambivalence of Irish constitutional nationalism', *Radical History Review*, no. 104 (2009), pp. 57–76.

ERICA S. DOHERTY completed her PhD, on the subject of 'T.P. O'Connor and the Irish Parliamentary Party, 1912–24', at Queen's University Belfast, and graduated in 2013.

GABRIEL DOHERTY is a college lecturer in modern Irish history in the School of History, University College Cork.

JAMES DOHERTY is a second-year PhD student at the University of Southampton. The title of his thesis is 'The Liberals and the Irish Parliamentary Party, 1910–14'.

LAURENCE KIRKPATRICK is Professor of Church History in the Institute of Theology at Queen's University, Belfast. His specialist research covers several areas of church history, ranging from the Patristic era to the present century. He has conducted field research in China and India relating to Irish Presbyterian missions, in Manchuria and Gujarat respectively. He has also researched nineteenth-century Presbyterian activity in Connacht and First World War battlefields. His publications include *Presbyterians in Ireland* (Booklink, 2006) and *Made in China – but not as you know it* (Manleys, 2008), and he was a co-editor of *John Calvin: reflections of a reformer* (Union, 2009). He has contributed to numerous television documentaries and was historical consultant to the acclaimed 'An independent people', the BBC Northern Ireland series on Irish Presbyterianism first broadcast in 2013.

MARTIN MANSERGH spent seven years in the Departments of Foreign Affairs and the Taoiseach before resigning in 1981 to take up the position of political and Northern Ireland advisor to the then leader of Fianna Fáil, Charles Haughey (a position he subsequently held under Albert Reynolds and Bertie Ahern). The son of prominent historian Nicholas Mansergh, he is a distinguished historian in his own right, having published on a wide variety of topics relating, in particular, to modern Irish history. He is currently a member of the Government's Advisory Group on Commemorations.

CONOR MULVAGH has recently completed a PhD entitled 'Sit, act, and vote: the political evolution of the Irish Parliamentary Party at Westminster, 1900–1918' under the supervision of Professors Diarmaid Ferriter and Michael Laffan. He completed an MPhil in modern Irish history (Trinity College Dublin) in 2008, where his thesis considered the interactions between John Redmond and the Roman Catholic hierarchy. He currently lectures on Northern Nationalism (1920–1998) and the 1916 Rising at University College Dublin. His research interests include constitutional nationalism, the Irish Volunteers, the Ulster crisis and partition, and the organisation of political parties.

DAITHÍ Ó CORRÁIN is a lecturer in history at St Patrick's College, Drumcondra (a college of Dublin City University). He has undertaken extensive research in the following areas: Irish political violence; the Irish revolution, 1912–23; north–south relations; the Northern Ireland troubles; church–state relations; Ireland in the 1950s and 1960s; and ecumenism. He is the author of *Rendering to God and Caesar: the Irish churches and the two states in Ireland, 1949–73* (Manchester, 2006) and co-author (with Eunan O'Halpin) of *The Dead of the Irish Revolution, 1916–21*, which will be published by Yale University Press. He is editor, with Professor Marian Lyons (National University of Ireland, Maynooth), of the 'Irish Revolution, 1912–23' series, published by Four Courts Press. The first volume, on Sligo, was published in November 2012. He is currently working on a history of the Irish Volunteers from 1913 to 1918.

JOHN O'DONOVAN completed his master's thesis at University College Cork on 'William O'Brien and the United Irish League in Cork' in 2012. His major research interests include Cork 1890–1912, the life and career of D. D. Sheehan, the United Irish League, the All-for-Ireland League and Irish nationalism 1890–1922. He has published articles in *Saothar: Journal of the Irish Labour History Society* and the *Journal of the Cork Historical and Archaeological Society*, as well as contributing a chapter to Brian Casey (ed.), *Defying the Law of the Land: Agrarian Radicals in Irish History* (Dublin, 2013). His current project is a study of the 'Baton Convention' of February 1909.

ANDREW SCHOLES studied at Queen's University, Belfast, completing a BA in history and theology in 2003 and an MA in Irish history in 2004. His research interests are focused on late nineteenth- and twentieth-century British and Irish political and religious history. He is the author of *The Church of Ireland and the Third Home Rule Bill* (Dublin, 2009).

MATTHEW SCHOWNIR is a graduate student of Purdue University, Lafayette, Indiana, USA.

Introduction

The crisis that followed the introduction of the third Home Rule bill at Westminster on 11 April 1912 was a defining one in both British and Irish history. For decades, however, it has been, at best, on the periphery of the collective memory of the events of the early twentieth century of both peoples. The reasons for this are not hard to find. In Britain the cataclysm of the First World War tended to eclipse the other seminal events that were occurring at that time – including the demand for the extension of suffrage to women, the industrial unrest of the pre-war period and the post-war rise of the Labour Party at the expense of the Liberals – before, in turn, being virtually erased from popular remembrance and being replaced by the apparently 'good war' of 1939–45. In Ireland most historically minded citizens found the 1916 Rising, the subsequent rise of republicanism and the collapse of the Home Rule cause in the 1918 general election, the War of Independence, partition, Treaty split and Civil War more than enough to digest, and by degrees the events of 1912–14 ebbed to a point where, for most people, they reposed in obscurity, if not entirely in peace.

If there is a theme running throughout the diverse collection of essays in this volume, it is that this collective amnesia was unfortunate (for many reasons), is to be regretted and, where possible, should be corrected – for what happened in these islands between 1912 and 1914 was a series of political seismic shocks that will forever register high on the Irish and British historical Richter scales. The almost daily confluence of dramatic developments experienced during these years simply has not happened very often over the centuries, and if, in this case, what was seldom may not have been entirely wonderful, it was certainly important – *very* important.

It was in recognition of this significance that the School of History,

University College Cork, as part of its broader programme of events designed to mark the revolutionary decade in modern Irish history, convened a major public conference in the university in October 2012. Over the two days of the event approximately 200 academics and members of the public heard and discussed, in formal session and in informal discussions, manifold aspects of the crisis over the Home Rule bill. At the end of the programme the overwhelming consensus among all participants – speakers and audience members alike – was that the proceedings should be published. To that end selected participants in the symposium were given an opportunity, on the basis of the discussions at the conference, to refine their ideas before submission of their final texts. The resulting volume is one that contains a multiplicity of views on the third Home Rule crisis, some of them, as one would expect, at odds with each other. There is no single 'line' or interpretation evident here, no over-arching 'meta-narrative', save, perhaps, a refusal to be unduly influenced by the subsequent development of the 'Irish' and 'Ulster' questions – matters to which the attention of future conferences and volumes in the series will be directed. In the meantime, I trust that the reader shall have as much pleasure in reading the various papers as I have had in collating and editing them.

Gabriel Doherty
School of History
University College Cork

The 1912 Home Rule bill: then and now

Dominick Chilcott

I applaud the vision of the School of History, University College Cork, in organising this conference. It seems exactly right, for reasons on which I intend to elaborate further, that the events that form its theme should be held up to the light of objective, modern scholarship and re-evaluated. The Minister of Justice, Equality and Defence, Alan Shatter, put it very well in his statement to the Dáil, earlier this year, announcing the pardon for Irish soldiers who had deserted their posts in order to join the Allies to fight against Nazi Germany in the Second World War. Mr Shatter said that in the time since the outbreak of the Second World War 'our understanding of history has matured. We can re-evaluate actions taken long ago, free from the constraints that bound those directly involved and without questioning or revisiting their motivations. It is time for understanding and forgiveness.'

Before going any further, I should offer a health warning and make a plea. At the de la Salle boarding school in Ipswich, where I was educated, I had to choose, at age fourteen, which subjects to study for 'O' level, the equivalent of the Irish junior certificate. For some

Byzantine timetabling reason, we faced a straight choice between music and history. I chose music. I am confident, therefore, that, by a long distance, I must be the least qualified of all the speakers at this conference. So it is with an entirely appropriate sense of humility that I deliver this address to the cream of Irish, British and international scholars of this tumultuous period in British and Irish history.

I make one plea to this audience. Contested history is a subject best left to historians; governments enter the territory at their peril. There are many examples where modern interpretations of historic events by governments have caused tension in international affairs. Perhaps one of the best-known recent cases was the law passed by the French parliament in January 2012 making it a crime publicly to deny that the killings of Armenians in the Ottoman Empire in 1915 constituted genocide, an action that provoked an angry response from Ankara. I obviously want to avoid prompting that sort of controversy. So to be clear, where I touch on the events of 100 years ago, these are my personal reflections. I am entirely responsible for their accuracy or otherwise. They are not the policy positions of the British government. And someone who stopped studying history when he was fourteen is delivering them. So be gentle with me.

The title of this speech is 'The 1912 Home Rule bill: then and now'. The 'now' is significant. The ambassador's job is to promote his country's interests in his host country. Happily, relations between Ireland and Britain have never been stronger or more settled than now. We both have governments committed to accentuating the positive in our relations. The 'joint statement' agreed by the Taoiseach and the Prime Minister in March sets out a new narrative for our relations, one that is no longer dominated by Northern Ireland but focuses more on promoting jobs and economic growth and working together in the European Union and in the wider world. We both recognise the very high value our economies have for each other. The United Kingdom is Ireland's biggest trading partner. Ireland is the UK's fifth biggest export market. When one of us is in difficulty, it affects the other. When one of us is growing fast, it helps to promote growth in the other. We are increasingly interdependent. It has never been less true that England's or, more correctly, Britain's difficulty is Ireland's opportunity. As two very open economies, we sink or swim together.

The greatly improved state of affairs between our two countries is due to a number of factors. Firstly, ever since our entry into the European Economic Community in 1973, British and Irish ministers and officials have been cooperating and building alliances on European issues. We often have a very similar approach to European Union business. Secondly, the successful design and implementation of the peace process in Northern Ireland saw our two governments sustaining an unprecedented level of cooperation at the highest level over a number of years as we worked towards a common goal. And thirdly, Queen Elizabeth's visit to Ireland last year removed any lingering inhibitions that the British or Irish people might have felt about expressing our regard and indeed affection for each other. A very important stage in that historic visit, of course, took place here in Cork. None of us will quickly forget the sight of the Queen joshing with the stallholders in the English Market or enjoying a walkabout with the people of the city.

Why is this relevant? Both governments and the vast majority of our two peoples want to strengthen our bilateral cooperation since it is so clearly to our mutual benefit. But there remains a very small minority who feel differently. They may wish to exploit the decade of centenaries for their own nefarious purposes. We mustn't allow them to wind the clock back. One of the best ways of preventing this is for both governments and for scholars and historians from our two countries and from other parts of the world to come together in a spirit of transparency and truth seeking to commemorate the past. We should make this as inclusive an endeavour as we can. We are not trying to hide from the past or cover it up – on the contrary.

We know that some of it will be uncomfortable. And we recognise how important an understanding and knowledge of the past is to our separate senses of national identity.

In her speech at Dublin Castle, the Queen said we should 'bow to the past but not be bound by it'. Those words carried extra force as, earlier in the day, she had indeed bowed her head at the Garden of Remembrance as she laid a wreath in memory of those who gave their lives in the cause of Irish freedom. And as President McAleese said during the Queen's visit: 'We cannot change the past. But we have chosen to change the future.' The British government is working closely with the Northern Ireland Executive, the Irish government and others to commemorate the different anniversaries in a way that promotes reconciliation and healing. Events like this conference are an opportunity to come together in a spirit of mutual respect and in a manner that emphasises the importance of forbearance and conciliation.

The decade of centenary commemorations has had an encouraging start. The First Minister of Northern Ireland, Peter Robinson, gave a ground-breaking lecture on Carson and unionism in Dublin earlier in the year. The then-British Minister of State in the Northern Ireland Office, Hugo Swire, delivered the John Redmond lecture at Waterford in April. A small exhibition, commemorating the third Home Rule bill, opened in Westminster in March and has travelled to Dublin and Belfast since. The big parade on the anniversary of the Ulster Covenant passed off peacefully and in something of a carnival atmosphere.

Despite my disclaimer earlier on, I would like to offer some thoughts on the third Home Rule bill and its aftermath. It's hard to read about those times without coming away with a strong admiration for John Redmond. There is no doubting his parliamentary talents. The deal he struck with Asquith, whereby the Irish Party supported the Liberal government's Parliament Act, which restricted the power of the House of Lords, in exchange for commitments on Home Rule, was the game-changer. The methods he used to pursue his ambition of Home Rule for a united Ireland commend him highly. He eschewed violence and revolution. He was a moderating influence as the leader of the Irish Volunteers. His constitutionalist and parliamentary approach achieved a lot. He not only exploited an opportunity in British politics to get the third Home Rule bill introduced to parliament, but he navigated it onto the statute book a month after the start of the First World War.

Another reason for warming to Redmond was the position he took at the outset of the First World War. He realised that this was not a war of two morally equivalent parties, as some have presented it. There was an aggressor and at least one neutral victim – a small Catholic country, Belgium. It was the violation of Belgium's neutrality, of course, that triggered Britain's entry into the war. The expectation was that, like previous European wars, this war would be relatively short. The fighting in the Franco-Prussian war of 1870–1 had lasted only six months. The industrial-scale slaughter of the First World War that would last more than four years and take the lives of a million men in the British armed forces, including over 40,000 Irishmen, could not have been foreseen in August 1914. So I'm with the former Taoiseach, John Bruton, in believing that Redmond's call for Irishmen to join the army in September 1914 should be judged by what he was trying to achieve at the time. His aim was to persuade Ulster unionists voluntarily to come in under a Home Rule government in Dublin. His goal was 'unity by consent'. He hoped that the experience of fighting shoulder to shoulder would bind together Ulster unionists and Irish nationalists.

It didn't work, as we know. The war was far longer and bloodier than anyone had expected. The Liberal government, crucial for Home Rule, collapsed during the war. And it is probably fair to say that, like many nationalist leaders of the time, Redmond did not understand Ulster well and underestimated the intensity of unionist opposition to Home Rule. His reputation survives in Westminster to this day. His bust stands just outside the members' dining room in the House of Commons – a tribute to an outstanding parliamentarian and political leader who believed passionately in Irish unity and self-government and sought to achieve those aims through constitutional and peaceful means.

The assessment of Edward Carson, the statesman who began his career as a barrister in Dublin, and the Ulster Covenant are, in terms of the methods they advocated, less straightforward. Of course, the Covenant expressed the reasons why unionists were so opposed to Home Rule. They feared Home Rule or 'Rome Rule' would undermine their civil and religious freedom. They worried about its effect on the more advanced, industrial economy of Ulster. And they thought their interests were being cynically sacrificed to the demands of the Irish Party by a Liberal government desperate to keep itself in power. As the Emeritus Professor of Irish studies at Queen's University, Belfast, Brian Walker, has said, these arguments from a unionist point of view were not unreasonable. The Ulster Volunteer Force was established in 1913 and equipped with rifles in a clandestine operation in April 1914. The creation of the Irish Volunteers was, of course, the nationalists' response. To quote Professor Walker again:

> It is possible to claim that the Ulster Covenant served to protect the interests of Ulster unionists in the six counties of what became Northern Ireland. At the same time it helped to justify the threat or use of force which led to the rise of armed resistance and Irish separatism in the rest of Ireland.[1]

For much of the twentieth century, the people of these islands lived

---

1   *The Irish Times*, 27 September 2012.

with the legacy from that time, of the gun being at the centre of Irish politics. We must hope that, with the success of the peace process in Northern Ireland, the use or threat of violence has finally been replaced by democratic principles and consent. I believe that this conference and similarly inclusive events, which re-examine and commemorate, as dispassionately as we can, the years leading up to Ireland's independence, will help cement a culture of greater tolerance, understanding and reconciliation in our politics.

This conference took place in the week that the United Kingdom and Scottish governments reached an agreement to provide for a referendum on Scottish independence. The story of constitutional developments on these islands clearly has some distance to run. This week's agreement will ensure the referendum in Scotland is legal, fair and decisive and commands the confidence of all sides. The people of Scotland will have a single-question referendum on independence, based on the principles set out for referenda held across the United Kingdom. There will be a clear choice: partnership within the UK or separation without it. Of course, the British government adheres to the view that any decisions on Scotland's future are for people in Scotland to decide. We believe that the principles of free debate and governance by consent which underlie the process in Scotland are universal values.

It would be foolish to draw very close parallels to developments in Scotland today and Ireland 100 years ago. The context and circumstances are very different. And thankfully one way in which they are different is the absence of the threat or use of violence in the process in Scotland.

I think John Redmond would approve.

1

When histories collide: the third Home Rule bill for Ireland

Thomas Bartlett

The narrative is well known.[1] On 11 April 1912 the British Prime Minister, Herbert Henry Asquith, introduced in the British House of Commons the third Home Rule bill for Ireland. Two previous Home Rule bills, both introduced by William Ewart Gladstone, in 1886 and 1893 respectively, had failed, the first in the House of Commons, the second in the House of Lords. The third Home Rule bill, however, had every chance of passing into law, for the Parliament Act of 1911, carried with Irish Party support, meant that the House of Lords could delay designated legislation for only three years – which meant that, all things being equal, Irish Home Rule would become law in 1914. But if this was the major difference between this Home Rule bill and the earlier ones, there was still a remarkable similarity, principally in what was on offer, between all three. As with the 1893 Bill, though not with that of 1886, which had provided for no Irish representation, forty-two Irish MPs would continue to attend at Westminster – which would of course be supreme – and Ireland would remain an integral part of the

---

1   Unless otherwise stated I have drawn on *The Irish Times* supplement to commemorate Home Rule, published on 25 April 2012, to supply the background information for this article, especially the essays contributed by Mark Hennessy, Jonathan Bardon and Michael Laffan.

Empire and United Kingdom. The proposed new legislature to be set up in Dublin would have two chambers: a senate with forty members, and a lower house with 164 members. However, the term 'legislature' is undoubtedly rather extravagant, for the powers to be delegated to the new assembly were extremely limited. Matters relating to the monarchy, marriage (a hot topic at the time because of the *Ne Temere* decree),[2] the military, peace or war, foreign affairs, coinage, the law of treason, and trade and navigation – even lighthouses and, curiously, trademarks – were to be outside its remit, while others – such as policing, tax collection, old age pensions, land purchase, national insurance and even the post office – could possibly be delegated to Dublin, but only after a period of years. We may note that in a marked departure from proposals in the earlier Home Rule bills, that proposed by Asquith stipulated that there could be no Irish interference with the existing Irish civil service.[3] In addition, a lord lieutenant would reside, as before, in Dublin, but now he would have real power, with the authority to approve or veto legislation, or to delay action of any kind. Admittedly, a sum of around six million pounds would be transferred annually from the British Exchequer, but even here there was a humiliating condition: the money would be paid only in proportion to the receipt of annuities due under the various land acts of the previous twenty years. If Irish farmers failed to pay up, funds from the British Exchequer to Ireland would dry up. Uncharacteristically – for he had accepted the rest without demur – John Redmond, leader of the Irish Party, was moved to complain that this safeguard for the British Treasury meant that 'the whole revenue of Ireland is thus held in pawn'.[4] By any standards, the third Home Rule bill offered a derisory amount

---

2   The *Ne Temere* decree was issued in 1907 under Pope Pius X; it refined canon law in respect of marriage for practising Roman Catholics.

3   M. Maguire, *The Civil Service and the Revolution in Ireland, 1912–38* (Manchester, 2008), pp. 12–15.

4   J. Redmond, *The Home Rule Bill* (London, 1912), p. 23.

of devolved government to Ireland: a legislature shorn of legislative powers, whose prime function, as envisioned in the days of Gladstone, was to act as a collector of British taxpayers' money previously advanced to Irish tenants to enable them to buy their holdings. Thirty years and more of constitutional and political struggle had, it seemed, produced a legislative mouse.

And yet, as is also well known, this excessively modest measure instantly provoked a series of extravagant, not to say hysterical, reactions that within a short time brought Ireland to the verge of a civil war. Even before Asquith had introduced his bill at Westminster, a nationalist crowd estimated at a half million strong had gathered in anticipation in Dublin city centre to acclaim the coming triumph. When Asquith did introduce the bill, Redmond declared flatly that 'I personally thank God that I have lived to see this day' and he hailed the third Home Rule bill as no less than a 'great treaty of peace between Ireland, England and the Empire'.[5] When Asquith visited Dublin in July 1912 he received a rapturous reception at the Theatre Royal: 'the entire audience rose to their feet,' reported *The Irish Times*, 'and waving hats, handkerchiefs and papers, cheered enthusiastically with a growing rather than a diminishing volume of sound … for close on five minutes.'[6] Given the extremely limited amount of devolved government on offer, such euphoria, such triumphalism, is hard to explain.

And, of course, on the opposite side of the case, Conservative and unionist fury at Asquith's action appeared equally unwarranted. Two days before the bill had been introduced, Andrew Bonar Law, leader of the Conservative Party, with Sir Edward Carson, leader of the Irish unionists at his side, had reviewed a march past at Balmoral, near Belfast, of over 100,000 opponents of the proposed Home Rule bill and Bonar Law had pledged his party's support in their resistance to that

5   *House of Commons Debates*, Fifth series, vol. 36, 11 April 1912, col. 1452.
6   *The Irish Times*, 20 July 1912.

measure. On 12 July he went further: he warned that there were 'things that were stronger than parliamentary majorities', and some weeks later, he notoriously averred that 'I can imagine no lengths of resistance to which Ulster can go in which I should not be prepared to support them.'[7] Mobilisation against Home Rule proceeded apace. On 'Ulster Day', 28 September 1912, against a background of sectarian rioting in Belfast and elsewhere, and expulsions of Catholics and other deviants from the shipyards, Sir Edward Carson became the first to sign the Ulster Covenant at Belfast City Hall, in which document he and his fellow signatories pledged to use 'all means which may be necessary to defeat the present conspiracy to set up a Home Rule Parliament in Ireland'. Within weeks, some 500,000 others, men and women, had followed his example and signed. Quite what 'all means that may be necessary' signified became clear over the subsequent months, with the purchase of arms, the drilling of armed men, the formation of the Ulster Volunteer Force (UVF) and gun-running at Larne and elsewhere in 1913. And these developments were mirrored on the nationalist side by the later formation of a corresponding force, the Irish Volunteers, and by the attempt to secure arms from abroad. As tempers flared, military preparations increased and the political temperature rose, it seemed that a civil war between opponents and supporters of the third Home Rule bill was inevitable, probably some time in 1914.

So far so conventional. Yet the puzzle remains: how could such a truncated piece of proposed legislation, one devoid of any Irish nationalist input, and one deliberately designed to set up such a toothless institution, arouse such elation on the one part and such horror on the other, so much so that civil war would quickly appear unavoidable?

In his review of Anglo-Irish constitutional relations between 1912 and 1972 Nicholas Mansergh addressed this question of the glaring

---

7   N. Mansergh, *The Unresolved Question: the Anglo-Irish settlement and its undoing 1912–72* (New Haven, 1991), pp. 53–4.

disparity between what was offered and the extreme reactions that the bill produced. So far as Redmond was concerned, Mansergh noted, the limited nature of the bill was very much a secondary consideration. For him, and by extension nationalist Ireland, '[the bill] proposed to reconstitute a parliament for Ireland, all Ireland', and 'it was the "example" of [the parliament at] College Green that counted, not the powers or the lack of them to be vested in it'. Once a parliament was restored, Mansergh continued, Redmond believed that 'much else would be added and the psychological gain would more than compensate for restrictions that were little short of humiliating'.[8] There is undoubtedly much in this insight; and unionists at the time would have concurred that the third Home Rule bill represented precisely that 'thin end of the wedge' (or staging post to complete separation of Ireland from Britain) that they feared would mean ruination and destruction for them. Whatever else, the Home Rule parliament envisaged in 1912, precisely because it was so evidently flawed in its structure and restricted in its powers, could never prove a final settlement, and therein lay the danger for unionists.

Further unionist objections, though the word seems inadequate, to Home Rule for all Ireland have been well rehearsed in the literature. Unionists claimed – possibly with an eye to winning British support – that Home Rule would strike a blow at the integrity of the British Empire, even presage its break-up. Then there was the self-pitying charge that Home Rule was 'the most nefarious conspiracy that has ever been hatched against a free people' and that unionists had done nothing to deserve being prised from the embrace of mother England and handed over to their enemies. As Carson put it (quoting a report produced by the Belfast Chamber of Commerce protesting against the 1893 Act): 'We can imagine no conceivable reason – no fault that we have committed – which will justify the treatment which this Bill

---

8   *Ibid.*, p. 53.

prepares for us.'[9] It was confidently asserted that Home Rule must mean both financial ruin, with Ulster money being drained to bail out feckless southern peasants, and industrial decay, since a Dublin parliament dominated by agriculturalists would legislate against the industrialised north-east. Home Rule, as well, would produce social chaos, with those, as Carson put it, 'whose capacity has never been applied towards the practical advancement of the material interests of the country', men who were demonstrably unfitted to rule, being placed over the natural governors.[10] Home Rule in short was 'ridiculous', for it was a farcical proposition that the Irish could govern themselves, and the thing must end in complete ruination.[11] Lastly, Home Rule was Rome Rule: as the Rev. Dr William McKean, a former Presbyterian moderator, put it in his sermon on 'Ulster Day' 1912: 'The Irish Question is at bottom a war against Protestantism; it is an attempt to establish a Roman Catholic Ascendancy in Ireland to begin the disintegration of the empire by securing a second parliament in Dublin.'[12]

And yet, while conceding that unionist fears and anxieties – and determination to resist Home Rule – were undoubtedly real, it is still difficult to reconcile the modest measure of devolution on offer with the apocalyptic consequences that unionists argued would inevitably flow from it, or indeed with the triumphalism with which nationalist Ireland viewed the proposed measure. Perhaps one way of doing so is to concede from the beginning that Home Rule itself was not at stake here, that is to say, that the crisis sparked off by the third Home Rule bill was not really about Home Rule at all: that in essence Home Rule was always more about image than substance.[13]

---

9   *House of Commons Debates*, Fifth series, vol. 39, 13 June 1912, col. 1070.

10   *Ibid.*, col. 1071.

11   *Ibid.*

12   Quoted in J. Bardon, 'The day Ulster first said No', *The Irish Times* Supplement on Home Rule, 25 April 2012, p. 12.

13   A. Jackson, *Home Rule: an Irish history, 1800–2000* (London, 2003), p. 2.

And that image, for both unionists and nationalists, was refracted through Irish history.

When Asquith rose in the Commons to propose his Home Rule bill 'for the better government of Ireland', he declared that it signalled 'the most urgent and most momentous step towards the settlement of the controversy which, as between ourselves and Ireland, has lasted for more than a century'.[14] Asquith's time frame – more than a hundred years – for the Irish demand for Home Rule may have struck some of his listeners as rather odd. After all, Gladstone's conversion to Home Rule had been in 1886, just under thirty years earlier, and while Irish demands for home government under Isaac Butt and Charles Stewart Parnell had been heard ten years earlier, the first use of the term 'Home Rule' appears to have been in 1873: a long way short of that century of struggle to which Asquith alluded. It is possible that he was including Daniel O'Connell's campaign in the 1840s for Repeal of the Union or 'Simple Repeal' in his passing reference to the chronology of the Home Rule agitation. After all, in a real sense, O'Connell not only pioneered the notion of the repeal of the Act of Union – and thus devolved government, however ill-defined, for Ireland – but he also created strategies, particularly electoral strategies, and institutions – the Loyal National Repeal Association and mass meetings – which later Home Rulers would make use of (and which their unionist opponents would copy).[15] We are, however, even with O'Connell's campaigns, some way short of the hundred years that Asquith mentioned, but we are approaching that period to which nationalists of all hues, and many Liberal politicians, looked back to with unashamed nostalgia and admiration: 'Grattan's Parliament'.

It is difficult nowadays to appreciate how much the perceived historical record of the last two decades of the eighteenth century

---

14   *House of Commons Debates*, Fifth series, vol. 36, 11 April 1912, col. 1424.
15   Jackson, *Home Rule*, p. 13.

weighed and played upon the imagination of those seeking Home Rule a hundred years on and was a constant source of inspiration. The years 1782–1801 appeared to be characterised by amazing triumphs: it was self-evidently a period of Home Rule under the guidance of Protestant patriots such as Henry Flood and Henry Grattan, and devolved government in the 1780s had also apparently sparked a surge in economic prosperity. In addition, the role played by the citizen-soldiers, the Volunteers of 1782, was particularly relished and even the United Irishmen, with their non-sectarian message and their union of Catholic, Protestant and Dissenter, offered proof that Irish people could cooperate together and need not always be at each other's throats. True, it had all ended in the carnage of 1798 and the resulting Act of Union, but many believed that the rebellion had been deliberately exploded by the British government in order to furnish the pretext and provide the opportunity to end the independent Irish parliament.

It mattered little that the historical record was far removed from the perception of a golden age. In reality, neither Grattan nor Flood had much influence with the new constitutional dispensation after 1782; what prosperity there was appears unrelated to the 'revolution of 1782', as some dubbed it; and, as the rebellion of 1798 made clear, it was not too difficult to stir up sectarian passions. Such criticisms – whether made at the time ('a most bungling imperfect business', claimed Theobald Wolfe Tone) or later (an 'Ascendancy charade' or 'noisy sideshow', as D. P. Moran and Daniel Corkery respectively dismissed the so-called 'Grattan's Parliament') – mattered little and were easily brushed aside.[16]

Allusions to the halcyon days of Grattan's parliament abound in the debates and arguments that surrounded the entire Home Rule agitation from the 1870s down to 1912 and beyond. W. E. Gladstone,

---

16 Mansergh, *Unresolved Question*, p. 12.

for example, was enormously influenced by W. E. H. Lecky's multi-volume depiction of Grattan's parliament as a sort of golden age in which rank, loyalty and nationality were to be found fused together in the interests of the whole Irish people. It was in vain for Lecky, a Unionist MP for Trinity College Dublin, to protest that the preconditions for something like 'Grattan's parliament' simply did not exist in late nineteenth-century Ireland and that his historical writings did not support the nationalist cause. Gladstone disagreed: unionist opposition to Home Rule was brushed aside by reference to the strong role played by Protestants in Grattan's parliament. And he frequently alluded to the gallant Presbyterian farmers turning out against the king's soldiers during the 1798 rebellion, making the point that their inner nationalism would re-emerge under devolved government and that their opposition to Home Rule was essentially bogus. As for Redmond, he yielded to none in his admiration for Grattan's parliament, an institution that, he declared, 'possesses today the enthusiastic and affectionate remembrance of the Irish people'. Redmond was even on record as claiming that with all its 'disqualifications' ('a parliament in which no Catholic could sit; for election to it no Catholic was allowed to vote') he would prefer taking back Grattan's parliament 'tomorrow' to continued rule under the union.[17] And he revered Grattan and Flood, indeed he saw himself acting as a latter-day Grattan or Flood when Home Rule was secured. Neither rebel nor fanatic, 'Redmond's natural pose', intoned *The Times* of London in his obituary, 'was that of the eighteenth-century patriot, a Grattan or a Flood.'[18]

Viewed in this light, it is clear that just as Grattan's parliament was forever associated with the Volunteers of 1782, so too a reborn Volunteer formation would have been needed to safeguard whatever Home Rule was achieved. Now, it is frequently asserted that the Irish

---

17 *House of Commons Debates*, Fifth series, vol. 39, 13 June 1912, col. 1087.
18 *The Times*, 7 March 1918.

Volunteers of 1913 drew their inspiration from the recently formed Ulster Volunteers, and certainly Eoin MacNeill in his famous article 'The North Began' pointed to their example. The emergence of the Irish Volunteers at that time may, however, be regarded as much a coincidence as a direct emulation of the Ulster Volunteers. It was accepted on all sides of nationalist opinion that the major flaw in Grattan's parliament had been the decision to disband the Volunteers. MacNeill in his article had explicitly evoked the example of the earlier Volunteers of 1782: 'their disbanding led to the destruction alike of self-government and of prosperity'.[19] And that well-known Home Ruler Patrick Pearse, when he appealed for Volunteers to be set up in 1913, stated that this time there would be no standing down: if the Volunteers of 1782 had not handed in their arms, Pearse said, there would have been no Union, no Famine and no emigration.[20] Fifty years later, Éamon de Valera, in his foreword to F. X. Martin's collection of documents on the Irish Volunteers, explained that the new Volunteer army was 'a heaven-sent opportunity to repair the mistake made when the Volunteer organisation of 1782 was allowed to lapse'.[21] UVF or no UVF, the lesson of history was that a Volunteer force was needed to safeguard Home Rule.

In short, nationalist Ireland, led by John Redmond, was prepared to settle for a cash-strapped assembly with little power because it appeared to offer the recreation of the glories of Grattan's parliament. When defended by an army of Volunteers on the model of 1782, its existence would be safeguarded and its quest for more power presumably enhanced. It was, it may be argued, this fixation with a largely fictitious image of the last period of self-government, or

---

19   MacNeill's article is reprinted in F. X. Martin (ed.), *The Irish Volunteers* (Dublin, 1963), pp. ix–x.
20   J. Augusteijn, *Patrick Pearse: the making of a revolutionary* (London, 2010), p. 233.
21   Martin (ed.), *Irish Volunteers*, p. v.

Home Rule, at the end of the eighteenth century that explains Redmond's, and nationalist Ireland's, embrace of a devolved scheme of government in 1912 that was almost certainly unworkable.

Unionists, by contrast, had little time for Grattan's parliament or the Volunteers of 1782. True, some of them took pride in their Presbyterian forebears who had turned out in 1798 against crown forces at Antrim, Saintfield and Ballynahinch, but their ancestors' resistance to oppression in 1798, the 'year of liberty', offered a useful precedent for armed resistance to oppression in 1912; it most certainly did not reveal Ulster Presbyterians to be closet Home Rulers. This is not to say that Irish history, or examples drawn from Irish history, played little part in unionist opposition to Home Rule. On the contrary, such opposition to Home Rule was firmly rooted in Irish history. The unionist battle anthem was, after all, 'O God our help in ages past', and while Carson would often allude to differences between unionist and nationalist based on 'traditions, ideas and race', he also pointed to 'deep-rooted historical questions' that divided one community from the other.[22]

The difference between unionist and nationalist lay in the periods of Irish history from which they strove to draw lessons, examples, inspiration or warnings. Just as nationalists sought to emulate Grattan's parliament, unionists preferred to contemplate the seventeenth century in Irish history, and within the seventeenth century, it was chiefly the Ulster plantation, the Irish rebellion of 1641 and the Williamite wars of 1688–91 from which they drew appropriate lessons. These years, beginning with the plantation, continuing with the rebellion of 1641 and concluding, after a series of heart-stopping reverses and glorious triumphs, with Protestant victory at the Boyne (1690) and Aughrim (1691) were of abiding interest to Irish Protestants. The plantation had proved a success, and this could be seen in the clear way that 'Ulster', and particularly Belfast and its environs, had through its industry and

---

22 *House of Commons Debates*, Fifth series, vol. 39, 13 June 1912, col. 1074.

commerce decisively detached itself from Ireland by the end of the nineteenth century. Home Rule was seen as an attempt to undo the plantation and had to be resisted on that count. As well, and probably more important, Catholic treachery and cruelties in the Rebellion had been well documented at the time and they had been retold over and over in subsequent centuries. Sir John Temple's *Irish Rebellion* (1646), with its lurid stories of Catholic excesses against defenceless Irish Protestants – such as drowning, boiling, hanging, stabbing, burning and robbing them – had frequently been reprinted and may be deemed pre-eminent among the literature of Irish atrocity. By the end of the nineteenth century the ghastly crimes attendant on the 1641 rebellion were being recalled in the public prints, on Orange Lodge banners and in quasi-scholarly productions. In particular, further selections from the 1641 depositions, or eyewitness accounts of atrocities that Irish Protestants suffered at the hands of Irish Catholics in the 1640s, were being published to acclaim (and to denunciation, from those who argued that such testimony was entirely suspect).[23]

Later additions to the Irish Protestant canon of atrocity tales had come from Archbishop King's *State of the Protestants of Ireland* (1691) in which Irish Protestant resistance to tyranny and oppression – as threatened by James II and his 'Catholicke designe' – was not only fully justified but was shown to be a Godly duty. James had 'designed', wrote King, 'to destroy and utterly ruin the Protestant religion, the liberty and property of the subjects in general and the English interest in Ireland in particular and alter the very frame and constitution of the government' and on these grounds he had to be resisted. To Irish Protestants it looked as if Asquith and Redmond were embarked on a similar undertaking. But King spelled out especially the dreadful social

---

23 Mary Hickson presented a number of the depositions in her *Ireland in the Seventeenth Century* (2 vols, London, 1884). Her 'Protestant' reading of the rebellion drew the ire of Thomas Fitzpatrick, in his *The Bloody Bridge and Other Papers Relating to the Insurrection of 1641* (Dublin, 1903).

revolution attempted by the Stuart king and his agents, in which those of mean condition and poor understanding – 'the scum and rascality of the world' fit only to be 'hewers of wood and drawers of water' – were catapulted to positions of authority simply because they were Catholics, and he instanced as example 'one that was no other than a cowherd to his Protestant landlord was set before him on the bench as a justice of the peace'.[24] For Irish Protestants, King's book detailed the social chaos attendant on Catholics gaining power over them.

The trilogy of works in Irish atrocity literature was completed by Sir Richard Musgrave's *Memoirs of the Different Rebellions in Ireland* (1801). He reaffirmed from his compilation of atrocities committed by Catholics during the 1798 rebellion that Catholicism was, and remained, a cruel and oppressive religion, and he confirmed that Catholics must never be permitted to assume a position of authority over Protestants.

There were other motifs drawn from the seventeenth century: a compact with God to resist oppression, a tradition of self-reliance in the face of danger and a conviction that a besieged Protestantism would ultimately triumph – hence the Covenant of 1912, which was inspired by the Solemn League and Covenant of 1643 against Popery and Prelacy. Hence, too, the Ulster Volunteer Force of 1913, which was most likely modelled not on the Volunteers of 1782, but on the Yeomanry of the 1790s and, even further back, the Laggan army, an armed body swiftly mobilised by Protestant settlers in the west of Ulster in the face of Catholic onslaught in 1642. And hence, lastly, the overwhelming presence of siege imagery in Protestant rhetoric at the time of the Home Rule crisis. Speaking at the massive Balmoral rally of Easter 1912, Bonar Law had recourse to the by now familiar language of an Ulster under siege:

---

24 W. King, *The State of the Protestants of Ireland under the late King James's Government* (London, 1691), pp. 6–7, 22, 27, 29.

Once again you hold the pass – the pass for the Empire. You are a besieged city. The timid have left you; your Lundys have betrayed you but you have closed the gates ... a boom [has been set up] against you to shut you off from the help of the British people. You will burst that boom.[25]

To conclude: the limited, indeed drastically truncated terms of the third Home Rule bill are almost entirely irrelevant; few of the half million or so who pledged undying opposition 'by all means necessary' to the bill going through the House of Commons had any idea of its terms and conditions. They viewed the whole project through the lens of history, especially the history of the seventeenth century; and in this stark glare any measure of devolved government that put Catholics in charge must prove not just threatening or dangerous, but potentially catastrophic. Home Rule, 'a term redolent of family values and fireside comfort', or so nationalists thought, when viewed through the prism of seventeenth-century Irish history became a fearsome thing for unionists.[26] As in the seventeenth so too in the twentieth century: the issue had never been about politics; it was what it had always been – 'a struggle between the loyal for existence and the disloyal for supremacy'.[27] By contrast, Irish nationalists were not just content, but were euphoric at the prospect of what many saw as the recovery of Grattan's parliament, an institution forever associated with patriotism, economic prosperity and communal goodwill. Its profound flaws were ignored, just as the faults of the third Home Rule bill were dismissed as inconsequential. What mattered was the image; the substance could wait. It was the collision of those rival or mutually exclusive views of the Irish past that was to lead to the very real prospect of civil war after the third Home Rule bill was introduced.

---

25 I. McBride, *The Siege of Derry in Ulster Protestant Mythology* (Dublin, 1997), pp. 67–70, *passim*.
26 Jackson, *Home Rule*, p. 2.
27 A. Jackson, 'Unionist politics and Protestant society in Edwardian Ireland', *Historical Journal*, vol. 33, no. 4 (1990), p. 864.

2

The politics of comparison: the racialisation of Home Rule in British science, politics and print, 1886–1923

Matthew Schownir

In the months leading up to the reading of the second Irish Home Rule bill in 1893, two leading Members of Parliament traded rhetorical blows in the pages of the *North American Review* over the issue of Irish self-government. The Duke of Argyll, a leading unionist, reminded his American audience of the support he had given to the federalist cause during their 'great Civil War' three decades past. In that war, the Duke 'felt that the "North" was in the right, and that the cause of civilisation was at stake' in the union's fight with the secessionists. For Argyll, the debate over Irish Home Rule was no different. Catering at once to New England sympathy and nomenclature, the Duke claimed that Irish self-government could be summarised 'in one well-known word – "Secesh"'. After all, English rule and law had only benefited the Irish, 'due to the utter absence of civilising institutions' before English conquest. Regrettably, even under such benevolent rule there was 'the survival in Ireland of semi-barbarous habits that were peculiarly Irish', including a 'contentment with a very low standard of life'.[1]

---

1   The Duke of Argyll, 'English elections and home rule', *North American Review*, no. 429 (August 1892), pp. 129–35.

The response to Argyll's editorial came from none other than William Gladstone, Liberal prime minister and architect of the Home Rule legislation in question. Though Gladstone dismissed the Duke's disdain for the Irish character, he insisted that England's 'feebler sister' would retain that love of law that the English had bestowed on the island. After all, wrote Gladstone, even Lord Salisbury had wondered whether the heavy-handedness of British rule over Ireland could be blamed for the 'lag' of the Celtic race. It was time to give the Irish a degree of self-rule and prove that England's civilising instruction had left a positive mark on the Irish people.[2]

Victorian debates over the Irish question have long been examined by historians of Great Britain. The imposing amount of literature on the topic reveals the complexity of the political, social and economic relationships between Britain and Ireland that made the latter only a junior partner in the United Kingdom for over a century. One important aspect of this relationship is, however, often overlooked. As high-lighted in the anecdote above, discussions of the Irish question often involved, in explicit or implicit language, an indictment of the Irish racial character, a topic that inherently involved comparisons with England's self-prescribed Anglo-Saxon lineage. This was especially the case among opponents of Home Rule, who sought to emphasise perceived racial differences between the Irish and British races as a political tool to combat Irish self-government and maintain British hegemony.[3]

The politics of comparison over Ireland in the late nineteenth and early twentieth centuries followed the decision to grant self-

---

2   W. E. Gladstone, 'A vindication of home rule: a reply to the duke of Argyll', *North American Review*, no. 431 (October 1892), pp. 388–93.

3   For some of the more comprehensive political histories concerning the Irish question, see D. G. Boyce, *The Irish Question and British Politics, 1868–1996* (Houndmills, 1996) and *Englishmen and Irish Troubles: British public opinion and the making of Irish policy, 1918–22* (Cambridge, Mass., 1972); G. K. Peatling, *British Opinion and Irish Self-government, 1865–1925: from unionism to liberal commonwealth* (Dublin, 2001).

government to other parts of the Empire. Britain's white settler colonies of Australia, New Zealand, Canada and Newfoundland all acquired responsible self-government decades before Irish Home Rule was even proposed. What made Ireland unique from Britain's other imperial possessions was its proximity to, and historical dominance by, England, as well as its 'Celtic' racial heritage. These factors complicated discussions on Home Rule in parliament and in British society at large, and the language of Irish racial fitness can be traced from the first of the Government of Ireland bills (hereafter referred to as the Home Rule bills) in 1886 to the fourth and final iteration in 1920.

This essay uses the four Home Rule bills as focal points to investigate the racialisation of such a sensitive and volatile subject in British social thought. The conceptualisation of the Irish race, as it pertained to political debate, is vital to understanding why Home Rule was so divisive and fought over so bitterly, not only by the political parties in Westminster, but also in newspapers, magazines, scientific journals and popular caricatures of the day. These perceptions, reflected in all facets of British society, are frequently ignored by a scholarly literature that often focuses on the parliamentary machinations and great political figures of the day.

The aim of this essay is to demonstrate the issue of Home Rule as a racialised topic of political contention, a notion articulated through Victorian scientific thought and popular media, as well as by the rhetoric within parliamentary debates. In this instance, racial difference was accentuated by those in Britain wishing to maintain control over Irish affairs; this was often accomplished by drawing racial comparisons between a weak, backward Celtic race and a virile Anglo-Saxon British national persona. This racial component of Home Rule comprises a key element to understanding the broader historical issue of the Irish question in the late nineteenth and early twentieth centuries.

This approach correlates with emerging aspects of the historiography of this topic. While political histories have dominated discussions of the Irish question in general and Home Rule in particular, scholars have increasingly argued for more nuanced approaches. Historians such as L. P. Curtis and Sheridan Gilley first broached the subject of a Victorian construction of Celtic racial identity in the late 1960s and early 1970s. Although their scholarly debates called into question entrenched understandings of race surrounding Anglo-Irish relations in the Victorian period, it was generally treated as an isolated phenomenon by successive literature on the Irish question. Fortunately, several scholars have recently begun to revisit the intersection of racial ideas and politics concerning Victorian and Edwardian conceptualisations of imperialism and federalism, particularly British notions of racial compatibility within different parts of the Empire. This essay similarly seeks to include formerly buried factors in the Anglo-Irish relationship before Ireland became an independent state.[4]

A considerable link connects the four Home Rule bills of 1886, 1893, 1914 and 1920, influencing the politics and social discussion of Irish self-rule. This time frame supersedes Curtis' argument for the culmination of Anglo-Saxonism as a political factor by the turn of the twentieth century; rather, the racialisation of the Anglo-Irish relationship continues well after the supposed decline of Anglo-Saxonism after the 1890s. Various areas of British society harboured Anglo-Saxonist attitudes of comparison toward the Irish Celt that emerged in Home Rule debates. Popular magazines and newspapers

---

4   L. P. Curtis, Jr, *Anglo-Saxons and Celts: a study of anti-Irish prejudice in Victorian England* (New York, 1968) and *Apes and Angels: the Irishman in Victorian caricature* (Washington, 1971); S. Gilley, 'English attitudes to the Irish in England, 1780–1900', in C. Holmes (ed.), *Immigrants and Minorities in British Society* (London, 1978); R. Douglas, L. Harte and J. O'Hara, *Drawing Conclusions: a cartoon history of Anglo-Irish relations, 1798–1998* (Belfast, 1998); M. de Nie, *The Eternal Paddy: Irish identity and the British press, 1798–1882* (Madison, 2004); R. Mohanram, *Imperial White: race, diaspora, and the British Empire* (Minneapolis, 2007); D. A. Valone and J. M. Bradbury (eds), *Anglo-Irish Identities, 1571–1845* (Lewisburg, 2008); D. Bell, *The Idea of Greater Britain: empire and the future of world order, 1860–1900* (Princeton, 2007); P. Cain, 'Empire and the languages of character and virtue in late Victorian and Edwardian Britain', *Modern Intellectual History*, no. 2 (2007), pp. 1–25.

depicted the Irish as a race of buffoons who knew nothing but how to bring disaster upon themselves and could not manage their own affairs without the civilising tutelage of Britain. In intellectual circles, celebrated anthropologists, ethnologists and social commentators referred to pseudoscientific evidence to explain Celtic helplessness and degradation, and to prove English racial superiority. Finally, these racialising exhortations found root in the political sphere, as prominent parliamentary figures defended their respective positions on Home Rule with the patronising language of race.[5] By taking examples from each of these areas of British society at the time of the four Home Rule bills, this essay points to a firm trajectory of racialised thinking over the course of five decades, which obscured the otherwise political issue of Home Rule in British dialogues.

The racialisation of the Irish question

The Irish question, as conceptualised by British politicians in the Victorian period, was born of the paternalist relationship created by the Act of Union.[6] As originally envisaged, the structure of Irish governance within the union smacked of colonial uplift: Ireland could vote a small number of representatives to the imperial parliament at Westminster, but Ireland proper remained under the supervision of a non-Catholic viceroy lord lieutenant appointed by London. Hence, an exercise in civilised democracy was balanced by a firm British hand on the ground in Ireland.

To many British, closer association under the union provided a unique opportunity for the Irish to learn from a stronger and civilised

---

5   For a continued discussion of a racialised Anglo-Irish relationship in the twentieth century, see R. M. Douglas, 'Anglo-Saxons and Attacotti: the racialisation of Irishness in Britain between the world wars', *Ethnic and Racial Studies*, vol. 25 (January 2002), pp. 40–63.

6   D. G. Boyce argues that the specific moment the Irish question entered British politics was after Lord John Russell's speech of 13 February 1844 in the House of Commons, in which Russell motioned to regard Ireland as an occupied, rather than governed, territory. See Boyce, *The Irish Question and British Politics*, p. 1.

England. In voicing its support for the proposed union in 1799, *The Times* predicted that 'nothing can tend to humanise the barbarous Irish as an habitual intercourse with this country and the opportunities of observing the civilised manners of those who are from it'. The creation of the union inspired hope in a civilising mission to 'remodel Ireland politically, economically, and morally', an effort that, in the minds of many British, bore little fruit in the following decades.[7] The Whig party particularly embarked on various reforms of land law, franchise expansion and religious disestablishment, both to quell opposition to British rule and to reverse the endemic poverty of the Irish that 'depraved and vitiated their characters, and fitted them for the commission of every crime'.[8]

Regular agrarian raids and a peasant revolt in the 1830s, however, convinced the government that the Irish had not reached the state of civilisation it had once hoped for. Richard Lalor Sheil, a prominent Irish MP, delivered a scathing indictment of the failings of the union before parliament in 1833, claiming after a recent tour of the island that 'the mass of the people are in a condition more wretched than that of any nation in Europe; they are worse housed, worse covered, worse fed, than the basest boors in the provinces of Russia'.[9] The potato famine of the 1840s and 1850s marked a turning point for Britain's Irish hopes; post-famine attitudes at Westminster focused on suppressing nationalist sympathy and efficiently ruling Ireland, rather than rehabilitating it. The Irish question took shape as finding the best way of upholding British institutions effectively, and any residual virtues of civilisation that could rub off on the Irish were seen as a secondary benefit of British rule.[10]

The nineteenth century also introduced a language of racism as men of science began categorising humanity into hierarchical groups,

---

7   Quoted in de Nie, *Eternal Paddy*, pp. 3–4.
8   B. Jenkins, *Irish Nationalism and the British State: from repeal to revolutionary nationalism* (Montreal, 2006), p. 35.
9   Jenkins, *Irish Nationalism and the British State*, pp. 36–7.
10   de Nie, *Eternal Paddy*, pp. 3–4.

gauging innate capacities and framing discussions of peoples in terms of generalised racial differences. In 1813 the English ethnologist James Cowles Prichard published his *Researches into the Physical History of Man*, a study that attempted to link physical appearance with cognitive ability in an effort to classify Europeans into four distinct groups that shared common peculiarities. Craniologists such as Anders Retzius and F. J. Gall also developed physiognomy as a correlative to emerging ethnological theories by applying quantitative measurements of jaw and forehead angles to prescribe inherent mental capacities in different types of humans.[11] In 1862 acclaimed physiognomist John Beddoe published *Races in Britain*, a seminal book that provided the basis of scientific racial comparison for the rest of the century. By applying his callipers to skulls throughout the British Isles, Beddoe developed an 'Index of Nigressence' that attempted to measure how close various peoples were to the African Negro. A self-styled expert on Ireland, Beddoe undertook many scientific excursions to each of the island's counties and eventually concluded that the modern Irish skull was 'usually rather long, low, and narrow' when compared to the average English skull. From this comparison he inferred that the Irish were in fact 'European Negroes'.[12]

But even before Beddoe's scientific approach claimed an empirical link between the backward Irish and primitive Africans, popular depictions of the Irish as ape-like and bestial were already in circulation in British popular discourse. One infamous example is found in the popular humour magazine *Punch*, in which a cartoon drawn for the 4 November 1843 issue features the 'Irish Frankenstein' of the repeal movement. Wielding a shillelagh and featuring torn, ill-fitting

---

11   de Nie, *Eternal Paddy*, p. 5; M. F. Jacobson, *Whiteness of a Different Color: European immigrants and the alchemy of race* (Cambridge, 1998), pp. 32–3; Curtis, *Apes and Angels*, pp. 10–11.
12   J. Beddoe, 'The Kelts of Ireland', *Journal of Anthropology*, no. 2 (October 1870), p. 118.

clothes, a gangly Irishman with dark skin, unruly hair and a simian face violently threatens John Bull, with the word 'Repale' written across his chest. This simianisation and dehumanisation of the Irish in popular caricature was typical of *Punch* and other popular publications of the nineteenth century, a stereotype that Beddoe's index seemed to confirm formally using 'scientific' evidence.[13]

Finally, the publication of Charles Darwin's *The Origin of Species* and *The Descent of Man*, in 1859 and 1871 respectively, introduced the idea of evolutionary theory to European science and discussions of race. Darwin's contribution to the discourse cemented an ideological shift away from a 'monogenistic' approach to humanity inspired by the long-held belief in the creation story of Christianity, to a secular 'polygenism' in which all humans were not assumed to derive from Adam but from different hereditary origins that directly affected the innate characteristics of different human 'races'.[14]

Emerging trends in physiognomy, evolutionary theory and anthropology heavily influenced British attitudes towards the Irish in the Victorian era, by which Britons conceived of distinct racial boundaries within the United Kingdom. New scientific ideas provided tangible 'evidence' for why the backward Irish did not have the same inherent love of law, democratic institutions and progress as the English, Scottish and Welsh. Racial typology neatly explained historic Irish predicaments and English hegemony: the Irish were a Celtic race, inclined to a decadent tribal culture and never 'Romanised', whereas the Anglo-Saxon lineage of the English (which was, rather ambiguously, shared at least in part with the Welsh and lowland Scots) prescribed a people with 'a particular genius for governing themselves' and the ability to reason into existence institutions that upheld justice and liberty. The negative traits of the Celtic Irish could indeed be

---

13   de Nie, *Eternal Paddy*, p. 10; Douglas *et al.*, *Drawing Conclusions*, p. 40.
14   N. Stepan, *The Idea of Race in Science: Great Britain 1800–1960* (Hamden, 1982), pp. 1–2.

predicted in 'observable physical differences', such as skin and hair colour and the angles of their skulls. The stereotypical 'Paddy' (and the female version, 'Fanny') typified in British popular discourse was always 'a Celt, a Catholic, and a peasant'. These three characteristics, as well as the popular and scientific portrayal of the simianised Irishman, provided racial ammunition when the Irish question took a new turn in the latter half of the nineteenth century as Home Rule was first discussed and eventually tried as a solution to Britain's Irish woes.[15]

As various settled parts of the Empire acquired dominion status and responsible government throughout the course of the century, the idea of Home Rule increasingly enjoyed circulation in Britain as a viable option to the Irish question, beginning in the 1860s. Many prominent political leaders regarded Ireland's continuing problems to be, at least in part, a consequence of distant British rule. The most influential of these was William Gladstone, who eventually became the writer and sponsor of the first two Home Rule bills.

Home Rule drew passionate criticism from several corners of British society, however, even before it took legislative form. Many intellectuals cited the Irish's deficient racial traits that made Home Rule untenable. Historian and Anglican priest Charles Kingsley wrote how he was 'haunted by the human chimpanzees' he saw during a trip to Ireland in 1860. 'I don't believe they are our fault … they are happier, better, more comfortably fed and lodged under our rule than they ever were.' Goldwin Smith, political essayist and historian, was of the opinion that 'the clannish Celt preferred subservience to a king or despot to freedom', compared to the Anglo-Saxon, who had an innate love of law, parliament and free institutions. Albert Venn Dicey, who became one of the most outspoken unionist voices against Home Rule, and pub-

---

15   J. H. Murphy, 'Broken glass and batoned crowds: Cathleen Ni Houlihan and the tensions of transition', in D. G. Boyce and A. O'Day (eds), *Ireland in Transition, 1867–1921* (London, 2004), pp. 114–5; Curtis, *Anglo-Saxons and Celts*, pp. 6–7; Jacobson, *Whiteness of a Different Color*, p. 48; de Nie, *Eternal Paddy*, p. 5.

lished four books on the topic, argued that the civilised and uncivilised races of the world were locked in an eternal conflict, and the Irish, being of the latter group, were fundamentally unfit to govern themselves.[16]

Anthropologists also sought to portray Home Rule as a scientific impracticability. At a meeting of the Anthropological Society of London in 1869, J. Gould Avery presented a paper in which his proclaimed objective was 'to show that the position of the Irish people in relation to England, and the alleged severity and badness of the English government, arise from and illustrate the racial characteristics of the Irish themselves'. Avery went on to argue that the Irish were inherently given to filth, idleness and drunkenness; were hostile to the concept of law; and possessed an overactive imagination that nevertheless prevented them from achieving any cultural edifice of value. Though maintaining he had no interest in political matters, he took the opportunity to reject any notion of Home Rule for the Irish, claiming that 'to govern the different races of men, you must study their peculiar racial characteristics and tendencies, and treat them accordingly', and that 'but for the interference of the English, the native people [of Ireland] would have utterly destroyed each other long ago'. Respondents to Avery's paper agreed that 'a parental government would suit the Celt … you cannot lead him as we are led', and 'if only those in authority would but take the trouble to make themselves acquainted with certain race distinctions – in fact, become anthropologists – there would be fewer political mistakes than ruled at present'.[17]

The following year, Celtic expert Henry Hudson, alongside Beddoe, spoke to another meeting of anthropologists to 'depict the marked characteristics of the Irish Celtic race, and to draw conclusions

---

16   Curtis, *Anglo-Saxons and Celts*, pp. 83–4; A. V. Dicey, *England's Case Against Home Rule* (Richmond, 1886), p. 75.
17   J. G. Avery, 'Civilisation: with especial reference to the so-called Celtic inhabitants of Ireland', *Journal of the Anthropological Society of London*, vol. 7 (1869), pp. 221–37, *passim*.

from thence as how they ought to be governed'. Hudson went on to say that the Irish were warlike, hasty, improvident and inherently 'clannish, from a want of individual reliance', hence unable effectively to rule themselves like the Saxon race. Hudson admitted he found his sudden interest in the topic piqued by recent talk about 'giving contentment to the Irish as a nation' in order to 'conquer England's great difficulty', namely, the Irish question.[18]

The first bill, 1886

The controversial introduction of the first Home Rule bill by Gladstone and the Liberals has been thoroughly documented by political historians. It will suffice to say here that the January 1886 elections turned out a sufficient number of Irish nationalist MPs to enable them to form a ruling coalition with the Liberals, which they did under the condition that an Irish Home Rule bill would be advanced in the spring sessions. The promise of such a piece of legislation was divisive enough to split the Liberal Party in two; those disaffected by Gladstone's concession to the Irish nationalists absconded from the party altogether to form a new bloc, the Liberal Unionists, who were devoted to killing any parliamentary measure that proposed giving Home Rule to Ireland. The Unionists allied themselves with the Conservatives for that express purpose; after two months of debate over the bill, from its first reading in April to its third in June, this alliance outnumbered the Gladstonians and Irish to vote it down. In a fatal political move, Gladstone took the matter to the country and called for a new general election in July, as a result of which the Conservative/Unionist bloc was voted overwhelmingly into power.[19]

18   H. Hudson, G. H. Kinahan and J. Beddoe, 'Three papers: On the Irish Celt, On the race elements of the Irish people (abstract), and On the Kelts of Ireland (abstract and comments)', *Journal of the Anthropological Society of London*, vol. 8 (1870–71), pp. 179–80.
19   P. Davis, 'The Liberal Unionist party and the Irish policy of Lord Salisbury's

Britain's print media reflected the importance of Home Rule in the popular arena. From the time Gladstone first announced his plans to introduce Irish governmental legislation to parliament, Home Rule received significant coverage in leading political periodicals. In the *Fortnightly Review* political (and racial) ideologies battled in the editorial pages. Frank Harris, a journalist born in Ireland to Welsh parents, argued that the union formed more than eighty years earlier should 'on no account be relaxed', and claimed that 'Ireland is not a nation', citing 'no distinctive, honourable past, no distinctive language, literature or art'. In *The Contemporary Review*, J. D. Campbell, the marquis of Lorne, urgently warned that Ireland was so poor that it would 'perish' if England removed itself from its direct governance.[20]

The twin notions of violence and Irish nationalism pervaded the public discourse over the first Home Rule bill. The memory of agrarian theft and violent revolts against British landlords in the 1860s and 1870s, as well as the 1882 assassination of Lord Frederick Cavendish, the chief secretary for Ireland, convinced many among the British public that Home Rule would either lead to more violence against the British and Protestants in Ireland, or be viewed as capitulation by the government to Irish terrorism. Jesse Ashworth, a retired Primitive Methodist preacher, asked, 'What, we ask, are the laws which Irish Roman Catholics choose to break – are they the laws enforced against them by the hated Saxon? In answer, they are the laws of Jehovah Himself; laws against murder, injustice and crime.' *Punch*, too, mockingly depicted a chaotic parliamentary scene in one of its cartoons, with the caption reading 'The Irish House. Moved from Westminster to Dublin', implying that any instance of Irish convening to discuss politics invariably involved violence.[21]

---

government, 1886–1892', *The Historical Journal*, no. 1 (March 1975), p. 86.

20 A. Parry, 'The Home Rule crisis and the "Liberal" periodicals 1886–1895: three case studies', *Victorian Periodicals Review*, no. 1 (Spring 1989), pp. 18, 22.

21 G. Goodlad, 'British Liberals and the Irish home rule crisis: the dynamics of

There were a few publications that took a dissenting stance, but these, too, carried hints of paternal racism. *The Daily News*, the only London paper that supported Gladstone's Home Rule project in 1886, said it was ready to 'hope and trust that Irish human nature is so much like other human nature, that the right and privilege of self-government will make Irishmen more contented, more prosperous and more neighbourly than they have been at any former period of our history'. The author did, however, add that a single, centralised Irish ruling body in Dublin would be better for Britain because it would be easier for London to monitor and control.[22]

Language in the parliamentary debates between supporters and opponents of Home Rule also took on a noticeably racialised tone. Unionists in Gladstone's government invoked Britain's dire responsibility to upholding true civilisation in Ireland. The lord chancellor of Ireland, Lord Ashbourne, declared that the island 'must always be ruled', ensuring that 'life, property, and liberty must be preserved there. Those are the conditions of every civilised society.' John Morley, the chief secretary of Ireland, cited the economic, religious and 'curious perversities of the geographical mixture of religion and race in Ireland', honouring the union's 'terrible task' in 'welding all these elements into a corporate whole and stable society'.[23]

It was, however, the Liberal Unionists who played most strongly on Ireland's racial makeup. Joseph Chamberlain, a Radical Liberal, who led the unionist defection from his party, argued that Ireland 'is not a homogenous community … it is a nation which comprises two races and two religions', and that if greater material benefits

---

division', in D. G. Boyce and A. O'Day (eds), *Gladstone and Ireland: politics, religion and nationality in the Victorian age* (Houndmills, 2010), p. 91.
22 *Ibid.*, pp. 92–3.
23 *House of Commons Debates*, Third series, vol. 302, 21 January 1886, col. 78; 9 April 1886, vol. 304, col. 1265.

were bestowed upon the poorer, Catholic race, 'you will do more for its pacification than any political scheme or any constitutional change'.[24] George Goschen, a Scottish MP representing Edinburgh, had perhaps the most vitriolic words for the bill:

> Can he [Gladstone] not see that, without looking upon the Irish people as lost to the common virtues of civilised communities, we may think that they are not such an angelic people as to be likely to be suddenly transformed at one stroke of the pen, and all at once endowed with the faculty of governing themselves? No people with such antecedents as the Irish could be suddenly trusted with the unexampled powers which he proposes to confer on them.[25]

For his part, Gladstone rebuked his opponents for their Irish prejudices. At the opening of the Home Rule bill's debate, he declared that Irishmen deserved free institutions as much as Englishmen or 'Scotchmen' did. Even he, however, engaged in racialising language when discussing the subject. Responding to Queen Victoria's opening of parliament in January 1886, in which she strongly warned against any change in the union with Ireland, Gladstone remarked that 'a fair and a proper view to take of this matter is not to judge Ireland by any abstract standard of peace and order; but she must be judged by the various circumstances connected with her history and race, and the position of her inhabitants'. Still, his words were more benign than his Conservative counterpart, Lord Salisbury. In a speech for his supporters between sessions, Salisbury disparagingly compared Home Rule to the ludicrous idea of granting democracy to the lowly and backward Hottentots; his resolve was bolstered by his claim that the Irish had become 'habituated to the use of knives and

---

24 *Ibid.*, 9 April 1886, vol. 304, col. 1200; 7 June 1886, vol. 306, col. 1164.
25 Davis, 'The Liberal Unionist party', p. 97.

slugs' to get what they wanted from London, and Home Rule would be tantamount to state capitulation.[26]

The discussion of the first Home Rule bill was invariably tied in with discussions of Irish racial character, a product of Victorian scientific developments that focused on outwardly determining the characteristics and even innate capacity of a particular people. Such a divisive issue brought out the worst in many Britons in terms of fear-mongering and stereotyping, but this was justified under the aegis of scientific 'fact'. This trend continued for the rest of the nineteenth century, most evident in Gladstone's second attempt at granting Home Rule to Ireland.

The second bill, 1892–3

The second bill began life in much the same way as its predecessor. The electorate voted enough seats for Gladstone's Liberal Party to form a minority government with the Irish nationalist MPs and again Gladstone prepared a Home Rule bill for parliamentary review. The political and intellectual climate had, however, changed in the interim. The Irish nationalist leader Charles Parnell had died in 1891, following his highly publicised divorce scandal, which had precipitated a split leadership in the Irish Party. Without the polarising figure of Parnell in the headlines, the Irish question commanded less public attention than at the time of the first Home Rule bill, as the issue took a back seat to social reforms and questions of voting franchise expansion.[27]

Additionally, a general shift in the intellectual approach to ethnography changed the foundation upon which Irish racial characteristics were constructed. Archaeologist and sometime Liberal Unionist MP John Lubbock set out to reinterpret the works of Beddoe and other anthropologists just after the battle over the first Home Rule

---

26 *House of Commons Debates*, Third series, vol. 304, 8 April 1886, col. 1040; vol. 302, 21 January 1886, col. 91; Curtis, *Anglo-Saxons and Celts*, pp. 102–3.

27 Davis, 'The Liberal Unionist party', p. 102.

bill. Lubbock's argument that 'English, Irish, and Scotch are all composed of the same elements, and in not very dissimilar proportions' represented the general intellectual shift of the day. Citing a common origin and prehistoric interracial mixing of the peoples inhabiting the British Isles, Lubbock concluded that the Irish did not have their own nationality from which to argue for a government separate from that of Great Britain. In his studies, Lubbock singled out Home Rulers for creating a fictitious Irish nationhood to disrupt British politics.[28]

One constant between 1886 and 1892 was the Conservative–Unionist alliance, and its commitment to defeating Irish Home Rule. One of the primary charges levelled against Home Rule was that Irish responsible government, and the acolytes of Parnell who pushed for it, did not represent the true wishes of the Irish people. Conservatives and Unionists argued that organised nationalism 'was a largely ephemeral phenomenon which had astutely exploited agrarian discontent', but would lose its appeal once material problems were properly remedied by the government. The focus on the material conditions of the Irish echoed the argument of Chamberlain in 1886. That this focus never seemed to come about was owed in part to the reluctance of unionists to infringe on the prerogative of Irish landlords, who were traditionally supporters of the Conservative Party. Introducing reforms that would strengthen the poor agrarian tenantry against their landlords would endanger the Unionist alliance with the Tories; nonetheless, a series of concessional Land Acts was gradually extended by those who opposed Home Rule as a political principle and overt solution to the perceived Irish question.[29]

Individual political rights became a major point of contention in the parliamentary debates over the second iteration of Home Rule

---

28   J. Lubbock, 'The nationalities of the United Kingdom. Extracts from letters to the "Times"', *The Journal of the Anthropological Institute of Great Britain and Ireland*, vol. 16 (1887), pp. 418, 420.

29   Davis, 'The Liberal Unionist party', pp. 97, 103.

in 1892–3. Again the topic took on a language that carried racial undertones, and this time Irish nationalists sought to confront the racial aspect head-on. Thomas Sexton, an Irish MP in the Commons, asked during the second reading of the Local Government (Ireland) bill why ordinary Irishmen could not enjoy the same rights in the franchise as their English or Scottish counterparts, adding 'why should Irishmen be supposed to be naturally more corrupt, dishonest, or criminal than the men of any other race?' Michael Davitt, representing Cork, when speaking on the second reading of the second Home Rule bill, accused the opposition of being 'blinded by bigotry and race hatred', otherwise they would 'recognise and acknowledge the services which Ireland is rendering to Great Britain and to the Empire'. William Redmond, a rising nationalist politician in the Commons, and brother of the Irish Party leader, pointedly confronted the racial assumptions of the unionists:

> You Englishmen – many of whom have never been in Ireland – whose information is extremely limited, to sit there and waste the time of your country – simply because you think yourselves superior to Irishmen, and better able to judge what is good for them locally than they are themselves ... make yourselves the laughing stock of the whole world.[30]

Salisbury's answer lay in his assertion that 'incurable differences' existed between the Irish and English races, in that the Irish believed themselves to have a distinct and separate nationality from the peoples of Great Britain. The definition of 'nation' was left unexplained in Salisbury's statements, but his disdain of the 'quarrelsomeness' of the Irish was rather less ambiguous in his speeches. For his part, Chamberlain's response to nationalist arguments was also dismissive:

---

30 *House of Commons Debates*, Fourth series, vol. 4, 19 May 1892, col. 1335; vol. 11, 11 April 1893, col. 60; vol. 4, 23 May 1892, col. 1587.

'I would be inclined to pay more attention to these flowers of rhetoric if I did not know that it is "only Pretty Fanny's way".' As with the first bill, George Goschen again stuck to his racialised historical perspective to argue that 'the Celtic races have never displayed that kind of cool patience and coolness of dealing which has always characterised the Parliaments of Anglo-Saxons'. These examples should not overshadow the fact that many other opinions were brought forth by Unionists and Conservatives to demonstrate the folly of Home Rule for Ireland, including financial and strategic concerns, as well as the protection of the Protestant minority centred in Ulster. It is important to note, however, that concepts of the Irish as a race were as embedded in the official dialogue over the second bill as was the case six years earlier.[31]

In the popular media, the topic of Home Rule lay largely dormant between the death of the first bill and the introduction of the second in 1893. Historian Ann Parry has written that the three most popular periodicals of the day that discussed Liberal ideas and politics published only nineteen articles on Ireland from 1886 to 1891. One of these, *The Nineteenth Century*, began publishing numerous essays by influential unionist intellectual A. V. Dicey, beginning in 1892. Dicey's long-standing Liberal credentials provided him an authority with which he could publicly question Gladstone's integrity and motives, while negatively eulogising Parnell by portraying the man 'in his true colours, revealing the type of race to which he belonged'. Additionally, journalist Thomas Lister published his account of a happenstance meeting on a passenger train one evening between himself and Parnell, whom Lister could only describe as cunning, ambivalent and possessing the suspicious temperament typical of an Irishman. This defamation of Parnell's character helped the magazine push a negative portrayal of Home Rule, Irish nationalism and the Irish race in general.[32]

---

31   *Ibid.*, vol. 4, 23 May 1892, col. 1545; vol. 11, 17 April 1893, col. 468.
32   Parry, 'The Home Rule crisis', pp. 26, 28.

Popular cartoons also impugned the character of Parnell and the Irish nationalist platform in the years leading up to the revived debate over Home Rule. *Fun*, a satiric magazine that rivalled *Punch* in London, ran a cartoon in 1890 entitled 'The Two Parnells', in which Parnell was at once portrayed as both patriot and traitor to Ireland for his disreputable behaviour. This realistically human caricature was rather more forgiving of Irish stereotypes than that seen in *Judy* on 20 September 1893. In this cartoon, Salisbury is seen booting out of parliament the second Home Rule bill, portrayed as a diminutive Irishman with torn rags as his clothing.[33]

The fate of the second Home Rule bill was accurate to *Judy*'s portrayal. Though the measure passed the Commons with the numerical superiority of Liberals and Irish nationalist MPs, it foundered in the Conservative-dominated House of Lords in September 1893. Lord Salisbury's successful resistance to the second iteration of Home Rule led to Gladstone's resignation as prime minister a few months later and the end of his political career. With the subsequent dominance of Conservative governments, Home Rule remained a muted issue for nearly two decades. The dialogue surrounding Gladstone's two Home Rule bills, however, suggests that many Britons holding positions of public and intellectual influence in society felt little reason to change their minds about the basic make-up of the Irish racial character.[34]

The third bill, 1910–14

As with the hiatus between the first and second attempts at Home Rule, the years between the second and third bills witnessed a general decline of interest in the Irish question on the part of the British public. The ongoing infighting of Irish nationalists, the reduction of agrarian crime and the influx of thousands of immigrants into London

---

33 Douglas *et al.*, *Drawing Conclusions*, pp. 122, 126.
34 Curtis, *Anglo-Saxons and Celts*, p. 103.

helped shift public attention away from Irish nationalist aspirations. Additionally, international events concerning the Empire, such as Fashoda, the Jameson raid and the Second Boer War, as well as the balance of power on the continent, caused Britons and their leaders more anxiety than the apparently defunct issue of Home Rule.[35]

Some scholars of *fin de siècle* Britain argue that a shift in national identity occurred in the early twentieth century, particularly after the military setbacks in the Second Boer War, the entente with arch-rival France, and the comparative weakening of British industrial and commercial strength with respect to the emerging powers of Germany and the United States. These and other factors point to a gradual decline in the belief of Anglo-Saxon superiority within Britain. Though Chamberlain and public intellectuals hailed the prominence of perceived Anglo-Saxon countries in world affairs, Britons were not as secure in the belief that it was their civilisation leading global progress.[36]

L. P. Curtis argues for a spike in Anglo-Saxon ethnocentrism in the mid-1890s, after which more attention was given to 'environmentalist' than to 'hereditary' explanations of race. In the years immediately after the second Home Rule debates, the publications of William D. Babington's *Fallacies of Race Theories as Applied to National Character* (1895) and John M. Robertson's *The Celt and the Saxon* (1897) helped dispel some of the comparative assumptions laid down by physiognomists and ethnologists earlier in the century. These two anthropologists specifically targeted the Anglo-Saxonism that tainted the scientific inquiries of such men as the Duke of Argyll, Goldwin Smith and John Beddoe; Babington and Robertson argued for

---

35   T. C. Kennedy, 'Troubled Tories: dissent and confusion concerning the party's Ulster policy, 1910–1914', *Journal of British Studies*, no. 3 (July 2007), p. 570.

36   For the political and psychological impact of international events at the turn of the century, see J. Charmley, *Splendid Isolation? Britain, the balance of power and the origins of the First World War* (London, 1999) and A. Friedberg, *The Weary Titan: Britain and the experience of relative decline, 1895–1905* (Princeton, 1988); also Bell, *The Idea of Greater Britain*, pp. 58, 164, 228–46.

environmental factors, instead of inherent Celtic racial characteristics, as the explanation of the perceived differences between the Irish and the Scottish, Welsh and English races. Although a general shift back to a monogenetic 'brotherhood of races' began by the turn of the twentieth century, a focus on racial characteristics through non-adaptive traits could still be found in the emerging literature, such as A. H. Keane's 1900 publication *The World's People*. As the racial basis for anti-Irish prejudice remained the subject of scientific dispute, however, the Irish question again assumed tangible form in the years immediately preceding the First World War.[37]

Hostilities between Catholics and Protestants in Ireland always concerned British lawmakers. The 'Ulster question' proved a perennial stumbling block for both Home Rulers and unionists seeking a solution to the nationalist movements within Ireland, and politicians of all stripes feared Ulster to be an entity irreconcilable with the Catholic counties of the south; indeed one of the motivations for unionists to keep the United Kingdom intact was to avoid having to deal with an increasingly militant Protestant population in Ulster. By 1910, however, tensions came to a head as a new Liberal government under the leadership of Herbert Asquith announced a third Home Rule bill in return for Irish nationalist support in keeping his government in office.[38]

What made this bill exceptional was the political manoeuvring that virtually ensured that Home Rule would become a reality, despite the same Conservative hostility in the House of Lords that killed the bill of 1893. Asquith, more forcefully creative than Gladstone in navigating the halls of power at Westminster, devised the Parliament Act in 1911, which replaced the unlimited veto of the Lords with a two-year delaying power, after which a bill again vetoed in the Lords would become law with the king's assent. This bypass mechanism

---

37 Curtis, *Anglo-Saxons and Celts*, pp. 104–5; Stepan, *The Idea of Race in Science*, pp. 90–1.
38 Peatling, *British Opinion and Irish Self-government*, pp. 67–8.

gave a new urgency to the issue of Home Rule. The Orange Order, a group that believed in the racial superiority of Anglo-Saxon Protestants over Irish Catholics, began arming Ulstermen on the pretext that Home Rule would subvert the religious and civil freedom of Protestants. In 1912 the Ulster Volunteer Force was formed, soon followed by the nationalist Irish Volunteers. If Home Rule seemed now a virtual inevitability, so did civil war.[39]

Before the outbreak of the First World War, which swayed parliament both to pass the Home Rule bill and to suspend its enactment until the termination of the war, a sudden resurgence of Anglo-Saxonist hostility to the Irish accompanied the political turmoil of the day. The leader of the Conservative opposition, Arthur Balfour, was not the ardent supporter of racial differences between the Irish and British that his predecessor Lord Salisbury had been. Balfour, however, like Salisbury, did not believe in Irish nationality and warned that Home Rule would lead to national disintegration for Great Britain. Some of Balfour's fellow Conservatives were not as outwardly progressive in terms of racial equality. James Hope, MP for Sheffield, argued in the Commons that 'race is a more potent factor than religion' in the Irish conflict, and Joseph Larmor from Cambridge stated his belief that the Irish only did well when working in interracial harmony with the English and Scottish within the context of the United Kingdom, where 'we find the true record of their race' in a supporting role to Great Britain.[40]

The media also provided many explicit examples of racial stereotyping. In its 15 January 1913 issue, *Punch* featured a cartoon of an apelike representation of the Home Rule bill, carrying a massive shield emblazoned with the words 'Parliament Act' and holding hostage a gagged Minerva, the goddess of wisdom, as the foolish bill marched toward the House of Lords. Another cartoon from October of the

---

39   J. J. Lee, *Ireland: 1912–1985* (Cambridge, 1990), pp. 2, 8–9.
40   Curtis, *Anglo-Saxons and Celts*, p. 106; *House of Commons Debates*, Fifth series, 8 May 1912, vol. 38, cols 462–3, 626.

same year featured Irish Party leader John Redmond herding a number of pigs, each named after an Irish county. Between 1912 and 1914 *The Times* repeatedly emphasised 'the general backwardness of the southern Irish race', which it characterised as the 'disloyal, retrograde majority'. The editor of *The Times*, Geoffrey Robinson, even editorialised that those in the north of Ireland were of a 'virile and honourable race' and called for unionists to 'fight for the integrity of the Empire'.[41]

In August 1914 the war on the European continent ended all parliamentary debate and caricature on Home Rule, its progress suspended in favour of state unity during the crisis. Such was the sudden shift in events that the foreign secretary, Sir Edward Grey, told the Commons that Ireland 'was the one bright spot' in British politics. Irish leaders such as Redmond and the militant nationalist Tom Kettle were eager to prove their goodwill to the crown by committing units of the Irish Volunteers to the war effort, hoping for a decisive settlement of the Home Rule debate at war's end. This brief moment of solidarity quickly became overshadowed by the circumstances of the war that touched off the violent beginning of Irish independence.[42]

The fourth bill, 1920–21

Although Irish nationalist leaders encouraged their supporters to fight for Britain against the Central Powers in 1914, most young Irishmen refused to fight in a war in which they had no stake, even if Britain claimed to fight for the rights of small nations like Belgium. Meanwhile, Irish militants sought to use the war as an opportunity to win Irish sovereignty by force while Britain's forces were largely deployed

---

41   Douglas *et al.*, *Drawing Conclusions*, pp. 165, 168; T. C. Kennedy, 'Hereditary enemies: home rule, unionism, and *The Times*, 1910–1914', *Journalism History*, no. 1 (Spring 2001), pp. 37, 39.
42   D. G. Boyce, 'A First World War transition: state and citizen in Ireland, 1914–19', in Boyce and O'Day (eds), *Ireland in Transition*, pp. 93–4.

elsewhere. The failure of the Easter Rising of 1916 in Dublin led to the execution of a number of nationalists involved in the rebellion and their deaths galvanised nationalist fervour across Ireland. Furthermore, in early 1918 the British government reversed the earlier decision not to introduce conscription to Ireland; as the German spring offensive threatened to overwhelm the exhausted British armies, an attempt was made to apply conscription to Ireland. In the wake of these events, the anti-Home Rule Sinn Féin nationalist party won a majority of Irish parliamentary seats in the 1918 general election and promptly declared Irish independence from Great Britain.[43]

By the time David Lloyd George's Liberal–Conservative coalition government formulated a fourth Home Rule bill two years after the end of the war, the legislative process in London was running separately from actual events happening in Ireland. The Irish Republican Army (IRA), formerly the Irish Volunteers, was fighting a guerrilla war against regular British forces and their Black and Tan/Auxiliary paramilitary allies. Despite this, politicians at Westminster still worked on a Home Rule bill that was supposed to safeguard the union. While this farce of a bill was read and debated in parliament, the racialisation of Home Rule persisted, albeit in attenuated form. Conservative William Gritten of Hartlepool hearkened to his intellectual predecessors of the late nineteenth century when he remarked of the Irish, 'That race is on account of its temperament happiest when firmly governed', but Ernest Wild, a Conservative from West Ham, claimed it was 'a slur upon the British race that we have given autonomy, freedom, and contentment to every race that we have had to do with except Ireland'.[44]

Popular caricature of the Irish had by 1920 lost much of the simianised tropes it had once relied on, though the occasional

---

43   *Ibid.*, pp. 99–100, 105–7; Y. Taouk, '"We are alienating the splendid Irish race": British Catholic response to the Irish conscription controversy of 1918', *Journal of Church and State*, no. 3 (June 2006), pp. 602–4.

44   *House of Commons Debates*, Fifth series, vol. 127, 30 March 1920, cols 1217, 1204.

cartoon still featured hints of old stereotypes. One *Punch* cartoon entitled 'A test of sagacity' from February 1920 depicted Lloyd George as a music hall entertainer introducing a pig to his audience, which was entrusted to spell out 'Home Rule' with lettered cards. This bestial symbolism of the Irish was by this stage a rarity, however, with most well-known Irish figures portrayed as human beings who held troublesome political views rather than having violent, primitive characteristics. This graphical shift paralleled a larger intellectual shift away from the discredited merits of physiognomy in the scientific sphere. The rise of psychology and non-hereditary anthropology paralleled an increasing interest in eugenic theory, led by Francis Galton, Charles Darwin's cousin. Though eugenics did not enjoy the same prominence in Great Britain as it did in Germany and the United States in the early twentieth century, it continued to shape the debate on ideas of racial fitness and the innate capacities of some humans in relation to others. The anthropologists of the upper and middle classes, meanwhile, increasingly put aside prejudices favourable to the Anglo-Saxon heritage to empathise with, and seek better to understand, the various peoples within the British Empire.[45]

Although the fourth and final Home Rule bill passed into law in June 1921, hostilities prevented its provisions from being enacted anywhere but Northern Ireland. The signing of the Anglo-Irish Treaty in December of the same year led to the creation of the Irish Free State, an independent political entity that maintained connections with London through the Commonwealth. Lloyd George's peace overtures to the Sinn Féin nationalist leaders helped stabilise British attitudes towards Ireland for a time, if only to put the Irish question finally to rest. Political journalist John Lawrence Hammond wrote in July 1921 that 'England ... only wants to get Ireland off its hands', while

---

45 Douglas *et al.*, *Drawing Conclusions*, p. 192; Stepan, *The Idea of Race in Science*, pp. 111–5; E. Barkan, *The Retreat of Scientific Racism: changing concepts of race in Britain and the United States between the world wars* (Cambridge, 1992), p. 25.

The Daily News ironically declared it was 'the opinion of the civilised world' that Ireland should have its own state. Kevin O'Shiel, an Irish official responsible for renegotiating the boundaries between the Free State and Northern Ireland, visited England in 1923 and recalled the different attitude towards the Irish as a race. He felt 'a conviction (for the first time perhaps) that we are possessed of some at least of those qualities of purpose, tenacity and moral courage which English people have been largely brought up to believe are the particular and exclusive monopolies of the Anglo-Saxon race'.[46]

Conclusion

Analysing the racial component of Irish Home Rule as perceived by Britons in the late nineteenth and early twentieth centuries illustrates an important, though often-overlooked, element of the so-called Irish question. Encompassing the span of five decades amid a rapid change in international, scientific and socio-cultural circumstances, the dialogues surrounding these pieces of legislation help illuminate the prescriptions placed on others under British hegemony. In trying to reconcile a historically imperial and artificially domestic relationship with Ireland, part of England's identity as the superior, 'civilising' race in the United Kingdom allowed notions of racial comparison between Anglo-Saxons and Celts to manifest themselves within the political, intellectual and popular discourse of the times.

One problem raised by this multi-layered examination is the effect of paternalistic and racialising English attitudes towards other parts of the United Kingdom. By and large, Welsh and Scottish participation in British derogations towards the Irish were coherent and unremarkable insofar as they followed the English Anglo-Saxonist lead, without reference to their supposed Celtic heritage. Occasionally politicians

---

46 Peatling, *British Opinion and Irish Self-government*, pp. 98–9; Lee, *Ireland*, pp. 144–5.

would point to the Welsh and Scots in Britain as successful recipients of Anglo-Saxon civilisation, as George Goschen (a Scot) did in 1886; so too did the anthropologist Robert Knox, arguing for Scottish lowlander racial affinities with their English cousins. Though men such as Salisbury spoke often of a 'Celtic fringe' that encircled Anglo-Saxon England, Celtic identity in Scotland and Wales was simply not as pronounced at this time as it was in Ireland. Prescribed identities of the Scots by both themselves and the English were in particular flux in the late nineteenth century. As Colin Kidd has proposed, Scottish and Welsh racial identities were often historicised, with ostensibly voluntary cooperation in the union counting much towards the 'progress' of the respective races therein.[47]

The racial undertones at work in dialogues over Irish Home Rule raise many questions about English (and British) ideas of national and imperial identity in the modern era. What other factors contributed to conceptualisations of the national self? To what extent did Britain and its peoples rely on race, class, gender and religion to construct an identity? How much did self-perception rely on imperial influence over others? How did the semi-autonomous members of the Commonwealth reinforce or cast doubt on British self-perceptions, as Ireland had done? The conceptual space afforded by a more inclusive study of race within British politics provides broad opportunities of interpretation for historians of the British Isles and the Empire.

With these questions in mind, the aim of this essay is to promote future considerations of the politics behind the Irish question, and of British social thought in general. A more nuanced appreciation of the staying power of racial thought within Victorian and Edwardian society may go far to enrich the history of British politics of those and later periods.

---

47 C. Kidd, 'Race, empire, and the limits of nineteenth century Scottish nationhood', *The Historical Journal*, no. 4 (Dec. 2003), pp. 874, 891–2.

3

Literary provocateur: revival, revolt and the demise of the *Irish Review*, 1911–14

Kurt Bullock

A letter to the editor of the *Irish Review* (1911–14) published in December 1913 opened: 'I think, Sir, the open court of your pages might perform a useful service to the whole country, if you could elicit constructive suggestions from Irishmen of whatever party regarding the problem in statesmanship which is presented by Ulster.'[1] This comment came from 'An Ulster Imperialist', an anonymous but invited contributor on the Home Rule dilemma in five editions of the *Irish Review* over the previous two-and-a-half years. By December 1913, however, the *Irish Review* was no longer soliciting the 'Ulster Imperialist' to write articles – nor was it offering an 'open court' of opinion on Home Rule, or, for that matter, any social, cultural or political issue. Sharing the pages of the December 1913 issue with the Ulster Imperialist's epistolary plea for equanimity, in fact, were Thomas MacDonagh's 'Marching song of the Irish Volunteers' and Eoin MacNeill's 'Manifesto of the Irish Volunteers' – these latter two

---

1   'An Ulster Imperialist', 'The problem – a letter to the editor', *Irish Review*, vol. 3, no. 4 (December 1913), p. 497.

articles following immediately the letter from 'An Ulster Imperialist', which had received initial placement in that issue's pagination.[2] The *Irish Review* – a publication, according to its banner, dedicated to 'Irish literature, art & science' – had turned suddenly, aggressively nationalist in the midst of the quandary over the third Home Rule bill.

It had not always been that way. Founded and financed in early 1911 by David Houston, and operated primarily with the voluntary assistance of Padraic Colum and Thomas MacDonagh, the *Irish Review* truly was a major anthology of the Irish literary revival and precursor of the literary-minded 'little magazines' that would proliferate throughout the decade. Its roll-call of authors during nearly four years of publication claimed the likes of William Butler Yeats, George Moore, James Stephens, Katherine Tynan, George Russell, Douglas Hyde, Daniel Corkery and Oliver St John Gogarty. A regular contribution in Irish from Patrick Pearse attested to the journal's interest in Gaelic restoration; illustrations supplied by, among other noted artists, William Orpen and Jack Yeats confirmed its revivalist breadth beyond the literary. Mary Colum noted that 'the older and established men of letters did not want to be brushed aside by obstreperous youth in a new Irish periodical; they were bent on sending in their contributions'.[3] The majority of the *Irish Review*'s pages did, in fact, reflect the ongoing cultural revival. The May 1912 issue, for instance, held fifty-six pages of editorial matter, with forty-four of those pages devoted to fiction, poetry, illustration, art-exhibition review, social essay and poetry translation; the other twelve contained two counter-balancing political articles: Arthur Griffith's 'Home rule and Irish unionists' and a piece entitled 'A light

---

2   T. MacDonagh, 'Marching song of the Irish Volunteers', *Irish Review*, vol. 3, no. 4 (December 1913), pp. 500–2; E. MacNeill, 'Manifesto of the Irish Volunteers', *Irish Review*, vol. 3, no. 4 (December 1913), pp. 503–5.
3   M. Colum, *Life and the Dream: memories of a literary life in Europe and America* (New York, 1947), pp. 157–8.

on Ulsteria', published by an anonymous 'Ulster Protestant'.[4] Even amidst political turmoil, most notably the third Home Rule debate, the *Irish Review* initially sought to provide a balanced and principally moderate perspective on partisan affairs.

Interestingly, the lifespan of the *Irish Review* matches almost perfectly the third Home Rule dispute, and the writings of the aforementioned 'Ulster Imperialist', as well as those by Griffith, the 'Ulster Protestant' and numerous others, serve as a measure not only of the 'Irish Question' rampant in those years but also a notable shift in the editorial practices of the *Irish Review*. Its first edition, in March 1911, claimed that it was a monthly periodical 'founded to give expression to the intellectual movement in Ireland' and declared it would 'note current affairs in their historical rather than in their political aspect', favouring no political party.[5] Indeed, that egalitarian position held true through its initial two-and-a-half years under the editorship of first Houston and then Padraic Colum, with MacDonagh serving as assistant editor to both. That changed, however, when MacDonagh instigated the sale of the *Review* by Houston to Joseph Plunkett in June 1913, in the process undermining his good friend Colum. Immediately, its editorial philosophy veered noticeably towards pugnacious political effrontery and any modicum of balance as regards the Home Rule question was eradicated.

At that point the *Irish Review* clearly epitomised its classification under 'political revival' rather than 'literary' or 'cultural' by Tom Clyde in his *Irish Literary Magazines: an outline history and descriptive bibliography* – even if that had not always been the case.[6] Yet I would suggest that the *Irish Review* under MacDonagh and Plunkett

---

4   A. Griffith, 'Home rule and Irish unionists', *Irish Review*, vol. 2, no. 15 (May 1912), pp. 113–8; 'An Ulster Protestant', 'A light on Ulsteria', *Irish Review*, vol. 2, no. 15 (May 1912), pp. 119–23.

5   'Introduction', *Irish Review*, vol. 1, no. 1 (March 1911), pp. 1–2.

6   T. Clyde, *Irish Literary Magazines: an outline history and descriptive bibliography* (Dublin, 2003), p. 34.

remained a periodical devoted to the literary revival, its content of political as opposed to cultural articles remaining proportionately consistent throughout the nearly four years of its publishing life. Rather, it was the tone of political articles – despite how relatively few they were – these editors chose to publish in the *Review* during its final year-and-a-half that has secured the periodical its label of 'political'. No longer treading the middle ground of Irish politics, the *Irish Review*'s belligerent voice was directed squarely at the timorous leadership of Irish Party political leaders such as John Redmond and the hegemonic British forces throttling Irish hope of Home Rule.

Scant analysis of the *Irish Review* exists, unfortunately, the periodical receiving mere mention – if that – in even the most noted scholarly critical appraisals of Ireland in the early 1900s. Patrick Maume's *The Long Gestation: Irish nationalist life, 1891–1918* is exemplary here, offering only a parenthetical notation of the *Irish Review* turning into a 'Volunteer mouthpiece'.[7] Meanwhile, Johann Norstedt, in his 1980 biography of Thomas MacDonagh, provides five pages of largely historical commentary on the *Irish Review*,[8] while MacDonagh's earlier biographers, Edd and Aileen Parks, provide the journal with a nondescript reference.[9] Plunkett's recent biographer, his great-niece Honor Ó Brolcháin, provides undocumented commentary on the final year-and-a-half of the *Irish Review*'s run, with no trace of critical analysis or scholarly citation;[10] nor does any academic appraisal appear in the memoir by her great-aunt, Geraldine Plunkett Dillon (Plunkett's sister), edited by Ó Brolcháin.[11] The most extensive assess-

---

7   P. Maume, *The Long Gestation: Irish nationalist life, 1891–1918* (New York, 1999), p. 156.
8   J. Norstedt, *Thomas MacDonagh: a critical biography* (Charlottesville, 1980), pp. 96–101.
9   E. W. Parks and A. Parks, *Thomas MacDonagh: the man, the patriot, the writer* (Athens, 1967).
10   H. Ó Brolcháin, *16 Lives: Joseph Plunkett* (Dublin, 2012).
11   G. Plunkett Dillon, *All in the Blood: a memoir of the Plunkett family, the 1916 Rising, and the War of Independence*, ed. H. Ó Brolcháin (Dublin, 2006).

ment appears in a 1969 dissertation by Daniel Sullivan on literary periodicals of the time, though his consideration of the *Irish Review* is limited largely to chronological contextualisation.[12] The perspective offered by Maume and Sullivan – that the *Irish Review* was politically militant and that this militancy grew out of socio-cultural conditions – persists, unfortunately, despite the periodical's primary role as a representative document of the literary revival. Even at the height of tension in Dublin, during the autumn of 1913 and the Lockout, the *Review*'s content was heavily literary and cultural; the October 1913 issue, for example, contained thirty-eight pages of fiction, poetry and socio-cultural essay, and only eighteen pages of material that could be deemed 'political' – and six of those were 'Poems of the Irish rebels' translated by Pearse and a one-page review of Frank Cruise O'Brien's *Proportional Representation*. As Denise Ayo notes in a recent article, whose focus is Mary Colum, the *Irish Review*'s 'nationalistic turn in 1913 ... historically characterises its entire existence'.[13] The persistence of such an unfortunate simplification has been reified over scores of years by critics such as Gal Gerson, who brand MacDonagh and Plunkett as 'radical nationalists' who used the *Irish Review* to promote 'overtly revolutionary politics', with the periodical serving as a 'revolt of avant-garde intellectuals' – a simplistic extrapolation at best and arguably misjudged.[14]

It is undoubtedly true that the *Irish Review* altered the tone of its articles during the third Home Rule crisis, even if the proportion of content, cultural to political, remained the same throughout the periodical's history. Tracing, most notably through the writings of

---

12   D. J. Sullivan, 'The literary periodical and the Anglo-Irish revival, 1894–1914' (PhD dissertation, University College Dublin, 1969), pp. 100–15, 231–9.

13   D. Ayo, 'Mary Colum, modernism, and mass media: an Irish-inflected transatlantic print culture', *Journal of Modern Literature*, vol. 35, no. 4 (Summer 2012), p. 111.

14   G. Gerson, 'Cultural subversion and the background of the Irish "Easter poets"', *Journal of Contemporary History*, vol. 30, no. 2 (1995), pp. 333–4.

the 'Ulster Nationalist', the moderately framed agenda of Home Rule as portrayed in the *Irish Review*, however, demonstrates the general tact with which Houston and then Padraic Colum addressed Ireland's most contentious issue of the time. The 'Ulster Imperialist' appears in the second issue of the *Irish Review* in April 1911, again six months later, and once more five months after that. These first three articles, commissioned by Houston, focus on articulating an Irish nationalism that can fit within a British imperialism and conveying the concerns of Ulster unionism – not of England – that are proving an impediment to Home Rule. Says the 'Ulster Imperialist', 'One cardinal mistake of the English is the way they often think of, and talk of, the United Kingdom and the British Empire as if these were actually the English Kingdom and the English Empire.'[15] He notes the failure of 700 years to curtail an Irish nationalism and argues that the Empire must instead work at developing 'its multiple Nationalities, present or future, to the limit of which each is capable'.[16] Thus he distinguishes between a 'real Nationalism' which is 'permanent' and a 'political Nationalism' that he finds 'temporary' and 'accidental'. Says the 'Ulster Imperialist' somewhat reductively:

> One may believe Home Rule to be good or bad according to one's political party, but Home Rule has nothing whatever to do with the existence of Nationality … for Ireland has never had genuine Home Rule since the twelfth century, and there was little enough National Irish sentiment before that date.[17]

He believes that, eventually, nationalism and unionism will 'fuse into

---

15   'An Ulster Imperialist', 'Nationalism and imperialism', *Irish Review*, vol. 1, no. 2 (April 1911), p. 66.
16   *Ibid.*, p. 65.
17   *Ibid.*, p. 68.

a true Nationality', and that Ireland then 'cannot but see that she will owe a deep debt of gratitude to the British Empire'.[18]

To do so, however, the 'Ulster Imperialist' insists that Ulster and the other provinces must recognise that their parochial and provincial allegiances exist beneath their national and imperial obligations. He mordantly, if not sardonically, laments 'the now prehistoric epoch of dynamite and landlord-shooting' that has transpired, rooted in sectarian bigotry.[19] He equally recognises that 'there is a small number of Ulster Protestants who quite sincerely believe that they would be burned by an Irish equivalent of the Inquisition if an Irish Parliament were established, in which Roman Catholics would be in the majority'.[20] Likewise, he empathises with the Catholic who has been conditioned to believe that Protestants want 'nothing better than to exterminate him and all of his faith'.[21] He deems the intolerance to be rooted in 'the men of the Eighties' who 'are still at the head of political forces'.[22] Though his attitude may sound at times supercilious, at others simple-minded, the 'Ulster Imperialist' appears to be walking the middle of the road on Home Rule, stating that 'whatever "England-Over-All" may have meant in the past there is no future for it among the white Nations which compose the Empire'.[23]

There is little new here to those of us sitting a century hence. As Peter Cottrell summarises in *The War for Ireland*, 'Home Rule was nothing less than Rome rule' for the Protestants of Ulster, even as it did not go far enough for the republicans – yet it 'was sufficient' for 'the bulk of Irishmen'.[24] Even though, as J. J. Lee points out, Home

---

18 'An Ulster Imperialist', 'True and false imperialism', *Irish Review*, vol. 1, no. 8 (October 1911), p. 387.
19 'Ulster Imperialist', 'Nationalism and imperialism', p. 71.
20 'An Ulster Imperialist', 'An appreciation of the situation', *Irish Review*, vol. 2, no. 13 (March 1912), p. 6.
21 'Ulster Imperialist', 'Nationalism and imperialism', p. 70.
22 *Ibid.*, p. 69.
23 'Ulster Imperialist', 'True and false imperialism', p. 386.
24 P. Cottrell, *The War for Ireland: 1913–1923* (Oxford, 2009), p. 24.

Rule 'did not propose anything so extreme as an Irish republic', it nonetheless 'provoked' an 'indignant response'.[25] While the Ulster unionists were developing 'The Solemn League and Covenant', with its biblical overtones, hot on the heels of the removal of the House of Lords' veto and Herbert H. Asquith's subsequent 1912 Home Rule bill, John Redmond was scoffing at the implied appeal to force as 'playing at rebellion'.[26] Yet the militarisation of the Ulster Volunteer forces led Patrick Pearse to comment that he thought 'the Orangeman with a rifle a much less ridiculous figure than the nationalist without a rifle'.[27] The lines were blurry: in April 1912, Arthur Balfour stated in the House of Commons that Home Rule 'privileges ... if Ireland be a nation, are not nearly enough', and three months later, speaking in Dublin, Asquith declared that 'in every relevant sense of the term, Ireland is a nation'.[28] Yet Lord Hugh Cecil, speaking in the House of Commons that same year, suggested that Irish nationality 'can never be anything but shameful to themselves and dangerous to the empire. Let them feel the real pride of citizenship in the great nation to which they and we belong.'[29]

It was this muddle of messages that the 'Ulster Imperialist', in the pages of the *Irish Review*, attempted to navigate and articulate in two further articles, appearing in September 1912 and July 1913. His appraisals, meanwhile, became the target for others, courtesy of the *Irish Review*. In its pages, Arthur Griffith responded to his first article by accusing him of 'recognition of English, Scots, and Welsh as British citizens' but the 'relegation of the people' of 'Ireland to the status of British subjects'. States Griffith:

---

25   J. J. Lee, *Ireland 1912–1985: politics and society* (Cambridge, 1989), p. 7.
26   *Ibid.*, p. 18.
27   P. Pearse, 'From a Hermitage', *Irish Freedom* (November 1913), reprinted in *The Collected Works of P. H. Pearse: political writings and speeches* (Dublin, 1916), pp. 139–211.
28   Quoted in D. Ferriter, *The Transformation of Ireland* (Woodstock edition, 2005), p. 123.
29   *Ibid.*

The 'Ulster Imperialist' is glad to boast that he is a citizen of the British Empire. I suggest the Irishman who is proud to boast himself a citizen of the British Empire will discover his long lost brother when he finds the Scotsman who is proud to boast himself a citizen of the English Empire.[30]

There resides a distinction for Griffith between 'Irishmen who think they are Imperialists and Irishmen who know they are Nationalists'.[31] He states:

> The Irish have learned to complain and whimper and even to appeal to their enemies, but they have not learned to admit defeat. Centuries of cruel punishment, because they kicked against the pricks, have taught them a mean wisdom – to dodge the lash and flatter the overseer. But it has not forced them to throw up their hands and cry, 'We surrender'. In seven hundred years that cry has never been forced from the throat of the Irish people. Such stubbornness has irritated the English mind much more than our unsuccessful insurrections.[32]

For Griffith, 'the acceptance of the British Empire is the acceptance of English ascendancy', and his views are echoed, though in much more mellow terms, by others in the pages of the *Irish Review*.[33] Arthur Burrowes, for instance, insists that 'politics are no longer inspired by the extremes that end in the prison cell or on the scaffold', and that currently 'the extremest extreme of our extreme politicians' tell Irish youth 'their supreme duty is to live, not die, for their country'.[34] As to Home Rule, Burrowes forewarns, 'the more we depend upon Great

---

30 A. Griffith, 'True and false imperialism', *Irish Review*, vol. 1, no. 6 (August 1911), p. 269.
31 *Ibid.*, p. 272.
32 *Ibid.*, p. 270.
33 *Ibid.*
34 A. Burrowes, 'Fleshpots and freedom', *Irish Review*, vol. 1, no. 9 (November 1911), p. 417.

Britain financially, the more dependent we shall be politically'.[35] These articles demarcating the nationalist edge, it should be pointed out, appear while Houston is not only owner but also actively editor of the *Irish Review*. Once Houston turns editorship over to Colum, the more zealous exhortations of Irish nationalism disappear from the periodical's pages.

They are replaced, notably, by a series of articles running counter to the hardline nationalist agenda – articles that, as with those by the 'Ulster Imperialist', appear under anonymous authorship. In fact, they are indebted to the 'Ulster Imperialist', it would seem, for the *Irish Review* under Colum now sports, as authors, 'An Ulster Scot', 'An Ulster Protestant', and 'Another Irish Protestant'. These articles appear within a five-month period during the summer of 1912, likely as a response to Asquith's Home Rule bill itself. In 'A light on Ulsteria', published in May 1912 as a counter-argument to Griffith's article, the 'Ulster Protestant' claims that 'reasonable men' realise that 'Ireland is progressing without Home Rule' as is and chastises the nationalist who 'first throws mud and then threatens violence', singling out Professor Thomas Kettle of University College Dublin, a colleague of MacDonagh's. He insists, meanwhile, that 'Irish Protestants gladly bear witness to the high and beautiful morality inculcated and practised by their Catholic fellow-countrymen' and, with more than a hint of absurd condescension, that 'there is not a Protestant home in Ireland that interferes with the religion of its Catholic servant'.[36] Not so, counters 'Another Irish Protestant', writing in response to the 'Ulster Protestant' a month later: '[T]he average uneducated Ulster Protestant (as well as many who are supposed to be educated) believes that Catholicism is a colossal system of fraud and organised iniquity.'[37]

---

35   *Ibid.*, p. 417.
36   'Ulster Protestant', 'A light on Ulsteria', p. 121.
37   'Another Irish Protestant', 'Another light on Ulsteria', *Irish Review*, vol. 2, no. 16 (June 1912), p. 221.

Yet whereas 'Another Irish Protestant' believes 'this talk of fighting is mere bluff' espoused by 'a very small fraction of the more ignorant and stupid',[38] the 'Ulster Scot' – in yet another response published a month later – disagrees, declaring the Ulster unionist to be 'no coward', even if, at present, he does not know whom he will be fighting – the 'Papishes' or the British military effecting undesired Home Rule.[39] 'There will doubtless be some broken heads before Home Rule comes into force', declares the 'Ulster Scot', commenting that as 'extreme are the speeches of the Ulster Unionist leaders, they are mild and weak compared to the opinions openly expressed by the rank and file'.[40]

One is left to wonder what the poor reader of the *Irish Review* was to believe!

Into the fray steps again the 'Ulster Imperialist' to elucidate the facts and mend fences. 'As soon as we get the first cold douche of common sense into Irish politics,' he says in a September 1912 article, 'we will grasp the fact that Irish unionism and Irish nationalism are obverse and reverse of the same coin, and the coin is one that passes current the world over – namely, the objection of mankind to all outsiders who meddle in what is not their business.'[41] The British Empire, he reasons, is predominantly Protestant, its centre in Westminster, and so the interests of the Church of Rome 'are looked after by a mere handful of Catholics'; meanwhile, 'if the Pope himself were installed in Dublin Castle, there would be little or nothing in Ireland for him to control that he does not already control quite as efficiently from Rome'.[42] Ultimately, he says, 'the politics of the most extreme Orangeman and the politics of the most extreme Sinn Féiner are absolutely

---

38 *Ibid.*, p. 221.
39 'An Ulster Scot', 'The denial of north-east Ulster', *Irish Review*, vol. 2, no. 17 (July 1912), p. 233.
40 *Ibid.*, p. 230.
41 'An Ulster Imperialist', 'On history repeating itself', *Irish Review*, vol. 2, no. 19 (September 1912), p. 342.
42 *Ibid.*, p. 337.

identical, save that one is directed against the Vatican and the other against Westminster'.[43]

This salvo by the 'Ulster Imperialist', it should be noted, concludes a five-month onslaught of politically charged articles, including a potent avowal by Arthur Griffith in May 1912 – his second and final article to be published in the *Irish Review*. In that article, he declares that the 'ideals of nationalism are not to be bought and sold', and that Asquith's bill 'does not alter that status of Irishmen by an inch' – that it 'recognises no Irish nation' and 'might equally apply to the latest British settlement on a South Sea Island', leaving the Irish 'impotent'.[44] It appears, though, that Padraic Colum, now fully in charge of the *Irish Review*, grew weary of these brow-beating articles solicited by Houston; his editorial content from this point on dismisses the Ulster rupture all but entirely, choosing to focus instead on more socially conscious issues that pertain – or do not – to impending Home Rule: Patrick Pearse on education, Hannah Sheehy-Skeffington and Frederick Ryan on women's suffrage, Justin Phillips on land purchase, James Meredith on proportional representation. These all are matters, it is true, that assume the passage of Home Rule, in some amended form or another – rhetoric that aligns with what Diarmaid Ferriter refers to as a 'mass movement' in Ireland that had a 'constitutional focus'.[45] Yet more than ever, the *Irish Review* under Colum returns to its initial emphasis – the 'intellectual movement' in its 'application of Irish intelligence to the reconstruction of Irish life'.[46] While, as Mary Colum recalls, Padraic Colum 'fancied himself as a political commentator', it should be noted that Padraic contributed no signed political commentaries in the *Irish Review*, only poetry and literary criticism.[47] As principal editor

---

43   *Ibid.*, p. 342.
44   Griffith, 'Home rule and Irish unionists', pp. 114–5.
45   Ferriter, *The Transformation of Ireland*, p. 117.
46   'Introduction', *Irish Review*, p. 1.
47   Colum, *Life and the Dream*, p. 158.

of the *Review* from late spring of 1912 to the end of summer 1913, he effectively shied away from the political volatility surrounding the Home Rule bill, opting instead impassively to tread a path of political indifference.

The editorial tone of Colum's publication, then, was no match for the nationalist venom produced by the *Irish Review* under the ownership of Joe Plunkett and control of Thomas MacDonagh beginning in late summer 1913. I wish to contend, in fact, that Colum's passivity in articulating the 'Irish Question', particularly as it related to Home Rule, provoked the more politically uncompromising MacDonagh into instigating David Houston's June 1913 sale to Plunkett. MacDonagh's disenchantment with the literary revival and cultural nationalism, I maintain, drove him to undermine both the editorship of Colum and the egalitarian intent of the periodical, transforming the *Irish Review* and stifling the mediated Home Rule rhetoric of the 'Ulster Imperialist', among others. With a circulation never exceeding 2,300, at no time did the *Irish Review* prove a self-sustaining enterprise, despite the voluntary services of its staff and complimentary contributions of its writers; additionally – with Ernst Manico, the periodical's printer, indicating to Houston how Colum's sloppy editing was causing delays and increasing costs – Houston grew increasingly displeased with Colum's editorship. Just over one year after relinquishing the editorship to Colum, Houston sought to sell the *Irish Review*, leaving Colum to frantically seek financial backing from past supporters such as George Roberts, Lord Dunsany and Alice Stopford Green in order to retain his editorship.

Colum's efforts were to no avail and MacDonagh, unbeknownst to Colum, recommended the sale of the *Irish Review* to Plunkett. Only twenty-five years of age, Plunkett had no personal income, aside from an allowance from his mother, yet MacDonagh, having served as his Irish tutor since 1909, was well aware of the Ascendency-class family's financial assets and nationalist leanings. First learning on a Saturday evening, 14 June, of the potential sale by Houston to Plunkett, Colum visited Plunkett the next day and implored him to delay his purchase until Wednesday 18 June at the earliest; instead, Plunkett met with Houston and Manico the next morning, 16 June, and, according to Houston, 'within twenty minutes we had the agreement written, signed and witnessed'.[48] Colum was not blind to the coup that had taken place, writing to Houston immediately after his ousting: 'I regarded the *Irish Review* as a rudimentary organ of free opinion in Ireland. That is the reason I regret it will have ceased to exist as such after the July issue.'[49] Crucially, Colum clearly recognised – even if Houston did not – that this sale constituted a drastic change in the editorial direction of the periodical. And it is in the July 1913 issue – Colum's last as editor – that Colum provided the 'Ulster Imperialist' with one last platform for his centrist rhetoric. The 'Ulster Imperialist' concluded that article with this thought:

> Whatever our politics, we have all got to live together in our little island, and a time is approaching when both sides may have to concede something to the other in order that the next chapter may begin with as much good will as is attainable in this once distressful country.[50]

Save for the 'Ulster Imperialist's' plea in his letter to the editor some five months later – an inclusion by MacDonagh and Plunkett that could be considered parodic, perhaps even contemptuous, of Colum's editorial decisions – the middle ground of Irish politics would never again grace the pages of the *Irish Review*.

---

48 David Houston to Thomas MacDonagh, 16 June 1913, Thomas MacDonagh papers, MS 44,328/2, National Library of Ireland (NLI).
49 19 June 1913, *ibid*. Colum's remarks were made in a letter he had sent to Houston, and which Houston then directly quoted in his letter to MacDonagh.
50 'An Ulster Imperialist', 'Half-time', *Irish Review*, vol. 3, no. 29 (July 1913), p. 237.

For MacDonagh and Plunkett there could be no concession and the *Irish Review* would no longer be the 'open court of opinion' so desired by the 'Ulster Imperialist' and Colum. MacDonagh's intentions for the publication were made evident in a letter to his friend Dominick Hackett in March 1911, shortly after the periodical's inaugural issue: 'The *Review* will speak for itself, and say something for me too.'[51] In the second issue following Colum's departure, MacDonagh and Plunkett replaced the word 'science' in the *Irish Review*'s banner with the word 'politics' – and those politics were decidedly rebellious. Take, for instance, MacDonagh's translation of an Irish poem in that issue, which declared that the poet will 'befriend and defend' Ireland during 'battle's contention', or his 'Marching song of the Irish Volunteers' but three months later, the chorus of which proclaimed 'our ranks we band in might', while the eight verses outlined the millennium of conquerors to Ireland's shore – including the 'evil hour' whence came the Normans, though Ireland 'has yielded not' and currently 'unconquered stand[s] and waits the word'.[52] The following summer MacDonagh wrote an anonymous first-person account of the Howth gun-running, proclaiming 'the incompetence and dishonesty of the British authorities' while asserting 'that if the leaders of the Irish people act strongly and decisively, they can succeed' in claiming 'national victory'. He added: 'The men who ruled Ireland in the past under Tory regime and Liberal regime lost their power on the 26th of July [1914]' – the day of the Howth gun-running.[53] Further articles demonstrated an ambition to attack British hegemonic practices in Dublin newspapers, such as James Connolly's 'Labour in Dublin',

---

51 Thomas MacDonagh to Dominick Hackett, 29 March 1911, MacDonagh papers, MS 10,854/5, NLI.
52 T. MacDonagh, 'Druimfhionn donn dilis', *Irish Review*, vol. 3, no. 31 (September 1913), p. 359.
53 T. MacDonagh, 'Clontarf 1914', *Irish Review*, vol. 4, no. 14 (July–August 1914), supplement.

published at the height of the Dublin Lockout,[54] or Sir Roger Casement's series of articles on British plans to eliminate Cobh as a port of call.[55] Under MacDonagh and Plunkett, the *Irish Review* aimed at nothing less than to subvert and disrupt the stranglehold of journalistic censure practised by British authority in Irish papers of the time, displacing Colum's tepid cultural nationalism with their own confrontational political nationalism and providing a voice to Irish positions that would never see the light of day in the larger Dublin newspapers.

For MacDonagh that purpose of proclaiming the Irish nationalist political cause came well before the crisis in Dublin during the autumn of 1913. As early as March 1909, in fact, MacDonagh talked at length with W. B. Yeats about 'the destructiveness of journalism here in Ireland', asserting that 'the habits of thought of current Irish journalism' were to blame for 'infecting Irish not only with the English idiom' but also with English ideas.[56] MacDonagh claimed a 'baptism in nationalism' while teaching at St Kieran's college in Kilkenny in 1902,[57] and Desmond Ryan – a later student of MacDonagh's at St Enda's, Pearse's bilingual school – recalls him saying that prior to Kilkenny, he had been 'the greatest West Britisher in Ireland'.[58] Joining the Gaelic League in February 1902, MacDonagh would spend that summer on the Aran Islands, then leave St Kieran's the following summer because the college refused to teach the Irish language. He became a leader and public speaker on behalf of the League, first in Fermoy and then in Dublin, following his 1908

54   J. Connolly, 'Labour in Dublin', *Irish Review*, vol. 3, no. 32 (October 1913), pp. 385–91.
55   Sir Roger Casement, 'From "Coffin ship" to "Greyhound"', *Irish Review*, vol. 3, no. 36 (February 1914), pp. 609–13; vol. 4, no. 37 (March 1914), pp. 1–11; vol. 4, no. 38 (April 1914), pp. 57–67.
56   W. B. Yeats, *The Collected Works of W. B. Yeats: autobiographies* (vol. 3), eds W. H. O'Donnell and D. N. Archibald (New York, 1999), p. 360.
57   Thomas MacDonagh, Notebook, *c.* 1903–6, MacDonagh papers, MS 44,342, NLI.
58   D. Ryan, *Remembering Sion: a chronicle of storm and quiet*, (London, 1934), p. 95.

relocation to teach for St Enda's, and also served as an Irish tutor to others – including Plunkett.

But a disenchantment with cultural nationalism was replaced by a desire for political nationalism at that point – perceived, most notably, in MacDonagh's 1908 play *When the Dawn is Come*, performed at the Abbey Theatre that autumn, about 'a time of insurrection', of 'getting up the rising', as he refers to the drama in a letter to Hackett.[59] Correlative with this was MacDonagh's work at St Enda's, where 'we are carrying out our ideals', he tells Hackett, performing 'work for the country, directly for the country, and that is a great deal'.[60] Other letters to Hackett around this time detail MacDonagh's dissatisfaction with the Gaelic League, particularly regarding debate over whether Irish should be compulsory in schools. Yeats details a conversation with MacDonagh on 6 March 1909 in which the latter claimed he was 'losing faith in the League', and that the move toward nationalism was 'practically dead, that the language would be revived but without all that [MacDonagh] loved it for'.[61] Two weeks later, following another meeting with MacDonagh, Yeats records him as being 'very sad about Ireland'.[62] Mary Colum recalls in her memoir how MacDonagh lamented 'the country will be one entire slum unless we get into action', and that 'in spite of our literary movements and Gaelic Leagues it is going down and down. There's no life or heart in the country.'[63] MacDonagh's further correspondence with Hackett further illustrates that as far back as March 1911 he was clearly agitated by the shortcomings of Arthur Griffith's Sinn Féin movement, 'the question of finances of Home Rule', the 'Home Rule fiasco', and the 'disaster' of John Redmond's 'resolution'.[64] Securing

---

59   MacDonagh to Hackett, 10 April 1908, MacDonagh papers, MS 22,934, NLI.
60   *Ibid.*, 5 November 1908.
61   Yeats, *The Collected Works*, p. 360.
62   *Ibid.*, p. 373.
63   Colum, *Life and the Dream*, pp. 237–8.
64   MacDonagh to Hackett, 29 March 1911, MacDonagh papers, MS 22,934, NLI.

the *Irish Review*, then, served as nothing less than MacDonagh's ambition to respond forcefully to his personal concerns over the fate of Irish nationalism and, crucially, the third Home Rule impasse.

The final issue of the *Irish Review*, published in November 1914, included beneath the fourth and final 'Manifesto of the Irish Volunteers' the signatures of MacDonagh and Plunkett, along with eighteen others. The article itself unequivocally disbarred Redmond from 'any place in the administration or guidance' of the Irish Volunteers, as a result of his actions that 'throw the country into turmoil' and 'destroy the chance of a Home Rule measure' that would 'provide the free action of a National Government of [Ireland's] own'.[65] Copies of that issue were seized by British forces and the *Irish Review* – once a monthly periodical of 'Irish literature, art and science' that would favour no political party – was for all practical purposes censured. Said the undeterred MacDonagh in a letter to Hackett just weeks later: 'We are making preparations. Destiny will take charge of the issue', referring to 'the event' to come where he and others will be 'liberators … if necessary, by war'.[66] MacDonagh asserts that he remains among 'those who, under all circumstances and at all times, will and must be Irish rebels'.[67] The prescient Padraic Colum, in a letter to David Houston a year-and-a-half earlier, had said: 'If you do not perceive that MacDonagh had an interest in Plunkett's getting the *Review*, your judgment was very bad. In cases such as these bad judgment is something like a crime.'[68] That crime, if one were committed, was to close the 'open court' of 'constructive suggestions' in the *Irish Review*, move beyond a suspect Home Rule bill, and prepare Ireland not for literary revival, but violent revolution.

---

65 E. MacNeill, 'Manifesto of the Irish Volunteers', *Irish Review*, vol. 4, no. 42 (September–November 1914), pp. 281–3.
66 MacDonagh to Hackett, 15 January 1915, MacDonagh papers, MS 22,934, NLI.
67 *Ibid.*, 19 May 1915.
68 Houston to MacDonagh, 19 June 1913, MacDonagh papers, MS 10,854/5, NLI. See above, footnote 49.

4

Liberal public discourse and the third Home Rule bill

James Doherty

With the restoration of self-government for Ireland to the Liberal programme in the early 1910s, sectional causes that had laid claim to Liberal hearts and minds since Home Rule had been cleaned from the slate in 1895 had to be acknowledged and accommodated.[1] To assert Home Rule's contemporary relevance, its 1912 incarnation had to mediate a number of strands of principle and matters of practical concern to Liberals. Home Rule propagandists mounted spirited rhetorical campaigns, not least because of an awareness of the need to reanimate the issue of Irish self-government in Liberal Britain. The mantle of Home Rule was, accordingly, fitted to many purposes. It was used to persuade British working men that Irish self-government advanced their interests. In the same way, the interests of nonconformists, and Liberal imperial and free-trade views, could all be expressed by means of Irish self-rule. In the name of achieving their centrepiece policy, Liberal and Irish nationalist propagandists crafted arguments for Home Rule to suit most (though not, of course, unionist) tastes.

---

1   I am grateful to the Arts and Humanities Research Council for supporting the research on which this essay is based.

Two organisations in particular sought to reinvigorate British support for Home Rule. The Home Rule Council was a semi-detached Liberal Party organisation, chaired from 1909 to 1912 by the Liberal chief whip, Alexander Murray, Master of Elibank.[2] In addition to publishing books and pamphlets, the organisation convened public meetings to promote the Irish cause and sent activists and canvassers to assist in Liberal by-election campaigns. The Irish Press Agency, first established by the Irish Party in 1886, was headed, from 1908, by Stephen Gwynn, MP. Like its Liberal counterpart, the Irish Press Agency published books and pamphlets for British consumption and engaged in canvassing in English and Scottish by-elections. It also organised an ambitious speaking tour of a claimed 500 engagements in English constituencies in 1912, drafting forty-three Irish Party MPs for the purpose.[3]

A variety of British newspapers, representing Liberal, nationalist and Labour perspectives, promoted the cause of Irish liberty. The *Daily News and Leader*, *The Nation* and *Reynolds's Newspaper* reflected and circulated influential strands of Liberal opinion. Among nonconformist newspapers, the *Methodist Times* most faithfully supported the Irish cause. The halfpenny *Daily Citizen* provided a mix of support and criticism from a Labour perspective. A somewhat surprising outlet for radical arguments was the *Catholic Times and Catholic Opinion* (hereafter *Catholic Times*). Whilst its support for the nationalist cause was to be expected, the paper's advanced progressive editorial positions – particularly its support for the political organisation of labour – must have spoiled more than one Roman Catholic bishop's breakfast.

The Lepracaun Cartoon Monthly (hereafter *The Lepracaun*), a monthly satirical magazine published in Dublin, provided a distinctive commentary on the third Home Rule debates. The cartoons of *The*

---

2   *The Times*, 13 June 1912.
3   *The Freeman's Journal*, 10 August 1912.

Lepracaun's editor and principal illustrator, Thomas Fitzpatrick, were often unflattering to the Irish Party and its leader, John Redmond, but with the advent of the Home Rule bill, *The Lepracaun* presented the party in a consistently positive light, and saved its ammunition for the unionists and, occasionally, William O'Brien.[4] So apposite and well executed were its cartoons that thirty-eight of them were reprinted in the London monthly *Review of Reviews* from 1910 to 1914.[5]

What emerged from the welter of books, pamphlets, newspapers and journals was a coherent set of arguments for Home Rule, originating from English and Irish sources. Home Rule literature and politicians' speeches reprised rhetoric from the unsuccessful Home Rule campaigns of 1886 and 1893, but a number of new and contemporary themes were introduced. These arguments, old and new, arose from a cross-fertilisation of ideas from Irish nationalist intellectual to British Liberal, and from propagandist to politician, and vice versa. Liberal pamphlets drew upon nationalist speeches, Irish nationalist politicians wrote for Liberal newspapers, and newspapers and pamphlets supplied the stuff of platform oratory. T. M. Kettle arguably dominated the output of Home Rule propaganda, writing on all aspects of the Irish question with such effectiveness and elegance of language that his words were widely published and reprinted in British newspapers and journals. Nationalist MPs such as Stephen Gwynn and J. G. Swift MacNeill wrote both Irish Press Agency publications and articles appearing in English journals, while MP Jeremiah MacVeagh's *Home Rule in a Nutshell* was published by the Irish Press Agency in 1911, reissued by the Liberal Home Rule Council in 1912 and substantially serialised in the *Morning Leader* in the same year.

The circular nature of this exchange of ideas meant that

---

4   Thomas Fitzpatrick biography, from http://irishcomics.wikia.com/wiki/Thomas_Fitzpatrick_%281860–1912%29 (consulted 31 January 2013).
5   Data from British Periodicals Online, http://search.proquest.com/british periodicals/index (accessed 24 May 2012).

rhetoric in the British Liberal press was indistinguishable from the Irish nationalist position and, as often as not, was written by a nationalist. T. P. O'Connor, MP, wrote a weekly column for *Reynolds's Newspaper*, dealing almost exclusively with Irish Home Rule, from 1913. Nationalist civil servant T. P. Gill was an anonymous 'Special Correspondent' for the *Daily Chronicle* in 1914, while MacVeagh was among the Liberal Home Rule Council's most effective proponents in print and on the stump.[6] 'Liberal' rhetoric around the third Home Rule bill can therefore be said to be an amalgam of Liberal and Irish nationalist creation. Except for critical perspectives from some socialist-leaning organs, the messages for British audiences in 1912 from supporters of the Irish cause – Liberal, nationalist and Labour – were emphatic and consistent, and sought to overcome the obstacles thrown up in the previous Home Rule battles, as well as to assimilate new and competing popular demands.

Arguments for Home Rule

Pamphlets revived imperial and financial arguments for self-government from earlier campaigns, which abounded with examples and lessons from Irish and imperial history. As before, the most sensitive issue, and the one with which Home Rule propagandists felt that they had to deal with at greatest length, was the fear of sectarian discrimination against Protestants under a predominantly Roman Catholic Dublin parliament. The emotional potential of this issue to rouse an indifferent electorate in Great Britain was the hope of British and Ulster unionists, and the dread of Home Rulers. Opponents of Home Rule calculated that, as in 1886, fear of Catholic intolerance could submerge all the rational and carefully crafted arguments of the nationalist movement under a wave of Protestant sentiment. Of all the cries that might be raised against Irish self-government, 'Home Rule

---

6   *The Times*, 23 April 1932.

means Rome rule' was recognised – by both sides of the controversy – as the one appeal that could so inflame British Protestant opinion that the bill might be wrecked altogether. For this reason, the issues of religious intolerance and the relations of Protestant and Catholic under a future Dublin parliament were extensively discussed in the Liberal press and pamphlet debates. Nationalist supporters mustered a series of nuanced arguments to dispel the bogeys of Catholic domination and Protestant subjugation. They relied especially upon the contributions of Protestant Home Rulers, Anglican and nonconformist, by whose testimony it was hoped that British Protestant fears could be disarmed.

The Roman Catholic hierarchy in Ireland, English Protestant Sydney Brooks believed, supported Irish liberty only so long as it was sure Ireland would not get it.[7] Methodist minister Joseph Hocking concurred that the church did not, in fact, want Home Rule, benefiting so much, as it did, from the existing state of affairs. 'Under no Home Rule Government,' he wrote, 'could she rule so completely, so absolutely, as she does now. Under no form of self-government could she dictate her will as she dictates it now.'[8] In other words, fear of Rome Rule was fantastical, because it was almost impossible for Ireland (with the exception of Ulster) to be more subject to Rome Rule than it already was.[9]

Stern anti-Romanism was no bar to support for Home Rule. The Vatican, Sydney Brooks charged, cared little for Ireland, but greatly about England. The Holy See's main concern, he contended, was that a reduction in the number of Irish representatives sent to Westminster after the passage of Home Rule would deprive English Catholics of the crucial parliamentary support of the Irish nationalists.[10] The Irish

---

7   S. Brooks, 'Aspects of the religious question in Ireland', *The Fortnightly Review*, February 1912, p. 391.
8   J. Hocking, *Is Home Rule Rome Rule?* (London, 1912), p. 174.
9   *Ibid.*, pp. 128, 189.
10   Brooks, 'Aspects of the religious question', p. 392.

hierarchy, Brooks suspected, dreaded a loss of influence over the imperial parliament even more than it did the erosion of its overwhelming power in Ireland. Some Protestants believed the Irish Party was the pope's agency at Westminster, and nonconformists, in particular, believed the party had intruded an injunction of the Catholic Church over English legislation by voting against the Education bill in 1906.[11] In reducing Irish representation at Westminster, it was argued, the 'poisonous' influence of Rome in England could be diminished.

Viewed through a nonconformist prism, Irish Home Rule was a vehicle for intellectual, moral and spiritual self-improvement, a virtuous synthesis of evangelical and Liberal goals. Free Church Protestantism, it was held, would rise to the top of Irish society by virtue of its tolerance and the inspiration of its example. Its mission would be the liberation of the minds of the people.[12] 'Pat' (P. D. Kenny, Irish journalist and bitter Catholic critic of the church) expressed a spiritual dimension to Home Rule that many nonconformists could have supported: 'The real problem is to restore the use of their wits to the Irish people. *We want peasant proprietorship in mental freedom. We want self-governorship for the peasant* [emphasis in original].'[13] In other words, Home Rule for Ireland could mean Home Rule of the mind and spirit for the smallholder in his cottage. Dr John Clifford, paragon of nonconformist Liberalism, asserted that most free churchmen, British and Irish, could see the divine ordination of Home Rule, and answer the call of a mission to liberate and redeem Catholic Ireland.[14] Clifford and nonconformist Home Rulers were the inheritors, and most characteristic practitioners, of Gladstone's evangelical style of Home Rule politics.

The connection between Irish self-government and advancement

---

11   *The Baptist Times*, 14 May 1906.
12   W. Crawford, 'A nonconformist view', J. H. Morgan (ed.), *The New Irish Constitution* (Cork, 1912), p. 90.
13   Hocking, *Is Home Rule Rome Rule?*, p. 190.
14   *Daily News and Leader*, 13 April 1912.

of the cause of working men in Britain was a new feature of the 1912 Home Rule rhetoric. Earlier campaigns had claimed that a prosperous, self-governing Ireland would benefit the British industrial classes in practical terms, through more work, less wage competition and lower taxation.[15] In 1912, however, arguments for Irish Home Rule were crafted to persuade working men that they had a direct interest in the Irish national demand. A grant of self-government to Ireland would be, some Home Rule propagandists argued, a blow struck, directly, for democratic and social reforms for the British worker.[16] The *Catholic Times* asserted that the landowning class so hard at work against Irish Home Rule in 1912 had fought Englishmen's struggles for liberty and a political voice down through history. Ordinary men, who now held power under a democratic franchise, were encouraged to ask themselves why the opponents of Irish Home Rule should be taking up the issue with such bitterness and assiduity.[17] Was it not plain to the English working man, it asked, that opposition to Home Rule was opposition to him and to the removal of his grievances?[18] The English worker was urged to recognise the latter-day opponents of Irish Home Rule as the same historic enemies as those of his own dispossessed ancestors. Deliverance of both countries from 'titled English robbers', said socialist newspaper *The Clarion*, was what was needed for the social salvation of Ireland and England.[19]

An unorthodox view of socialism and Irish self-government was advanced by Harold Begbie in his 1912 book *The Lady Next Door*. Begbie asserted that the negative polarity of the two islands had produced a bizarre outcome aligning English Tories and Irish socialists against English socialists and Irish conservatives. Socialists in Ireland

---

15   F. W. Evans, *A Workman's View of the Irish Question* (London, nd).
16   For example, *Daily Citizen*, 18 January 1913; *Reynolds's Newspaper*, 11 February 1912; *Catholic Times*, 22 November 1912.
17   *Catholic Times*, 15 March 1912.
18   *Ibid.*, 26 June 1914.
19   *The Clarion*, 14 June 1907.

supported the union to escape what they thought would be the saturating conservatism of a Dublin parliament, while Irish conservatives dreamt of displacing a Protestant, industrial hegemony with a Catholic, agrarian one of their own.[20] This was of a piece with Irish-Ireland arguments in the Home Rule literature, which posited that the British and Irish nations were economically and spiritually misaligned, resulting in a disjuncture only capable of remedy by self-government.[21]

A few writers, arguing on behalf of the third Home Rule bill, speculated how a future Dublin government might remould Irish society in organically Irish ways. Though the bill itself was drafted by British ministers, with little reference to Irish ideas, some advocates of Irish self-government saw Home Rule opening up a new vista for Irish society: one in which the Irish way of life would be at once purified of corrupting Anglicisation and made more harmonious and prosperous. This was by no means a common theme in the Liberal and nationalist public discourse, but the presence of the argument points to a growing awareness of the Irish-Ireland movement, and a desire to explain its meaning to British audiences.

Ideas of romanticised agrarianism were popular at the time, in Britain as much as in Ireland. Home Rule and David Lloyd George's land campaign were presented as promising a sort of pastoral salvation for the British Isles, freeing the people of Ireland first and then those of England. Restoring the lands of the two islands to the people and returning to a simpler pattern of life, of tilling the soil and living off the produce of the land, would be to exchange the wretchedness of industrial life for something approaching paradise.[22] Ireland enjoyed an advantage, which England did not, in bringing this vision to fruition, in that Ireland's earthly paradise was as yet unspoiled.

---

20   H. Begbie, *The Lady Next Door* (London, 1912).
21   *Ibid.*, pp. 319–22; *Catholic Times*, 3 January 1913; Brooks, 'Aspects of the religious question', p. 392.
22   *Catholic Times*, 2 August 1912.

British rule, writers like Sydney Brooks asserted, was a corrupting influence in Ireland, one that had left Irishmen 'nondescripts, half-provincial English, half-renegade and emasculated'.[23] Others, like Harold Begbie, feared that the polluting way of life under the union would lead to the industrial anarchy and commercial brutality of England being reproduced in Ireland.[24] A government of Irishmen, guided by Irish ideas, would offer the chance of preserving the purity of the land, the air, and the spirit of the people themselves. For what was the use of Home Rule, if it meant importing the factories and squalid life of industrial England to Ireland?

From the Irish-Ireland viewpoint, a dystopian vision of Ireland, or a flabby West British imitation, was in prospect if Ireland remained under British rule. Government according to Irish ideas would mean following the Irish nature. Begbie asserted that the mass of the people of Ireland, Roman Catholic and agrarian, were naturally conservative. They did not desire change, but wanted peace and continuity. A fundamental clash of cultures, he claimed, went to the heart of the impossibility of benign English rule: the two nations were on different paths of destiny. One, England, was embarked on a course of materialism, accruing the wealth, power and social turmoil that her choice entailed. The other, Ireland, was seeking a national life without materialism, one in which a free people could till the land in harmony with nature and enjoy a simple life in which the spiritual remained the supreme reality.[25]

T. M. Kettle, writing of 'The Catholic future in Ireland', foresaw a return to the land, to the community and to the teachings of the Catholic Church, which, he believed, would result in a society built on agriculture, local industry and cooperation. This rejection of urbanism and unbridled capitalism was, he asserted, an expression of Catholicity and

---

23 *The Nation*, 12 October 1912.
24 Begbie, *The Lady Next Door*.
25 *Ibid.*, pp. 320–2.

of keeping faith with the Irish way of life.[26] Brooks argued that the independence of thought and social reordering, which innovations like agricultural cooperation and the Irish language were breeding in Ireland, were cultivating a generation of people possessing a strong national identity and a progressive and increasingly secular culture.[27] Like Kettle's vision, the future Ireland populated by this generation would be agricultural and cooperative, but it would be the product of dynamic, free-thinking minds, rather than the consummation of a Roman Catholic arcadia. Begbie, as a Methodist minister, could embrace neither the Catholic nor the secular point of view, but he nonetheless agreed that the Irish experiment of living without materialism would be an admirable one. A self-governing Ireland that was true to the 'backbone' of her past and her natural way of life promised to propagate, for her people, a contentment that England had lost.[28] In setting the Irish people free to follow their own path, England might be repaid by an example of national fulfilment and happiness.[29] He commended his British readers to give Ireland her chance to live national life in her own way. The English people should honour Ireland 'for her sense of nationality … revere her for the beauty and simplicity of her life … be interested in her choice of natural simplicity, and … help her with all the power they possess'.[30]

The Ulster crisis

Opposition from the Protestants of north-east Ulster was recognised by Liberal and nationalist supporters as the principal obstacle in the way of the third Home Rule bill. Home Rulers were confident, however, that Ulster Protestant resistance was unsustainable and that it would fall before reasoned arguments, a display of sensitivity to Protestant

---

26 *Catholic Times*, 3 January 1913.
27 Brooks, 'Aspects of the religious question', p. 392.
28 *The Freeman's Journal*, 9 September 1912.
29 Begbie, *The Lady Next Door*, p. 323.
30 *Ibid.*, p. 325.

sentiment and proffered legislative safeguards. The resistant population of 'Ulster' was, in their view, a minority within a minority within a minority. Home Rule propagandists went to great lengths to challenge the vaunted 'Ulster' opposition to Home Rule, pointing out that large sections of the population of Ulster desired Home Rule, as could be illustrated by the record of election results between 1885 and 1910. The consistently narrow rivalry of nationalists and unionists in election contests in the province was cited as proof that the voice of Ulster, as a whole, on Home Rule was by no means united in opposition.[31] It was rather, critics charged, *Belfast* resistance to Home Rule that was being amplified and exaggerated by unionists as representing the verdict of the whole of Ulster. To accept Belfast as being indicative of Irish opinion on Home Rule, one writer argued, was no more valid than to assume that Birmingham represented English opinion on protection.[32]

Home Rule proponents asserted that Irish Protestant fears were baseless. Under Home Rule, they pointed out, Protestants would remain under the protection of the imperial parliament. They numbered one million in a nation of four million and were a minority certainly not inferior in grit, nor in conviction, to their Catholic countrymen.[33] As for Belfast, its fortune had been made by the hard-working, tenacious and resilient character of its Protestant forebears. Why would their descendants allow a Dublin parliament to endanger Belfast's industrial pre-eminence, even if it tried?[34]

If there could be no accounting for irrational fears, Liberal and nationalist writers expressed the hope that one aspect of the Ulster-man's character would overcome his worries – his thrift. Cynics suspected that the overriding consideration for the Ulsterman was the likely effect of Home Rule on his pocketbook and that if it promised

---

31 *Daily News and Leader*, 9 February 1912.
32 Home Rule Council, *Home Rule ?s Answered* (London, 1912), pp. 42–5.
33 *The Nation*, 20 January 1912.
34 Hocking, *Is Home Rule Rome Rule?*, pp. 185–8.

to advantage his trade, his fears would quickly evaporate. *The Freeman's Journal* wrote that, Solemn League and Covenant or no, if a Dublin parliament reduced internal rail rates, nary 'a passive resister would insist on paying a higher rate', or if it introduced a scheme of compulsory purchase, not a single Orangeman would resent the title of peasant proprietor.[35] Harold Begbie believed the Protestant working class of Ulster would give more thought to their household economy than to fantastical spectres of popery, prophesying, in his poem 'Better Times':

> The Orange poor will toil, the rich make money …
> Workman and clerk, dismiss your dread,
> the Pope still in his prison lingers;
> Pirrie won't burn his boats, nor Ned [Carson] his fingers …
> But this will pass.
> The wise will own, while babies are born and trade increases,
> peace is better than being blown to pieces.[36]

The business owner's hard head, said Liberal propagandists, would overcome pledges to deny the legitimacy of a Home Rule parliament. The *Catholic Times* argued that a provisional government, setting itself apart both from a Dublin parliament and from Westminster, would involve disruption of trade and civil law. With these requisites of commerce in disarray, one could expect, at the least, mischief when 'some witty Irishman will order from a Belfast merchant or shopkeeper, and laugh while the creditor appeals to his precious Ulster Assembly to put the law in motion against the debtor in Cork or Dublin'.[37] Such considerations would surely give the merchants of Belfast pause for thought; but for the manufacturers of the linen trade and shipbuilding,

---

35 *The Freeman's Journal*, 23 August 1912, p. 6.
36 Lord Pirrie was the Liberal-supporting chairman of shipbuilders Harland & Wolff. *The Nation*, 18 October 1913.
37 *Catholic Times*, 30 August 1912.

the losses owing to interruption of supplies and receivables, and legal disputes, were potentially incalculable. Were the scions of industry really so rash as to risk insolvency on a speculative fear? Much of the Liberal press thought not. The Covenant-supporting business owners ran a political risk, too, for if Orangemen boycotted an Irish parliamentary election, they might find their seats taken by Labour representatives. An assertive and burgeoning Labour Party firmly entrenched in Belfast and environs, whose emergence was confidently predicted, would be a most unwelcome development for large employers in the city.[38] As for civil war, the *Daily Citizen* speculated that the industrialists of Ulster would not countenance it for a moment, calling it a 'mad enterprise' that would result in 'irreparable ruin'.[39] The business owners of Ulster might engage in bluff, but bloodshed was another matter.

The government's willingness to consider the reasonable concerns of the Protestant minority was proof, claimed its supporters, of its even-handedness and solicitousness of northern fears. There was, consequently, bafflement at the Orangeman's refusal of the hand of good faith, the intensity of his intransigence and the seeming disproportionality of his threatened rebellion. The adamantine position of the Ulster unionists, with its bellicose talk of arms, oaths and provisional governments, juxtaposed with the spectacle of broomstick-toting Orange *bandoleros* drilling, made the solemn oaths of the covenanters of September 1912 sound pretty hollow to critics. The expansive bombast of Sir Edward Carson in 1912, the 'black robes and masks ... [of] Adelphi actors', and the apparently feeble ability of his cohorts to deliver any meaningful action, invited ridicule, an invitation that Liberal propagandists were only too happy to oblige.[40]

'Ye Tale of Ye Pigge' in the *Daily Citizen* lampooned the Ulster unionists in the manner of an earthy Chauceresque tale. Two yeomen,

---

38   *Reynolds's Newspaper*, 13 July 1913.
39   *Daily Citizen*, 30 September 1913.
40   *Methodist Times*, 29 August 1912.

Redmond and Carson, shared ownership of a pig, but Carson, the owner of the animal's tail, disputed its direction of travel.[41] 'King Carson, a Renaissance masque' featured Cardinal Redmondo, Asquith as a stage-drunk royal porter and a haunted Carson, pretender to the throne of Ireland, trying to wash ghostly blood from his hands.[42] In 1913 the *Daily Citizen* portrayed arch-Tory Lord Halsbury commending Ulster to his fellows as 'the winning card', advising them to 'stick to Ulster and civil war 'til we scare the Coalition into a General Election', and so overturn the Parliament Act, the land campaign and Welsh disestablishment.[43]

Confidence in the Home Rule bill's ultimate triumph persisted in the Liberal press well into 1914, but doubts increasingly clouded this hopeful vision and confused counsels that were offered. Gary Peatling, endorsing the view of Patricia Jalland, has observed that Liberal journalists during the Ulster crisis 'fluctuated between coercion and conciliation' in a 'schizophrenic' manner.[44] It is certainly true that Liberal journals were at pains to urge the government to accommodate all reasonable concerns of Ulster unionists. In the effort to adopt a firm but conciliatory line, Liberal editors tended to tie themselves into knots. Arguments for peace – if not at any price, at almost any price – followed directly upon urgings to go 'full steam ahead' and uphold law and order.[45] Despite the inconsistency and equivocation of Liberal journals, however, by the spring of 1914 the dominant mood in the Liberal press was one of impatience with the government's inaction over Ulster and of urging a stiffening of position.

As early as 1912 there had been complaints that threats of civil war were going unpunished and that the words and actions of Sir Edward

---

41   *Daily Citizen*, 21 June 1913.
42   *The English Review*, May 1914.
43   *Daily Citizen*, 17 December 1913.
44   G. K. Peatling, *British Opinion and Irish Self-Government, 1865–1925: from unionism to liberal commonwealth* (Dublin, 2001), p. 79.
45   *The Contemporary Review*, October 1913.

Carson affronted the throne and parliament.[46] 'The Orangemen,' the *Daily Citizen* wrote, 'shriek their defiance of law and government … [yet] Mr Asquith suggests an informal tea-party for an exchange of views.'[47] It was warned that if the government did not deal promptly with the leaders, it would have to deal with a growing and emboldened army of their dupes.[48]

The popular appeal of Home Rule to the Liberal rank and file was stressed by reports of high feeling among the English and Scottish constituencies and large public demonstrations. By-election results, even when lost by the Liberal candidate, were pointed to as 'Home Rule majorities' if the combined Liberal and Labour vote exceeded that of the Conservatives.[49] In such circumstances, concession to cynical unionist threats was not only craven, Liberal critics charged, but foolhardy. Compromise, particularly in the form of an amending bill to exclude Ulster, was widely and sharply criticised.[50] In presenting the government with a choice between civil war and the exclusion of Ulster, *Reynolds's Newspaper* wrote, the Tories were, in fact, offering alternatives with only one outcome: the wrecking of Home Rule.[51] Like *The Nation* and *Reynolds's Newspaper*, the *Daily Citizen* claimed the government had endangered its whole position by not being more forceful. Large sections of the Liberal Party, it claimed, were growing exasperated by 'endless olive branches'.[52]

The inconsistency of the government's actions troubled many commentators. How, when it was expedient to turn a blind eye to rebellion in Ulster, could the government so swiftly imprison striking trade

---

46 For example, *The Nation*, 21 Sept., 5 Oct. 1912; *Catholic Times*, 30 August, 4 October 1912.

47 *Daily Citizen*, 13 November 1913.

48 *Methodist Times*, 26 September 1912; *Catholic Times*, 9 May 1913.

49 *Methodist Times*, 12 June 1913; *Reynolds's Newspaper*, 1 March 1914.

50 *Daily Citizen*, 25 May 1914; *Reynolds's Newspaper*, 15 February 1914; *The Lepracaun*, June 1914, p. 22.

51 *Reynolds's Newspaper*, 30 November 1913.

52 *Daily Citizen*, 25 and 26 May 1914.

union leaders? Why, *The Clarion* asked, did the government shrink from acting against 'shrieking misfits in trousers', while locking up others clad in petticoats?[53] The usually staid *Baptist Times* condemned the imprisonment of Jim Larkin in November 1913, while Sir Edward Carson roamed free, complaining that it rather looked as if there was one law for the poor and another for the rich.[54] The *Methodist Times* and *Catholic Times* both contrasted the swift response to Larkin's intemperate speeches, in fighting against actual evils, to the passivity that greeted Carson's seditious language about imaginary ones.[55] Not surprisingly, some of the harshest criticism came from the pro-Labour *Daily Citizen*. Larkin, whose only crime, the *Daily Citizen* asserted, was laying bare the squalidness of Dublin's sweated industries, was not to be tolerated, and 'with one consent the men of wealth and privilege, with the consent and approval of a Liberal Government, and a Liberal Attorney General, and a Liberal Lord-Lieutenant, sprang at him and flung him into prison'.[56] The newspaper asserted that 'the Dublin business has given rank and file Liberals the hump', prompting them to view the Liberal leadership in a new and unflattering light. Millions of labouring men, 'suckled on the Radical faith', the *Daily Citizen* suggested, would be soured on the party forever at the sight of leaders whom they had once admired locking up one of their fellows for asserting working-class grievances.[57]

Disregarding preparations for secession in Ulster might make sense from the point of view of party politics, *Reynolds's Newspaper* argued, but if it meant that the machinery of the law came to a halt because it was impolitic for the administration to prosecute one set of criminals, they would be encouraging other troublemakers, such as suffragettes and syndicalists.[58] *The Nation* censured the government for its uneven response

---

53   *The Clarion*, 4 October 1912.
54   *Baptist Times*, 21 November 1913.
55   *Methodist Times*, 13 November 1913; *Catholic Times*, 22 May 1914.
56   *Daily Citizen*, 13 November 1913.
57   *Ibid.*, 5 September and 12 November 1913.
58   *Reynolds's Newspaper*, 7 April 1912.

to Ulster unionists versus nationalists, charging that indifference, and failure to uphold the law, was bearing bitter fruit.[59] The role of the army and the Asquith ministry's unwillingness to use the levers available to it to bring officers to heel further piqued Liberal irritation. Newspapers questioned why pensioned officers 'like the grotesque Gen. Richardson' should not be struck off the Army List and stripped of civil honours for serving the dishonourable Ulster Volunteers.[60] *The Nation* criticised both parties for the weakness that scarcely veiled rebellion in Ulster was communicating to European capitals.[61] Orange defiance had become a real danger, many Liberal critics charged, because official dithering had allowed it to grow to such formidable and menacing proportions.[62]

Aristocratic lawlessness was an unprecedented phenomenon in modern memory; some Liberal commentators worried that the government was overawed by wealth and titles. In thinking that curbing the power of the House of Lords had emasculated the forces of reaction, *The Nation* asserted, Home Rulers had been mistaken.[63] The army and other powers of authority in the state were still in Tory hands and were ranged against the government in supporting the Ulster rebellion. Tory intrigues, wrote the *Catholic Times*, had succeeded in bringing royal pressure to bear against the Home Rule bill's enactment.[64] Having offered every possible means of compromise, *The Nation*, in its inconsistent fashion, urged that the administration should now prepare itself to meet Bonar Law and the Orangemen with their own weapons – those of steel.[65] In the summer of 1914, however, the government was still afraid to grasp the nettle.

---

59   *The Nation*, 11 April 1914.
60   *Ibid.*, 20 June 1914.
61   *Ibid.*, 13 June 1914.
62   *Ibid.*, 11 April 1914; *Reynolds's Newspaper*, 24 May 1914; J. A. Hobson, *Traffic in Treason: a study of political parties* (London, 1914), p. 50.
63   *The Nation*, 28 March 1914.
64   *Catholic Times*, 5 June 1914.
65   *The Nation*, 25 April 1914.

The reason why, many Liberal writers suggested, was that the status of the Ulster unionist leaders, as peers and privy councillors, rendered them immune from prosecution; a government pledged against wealth and privilege was, in fact, kow-towing to it. The government, argued *Reynolds's Newspaper*, ought to enforce the law every bit as rigorously against seditious aristocrats as against Irish nationalists fighting for liberty, or British workers demanding a living wage.[66] The English working man, it claimed, was 'a volcano of passionate resentment' over the blatant inequality before the law.[67] Carson and his followers, the *Daily Citizen* asserted, could utter any disloyal oath, even arm themselves openly, and the government would become ever more pliable.[68] This pandering to class privilege, *The Nation* wrote, was causing indignation in the Labour and Liberal ranks, at a time perilous to the cause of Liberalism.[69] In February 1914 the newspaper published a mock column from 100 years in the future, which stressed to its supposed 'readers' of 2014 that the mystification felt by the twenty-first-century historian studying Liberal tolerance of insurrection was shared by contemporaneous observers in 1914. They didn't understand it either.[70]

It was the inconsistent application of the law that occasioned the greatest consternation for Liberal writers. Leaders of causes allied to the progressive coalition of Liberals and Labour – suffragists and striking workers – were attacked and imprisoned; yet a Liberal administration was apathetic in the face of violent sedition led by lawyers and dukes. It was a shocking failure of nerve, or of sense, it seemed to many, that a Liberal government came down hard on the common men and women whose interests it was pledged to defend, whilst winking at the follies of what Liberalism's followers supposed were its mortal opponents.[71]

---

66 *Reynolds's Newspaper*, 15 March 1914.
67 *Ibid.*, 14 December 1913.
68 *Daily Citizen*, 13 November 1913.
69 *The Nation*, 15 November 1913.
70 *Ibid.*, 28 February 1914.
71 *Ibid.*, 20 June 1914.

The Liberal press was virtually as one in seeing Ulster as a Tory cat's paw to defeat democracy and the Parliament Act. The power of the House of Lords, Liberal writers recognised, was still at issue, making the passage of Home Rule a vital constitutional precedent to be set and one with repercussions for the future of Liberalism. 'Noble Syndicalists and Wreckers ... who do not care a rap about Ulster,' wrote *Reynolds's Newspaper*, were mounting 'a last desperate stand against the new Democracy which has crippled the power of the House of Lords'.[72] The *Baptist Times* suggested that the Tory Party was 'straining every nerve to get the Government out'.[73] British democrats, the *Catholic Times* claimed, wanted only to see the passage of Home Rule, the operation of the Parliament Act and the consequent humiliation of the House of Lords; upon delivery of these expectations the government's fate would rest in a general election in 1915.[74] To stray from the course commanded by the electorate, *The Nation* asserted, and to give in to demands for an appeal to the country, would be to wreck the Parliament Act upon its first trial.[75] Here was the prospect, as the newspaper put it, of a Liberal government, 'unbeaten in argument or the division lobby, reduced to ... the voluntary surrender of the weapon with which it had armed Democracy against the House of Lords'.[76]

A scathing critique of the government's handling of Ulster arrived in June 1914, with the publication of J. A. Hobson's *Traffic in Treason: a study of political parties*. Hobson bitterly criticised British unionists for cynically manipulating the Orangemen, but was scarcely less harsh on the Asquith ministry. He asserted that the social radicalism arising in the 1880s and 1890s had brought economic issues to the fore of politics, and as a consequence had set 'property against

---

72   *Reynolds's Newspaper*, 15 March 1914, p. 2 and 31 May 1914, p. 7.
73   *Baptist Times*, 11 October 1912.
74   *Catholic Times*, 3 July 1914.
75   *The Nation*, 17 August 1912.
76   *Ibid.*, 14 March 1914.

poverty, mastery against servitude, privilege against equality'.[77] Tories feared, Hobson wrote, that social reforms and redistributive taxation had summoned up 'an everlasting Lloyd George, who will leave them no peace, living or dead', exacting ever-larger tolls on their incomes and inheritances.[78] In reaction, the oligarchy sought to mobilise all its forces: the influential classes, the army and the crown. The Ulster crisis, he wrote, represented the testing of these subterranean levers of Toryism to bring the government to its knees, 'recapture the Constitution' and to fortify it against 'levelling' collectivist reforms.[79] The success of this retrograde enterprise, however, Hobson attributed chiefly to the complacency of the Asquith government. The very magnitude of the resistance which the cabinet had allowed to gather, supplied its argument for voluntary and unsolicited concessions.[80]

Unlike the Tory Party, Hobson asserted, which the Ulster crisis demonstrated had become 'thoroughly alive to the meaning of *real politik*', the middle-class leadership of the Liberal Party shrank from challenging foes to whom they instinctively, and fatally, deferred.[81] For Asquith and the Liberal leaders to contemplate the possibility of having to treat men of high social standing, whom they secretly admired, as they would do delinquents of the lower orders, was, for Hobson, quite inconceivable.[82] Middle-class timidity was costing Liberalism Ireland, the constitution and the longer struggle for democracy.[83] With Liberalism supine before unionist resistance, and with the Labour Party unready to pick up the reins, the only hope, in Hobson's eyes, was for organised working people and their trade unions to 'stiffen and ... direct' the Liberal Party from within. The party, he wrote, must

---

77   Hobson, *Traffic in Treason*, p. 10.
78   *Ibid.*, pp. 59–60.
79   *The Academy*, 27 June 1914; Hobson, *Traffic in Treason*, pp. 21, 59.
80   Hobson, *Traffic in Treason*, p. 50.
81   *Ibid.*, p. 61.
82   *Ibid.*
83   *Ibid.*, p. 62.

reconstitute itself with the 'active assistance of the people whom it ... professed to "trust", but ... always sought to "manage"'.[84]

The government's failure of nerve, and the sacrifice of matters of principle, like unitary Home Rule, provoked protest and despair among the party's supporters. For collectivist new Liberals, retreat in Ireland betokened the inability of a middle-class party vigorously to press the demands of an expanded democracy. For individualist radicals, a failure of Home Rule would represent the crumbling of one of the pillars of their belief, and with its collapse would fall Welsh disestablishment and abolition of plural voting. For a great many supporters, Liberalism was nothing if not the politics of conviction; abandonment of principle, as one newspaper warned, would result in the general election of 1915 being 'the Sedan of Liberalism'.[85]

The government's conduct regarding Ulster in 1913–14 was a point at which many British Liberals, like Hobson and C. P. Scott, became convinced that only a wholesale reconstruction of the party could save it.[86] Discontent in the party over Irish Home Rule in 1914 arose not because it diverted the party from the social-reform agenda, but because of the weakness of Liberalism that the bill's deeply flawed stewardship exposed. Knuckling under to threats of violence, egged on by the Tory Party, and with the connivance of the army and perhaps even the king, *The Nation* wrote in spring 1914, was tantamount to the party yielding up its life to its enemies.[87] 'Everything else in politics is either dead or dying,' the newspaper commented in 1913, 'or as yet unready to be born.'[88] For many contemporaries, friendly to Liberalism, the party's grievous inadequacy in the Ulster crisis signalled its own irredeemable demise.

---

84 *Ibid.*, pp. 62–4.
85 *Catholic Times*, 7 June 1912.
86 Peatling, *British Opinion*, p. 79.
87 *The Nation*, 14 March 1914.
88 *Ibid.*, 15 November 1913.

5

Ulster 'will not fight': T. P. O'Connor and the third Home Rule bill crisis, 1912–14

Erica S. Doherty

Considerable scholarly attention has been given to the events surrounding the introduction of the third Irish Home Rule bill in 1912 and the crisis that transpired over the following two years. During this period the Irish Party, chaired by the MP for Waterford city, John Redmond, lost considerable ground to its political opponents. The party refused to take the threat from Edward Carson, and the Ulster unionists he led, seriously until it was too late, believing instead that the nationalist viewpoint continued to have the full backing of the Liberal government for Irish Home Rule, when concessions demanded from them suggested otherwise. Most studies have understandably concentrated on the manoeuvrings and actions of the political heavyweights involved during the crisis, including Herbert H. Asquith (the British prime minister), Andrew Bonar Law (the leader of the Conservative Party), Edward Carson and John Redmond.[1] As a

---

1   A recent study by James McConnel on the Irish Parliamentary Party and the third Home Rule crisis has gone some way to broadening the historiographical focus on the subject. J. McConnel, *The Irish Parliamentary Party and the Third Home Rule Crisis* (Dublin, 2013).

consequence the roles of some of the less visible political actors involved, including T. P. O'Connor, the Irish Party's 'chief scout', have received little recognition.[2] This essay sheds new light on the third Irish Home Rule crisis by scrutinising the part played by O'Connor, demonstrating that he had an important role in the various negotiations that took place. It also assesses the extent to which he was to blame for the party not recognising the impact of Ulster unionist opposition on the Liberal government and considers if he was responsible for failing to notice the evident change in attitude in support of granting concessions to them.

T. P. O'Connor held a unique political position. Elected as MP for the Scotland division of Liverpool in 1885 (a seat that he held until his death in 1929), he was the only member of the Irish Party to sit for a non-Irish constituency. He was also president of the United Irish League of Great Britain, the party's grass-roots organisation there. Both positions enabled him to be recognised as the effective leader of the Irish in Britain. Having moved to London in 1870, O'Connor's long residence in England also resulted in important friendships with several British politicians, the most significant of these being David Lloyd George, the chancellor of the exchequer at the time of the introduction of the third Home Rule bill. This friendship was central to O'Connor's ability to act as chief scout and go-between on behalf of the Irish Party. Having spearheaded the Irish–Liberal alliance of the 1880s, which directly contributed to the introduction of the first Irish Home Rule bill in 1886, he became the key link between the Irish and Liberal parties. This alliance resulted from the Irish Party holding the balance of power in the House of Commons. In return for supporting the Liberals in government the Home Rule bill was introduced. Similar circumstances prevailed following the December 1910 general election, and with the introduction of the third Home Rule bill in April 1912 O'Connor's importance to the

---

2 A. C. Murray, *Master and Brother: Murrays of Elibank* (London, 1954), p. 23.

party once again peaked. By this stage he was recognised as part of its inner leadership circle along with John Redmond, John Dillon (the second most important party member) and Joseph Devlin (leader of the nationalists in Ulster). O'Connor's position within the party, his long-term residence in London and his close friendships with several British politicians enabled him to assume an important role during the third Home Rule crisis.

O'Connor's role during the crisis

From 1912 until the time when the Home Rule bill was placed on the statute book in September 1914 O'Connor committed his energies to four main activities, all of which were aimed at gaining Home Rule for Ireland. Firstly, he tried to persuade unionists, through his speeches and newspaper columns, that they had nothing to fear from an Irish Home Rule government. He argued that the idea of Catholic intolerance in a Home Rule Ireland was unfounded.[3] Instead, he maintained that an Irish parliament would not result in a growth of sectarianism or divisions along religious lines but would rather bring about 'the re-grouping of Irish politics and parties' along 'economic lines'.[4]

Secondly, he tried to convince both British public opinion and the government that they had little to fear from unionist threats of violence. To counteract the unionist anti-Home Rule campaign in Britain, he embarked upon an extensive tour, speaking at several locations throughout the country on the Home Rule issue. His stops included Newcastle, Cornwall, Cardiff, Edinburgh, Reading, Dumfries, Stockton, Scarborough, Aberdeen, Inverness, Dundee, Rochester and Peterborough.[5] Most of his speeches identified the

---

3   *The Freeman's Journal*, 25 May 1912.
4   *Reynolds's Newspaper*, 25 February 1912.
5   *Liverpool Catholic Herald*, 22 June and 3 August 1912; *Irish Independent*, 27 May 1912; 21 June 1913; 27 and 30 October 1913; 6, 10, 12, 13, 14 and 18 November

emptiness in the unionist threats, arguing that the campaign had already lost substantial support. From the platform he declared, Ulster 'will not fight' and 'Carsonism is breaking down already from the inside', losing the support of the Tories and many 'of those who had followed Sir Edward Carson in the opening stages of his campaign'.[6] He used similar arguments on several important governmental figures, in an attempt to encourage the Liberals to remain strong and not give in to unionist demands. For example, during a golfing holiday in Romford in August 1912 with Lloyd George, O'Connor was described by Marsh Lockwood, a friend of Bonar Law, as persistently harrying the chancellor of the exchequer regarding the Ulster issue. Lockwood recorded that O'Connor 'never leaves George. We generally breakfast together and T. P.'s whole time is occupied by proving how little is in the Ulster movement.'[7]

Thirdly, he campaigned to get Irish voters to vote for the Liberal Party in the various by-elections held in Britain. Irish Party manifestos produced by O'Connor and Redmond were issued in a number of constituencies, including Midlothian, Chorley and Reading.[8] The Irish Party's involvement in these electoral contests undoubtedly stemmed from the need to ensure that the Liberals remained in power for the sake of the Home Rule bill.

Finally, O'Connor acted as go-between and chief scout by actively participating in the various Home Rule negotiations that took place. The remainder of this essay will examine O'Connor's role during these negotiations, evaluating his importance and determining the extent to which he should be held responsible for the Irish Party's failure to take the unionist threats more seriously.

1913; 9 December 1913.

6   *Irish Independent*, 6 November; 30 and 22 October 1913.

7   Marsh Lockwood to Bonar Law, 22 August 1912, Bonar Law papers, BL/27/1/50, Parliamentary Archive, London.

8   *Irish Independent*, 19 August 1912; 13 February 1913; 1 November 1913.

The third Home Rule bill

Having been uninvolved in the initial formulation of the Irish Home Rule bill, the Irish Party was first introduced to it at two meetings at Downing Street towards the end of March 1912. The party delegation comprised Redmond, O'Connor and the party's MP for North County Dublin, John Joseph Clancy; Dillon joined them for the second of the two meetings.[9] In response to seeing the draft bill for the first time, the four members jointly penned a memorandum outlining desired amendments.[10] Although the memorandum addressed a number of issues, the primary focus rested on the bill's financial arrangements. The party hoped to achieve as much financial independence for the proposed Home Rule parliament as possible, in the belief that this would secure its continued existence once it was established. They demanded that the surplus given by the imperial parliament to the Irish administration should be greatly increased from the proposed £150,000, because this amount would, the delegation argued, 'be useless under the actual circumstances'.[11] In the end the surplus was increased to £500,000.[12] Overall, however, the party was unable to amend the terms of the bill to any great degree. When it was introduced into the House of Commons by Asquith on 11 April, it outlined proposals for the establishment of a Home Rule bicameral legislature in Dublin, with responsibility for Irish domestic laws. Several powers – including foreign affairs, international trade,

---

9   *Ibid.*, 21 and 25 March 1912. In the initial newspaper reports J. J. Clancy's attendance is not recorded. On 26 March 1912 the *Irish Independent* rectified its reporting on the two meetings, confirming that the North County Dublin MP was present at both.

10   A memorandum by the British cabinet member Herbert Samuel confirms the four Irish Party members as joint authors of this document. Memorandum by Herbert Samuel, 27 March 1912, Herbert Samuel papers, SAM/A/41/7a, Parliamentary Archive, London.

11   'The Home Rule bill: memorandum on certain points', David Lloyd George papers, LGP/C/20/2/13, Parliamentary Archive, London.

12   P. Jalland, 'Irish home-rule finance: a neglected dimension of the Irish question, 1910–14', *Irish Historical Studies*, vol. 23, no. 91 (1983), p. 238.

and the armed services – would be retained by Westminster, with a lord lieutenant representing the executive authority on behalf of the king in Ireland.

O'Connor's presence at the two Downing Street meetings and his involvement in helping to construct the party's memorandum are evidence that he had a significant role to play. Yet it is not here that the main crux of his involvement and importance lies. Rather, it rests in his position as go-between on behalf of the other Irish Party leaders. This proved most significant from September 1913 to March 1914, when he was responsible for relaying information regarding developments to his colleagues back in Ireland.

O'Connor as go-between

It is evident from O'Connor's correspondence, newspaper articles and speeches that, regardless of mounting opposition, he saw little threat to the Home Rule bill before 1914 and believed that its passing into law was a mere formality. This stance suggests that he may not have taken the unionist threat as seriously as he should have. However, when the bill was introduced in April 1912, the Irish Party was in a very strong position and any sense of the difficulties that followed could not have been foreseen. In spite of the creation of the Ulster Volunteer Force and Thomas Agar-Robartes' attempted (albeit failed) amendment of the bill advocating the exclusion of the four north-eastern counties (Antrim, Down, Derry and Armagh), O'Connor's attitude towards unionist opposition to the bill changed little. By September 1913 he was still confident that it would pass and that Ulster unionists would not take up arms. The Irish Party's position seemed safe to him; he referred to unionist threats of force as bluff, maintaining that Home Rule would not be responsible for causing a civil war in Ireland.[13] His opinion may have differed, however, had he

---

13 *Irish Independent*, 19 and 29 September 1913.

been aware that Bonar Law and Winston Churchill (first lord of the Admiralty) had met at Balmoral a few days earlier.[14]

O'Connor was not made aware of this secret meeting until 30 September, when he was informed during the course of a discussion with Lloyd George. He reported the information to Dillon and added that he had been asked 'to ascertain what the attitude of the Irish leaders would be' to the possibility of a conference that would 'involve the acceptance of the Ulster option'. It is clear from this report that he was led to believe that there was widespread Tory support for such a conference. He had been told that the outcome of the secret meeting had been the indication by Bonar Law that the 'Tory leaders would be ready to enter into conference' if Ulster were given the option by plebiscite to opt out.[15] Patricia Jalland has argued that during his meeting with O'Connor, Lloyd George 'gave a version of the truth which suited his purpose'.[16] This evaluation is valid. O'Connor was certainly left with the impression that the Conservatives wanted a conference, writing to Dillon that he believed the 'Tory Party as a whole … would grasp at any compromise which would save their faces'.[17] In reality, as Jalland rightly points out, only F. E. Smith, the earl of Birkenhead, 'had made such a suggestion'.[18]

This meeting, and the letter to Dillon, clearly outline the major difficulty that O'Connor faced in operating as the party's chief scout and go-between during the crisis: he was to a significant degree reliant upon receiving his information from others. As a result, his governmental sources could control what details the Irish Party received, something which proved beneficial to the Liberal government in its

---

14   A. O'Day, *Irish Home Rule: 1867–1921* (Manchester, 1998), pp. 255–6.
15   T. P. O'Connor to John Dillon, 30 September 1913, John Dillon papers, 6740/194, Trinity College Dublin (TCD).
16   P. Jalland, *The Liberals and Ireland: the Ulster question in British politics to 1914* (Brighton, 1980), pp. 149–50.
17   O'Connor to Dillon, 30 September 1913, Dillon papers, 6740/194, TCD.
18   Jalland, *The Liberals and Ireland*, p. 150.

attempts to forge an agreement on Ulster. For example, O'Connor was not told about secret talks being held between Asquith and Bonar Law from October to December 1913.[19] This problem notwithstanding, however, O'Connor was an important contact point and vehicle through which information was relayed between the Irish Party and the British government.

Having been given this new information, Dillon proved reluctant to advise O'Connor on the best course of action 'without full consultation with Redmond', adding that he would be surprised if Redmond agreed to 'enter into any private communication with ministers direct or indirect'.[20] This greatly frustrated O'Connor, who was particularly worried about a speech by Churchill scheduled to take place at Dundee. He warned his colleagues of the perils that they would face should Churchill make a speech in favour of Ulster exclusion.[21] It is evident that O'Connor fully expected his colleagues to take his advice and contact the government to outline the party's stance. He was, however, to be sorely disappointed, because Redmond proved reluctant to write to the prime minister.[22] O'Connor wrote to Dillon explaining that he thought this to be a 'grave political mistake'.[23]

Having had his recommendations rebuffed by his colleagues and under pressure from the Liberals to ascertain the Irish Party's stance, O'Connor took it upon himself to contact Churchill personally in an attempt to ensure that he would not make a speech which would undermine the Irish Party's position. In his letter he outlined the utter impossibility of excluding any part of Ireland from the area governed by a Home Rule parliament, adding that a postponement

---

19   A. Jackson, *Home Rule: an Irish history 1800–2000* (London, 2003), p. 146.
20   John Dillon to T. P. O'Connor, 2 October 1913, Dillon papers, 6740/196, TCD.
21   O'Connor to Dillon, 3 October 1913, Dillon papers, 6740/198, TCD; T. P. O'Connor to Joseph Devlin, 1 October 1913, John Redmond papers, MS 15,181/3, National Library of Ireland (NLI).
22   Dillon to O'Connor, 5 October 1913, Dillon papers, 6740/199, TCD.
23   O'Connor to Dillon, 6 October 1913, Dillon papers, 6740/200, TCD.

of the proposal would be infinitely better.[24] His efforts, however, proved fruitless; Churchill acknowledged north-east Ulster's claims for special treatment during his Dundee speech.[25] This setback was particularly disappointing for the Liverpool politician because he believed that it could have been easily avoided had the other Irish Party leaders heeded his advice and contacted Asquith when he had requested them to do so.

In a letter to Dillon dated 13 October 1913, O'Connor laid the blame squarely at Redmond's doorstep. With the latter having given a speech at Limerick outlining the Irish Party's position a few days after Churchill made his Dundee speech, O'Connor exclaimed, 'but why in God's name, did not Redmond communicate these views to Asquith? You would have saved the situation from the great embarrassment caused by Winston's speech. That speech would never have been delivered if my urgent entreaties had been listened to.' He continued, 'I knew what was coming and I gave you full warning.'[26] Despite his heartfelt protestations, and a letter explaining that Lloyd George had expressed the view that he would much prefer the exclusion of the four counties for a set period of five years, under the condition that they would come in automatically after that period and the Tories would take a pledge that they would not stoke up resistance, the other Irish Party leaders still refused to act upon O'Connor's advice.[27] It was not right, Dillon responded, to write to Asquith on this important issue without a direct request from the prime minister, adding that Churchill's speech 'has killed this proposal of the exclusion of Ulster'.[28] O'Connor did not, however, share the same outlook as Dillon. He sent one final letter

---

24   T. P. O'Connor to Churchill, 7 October 1913, Chartwell papers, CHAR 2/62, Sir Winston Churchill Archive, Cambridge.
25   *The Times*, 9 October 1913.
26   O'Connor to Dillon, 13 October 1913, Dillon papers, 6740/203, TCD.
27   O'Connor to Dillon, 15 October 1913, Dillon papers, 6740/205, TCD.
28   Dillon to O'Connor, 15 October 1913, Dillon papers, 6740/206, TCD.

protesting against the silence of his colleagues and the difficulties that this mistake was causing to their position.[29] Redmond did not meet with any member of the British government until the end of November.[30] By this stage it was clear that the Irish Party's reluctance had enabled their unionist opponents to seize the initiative, with O'Connor confirming that the cabinet now favoured some sort of proposal advocating the exclusion of part of Ulster.[31]

These exchanges between O'Connor and the other leaders identify his role within the party. His importance should not, however, be overstated. Whilst he was crucial in transferring information from the government and keeping the party informed of political developments, it is also evident that he was at all times subordinate to Redmond and Dillon. He failed to persuade them to contact the government to give the party's views and continually deferred to their decisions. Undoubtedly his colleagues valued his input, but his reluctance to define Irish Party policy to government suggests that he lacked not only the political clout but also, more importantly, the authority to do so. The party leadership operated as a cabinet, with decisions made jointly.[32] There was, nonetheless, a definite ranking system within the leadership circle. This is evidenced throughout O'Connor's personal correspondence as he continually sought direction from the other leaders, refused to act without first consulting them and deferred to their decisions.

Secrecy was also a key element that hampered O'Connor in his role and allowed the unionists to outflank their nationalist counter-parts. For example, Asquith met the Conservative leader, Bonar Law, for secret talks on 14 October, 6 November and 10 December 1913. O'Connor was unable to inform the Irish Party that such meetings

---

29   O'Connor to Dillon, 17 October 1913, Dillon papers, 6740/208, TCD.

30   D. Gwynn, *The Life of John Redmond* (London, 1932).

31   O'Connor to Dillon, 26 November 1913, Dillon papers, 6740/212, TCD.

32   S. Gwynn, *John Redmond's Last Years* (London, 1919), p. 64.

were taking place until 26 November.[33] He was also left in the dark regarding two meetings between Asquith and Carson on 16 December 1913 and 2 January 1914, in which the unionists were encouraged to formulate counter-proposals in writing.[34] These secretive meetings are a further indication that Redmond's refusal to heed O'Connor's warnings about the necessity of meeting the prime minister was indeed a grave mistake. The field had been left open for their unionist and Conservative opponents to impress upon the government that Ulster should be excluded from the Home Rule scheme.

By January 1914 both O'Connor and Dillon were encouraging Redmond to get in contact with Asquith.[35] The party's leader was adamant that the negotiations would come to nothing and concessions would not be granted to Ulster unionists.[36] A few weeks later, Redmond finally met the prime minister for face-to-face talks at Downing Street. The Irish Party leader was duly informed that the government now intended to introduce some form of concession, possibly in the form of 'Home Rule within Home Rule'.[37] While O'Connor holidayed with Lloyd George, both Devlin and Dillon crossed to London and, along with Redmond, drafted a letter outlining their objections to such a scheme.[38] Two meetings followed between the prime minister and the Irish Party leadership, with O'Connor, Lloyd George and Augustine Birrell (the chief secretary) joining the proceedings for the second meeting on 2 March. It was now clear that the British cabinet favoured some form of concessions. The Irish Party was presented with a scheme for Ulster exclusion

---

33   Jackson, *Home Rule*, p. 146; O'Connor to Dillon, 26 November 1913, Dillon papers, 6740/212, TCD.

34   O'Day, *Irish Home Rule*, pp. 258–9.

35   O'Connor to Dillon, 24 January 1914, Dillon papers, 6740/221, TCD; Dillon to O'Connor, 29 January 1914, Dillon papers, 6740/222, TCD.

36   John Redmond to John Dillon, 21 January 1914, Redmond papers, MS 15,182/20, NLI.

37   Jalland, *The Liberals and Ireland*, p. 191.

38   *The Times*, 13 January 1914; Gwynn, *John Redmond's Last Years*, p. 253.

based on a plebiscite in each county, with those that chose to opt out automatically coming under the jurisdiction of a Home Rule parliament after a period of three years.[39] Redmond and the party reluctantly accepted the proposal as a means of ensuring peace, but maintained that this would be their last word on the matter.[40]

This concession was extremely significant. Having refused previously to accept any major changes to the Home Rule bill, the party ended up agreeing to a change that violated the central premise that Ireland was a single political unit. It would also appear that this initial acceptance broke the Irish Party's resolve and opened the gates for further concessions. Just two days later Redmond was informed that the original time frame of exclusion had been extended to six years rather than the previously agreed three. He reluctantly acceded to this change.[41] This concession was crucial to the history of the Irish Party, as it represented the first time that it had agreed to any form of territorial exclusion, and this undoubtedly damaged its credibility amongst its supporters in Ireland.

So why did the party now abandon its original position and accept this crucial amendment to the Home Rule bill? This shift in stance can be attributed to the change that emerged within the Liberal government. From August 1913 onwards, the government came to favour some sort of concession being granted to the Ulster unionists. As the Irish Party relied heavily on the Liberals, there was therefore little (other than protest) that the party could do. It was also clear that the Irish Party was concerned that the entire Home Rule bill might be called into question if the deadlock was not broken, but they were adamant that the party would not concede any more ground. The Curragh mutiny and Larne gun-running, however, further confirmed

---

39 Interview at Downing Street, with the Prime Minister, no date, Redmond papers, MS 15,257/2, NLI.
40 Jalland, *The Liberals and Ireland*, p. 200.
41 F. S. L. Lyons, *John Dillon: a biography* (second edition, London, 1968), p. 348.

the newly weakened position of the party. In spite of this, O'Connor remained confident that the bill would be introduced, even if this required the introduction of safeguards to allay Protestant fears.[42] He still refused to acknowledge the seriousness of the unionist campaign in general and of the events that had transpired at the Curragh camp in particular, declaring that the incident had 'struck the heaviest blow in favour of Home Rule'.[43] Serious alarm did not register with him until the summer of 1914. When the Lords introduced an amendment for the exclusion of all nine counties of Ulster, the situation had reached political deadlock.

It was then that O'Connor first expressed concern that Asquith might demand more concessions from the Irish Party.[44] With little prospect of political movement and mounting pressure from the king, a conference was convened at Buckingham Palace in July to try to break the deadlock. The conference was, however, an 'unmitigated failure'.[45] The talks broke down over whether Fermanagh and Tyrone, which contained Catholic majorities, were to be excluded from the jurisdiction of a Home Rule parliament. The failure of the conference and the outbreak of European war further complicated matters for the Irish Party, and the best the party could achieve was the placing of the bill on the statute book, accompanied by a Suspensory Act for the duration of the war and with agreement that special provisions would be made for Ulster.

Conclusion

The concessions drawn from its leadership over the course of 1914, and in particular the Suspensory Act, denied the Irish Party its

---

42   *Reynolds's Newspaper*, 31 May 1914.
43   *Irish Independent*, 27 March 1914.
44   O'Connor to Redmond, 10 July 1914, Redmond papers, MS 15,215/A, NLI.
45   J. D. Fair, *British Interparty Conferences: a study of the procedure of conciliation in British politics, 1867–1921* (Oxford, 1980), p. 118.

victory. Consequently, what should have been the greatest moment for O'Connor and his colleagues – the passage of the Home Rule bill through parliament – was something of a let-down. L. W. Brady has commented, 'finally there was the parliamentary victory for Home Rule which turned out to be pyrrhic and where O'Connor totally underestimated the force of unionism and, the other side of the coin, was betrayed by his natural belief in the efficiency and supremacy of parliament.'[46] This essay has confirmed this view. O'Connor certainly failed to appreciate the impact unionist opposition had on the Liberal government during these years, and he did not interpret the significance in the shift towards the militarisation of Ireland caused by the creation of the two Volunteer forces and the landing of weapons at both Larne in April and Howth in July 1914. It is clear that the position of the Irish Party weakened considerably after the introduction of the Home Rule bill, to a point where it was forced to accept concessions that shortly before it would not have even considered. Unionist opposition worked to undermine the party's position and drive a wedge between the nationalists and the Liberals, yet even at the height of the crisis O'Connor and the party continued to believe that their position was safe.

Robert Kee has argued that 'one of the strangest phenomena of the time' was 'the virtual paralysis with which Redmond and the nationalists seem to have been afflicted when faced with such unmistakable evidence of the government's increasing reluctance and inability to support them', particularly from March 1914 onwards.[47] Could the Irish Party blame O'Connor, as chief scout and main contact between the party and the Liberals, for this lack of action? He undoubtedly had complete faith in the Liberal government and its support for the bill. As a result, he did not think that the Liberals

---

46   L. W. Brady, *T. P. O'Connor and the Liverpool Irish* (London, 1983), p. 172.
47   R. Kee, *The Green Flag: a history of Irish nationalism* (London, 1972), p. 490.

would reconsider their position on Home Rule or continually seek to squeeze concessions from the Irish Party. His unwavering trust in them was evidence of questionable judgement, and his ongoing denial of the threat posed by organised unionist opposition to Home Rule was a mistake.

As chief scout, it is arguable that he should have been more alert to the movements within the British cabinet and the impact of the unionist campaign. Nevertheless, it would be unfair to lay all the blame for not recognising the change in the government's mood on his shoulders. This essay not only confirms the general consensus amongst historians that the Irish Party as a whole failed to take the unionist threat seriously, thereby damaging its own position, but also contributes to an understanding of the Home Rule crisis by showing that the reasons for the party's lack of response were more complicated than is sometimes suggested. Factors outside its control have to be taken into consideration when evaluating its paralysis in the face of mounting opposition. The party as a whole certainly made a massive mistake in not taking the unionist threat seriously, as it did in believing that this threat would not impact upon the Home Rule bill.

By examining O'Connor's role during the crisis, however, it becomes clear that the party leadership was unaware of certain considerations that may have forced them into being more proactive. For example, O'Connor's ability to read the situation at several points during the crisis was severely limited by the fact that he relied on receiving his information from his British political friends, such as Lloyd George. As shown by the meetings conducted between Asquith and Bonar Law, secrecy played an important part in discussions at this time, with O'Connor being left in the dark about several developments. He remained at all times outside the hub of British power and could report back only the information that he had been given. Secrecy was thus a useful tactic for the Liberal government to use. Whilst it is generally agreed that the Irish Party and O'Connor should have taken the unionist movement more seriously, they were left unaware of the full extent to which the government was shifting towards granting concessions because they were purposely left in the dark regarding such developments. In addition, whilst O'Connor's refusal to recognise the threat of unionism appears incomprehensible, in hindsight, his outlook was in line with that of the rest of his party colleagues throughout this period. There was undoubtedly a degree of naivety on his part in thinking that the Irish Home Rule bill would pass easily. Both he and the party in general were too optimistic for their own good.

6

Myopia or utopia? The discourse of Irish nationalist MPs and the Ulster question during the parliamentary debates of 1912–14

Pauline Collombier-Lakeman

A number of the analyses of the Home Rule crisis of 1912–14 have stressed the lack of insight of both the British government and the Irish nationalists with regard to the issue of Ulster and unionism in Ireland. Patricia Jalland, for instance, blamed the British Liberals for not taking account of the Ulster problem early and thoroughly enough. She noted that '[t]he most important argument against [Prime Minister Herbert H.] Asquith's Ulster policy was that it overlooked the advantages to be gained from the Parliament Act by dealing with Ulster immediately'.[1] Irish nationalist MPs and their leaders, notably John Redmond, have also been judged rather harshly for failing to grasp the seriousness of the concerns and threats of the Irish unionists. Patrick Maume stated that while '[they] sincerely regard[ed] Irish Protestants as fellow-countrymen, they assumed Unionists "naturally" shared their brand

---

1   P. Jalland, *The Liberals and Ireland: the Ulster question in British politics to 1914* (New York, 1980), p. 66.

of patriotism and ignored the cultural and economic forces which led Protestant farmers and workers in the great Belfast export industries to support Unionism'.[2] John Redmond himself has been regarded by some as a 'tragic figure',[3] a 'fool' or even a 'servile traitor',[4] who 'first underestimated [the forces of violence], then allowed them to seize the initiative', and who, as a result, was 'deprived ... of the united Ireland he and other nationalists had always naively taken for granted'.[5]

Different accounts have emerged, however, and seem to testify somehow of a desire to re-examine the case of moderate nationalism, as they have shed a more positive light on the choices made and the results obtained by John Redmond and his followers. Kevin Myers, writing in *The Irish Times*, thus wrote of Redmond in 1996:

> [h]e was a pioneer; and as a pioneer, he was the first to take on the challenge of trying to persuade the unionists of Ulster to cease to be unionists. Like all who have tried since, he failed; and for that failure he has been vilified by republicans who have been as dismally unsuccessful.[6]

The same year, in one of the first fairly recent biographical works on the Irish Party leader, Paul Bew admitted 'a lack of insight into the intensity of Protestant fears' on Redmond's part, but warned at the same time that 'it would not be fair to say that Redmond was indifferent to unionist concerns'.[7]

To contribute to the debate surrounding the attitude of the Irish nationalist MPs towards Ulster and other Irish unionists during the

---

2   P. Maume, 'John Redmond – visionary, fool or traitor?', *The Irish Times*, 4 March 1993.
3   M. Laffan, 'John Redmond (1856–1918) and Home Rule', in C. Brady (ed.), *Worsted in the Game: losers in Irish history* (Dublin, 1989), pp. 133–41, in particular p. 139.
4   Maume, 'John Redmond'.
5   Laffan, 'John Redmond (1856–1918)', pp. 137–8.
6   K. Myers, 'A great reconciler is traduced again', *The Irish Times*, 23 April 1996.
7   P. Bew, *John Redmond* (Dundalk, 1996), pp. 33–4.

Home Rule debates of 1912–14, this essay will offer an analysis of the speeches delivered by some of the main figures of moderate Irish nationalism. A quantitative, computer-assisted method of discourse analysis, as well as a more qualitative approach, will be relied on to identify some of the arguments developed by the nationalist side during the main stages of the discussions at Westminster, and to show how the nationalists tried to respond to, and refute, some of the unionist objections to Home Rule. A closer examination of some features of Irish nationalist dialogue in parliament will demonstrate that the leaders of Irish nationalism may have failed to take into account the Ulster issue earlier because they actually believed in what could be regarded as a form of social or political utopia – Ireland as a politically autonomous nation in which Catholics and Protestants could be reconciled once and for all.

An overview of the main unionist arguments, 1912–14

Before dealing with the arguments of the Irish nationalists, it is necessary to present briefly those of the Irish unionists. For their leader, Edward Carson, Asquith's proposals in 1912 were simply 'ridiculous', 'fantastic', 'unworkable',[8] and could be regarded as a 'farce'.[9] The main reason why Carson rejected the bill so harshly was that he viewed the Irish question primarily as a religious issue and considered, as a result, that there were obvious and irreconcilable differences between Irish Catholics and Irish Protestants:

> Sir, it is a religious question added to various other questions. There is no doubt that the broad dividing line in Ireland in relation to this question of the Home Rule Bill can be broadly said to put on one side the Protestants, and on the other side the Roman Catholics. I know

---

8 *House of Commons Debates*, Fifth series, vol. 36, 11 April 1912, cols 1427, 1433.
9 *Ibid.*, col. 1438.

there are some Protestants, not many I think, who are Home Rulers, just as there are some Catholics, a great many I think, who are not Home Rulers. It is unfortunate that that should be the dividing line, but it is there and you cannot neglect it.[10]

As the end of this quotation shows, a tactic used by the unionist side was to minimise, as much as possible, the idea that there was widespread support for Home Rule in Ireland and to emphasise the political and socio-economic importance of Irish unionists, especially in the north. Carson thus warned the government that the 1912 bill was 'legislating against the sentiment of one-third of Ireland, and that not the least important part of the population'.[11] Captain Craig also asserted that just as 'the demand for Home Rule … in the last twenty-six years [had become] less and less accentuated amongst people of all classes and creeds … so the opposition to Home Rule in any form [had] steadily increased'.[12] As the debates went on, the determination of Irish unionists to resist any form of legislative autonomy for Ireland became stronger and threats of civil war were more real,[13] as Carson was able to boast that 'even in the threat of armed resistance, if it should ever be necessary … we have behind us … the whole force of the Conservative and Unionist Party'.[14]

---

10 *Ibid.*, col. 1440.
11 *House of Commons Debates*, Fifth series, vol. 53, 10 June 1913, col. 1473.
12 *House of Commons Debates*, Fifth series, vol. 36, 11 April 1912, col. 1438.
13 By the end of 1913 the government was made well aware of the extent of discontent in Ulster and the risks of civil war, thanks to two memoranda written by Chief Secretary Augustine Birrell ('Further Notes on the Movement in Ulster', November 1913, and 'Further Notes from Ulster', 4 December 1913, CAB 37/117/83 and CAB 37/117/85, British National Archives).
14 *House of Commons Debates*, Fifth series, vol. 53, 10 June 1913, col. 1465. Carson and Craig had committed to resist Home Rule by all means necessary as early as 23 September 1911, during the famous Craigavon meeting: 'We must be prepared, in the event of a Home Rule Bill passing, with such measures as will carry on for ourselves the government of those districts in which we have control. We must be prepared – and time is precious in these things – the morning Home Rule passes,

Irish nationalist responses

Irish nationalist responses to these arguments will be assessed here through the use of a discourse-analysis computer programme, Lexico 3, which was devised by French linguists from the Université de la Sorbonne Nouvelle, Paris 3.[15] Lexico was used to examine a sample of twenty-eight speeches delivered by six prominent figures of Irish moderate nationalism in parliament – John Redmond, John Dillon, William O'Brien, Timothy Healy, Joseph Devlin and T. P. O'Connor, during the First, Second and Third Readings of all three series of debates on Home Rule between April 1912 and May 1914. Lexico allows one to identify the importance of certain terms and phrases used in these speeches by assessing frequencies, listing word associations and contexts, and estimating the connections and echoes between the speeches of the various orators during the course of the debates. In order to study the way Irish nationalist leaders responded to Irish unionists, I first focused on words or phrases used more or less significantly in relation to the Ulster issue or to Irish unionism.

Reactions to threats of civil war

Mentions of a possible 'civil war' in Ireland are rather rare in the sample as the phrase was only used twenty-four times. The phrase appears to have been more frequently employed as the debates went on, as Figure 1, provided by Lexico, suggests.

---

ourselves to become responsible for the government of the Protestant Province of Ulster' (quoted in J. F. Harbinson, *The Ulster Unionist Party, 1882–1973: its development and organisation* (Belfast, 1973), p. 27). Southern unionists had opted for a very different position: 'We Irishmen, belonging to the three Southern Provinces, being of all creeds and classes, representing many separate interests, and sharing a common desire for the honour and welfare of our country, hereby declare our unalterable determination to uphold the Legislative Union between Great Britain and Ireland' (from *The Times*, 11 October 1911).

15   Université de la Sorbonne Nouvelle, Paris 3, *Systèmes linguistiques, enonciation et discours* (EA 2290) *et Secteur du traitement autonomique du langage*, http://www.tal.univ-paris3.fr/lexico/lexico3.htm (accessed 7 February 2014).

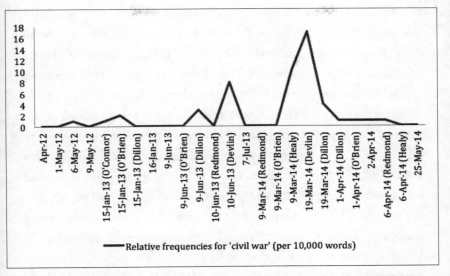

Figure 1: Relative frequencies of the phrase 'civil war' throughout the debates (April 1912 to May 1914)[16]

Figure 1 suggests that Irish nationalist leaders became more and more aware of the increasing likeliness of a civil war during the course of the Home Rule debates. When the contexts in which the phrase appears are examined in detail, however, one can't fail to notice that, in a significant number of instances, the prospect of a civil war suggested by Irish unionists was dismissed using derogatory terms such as 'humbug', 'hypocrisy', 'sham', 'bogus', 'mock', 'bluff' and 'unthinkable'. In other words, despite the toughening of the Irish unionist stance as the crisis developed, the increasing importation of weapons into Ulster, the military drills organised under the auspices of the Unionist Clubs

---

16   The entries on the x axis represent the dates on which the various speeches under examination were delivered, from John Redmond's speech on 11 April 1912 to William O'Brien's speech on 25 May 1914. The graph describes the distribution of the form 'civil war' throughout the speeches by calculating relative frequencies; in other words, the occurrences of the form are put in relation to the length of each speech (http://www.tal.univ-paris3.fr/lexico/manuelsL3/L3–usermanual.pdf, p. 27, accessed 7 February 2014).

or the Ulster Volunteer Force,[17] and the creation on the nationalist side of a rapidly growing body of Irish Volunteers,[18] the idea of an Irish civil war was publicly ridiculed by the Irish nationalist leaders as pure fiction. Negative structures, questions and hypothetical structures also served to question the legitimacy of threats, which were presented as uttered merely for show by the Irish unionists ('stage army', 'it was the next dodge in the party game of politics').[19] Such denials or, rather, dismissive tactics were not new in Irish nationalist discussion: in his 1912 book *The Justice of Home Rule*, Irish Party leader John Redmond had already minimised the danger, stating that 'there [was] no terror in the threats' of Orangemen, and denouncing such threats as 'stale and worthless', 'insolent bluffs … stupid, hollow, unpatriotic bellowings'.[20] What is more striking is that some of the Irish nationalist leaders continued to consider the unionist threats of violence as without substance until the last stages of the debates: not only did Redmond mention the phrase 'civil war' proper only once, but also, as Lexico shows, he did so as late as his speech of 6 April 1914.[21] A reason for

---

17   Jalland, *The Liberals and Ireland*, p. 134. See also Harbinson, *Ulster Unionist Party*, pp. 25–6, and A. Jackson, *The Ulster Party. Irish unionists in the House of Commons, 1884–1911* (Oxford, 1989), pp. 284–321.

18   Created in November 1913, the Irish Volunteers numbered 19,000 members by April 1914. Cabinet paper, 30 April 1914, CAB 37/119/60, British National Archives.

19   For instance: 'if we are to have revolution and civil war' (J. Devlin, 6 May 1912); 'Therefore, it is, I am convinced, that there would be no civil war and no bloodshed in Ulster' (J. Dillon, 9 June 1913); 'How can they say they would be justified in resorting to rebellion (…)?' (J. Dillon, 19 March 1914); 'Would any sane Britisher go to civil war for the difference between six years and 666 years? Is there any sane man amongst you who would let loose the fires of civil war for such a mere form?' (T. Healy, 9 March 1914); 'I must be allowed to say candidly that I do not believe, and I never have believed, in civil war in Ulster.' (J. Redmond, 6 April 1914); 'Now I am told that we are face to face with civil war, and why? For what purpose, for what reason, for what justification?' (T. P. O'Connor, 2 April 1914).

20   J. Redmond, *The Justice of Home Rule: A statement of Ireland's claims to self-government* (London, 1912), pp. 60–1.

21   It was only in May 1914 that Redmond admitted in a private letter to Asquith that 'the Nationalists of Ulster [were] seriously disturbed by apprehension of

Redmond's reluctance to talk about civil war for so long may have been that he was aware of the fact that such a situation would impair the work and credibility of a future independent Irish assembly. T. P. O'Connor noted in a letter addressed to John Dillon that Redmond believed that 'bloodshed and smouldering rebellion in Ulster' would be an 'immense drawback … to the working of the Irish Parliament'.[22]

Differences between the various Irish nationalist figureheads are worth noting and are illustrated in Table 1.

Speaker	Number of times 'civil war' is said	Total number of words used in speeches	Relative frequencies (per 10,000 words)	Exponent attributed by Lexico as an estimation of the over- or under-employment of the phrase 'civil war' by each speaker
J. Redmond	1	27,556	0	-3
W. O'Brien	2	25,240	0	0
J. Dillon	9	24,163	2	0
T. Healy	2	12,561	1	0
J. Devlin	12	15,190	7	+5
T. P. O'Connor	2	21,824	0	0

Table 1: Over- or under-employment of the phrase 'civil war' in the speeches of 1912–14 for each nationalist orator.[23]

isolated attacks on life and property.' Letter from Redmond to Asquith, 15 May 1914, Redmond papers, 15169, National Library of Ireland, Dublin, quoted by A. C. Hepburn, *Catholic Belfast and Nationalist Ireland in the Era of Joe Devlin 1871–1934* (Oxford, 2008), p. 148.

22 Letter from T. P. O'Connor to J. Dillon, 26 November 1913, John Dillon papers, 6740/212, Trinity College Dublin, quoted in Hepburn, *Catholic Belfast and Nationalist Ireland*, p. 146.

23 Table 1 represents *spécificités* – i.e. characteristic elements or increments in the corpus. The headings of columns one to five indicate the meanings of the entries in these columns. Column five gives two indications. First, the + or − signs show the over- or under-use of a specific form ('civil war') in the selected parts of the corpus. Second, the figures associated with the + or − signs in this column are exponents representing the degree of significance of the difference. In other words, the table describes how, in the case of specific orators (J. Redmond, J. Devlin), the form 'civil war' comes up more often or less often than would have been expected

Lexico not only confirms that, in relation to other speakers, John Redmond under-used the phrase 'civil war', but it also shows that Joseph Devlin over-employed it. The latter associated it recurrently with words or structures that were meant to cast doubt or discredit it ('if we are to have revolution and civil war', 'it was the next dodge in the game of party politics', 'they would threaten you with civil war').[24] Anthony C. Hepburn notes that 'privately too, Devlin told several parliamentary colleagues that he believed "Ulster" was "bluffing"'.[25] Devlin had been the MP for West Belfast since 1906 and despite being at the head of the Catholic Ancient Order of Hibernians since July 1905, he was no supporter of sectarian strife: as Hepburn reminds us, Devlin was 'well aware of the dangers of a sectarian appeal', and 'knew from early days that for Home Rule to succeed at least some Protestants – and what he called "the Orange democracy" – had to be won over'.[26] He may also have underestimated the possibility of civil war simply because, as he underlined in a private memo in February 1914, he represented an area where sectarianism played a key role and whose constituents were the most likely to suffer in case of an armed conflict:

> We have exceptional sources of information in regard to the Ulster movement, and we are convinced that its danger is grossly exaggerated … In Belfast … where the Catholic and Protestant home rulers would be among the first victims of any outbreak among the Orangemen, the home rulers regard the whole thing with absolute contempt.[27]

---

in a distribution at random (http://www.tal.univ-paris3.fr/lexico/manuelsL3/L3-usermanual.pdf, p. 29, accessed 7 February 2014).

24 *House of Commons Debates*, Fifth series, vol. 38, 6 May 1912, col. 103; vol. 59, 19 March 1914, cols 2277–86.

25 Hepburn, *Catholic Belfast and Nationalist Ireland*, p. 144.

26 *Ibid.*, p. 93.

27 'Mr Devlin's memo', 20 February 1914, Redmond Papers, 15181/3, National Library of Ireland, Dublin quoted by Hepburn, *Catholic Belfast and Nationalist Ireland*, p. 148.

The speeches of John Dillon, John Redmond or William O'Brien were characterised by greater ambivalence. While all three denied the possibility of a civil war, they did, at the same time, acknowledge the reality and extent of the political opposition to Home Rule in Ireland, especially in the north. John Dillon, for instance, admitted:

> there is no section of the Irish people in favour of exclusion of Ulster as a settlement. I include in that the men of Ulster themselves. I entirely agree and recognise, and I deplore being obliged to recognise it, that the overwhelming majority of the Protestants of Ulster are bitterly hostile to Home Rule.[28]

John Redmond also acknowledged a 'genuine' and 'vehement' opposition to the third Home Rule bill but dismissed it at the same time as 'an opposition which thinks it can kill a Bill it hates and dislikes'.[29] For the leader of the Irish Party, threats of civil war were dismissed because they could not represent a genuine form of democratic opposition; a civil war could be nothing else than a 'rebellion', as Devlin also pointed out. Talk of civil war was regarded as mere talk or just for show, and it was seen purely as a political tactic used by the unionists in the 'party game of politics' and to be dismissed as such. Besides, minimising as much as possible resistance to the bill was all the more crucial for the Irish nationalist leaders since, as A. C. Hepburn underlines, 'evidence of strong popular Protestant feeling against Home Rule ... was not the message they wanted to go out to the British electorate'.[30]

Like Dillon or Redmond, O'Brien in 1913 stressed 'the sincerity of the Ulster Protestants and covenanters' and recognised that 'they [had] ... the power of making the life of the Irish Parliament almost

---

28   *House of Commons Debates*, Fifth series, vol. 60, 1 April 1914, col. 1210.
29   *Ibid.*, 6 April 1914, col. 1663.
30   Hepburn, *Catholic Belfast and Nationalist Ireland*, p. 142.

unbearable'.[31] Unlike them, however, he had expressed an early aware-ness of unionist discontent. Estranged from the Irish Party since March 1909, when he had formed his own organisation – the All-for-Ireland League – O'Brien had foreseen in a letter to Asquith in November 1911 that 'little as the threats of actual civil war need to be regarded, it [was] only too certain that discontent and exasperation in the North Eastern counties of Ulster would be a most grievous addi-tion to the difficulties of an infant Irish legislature'.[32] In January 1913 he again stressed, with more vigour, that '[the] opposition of Ulster [had to] be treated with all respect. Doubtless it [was] a genuine and sincere expression of the fixed determination of determined men.'[33] While other nationalist leaders were never overtly critical of British proposals and strategy, O'Brien's speeches in parliament show that he blamed the government for not taking action early enough to address Irish unionist concerns.[34]

To violence and threats of civil war, which would divide Ireland, Irish nationalist leaders proposed the ideal of a united nation, in which Catholics and Protestants, nationalists and unionists, could be reconciled.

---

31   *House of Commons Debates*, Fifth series, vol. 46, 15 January 1913, col. 2191.
32   Letter from W. O'Brien to H. Asquith, 4 November 1911, H. H. Asquith papers, MS 36/7–9, Bodleian Library Oxford (copy available in Lloyd George papers, C/6/11/10, House of Lords Record Office).
33   *Weekly Free Press*, 11 January 1913.
34   See, for instance, *House of Commons Debates*, Fifth series, vol. 53, 9 June 1913, col. 1332: 'there has been made on the authority of the Government no proposal which goes to the root of the Ulster difficulty, or which ought to give them any reasonable hope of disarming the opposition of the minority in Ireland'; vol. 59, 9 March 1914, col. 929: 'I cannot, therefore, lose a moment in expressing our disappointment that the ministry, after they have for the past two years, declined to make any substantial offer to Ulster ...'; vol. 60, 1 April 1914, col. 1243: 'I cannot congratulate either the Government or their Irish followers in regard to recent events. They may have postponed the trouble in Ulster, but they have demoralised their Army, they have swelled the head of the Covenanters, and they have destroyed their Irish settlement without pleasing anybody.' See also W. O'Brien, *Grattan's Home Rule, Gladstone's, and Asquith's* (Cork, 1915).

Dreaming a united nation

One argument of the unionists, whether British or Irish, was that Ireland was composed of 'two nations'. Such an idea was inconceivable for the Irish nationalist leaders. In Limerick, in October 1913, John Redmond stressed that 'the two-nation theory [was] to us an abomination and a blasphemy'.[35] Lexico highlights that the expression 'two nations' was resorted to only twice in the whole course of the debates – once by John Dillon when quoting Arthur J. Balfour and once by T. P. O'Connor. The latter was clearly not as assertive as Redmond: 'The contention of the right hon. Gentleman and other Members of that party is that there are two nations and two creeds in Ireland which are irreconcilable, and that there is a great gulf between them today. I do not deny it; I deplore it.'[36] But while he admitted that there might have been growing hostility and differences between the pro- and the anti-Home Rule factions in Ireland, he also expressed deep regret about it. This tends to suggest that he, like other nationalist colleagues, hoped to mend religious and political fences in Ireland.

Lexico actually reveals that terms such as 'Unionists', 'Catholics', 'Protestants' and 'Ulster' were often followed by the connector 'and'. When the forms 'Protestants and', 'Unionists and', 'Catholics and' and 'Ulster and' are examined within their broader contexts, it appears that Irish nationalist leaders often associated communities together – in phrases like 'Protestants and Catholics', 'Catholics and Protestants', 'Ulster and the rest of Ireland', 'Ulster and the Nationalists of the rest of Ireland', 'Unionists and Nationalists' – and thus recurrently stressed the idea of unity and harmony within the whole of the Irish population. The quotations Lexico gathered reveal that the Irish nationalist discourse could be, at times, saturated with terms and

---

35   Quoted in D. R. Gwynn, *The Life of John Redmond* (London, 1932), p. 232.
36   *House of Commons Debates*, Fifth series, vol. 55, 7 July 1913, col. 107.

images evoking the idea of a bond and a communion between all Irish people, whatever their creed or political affiliation: 'understand each other', 'friends', 'join hands together', 'live in harmony', 'trust', 'making peace', 'combined together', 'shook hands', 'bore arms together', 'kindly feelings between', 'our countrymen', 'uniting all Irishmen'. The use of verbs such as 'hope', 'desire', 'believe' and 'dream' emphasises that this united Ireland was an ideal and a construction.

As can be seen in the discourse of John Dillon or T. P. O'Connor, history had an important part to play in order to provide the reconciled nation with common memories: Protestant patriots, in particular Henry Grattan, were put forward as founding fathers of the Home Rule movement, and the period during which the so-called 'Grattan parliament' was in place (1782–1800) was presented as a golden age in the relations between Catholics and Protestants.[37] Historians have pointed out, however, that the Grattan parliament was not at all favourable to Catholics: not only was it exclusively composed of Protestants, but these Irish MPs, together with some members of the Irish privy council, proved extremely reluctant to extend the franchise to certain categories of Catholics.[38]

Idealising the past as a golden age helped Irish nationalist leaders forge another myth – the 'myth of union' or *mythe de l'unité* as Raoul

---

37 For instance: 'Such a statement is in the very teeth of history. Remember this: in 1708, when Grattan commenced his agitation for a free Parliament in Ireland, the Protestants of Ulster and the Catholics of that province combined together to win a free Parliament' and 'we have before us the uncontradicted record of one happy period of fifteen years, during which the Catholics and Protestants of Ulster – and even Belfast – shook hands, were friends, and bore arms together in the common cause of Irish liberty' (J. Dillon, 19 March 1914); 'Will [the hon. Gentleman] deny that Ulster and Ulster Protestants were the cradle of some of the movements for the liberation of Ireland and the Irish Parliament, and, above all, for equal rights for Catholics?' (T. P. O'Connor, 2 April 1914).

38 A. J. Ward, *The Parliamentary Tradition: Responsible government and modern Ireland, 1782–1992* (Dublin, 1994), p. 23. See also J. J. Lee, 'Grattan's parliament', in B. Farrell (ed.), *The Irish Parliamentary Tradition* (Dublin, 1973), pp. 149–59, especially pp. 154–5.

Girardet calls it in his work *Mythes et Mythologies Politiques*. Just as French historians Michelet or Lavisse wrote texts and books which, according to Girardet, put forward a 'single image … of harmony, balance and fusion' – i.e. the image of a 'united, indivisible and homogeneous Society for ever protected from rift and unrest, of an undivided mass of people filling each and every one of them with the comforting confidence that they were fully reconciled with one another' – Irish nationalist leaders were striving to break away from the unionist vision of the past and rebuild the past, and thus the nation, on new foundations. That entailed emphasising 'beneficial forces … such as converging interests, unity and cohesion' and rejecting 'evil forces … such as division, breaking-up, and separation [my translation]'.[39] In other words, turning events into myths and rewriting the past was a way for the Irish nationalist leaders to alleviate fears that Catholics might dominate the Protestant and unionist population of Ireland under a Home Rule parliament and to suggest a political alternative to strife and civil war.

Despite their attachment to the idea of a united Ireland, John Redmond and his supporters eventually agreed reluctantly to the exclusion of four Ulster counties for a limited period of six years as the bill was about to be discussed a third time by the Commons. It would seem that, by doing so, they betrayed the ideals in which they believed. Their discourse, however, shows that their attitudes concerning the issue of exclusion or partition were in keeping with the dream they had of keeping the Irish nation one and indivisible.

Attitudes to partition/exclusion

A first result Lexico brings to light is that Irish leaders did not necessarily use the same vocabulary to refer to the fact that Home

---

39 R. Girardet, '*Le mythe de l'unité*', in R. Girardet, *Mythes et Mythologies Politiques* (Paris, 1986), pp. 153–4, 158.

Rule was eventually not to apply to some of the Ulster counties. The word 'partition' was used only by Timothy Healy and William O'Brien who, at the time of the debates, no longer belonged to the Irish Party and can thus be regarded as outcasts from the mainstream of Irish nationalism. Figureheads of the Irish Party such as Redmond, Dillon, Devlin or O'Connor seemed to have preferred to talk exclusively of exclusion or, less frequently, division (employing terms such as 'division', 'dividing', 'divided', 'divide', 'exclusion', 'excluded', 'excluding' and 'exclude'). The difference in word use is significant, as it highlights Healy and O'Brien's different perception of the Ulster question. 'Exclusion' (and its variants) tends to focus on the fact that Home Rule was meant to apply to the whole of Ireland, but that a few Ulster counties might be left out of the scheme; it also tends to suggest that these counties would not be in a position to benefit from what Home Rule entailed for Ireland. 'Partition', in contrast, lays the emphasis on the main consequence of an exclusion of a number of Ulster counties, that is to say on the fact that Ireland would be split into separate entities and no longer united.

The figureheads of the Irish Party eventually accepted a limited scheme of exclusion of four Ulster counties – Antrim, Down, Derry and Armagh – but could not rally to the idea of a permanent exclusion of Ulster. Such a choice was going against the ideal they had of reconciling and uniting again together all the Irish people and was rejected in the House of Commons as well as outside parliament, as is shown by this quotation from a speech delivered by John Redmond in Newcastle-upon-Tyne on 14 November 1913:

> I say that the exclusion of Ulster or any part of Ireland would mean the ruin of its prosperity. But, ladies and gentlemen, to us exclusion would mean something more. It would mean the nullification of our hopes and aspirations for the future Irish nation. It would mean the erection of sharp, permanent, eternal dividing lines between Catholics

and Protestants, whereas our ideal has been an Irish nation in the future made up of a blend of all races, of all classes, and of all creeds.[40]

Permanent exclusion was rejected on the grounds that it was simply a political weapon used by the unionists and that it did not represent the aspirations of the Irish people, even in Ulster itself. In other words nationalist arguments lay on the assumption that the Irish nation was the type of nation Ernest Renan described, that is to say a nation emerging from a 'daily plebiscite', a group of people sharing common memories and common aspirations as well as the desire to live all together. This could be regarded as another myth, as Bernard Yack has pointed out – the 'myth of the civic nation', which 'foster[ed] the illusion that [the mutual association of citizens was] … based solely on consciously chosen principles', and that 'voluntary associations for the expression of shared political principle would be as conducive to toleration and diversity as their supporters expect[ed] them to be'.[41]

A certain moderation or restraint characterised the discourse of the leaders of the Irish Party when they evoked the possibility of the permanent exclusion of Ulster, which was described as 'unpopular', 'a blunder' or 'a deep and bitter wrench'. Only Devlin referred to a possible separation between north and south with the more serious and more obviously derogatory word of 'divorce', which he used in a speech in Portsmouth in October 1913: 'while the door was still open for conciliation and for concession there must be no divorce either of Ulster or of any portion of Ulster from the rest of Ireland.'[42] Not only does the word 'divorce' include obvious moral connotations, but it must be noted here that it is preceded by a clear negation ('no')

---

40   J. Redmond, *Ulster and Home Rule: A speech by John Redmond, at Newcastle-on-Tyne, November 14th, 1913* (London, nd), p. 9.
41   B. Yack, 'The myth of the civic nation', in R. Beiner (ed.), *Theorising Nationalism* (Albany, 1999), pp. 107, 115.
42   *The Times*, 23 October 1913.

as well as the modal verb 'must', which implies an obligation felt by the Irish nationalists themselves, Devlin included. Within the Irish Party, Devlin had been staunchly opposed to the policy of temporary exclusion until he was made to swallow it and sell it to the Ulster nationalists by Dillon and Redmond.

Healy and O'Brien were more radical when denouncing exclusion, as terms such as 'cut off' or 'deeper wound' found in their parliamentary speeches suggest. Both associated the possibility of an exclusion of some of the Ulster counties or, rather, a partition of Ireland with a much more potent and derogatory image – that of 'vivisection'. O'Brien's speeches included similar metaphors, since he also evoked images such as dissection, mutilation and surgery, through the use of terms and phrases such as 'dismemberment', 'mutilated', 'amputation', 'chopped up', 'carved out' and 'pieced together'.[43] These images were used by him not only in the House of Commons, but also outside parliament, as can be inferred by the following passages, taken from the pamphlet *Grattan's Home Rule, Gladstone's, and Asquith's*:

> Even should the Amending Bill of the future go no further, the Parliament will not be the Parliament of Ireland at all, but of an Ireland amputated of four of her richest and most historic counties as a minimum subject, indeed, to the lunatic condition that the amputation is only to last for 6 years … Because we abstained from joining [the Irish nationalist representatives] in publicly pledging Ireland by our votes to her own dismemberment, our generous adversaries, with their own hands stained with the blood of Ireland's mutilation, raised the cry that we had 'voted against Home Rule …'[44]

---

43 *House of Commons Debates*, Fifth series, vol. 59, 9 March 1914, cols 941–5 (T. Healy) and vol. 59, 9 March 1914, cols 929–32; vol. 60, 1 April 1914, cols 1242–54 (W. O'Brien).

44 O'Brien, *Grattan's Home Rule*, pp. 8, 31–3.

Likewise, in this speech delivered in Cork in May 1915:

> We warned you ... as to the Amending Bill for the mutilation of
> Ireland. We warned you that the Liberal Government were pledged,
> and are pledged up to the lips, to an Amending Bill that will partition
> and mutilate Ireland; we warned you that the majority of Ireland's
> own representatives publicly assented to that enormous crime against
> the integrity of Ireland, and that our own small Party was the only one
> that raised one voice of protest in the House of Commons against that
> abominable mutilation.[45]

In these metaphors, Ireland was considered as a person or, rather, a
body, which meant that it could be imagined or exist as a nation. In
turn such rhetoric stressed the idea that Ireland could be imagined or
exist as a nation only as long as its territorial unity was preserved and
its population remained united and governed by a single government
and parliament. These metaphors also highlight the extent to which
O'Brien and Healy had moved away from the Irish Party. The gap is
all the more evident when their use of language is compared to the
strikingly similar imagery that was being employed at the same time
by more radical separatists, such as James Connolly:

> This ... means that a local majority, in Belfast or Derry, for instance, are to
> be given the power to wreck their hatred upon Ireland by dismembering
> her, by cutting Ireland to pieces as a corpse would be cut upon the
> dissecting table. Cromwell, in his worst days, the Orange Order, in its
> most atrocious moments, never planned a more dastardly outrage upon
> the Irish nation than this.[46]

---

45   *The Situation in Ireland. Speeches of Mr. William O'Brien, MP, and Mr. Maurice
Healy, MP, delivered at a great open-air demonstration on the Grand Parade, Cork, 10th
May 1915* (Cork, 1915), p. 9.
46   J. Connolly, 'Ireland upon the dissecting table' reprinted in *Ireland upon the*

Myopia characterises a viewpoint that is unable to go beyond a limited scope and thus lacks insight or foresight. The term 'utopia' is applied to describe ideal communities or societies, which are presented as alternatives to the present. For French philosopher Paul Ricoeur, for instance, utopias are meant to reconcile irreconcilable groups and are meant to propose 'alternative ways of living which function on the basis of cooperation and equal relationships'.[47] Violence is rejected by the utopian discourse, which is supposed to convince through imagination rather than force.

What the study discussed in this essay helped to establish is that some of the most prominent figures of Irish parliamentary nationalism – such as Joseph Devlin or John Redmond – appear to have underestimated or denied the threats of civil war. Other figures – notably William O'Brien, who was outside the mainstream of the party – seem to have taken them more seriously. The lack of realism of some of the Irish nationalist leaders is even more blatant if one believes, like Alvin Jackson, that, had Home Rule been implemented in 1912 or 1914, it would have been likely that 'advanced separatists would have staged a revolt against a Home Rule administration' or that there would have been 'a conflict between the Ulster Volunteer Force and the Irish Volunteers'.[48] Such minimisation of unionist threats on the part of some of the Irish nationalist leaders can be interpreted as a strategy to sabotage and discredit unionist discourse and arguments, as well as a tactic to reassure pro-Home Rule Protestants, their British Liberal allies and British public opinion as to the prospects of Ireland under a Home Rule parliament. The nationalist discourse was all the more ambivalent as nationalist MPs had very

---

Dissecting Table: James Connolly on Ulster and partition (Cork, 1975), pp. 60–1.

47   P. Ricoeur, *L'idéologie et l'utopie* (Paris, 1997), p. 17.

48   A. Jackson, 'British Ireland: What if Home Rule had been enacted in 1912?' in N. Ferguson (ed.), *Virtual history: alternatives and counterfactuals* (London, 1999), pp. 185–227, especially pp. 217, 221.

different allies they were careful not to upset – on the one hand the British Liberal Party and on the other hand the Catholic Church.

Irish nationalist leaders appear also to have been trapped by long-established trends, myths and ideals in Irish nationalist discourse as well as Liberal discourse in Britain – notably an 'Irish myth of unity'. One could agree with Alvin Jackson when he writes that '[t]he vision of Home Rule as a pathway to Arcadia is rooted more deeply in Gladstonian optimism and myopia than in the politics of 1914'.[49] In other words, utopianism and myopia went hand in hand.

Ricoeur and others do emphasise that utopias are escapes from the actual and may be out of touch with reality. For French philosopher and historian Louis Marin, utopias are actually 'pure discourse'; they are 'accounts of the world involving ideal representations of history and of people which come to replace actual history and people'.[50] A. C. Hepburn notes in his recent biography of Joseph Devlin that the Home Rule debates of 1912–14 were a 'war of words', and that Irish nationalist MPs offered 'conciliation of Protestant Ulster by promises and the rhetoric of moderation, rather than by political concession'.[51] Redmond and his colleagues had made the choice to sit at Westminster and to play by parliamentary rules; as such they may have placed democracy and peace above violence, but they may also have placed persuasion, rhetoric and language above pragmatic responses and concrete political solutions to the Ulster issue.

---

49   *Ibid.*, p. 226.
50   Ricoeur, *L'idéologie et l'utopie*, pp. 406–7, 436 and L. Marin, *Utopiques: Jeux d'espaces* (Paris, 1973), pp. 87, 92.
51   Hepburn, *Catholic Belfast and Nationalist Ireland*, pp. 141, 151.

7

The All-for-Ireland League and the Home Rule debate, 1910–14

John O'Donovan

The All-for-Ireland League (AFIL) was one of the most interesting political groups to have existed during the 'long nineteenth century' of Irish history. Although generally nationalist in conception and composition, the AFIL's tone and message jarred quite heavily with those of the Irish Party. Nowhere was this more in evidence than during the tumultuous years between the two general elections of 1910 and the outbreak of the First World War. The conduct of the AFIL during this period was based on a strategy of propaganda (through its daily newspaper the *Cork Free Press*) and grass-roots political action. This strategy was a reflection of the AFIL's ideologically extreme positions. At a leadership level the AFIL's founder, William O'Brien, courted members of both the Conservative Party and the Ulster unionists, relying on his alliance with Tim Healy to gather support from his Liberal-leaning coterie. At a more local level the AFIL welded itself to the rural labour movement under the command of its chief organiser D. D. Sheehan, supported by a Cork city labour clique cultivated by Eugene Crean among others. Thus the AFIL attacked the Irish Party and its grass-roots affiliates – the United Irish League (UIL) and the Ancient Order of Hibernians (Board of Erin) (AOH-BOE).

A brief outline of the genesis of the AFIL is in order. The movement was a by-product of both the Parnell split and the Wyndham Land Act. Certainly it is true that relations between the chief actors in the drama of Irish nationalism post-Parnell were soured for a long period of time. The cosmetic reunion of the Irish Party in 1900 plastered over a number of deep-seated fissures. These were re-opened in the winter of 1902–3, when the land conference, comprising landlords and tenant representatives, produced a report into the future of land purchase. Its prime movers were O'Brien, Irish Party leader John Redmond and conference chairman Lord Dunraven. The relative success of the legislation spawned by the conference convinced O'Brien and his clique of followers that future conferences on a number of issues could lead to a possible Home Rule settlement by conference, conciliation and consent: the 'three Cs'. However, over the next seven years he was sidelined from the mainstream Irish Party, though he continued to build up an influential following in Cork and Munster generally. Much of this work was carried out by Sheehan, whose support for O'Brien rent the rural labour movement, but gained a crucial following for O'Brien and his ideas. Relations between O'Brien and his following and the Irish Party in general fluctuated from 1906, when an agreement was reached not to contest seats held by O'Brien and his followers in Cork and elsewhere. Although a cosmetic reunion was engineered in 1908, the unruly scenes of the Mansion House Convention in February 1909, when O'Brien was prevented from speaking on the new land bill, displayed the sea change in attitudes towards him by those purporting to represent mainstream nationalism. Later that year the AFIL came into embryonic existence and all outgoing O'Brienite MPs fought under its banner in the general election of January 1910.[1]

---

1   On this topic see J. O'Donovan, 'The Cork Advisory Committee, the Wyndham Land Act, and the restructuring of the United Irish League, 1904–1910' (MPhil thesis, University College Cork, 2011) and 'Daniel Desmond (D.D.) Sheehan (1873–1948) and the rural labour question in Cork, 1894–1910' in B. J. Casey (ed.), *Defying the Law of the Land: agrarian radicals in Irish history* (Dublin, 2013), pp. 220–37. For a narrative of the violence of 1910 see J. O'Donovan, 'Nationalist political

Following the election the AFIL was formally launched as a full-blown political movement in Cork on 31 March 1910. At the inaugural rally the decision of Redmond to support the prime minister, Herbert H. Asquith, and the Liberals was roundly condemned. O'Brien declared that the AFIL would not stand beholden to either English political party. In furtherance of this campaign the *Cork Free Press* was launched in June. The paper's appearance was attacked by the *Cork Examiner*, which saw the AFIL as 'under the protection of the Landlords Defence Association'; in retaliation the *Free Press* lambasted the *Examiner* for being 'the organ of the Molly Maguire secret society'.[2] A glance at the list of shareholders of the new company would have confirmed to an extent the *Cork Examiner*'s criticisms: the major shareholders in the paper included Dunraven, Colonel William Hutcheson-Poe, Lord Castletown and Lady Fitzgerald-Arnott, wife of the proprietor of *The Irish Times*. A number of smaller shareholders had, however, enlisted following a public meeting in February 1910; these included Mrs H. Mitchel Martin, sister of Fenian John Mitchel. Other money used to launch the paper came from an American-based group, the League of Federals, which sent £4,000 by way of Lord Dunraven and £500 to Healy, who later passed it on to O'Brien. The League of Federals was organised by Moreton Frewen, an uncle by marriage of Liberal cabinet member Winston Churchill. Frewen envisaged being able to challenge the Irish Party-affiliated United Irish League of America, but could not obtain support from any leading Irish-Americans for his schemes of federalism.[3]

---

conflict in Cork, 1910', *Journal of the Cork Archaeological and Historical Society*, vol. 117 (2012), pp. 37–52.

2   *Cork Examiner*, 14 June 1910; *Cork Free Press*, 16 June 1910. The 'Molly Maguires' was a pejorative term used to describe the AOH-BOE faction, whose president Joseph Devlin, a political protégé of John Dillon, was one of the principal leaders of the Irish Party. The AOH-BOE, principally based in the north of Ireland, had subsumed the United Irish League (UIL) after 1909.

3   F. K. Schilling, 'William O'Brien and the All-for-Ireland League' (BLitt thesis, Trinity College Dublin, 1956), pp. 112–5; A. J. Ward, 'Frewen's Anglo-American

With such an eclectic mix of shareholders, the *Cork Free Press* was a microcosm of the AFIL as a whole. This was further reflected in the paper's content, which carried copious reports from branches of the Land and Labour Association (LLA) and from the frequent meetings of the Cork United Trades and Labour Council (CUTLC). These were frequently juxtaposed with reports gleaned from the Conservative-leaning English press, such as the *Daily Telegraph*. Furthermore, its editorial stance (in spite of the frequent changes of editor) combined fervent anti-Irish Party rhetoric with consistent (and constant) argument in favour of conciliation with both English political parties and with unionists.[4] It also proclaimed that the AFIL would not align itself with either party, thus in O'Brien's eyes bringing back into practical play the famous dictum of Parnell during the 1880s of Irish nationalism being independent from English influence.[5]

It is hard to pin down exactly where the AFIL stood in the British political spectrum between 1911 and 1914. O'Brien's own nationalism was inspired by the idea of *jus soli* – law of the soil.[6] Following in the footsteps of Thomas Davis (like O'Brien a native of Mallow, County Cork), O'Brien acknowledged the existence of many strands of Irishness. As early as November 1892 he acknowledged during a lecture in Belfast: 'We are on the eve of a battle for our existence as a self-governing nation … What could be more useful at such an hour than to review those common interests, sympathies, and traditions which constitute us a nation as contra-distinguished from a faction?'[7]

campaign for federalism, 1910–21', *Irish Historical Studies*, vol. 16, no. 59 (March 1967), pp. 256–9.

4   P. Maume, 'A nursery of editors: the Cork Free Press, 1910–16', *History Ireland*, vol. 15, no. 2 (March/April 2007), available online at http://www.historyireland.com/volumes/volume15/issue2/features/?id=113924 (accessed 12 August 2009).

5   F. Callanan, *The Parnell Split* (Cork, 1992), pp. 201–2.

6   H. F. Kearney, *Ireland: contested ideas of nationalism and history* (Cork, 2007), p. 59; B. Girvin, *From Union to Union: nationalism, democracy and religion in Ireland – Act of Union to EU* (Dublin, 2002), pp. 30–1.

7   W. O'Brien, *Irish Ideas* (London, 1893), pp. 112–13.

Almost twenty years later, this thinking had not substantially changed, save for its increasing marginalisation among mainstream nationalism and unionism. The brief flowering of centrism as a viable political alternative between 1903 and 1905 was overshadowed by subsequent events. Almost all of O'Brien's influential supporters on the unionist side had been prominent figures during this flowering; the foundation of the Ulster Unionist Council in March 1905 was a clear signal that unionists in the north of Ireland did not subscribe to this line of thinking. It was this new, militant unionism with which the AFIL would have to work if it were to express *jus soli* in legislative reality.[8] Any hope the AFIL may have had in remaining totally independent in British politics was scuppered by the Irish Party's strong connections with the Liberal Party.[9] On the other side of the British political divide, the Conservative Party had shed progressives in favour of more austere policies. Nevertheless, a small, yet influential, minority argued for a federal solution of the Irish self-government question. It was this clique that allowed O'Brien and the AFIL to have a voice within Conservative politics. This minority, however, had been gradually losing its voice before 1910, and by the time Sir Edward Carson succeeded former Irish Chief Secretary Walter Long as leader of the Irish unionists, the prospect of a federalist solution in the medium term was remote at best.[10] By the dawn of 1911, nevertheless, the AFIL was viewed by many within the Irish Party as the Irish adjunct to the Conservative Party.[11]

---

8   A. Jackson, *Ireland 1798–1998: politics and war* (Oxford, 1999), pp. 152–5; A. Jackson, *Home Rule: an Irish history 1800–2000* (London, 2003), pp. 104–14; T. Bartlett, *Ireland: a history* (Cambridge, 2010), pp. 362–3.

9   G. K. Peatling, *British Opinion and Irish Self-government, 1865–1925: from unionism to liberal commonwealth* (Dublin, 2001), pp. 58–9, 63, 65–7. See, however, E. F. Biagini, *British Democracy and Irish Nationalism 1876–1906* (Cambridge, 2007), pp. 364–6.

10   J. Smith, *The Tories and Ireland: Conservative party politics and the Home Rule crisis, 1910–1914* (Dublin, 2000), pp. 22–30.

11   Joseph Devlin, one of the leaders of the Irish party, wrote to his Cork contact

This view of the AFIL was scarcely lessened during the constitutional crisis of 1910–11, which was sparked by the rejection by the House of Lords of the 1909 budget and led to two general elections during 1910.[12] Between the two elections, the AFIL made great play of denouncing the budget and its proto-socialist proposals, including increasing duties on spirits and introducing land taxes. This opposition increased its grass-roots support, in tandem with disillusionment with parliamentary politics among the Irish population as a whole. O'Brien's virulent attacks on Redmond and the Irish Party dented the idea of parliamentary action leading to a settlement of the Home Rule question. Furthermore, growth in the AFIL's support was an example of a conservative backlash against Liberal social radicalism, personified by Liberal chancellor David Lloyd George. This anti-radical coalition was, inevitably, unstable.[13] An opportunity to spread the AFIL's strength outside the confines of Cork city and county was thwarted in the December 1910 election due to lack of finance and organisation; it was also due to a solidifying of Irish Party support around the AOH-BOE, as well as the promise of the ending of the veto of the House of Lords. The *Cork Free Press* foresaw no real change at Westminster in the aftermath of the election, and on the issue of Home Rule argued:

The one hope for Ireland is to raise the question above mere Party strife and contention, to make its solution a great Imperial issue, and to convince the English people that Ireland can be trusted to work

---

John J. Horgan: 'There is no doubt about it that Healy and O'Brien are bent on destroying Home Rule if they can … there is nothing now hidden in the alliance that exists between them … [and] the Tories'; J. J. Horgan, *Parnell to Pearse: some recollections and reflections* (second edition, Dublin, 2009), p. 208.

12 For a classic account of the Lords versus Commons imbroglio over the 1909 budget, see G. Dangerfield, *The Strange Death of Liberal England* (London, 1997), pp. 28–36.

13 F. Callanan, *T. M. Healy* (Cork, 1996), pp. 470–1.

successfully any measure of Self-Government which may be conceded to her. That can only be done on Conciliation lines. It is by Conference methods that practical results can be attained and that Ireland's hopes will not again be doomed to disappointment. That is the bedrock fact in the situation, and until it is recognised and acted upon the Irish people will remain wandering in the wilderness.[14]

This was to prove the hallmark of the AFIL in the coming years: conference, conciliation and consent.

On 22 February 1911 Lord Lansdowne, leader of the Tories in the House of Lords, called for 'some form of compromise which will provide for the reconstitution of the House'. The *Cork Free Press* supported these calls, and argued that Redmond had chosen to forego 'his command of the balance of power to compel both English parties to club together and … come to a settlement on the Constitutional and Home Rule questions'.[15] The passage of the parliament bill through both Houses of Parliament vindicated the judgement of Redmond and the Irish Party in remaining part of the 'Democratic Alliance' (a phrase coined to describe the coalition of Liberal, Labour and Irish Party MPs). Yet not all Irish nationalists were pleased. Fr Richard Barrett, one of only a handful of clerical supporters of the AFIL, wrote to O'Brien that there would 'be great jubilation over the Veto Bill … Alas, poor Ireland.'[16]

Barrett's fears over the passage of the Parliament Act were shared by many within Ulster unionism. A rally at the home of Sir James Craig on 25 September 1911 attracted somewhere between 100,000 and 250,000 members of Orange Lodges, Unionist Clubs and the

---

14   *Cork Free Press*, 13, 31 December 1910.
15   *Ibid.*, 31 January, 23 February 1911.
16   C. O'Leary and P. Maume, *Controversial Issues in Anglo-Irish Relations 1910–1921* (Dublin, 2004), p. 12; Fr Richard Barrett to William O'Brien, 11 August 1911, William O'Brien papers, Box AR, item 92, UC/WOB/PP/AR 92, Special Collections, Boole Library, University College Cork.

County Grand Lodge of Belfast; the gathering marked the launch of the anti-Home Rule campaign in Ulster.[17] Frewen resigned as AFIL MP for North East Cork, after the bill had passed. He had been elected unopposed to this seat after O'Brien had been elected for both North East Cork and Cork city at the December 1910 general election, choosing to sit for the latter. His tenure as MP had been ceaselessly mocked by D. P. Moran in *The Leader*, who had taken to referring to the AFIL as 'the Frewenites'.[18]

The passage of the Parliament Act also had consequences on the Tory side; the rise of the radical Tories was a reaction to the conciliationist tendencies of Balfour and Lansdowne. An alliance between a Conservative Party out of power for five years, and Ulster unionists, who were divesting themselves of landed southern Irish unionism in favour of the militant, middle- and working-class unionism of the north-east of Ireland – an area where the loss or gain of a few seats could precipitate a new general election – promised to bear much fruit. The elections of Edward Carson as leader of the Irish unionists and Andrew Bonar Law as Conservative leader in late 1911 dramatically shifted the political landscape; now compromise was possible, but confrontation, too, was inevitable.[19]

O'Brien used the fact that the passage of the Parliament Act opened up the vista of a Home Rule bill in the immediate future to propound the AFIL's views to Asquith in November 1911. To him, the ideal solution was to grant Ireland full dominion status, similar to that enjoyed by Canada. While this was unattainable for the present,

17   P. Bew, *Ideology and the Irish Question: Ulster unionism and Irish nationalism, 1912–1916* (Oxford, 1998), p. 21.
18   *The Leader*, 11 February, 18 March 1911.
19   N. Harrington, 'The Last parliamentarian: the political career of John Redmond 1881–1918' (PhD thesis, University College Cork, 2008), pp. 179–80; G. D. Phillips, 'Lord Willoughby de Broke and the politics of radical Toryism, 1909–1914', *Journal of British Studies*, vol. 20, no. 1 (Autumn 1980), pp. 205–24; J. Loughlin, *Ulster Unionism and British National Identity Since 1885* (London, 1995), pp. 52–3; *Cork Weekly News*, 18 November 1911.

O'Brien offered two alternatives: 'Home Rule all round', that is 'a general Federal scheme, applicable to England, Scotland and Wales', and 'experimental Home Rule' with a limit of five years. While he did not expound precisely the details of the schemes and called for a conference once the bill was introduced, he stressed the need to soften the growing hostility of Ulster unionists to any measure of Home Rule, however limited: '[It] is only too certain that discontent and exasperation in the North Eastern counties of Ulster would be a most grievous addition to the difficulties of an infant Irish legislature.'[20]

O'Brien's overtures came at a time when Liberals were debating the future of Irish self-government. He and Asquith had publicly exchanged views on the subject on 2 November 1911, a fact that the *Cork Free Press* did its level best to highlight and contrast with the behaviour of the Irish Party, which seemed more engrossed in the details of the National Insurance bill. His suggestions may be seen in the context of his call, a few days after his exchange with Asquith, for both English parties to publish their proposals on Home Rule. To him, and despite the blow of losing support of some southern Irish unionists, the AFIL remained Ireland's only true ambassador at Westminster.[21]

In early 1912 the *Free Press* carried a leading article from O'Brien setting out the AFIL stall for the coming session of parliament, during which a Home Rule bill was to be introduced. He attempted to coax support for a measure of self-government, however limited it looked on first viewing. This was not a new strategy; O'Brien had adopted the same approach towards the abortive Irish Council bill of 1907. While he argued in favour of 'getting any measure, however small, on to the Statute Book', this was conditional: '*provided we are*

---

20 S. Warwick-Haller, 'Seeking conciliation: William O'Brien and the Ulster crisis, 1911–14', in D. G. Boyce and A. O'Day (eds), *The Ulster Crisis 1885–1921* (Basingstoke, 2006), pp. 151–2; *Cork Free Press*, 28 January 1914.
21 *Cork Free Press*, 3, 4, 6, 9, 10 November 1911.

not asked to sign our names to the forfeiture of any national principle [my emphasis]'.[22] This was a warning to the Irish Party that O'Brien and the AFIL would not tolerate Home Rule at any price. Such an attitude had already been seen in a leading article reacting to a speech by Carson to the Constitutional Club on 11 December 1911. The speech, the paper argued, set out the new policy of the Conservatives towards Ireland. Nationalists should 'no longer [be] absolutely dependent on the existence of a Liberal Government for Irish legislation … if the Liberals refuse to accede to the Irish demand, we have a second string in the shape of the Conservatives, on whom we can fall back'. The article preached caution, however, until the Liberals introduced their promised Home Rule legislation; if it did not live up to expectations, then the Redmondites should 'turn them out, and get land purchase, Private Bill legislation, Poor Law [reform] and educational reform … The day has gone by when our only hope of legislation depended on the vague promises of the Liberals.'[23] In spite of its previous declaration to be above British party politics, the AFIL very clearly considered unsettling the Democratic Alliance. O'Brien, addressing an AFIL rally at Killeagh in east Cork in January 1912, argued that the Irish Party would 'have to swallow' the Home Rule bill; a week later at Kanturk in north Cork he warned:

> Sir Edward Carson's mischief-makers and Mr Dillon's mischief-makers … are now rekindling the old fratricidal strife and war between the two races and the two creeds, which is infinitely a more dangerous obstacle to Home Rule than the Veto of the House of Lords … The Irish Party and their constituents have made their own bed and will have to lie upon it.[24]

The reference to 'mischief-makers' is important; a few weeks later

---

22   *Ibid.*, 10 February 1912; Schilling, 'William O'Brien', pp. 137–8.
23   *Cork Free Press*, 13 December 1911.
24   *Weekly Free Press*, 13, 20 January 1912.

the paper declared that 'we refuse to subscribe to the policy which bases the consummation of the National demand on the defeat and humiliation of a strong minority of the National forces'.[25] This ambiguous phraseology encapsulated the AFIL's message: was it talking about its own forces, or the forces in the north of Ireland open to compromise on the question of self-government?

Such an open-ended declaration on the issue of Home Rule led the AFIL to scrutinise carefully the Home Rule bill introduced on 11 April 1912. The re-appearance of Tim Healy on the Commons stage (he had been invited to take Frewen's vacant seat) bolstered the AFIL challenge to the bill. This was in contrast to the national convention of the Irish Party in Dublin on 23 April, which proclaimed 'unanimous acceptance' of the bill and, in the eyes of the *Free Press*, thereby pitched the question 'into the cauldron of English Party passions'. A speech by Redmond at Swindon a week later promising a 'full, free and frank' discussion of the bill was greeted with scorn by the AFIL, which challenged the Irish Party leader to remember the scenes that had disfigured the national convention of February 1909.[26] It was the financial clauses of the bill that proved to be the main stumbling block. The AFIL was not alone in this; many publications, ranging from *The Times* to *The Freeman's Journal*, queried the complex provisions drawn up by Postmaster General Herbert Samuel. Even the Irish chief secretary, Augustine Birrell, admitted that he could not follow Samuel's complex memoranda at cabinet meetings! Some, including the Tory federalist Leo Amery, argued that a binary solution was necessary: Ireland should receive full fiscal autonomy along the lines suggested by the Primrose Committee in 1911, or it should get no taxation powers at all.[27] In all, the *Free Press* concluded that,

---

25   *Ibid.*, 17 February 1912.
26   *Ibid.*, 27 April, 4 May 1912.
27   P. Jalland, 'Irish Home Rule finance: a neglected dimension of the Irish question, 1910–14', *Irish Historical Studies*, vol. 23, no. 91 (May 1983), pp. 237–45.

with the Imperial Treasury being the final arbiter of all income and expenditure in a nascent Irish parliament, the bill 'leaves us subject to the ravages of Lloyd George [and] gives us a smaller surplus than that awarded us in the Council Bill [of 1907] ... It is unjust and unworkable.'[28]

In tandem with the Insurance Act, which the AFIL frequently denounced at numerous grass-roots meetings throughout Cork city and county, Home Rule finance was to become a source of much criticism. This was due in no small part to the campaign for new land-purchase legislation, which was one of the central tenets of AFIL policy. For it a repeal of the Land Act of 1909 was essential, with a reworking of the machinery of land purchase in Ireland along the lines of the Wyndham Land Act necessary. Accordingly at a special AFIL convention in Cork on 25 May 1912 one of the resolutions passed condemned the lack of any provisions in the bill for completing land purchase, in spite of a pledge by Churchill in his Belfast speech that the Liberals would commit themselves to such a goal. Another resolution condemned the financial provisions, which would leave the proposed Dublin parliament with no means for undertaking development work 'except by means of Irish taxation ... or through loans on Irish security at a ruinous rate of interest'.[29] Despite strenuous efforts on the part of O'Brien and Healy in the Commons, amendments demanding changes in the financial clauses were defeated, and the AFIL abstained in all votes on Home Rule finance for the rest of the year. The *Free Press* decried the attitude of the Irish Party leadership towards the finances of Home Rule, declaring that the AFIL MPs were 'sent to Westminster to be Irish nationalists and not ... maids-of-fork of an English Liberal Party'. For this reason, AFIL MP Eugene Crean declared at a public meeting

---

28 *Weekly Free Press*, 1 June 1912.
29 *Ibid*; Schilling, 'William O'Brien', pp. 143–6.

at Barryroe near Clonakilty in August 1912 that the bill was not 'a final settlement of the National question ... [but] an experimental Act only'.[30]

The question as to exactly how experimental any measure of Home Rule would or could be was contested after September 1912, when thousands of unionists marched throughout Ulster in support of the Ulster Solemn League and Covenant, which was signed in hundreds of locations across the province on 28 September, 'Ulster Day'. To the majority of Ulster unionists, the complex shifting of priorities within Irish nationalism mattered little; many expected the horrors of the Parnellite agrarian struggle during the Land War to be visited upon their homes and premises under a Home Rule Ireland.[31] The Covenant was also partially a reaction to an attack perpetrated by the AOH-BOE on a group of Sunday school pupils from Belfast at Castledawson, County Londonderry, on 29 June.[32] Whatever the exact cause of the origins of the Covenant, reaction to its signing in Cork was one of worry. The unionist *Cork Constitution* warned that 'the Home Rule Bill cannot be forced upon the Statute Book by coercive means' and the *Free Press* echoed the Castledawson aftermath when it argued that Redmond, Dillon and Devlin had created 'a policy of religious ascendancy ... [that] has compelled the moderate Irish Protestant to seek protection in the arms of Sir Edward Carson's battalions'.[33] This showed the other facet of the AFIL's opposition to the Home Rule bill: in spite of provisions contained within it that outlawed the enactment of sectarian legislation in a Dublin parliament, there existed growing sectarian tensions in all parts of the island. These tensions were fuelled by the increasing

30   *Weekly Free Press*, 10, 17 August 1912; Schilling, 'William O'Brien', pp. 146–7.
31   D. W. Miller, *Queen's Rebels: Ulster loyalism in historical perspective* (second edition, Dublin, 2007), pp. 100–1.
32   A. T. Q. Stewart, *The Ulster Crisis* (London, 1967), pp. 59–68; Bew, *Ideology and the Irish Question*, pp. 54–70.
33   *Cork Constitution*, 30 September 1912; *Weekly Free Press*, 5 October 1912.

identification of the Irish Party with Catholic triumphalism, through the growing influence of the Board of Erin. By March 1913 RIC inspector general Neville Chamberlain reported that the board was now more influential within the Irish Party umbrella than the UIL.[34] One example of the attitude of many mainstream nationalists to the Ulster unionist position came in the form of an essay by Irish Party MP Richard Hazleton in *The Leader* in October 1912. Referring to the recent demonstrations in the province, he declared them to have 'failed dismally in [their] ... great purpose, which was to frighten and intimidate the British public into ... [believing] that, if the Government's programme is persisted in, there will be civil war in the North of Ireland'. It was, he argued, merely a stunt, in which the Tories had more than a hand, 'to force another general election'.[35]

Throughout 1913 the likelihood of a general election grew greater. Rejection of the Home Rule bill by the House of Lords on 30 January was greeted by the *Free Press*, however, with a hint of satisfaction: the tone of the rejection was not 'that of "No Home Rule". It is that of "This Bill and these methods will not do".'[36] In spite of this, plans by Ulster unionists to resist what they saw as the inevitable introduction of Home Rule gathered pace. Plans for a provisional government of Ulster were adopted by the Ulster Unionist Council, and Charles Craig, brother of James, made a speech in March in which he argued that money spent on rifles would be better than money spent on political ends.[37] These developments, in tandem with parallel campaigns for devolution, moved on through the spring. On 1 March the AFIL launched a campaign in Cork to call for an Irish convention to settle the Home Rule question by consent. Speaking

---

34   R. F. Foster, *Modern Ireland 1600–1972* (London, 1988), pp. 432–3; I. G. report, March 1913, CO 904/89, 390, British National Archives.

35   'The political position', *The Leader*, 19 October 1912.

36   *Cork Free Press*, 31 January 1913; see also issues dated 3, 4, 17, 29 and 30 January 1913.

37   D. Gwynn, *The History of Partition (1912–1925)* (Dublin, 1950), pp. 54–5.

at the meeting O'Brien made his position clear: 'There was one thing, and one thing only, which, as far as Ireland was concerned, could not be compromised on any possible conditions, and that was that Ulster must not be amputated from the fair lady of Ireland.' The Home Rule bill, in his opinion, was 'so grotesque a farce' that its rejection was inevitable. Conciliation and consent of those who were to be governed were critical in arriving at a satisfactory Home Rule settlement. Tim Healy, following O'Brien, condemned the bill for offering an Irish parliament a subvention just over three times as much as it would cost to run Cork city for a year. Lord Dunraven also gave a detailed critique of the bill, but said little about any proposed exclusion. Dunraven wished to bang the federalist drum, but O'Brien cautioned him against such a move, arguing privately that many AFIL grass-roots supporters would see it as watering down Home Rule.[38] In May, O'Brien launched a stinging attack on the Irish Party, claiming that Irish people 'can no longer pretend to accept this maimed and crippled Bill as a final and unalterable settlement (cheers)'. In June he followed up the Cork declarations by making an eloquent plea in the Commons during the fresh second reading of the Home Rule bill, which had been reintroduced on 9 June despite criticisms from Carson in particular, when he derided proceedings as 'sham and hypocrisy' in view of the escalation of tensions in Ulster.[39]

September 1913 saw the zenith of the AFIL campaign when Lord Loreburn, a Liberal peer who was the leader of federalist Liberals in the Lords, wrote a letter to *The Times* urging for a conference of party leaders to explore the prospects of 'cooperation for the good of Ireland'. O'Brien had had contact with Loreburn since July 1913,

---

38   *Cork Free Press*, 3, 4 March 1913; *Cork Weekly News*, 8 March 1913; Schilling, 'William O'Brien', pp. 150–2; J. Smith, 'Federalism, devolution and partition: Sir Edward Carson and the search for a compromise on the third Home Rule bill, 1913–14', *Irish Historical Studies*, vol. 25, no. 140 (November 2007), p. 502.
39   *Cork Free Press*, 19 May, 10 June 1913; P. Jalland, *The Liberals and Ireland: the Ulster question in British politics to 1914* (New York, 1980), p. 123.

when he had invited him to an AFIL rally in Cork, and the two men had met and corresponded in August.[40] Loreburn's letter came shortly after the Cork rally, which passed a resolution calling on the Liberals to advise King George V to call a conference to bring about settlements of both the Home Rule and the land-purchase questions. The *Free Press* argued such a conference would 'sap Edward Carson [of] … his English and Irish allies'; if the Democratic Alliance rejected such an offer, 'they must bear the burden of the fiery cross'.[41] In response to the Loreburn letter, Lord Dunraven proposed that Ulster unionism could be accommodated under federalist principles.[42] Carson, speaking at Durham, hinted at conditions for a settlement by consent, but dismissed the idea of a conference unless it considered 'the better government of Ireland'. Nevertheless the AFIL trumpeted the speech and the *Free Press* called on John Redmond to respond to Loreburn and Carson 'like a man'. Two scenarios were open to the government: agree to a conference, or call an election, which would turn out to be 'a referendum or an election on Marconi, Insurance, Land Taxes, Strike troubles and the internecine warfare between Liberalism, Labour and Toryism'.[43] Redmond at Cahirciveen, County Kerry, on 28 September, dismissed both the Loreburn and Carson proposals, declaring that the Irish Party 'would go on, and next year … witness the triumph of their cause'. Infuriated, the *Free Press* lashed out at Redmond, calling him '[an] Anti-Home

---

40   *The Times*, 11 September 1913; Callanan, *T. M. Healy*, p. 491; S. O'Brien, 'William O'Brien as a parliamentarian' in *Intimate notes about William O'Brien and some of his friends, by Mrs William O'Brien*, pp. 208–9, Sophie O'Brien papers, PR25/5, Cork City and County Archives (CCCA); P. Maume, *The Long Gestation: Irish nationalist life, 1891–1918* (New York, 1999), p. 137; Jalland, 'Irish Home Rule finance', pp. 126–7.

41   *Cork Free Press*, 16, 19 August 1913.

42   *The Times*, 24 September 1913; T. C. Kennedy, 'Troubled Tories: dissent and confusion concerning the party's Ulster policy, 1910–1914', *Journal of British Studies*, vol. 46, no. 3 (July 2007), p. 584.

43   *Cork Free Press*, 15, 16, 20, 24 September 1913; Smith, 'Federalism, devolution and partition', p. 503.

Ruler'; the paper also professed its astonishment at a report in the *Daily Chronicle*, in which Redmond admitted he had heard next to nothing of the debate around the Loreburn and Carson proposals.[44]

A number of speeches by leading British politicians in the wake of the Loreburn controversy were interpreted by the *Free Press* as proof that Cork with its 'Conciliation policy ... holds the field'. It was, however, clear that the Ulster question had shifted the dynamics of the debate. At Newcastle in late October Bonar Law was reported to have accepted a plan 'for an interchange of views with a view to a settlement by consent'. In practice, this led to a series of meetings between Asquith and Bonar Law in November and December 1913. Preoccupied by the labour troubles in Dublin during the autumn, the Irish Party was not in a position to influence these discussions positively. This theme was confirmed by Redmond at Newcastle in November. In response, O'Brien gave a fiery speech at Mitchelstown, during which he warned that Irish nationalists 'should be prepared to lay down our lives at least as cheerfully as the most warlike men in all the Ulster Volunteers (loud and prolonged cheering)'. In other words, a change of emphasis was needed. The *Free Press* argued that Redmond 'is such a wobbling mass of inconsistencies – a "political blanc-mange" as Mr Healy phrased it – that we cannot regard anything he says as final, and we know that if political exigencies are too strong for him he will eat his "no exclusion" Limerick speech'.[45]

---

44 *Cork Free Press*, 29 September, 1, 2 October 1913.
45 *Cork Free Press*, 27, 28, 29, 30, 31 October, 15, 17 November 1913; Smith, *Tories and Ireland*, pp. 118–9; Jalland, *Liberals and Ireland*, p. 170; J. McConnel, 'The Irish parliamentary party, industrial relations and the 1913 Dublin Lockout', *Saothar*, vol. 28 (2003), pp. 25–36; County Inspector's monthly report for Cork (East Riding), October 1913, pp. 258–9, CO 904/91, British National Archives; F. S. L. Lyons, *John Dillon: a biography* (London, 1968), pp. 335–7; A. O'Day, *Irish Home Rule 1867–1921* (Manchester, 1998), p. 257. Redmond had protested at Limerick on 12 October 1913 against dividing Ireland into two nations, which he described as 'an abomination'. Dangerfield, *Strange Death of Liberal England*, p. 111; J. P. Finnan, *John Redmond and Irish Unity, 1912–1918* (New York, 2004), pp. 61–2.

The reason for O'Brien's strong language at this meeting became clear a few days later, when *The Times* reported that the cabinet had proposed the exclusion of Ulster from the Home Rule bill. Infuriated, the *Free Press* poured scorn on Redmond, Dillon and the Board of Erin, who were 'ready to betray the ideal for which the Irish people have battled for a thousand years'. A speech by Liberal Lord Chancellor Lord Haldane at Birmingham on 1 December contained, according to the paper, a 'series of indirect rebuffs to Mr Redmond, who … has led them into a political impasse where riot and coercion stare them in the face'. Remarks by Carson the following day at Manchester were 'a denial of the exclusion policy', a policy that 'Home Rule all round' would nullify. A third meeting between Bonar Law and Asquith later in the month was trumpeted as 'an overwhelming triumph for the All-for-Ireland Party'.[46]

By the dawn of 1914 the AFIL grass-roots were losing their grip on the little political power they wielded. This was due in no small part to the effects of the 1911 Insurance Act, of which the AOH-BOE took advantage to solidify and increase its powers of patronage. One former member of the Cork Poor Law Board of Guardians argued that many AFIL activists defected after promises of 'basketfuls of Jay-Payships [justiceships of the peace]'.[47] Another reason for the decline in support was lack of money, which left them effectively powerless to counter Irish Party efforts to strike many of their supporters from electoral registers in Cork city and county. That Maurice Healy, the foremost legal advocate within the AFIL, had to appear at many revision court sittings robbed the movement of his formidable powers of critique at Westminster. At the corporation elections

---

46 *Cork Free Press*, 18, 19, 21 November, 3, 4, 5, 20 December 1913.
47 S. R. Day (ed.), *The Amazing Philanthropists, Being Extracts from the Letters of Lester Martin, P. L. G.* (London, 1916), pp. 144–8; Maume, *Long Gestation*, pp. 126–7. See, however, J. McConnel, ' "Jobbing with Tory and Liberal": Irish nationalists and the politics of patronage 1880–1914', *Past and Present*, no. 188 (August 2005), pp. 105–32.

in January, the Irish Party candidates routed the AFIL, 33 seats to 13. The *Free Press*, unsurprisingly, took the result very badly, arguing that English onlookers would see a picture of 'Mollies … dancing a war dance not only over the Protestant Unionist … but over the Catholic Nationalists who pleaded for the smallest measure of toleration for their Protestant countrymen in their native land'. In protest O'Brien resigned his Westminster seat, an action condemned by the Cork City UIL as designed 'to befoul and slander his fellow-countrymen in the English Press and so injure Ireland's claims for self-government'. An eve-of-election address issued by O'Brien on 27 January listed a number of proposals for settling the Ulster question, including proportional representation for Ulster constituencies in an Irish parliament. D. P. Moran, as ever, attacked O'Brien, claiming his 'antics … are only fit for a pantomime; he should dress himself up fittingly and jump about Cork striking left and right with a string of stage sausages'.[48]

This pantomime, though important in a local Cork context (O'Brien was re-elected unopposed on 18 February), was overshadowed by increasing militancy in Ulster and a concomitant growth in militancy in the rest of Ireland after the formation of the Irish Volunteers in November 1913.[49] Carson reluctantly agreed to a proposal from the Ulster Volunteer Force (UVF) in late January to allow guns and ammunition to be imported from Germany. The *Free Press* warned of 'the danger that the enormous masses of drilled and armed men now unquestionably enrolled in Ulster cannot be restrained … from enacting scenes of bloodshed and massacre such as would delay for another century the Union of Irishmen which ten years ago was all

---

48   Schilling, 'William O'Brien', p. 158; *Cork Free Press*, 17, 18, 22, 28 January 1914; *The Leader*, 14 January 1914.
49   D. Fitzpatrick, 'Militarism in Ireland, 1900–1922', in T. Bartlett and K. Jeffrey (eds), *A Military History of Ireland* (Cambridge, 1996), pp. 383–5.

but consummated'.[50] The Irish Party was also drawn into a state of anxiety; many of the rank-and-file were unaware of the pressures that Asquith and his cabinet were placing on the leadership quartet of Redmond, Dillon, Devlin and T. P. O'Connor.[51] In late February the *Free Press* attacked the quartet, claiming that they were 'reduced to a state of panic at the prospect of coming back to Ireland with nothing after all their magnificent promises and disastrous sacrifices'. Given O'Brien's numerous concessions to Ulster unionists over the previous two years, the words had a slightly ironic ring to them.[52] Nevertheless, in the context of hardening attitudes to Home Rule and Ulster by both English parties, and added to the dissociation of Irish separatist nationalists from the Irish Party – the breaking of a chain stretching back to Isaac Butt – the paper's words were prophetic.[53]

The opening of parliament on 9 February 1914 was given a special urgency in light of the increasing threat of rebellion in Ulster. O'Brien made an eloquent speech on 24 February pleading for generous concessions towards Ulster, but warning he would 'strenuously oppose exclusion'.[54] For a week, Asquith and the cabinet concluded long negotiations with both sides of the Irish political divide and on 4 March a scheme of exclusion devised by Lloyd George was agreed upon. The plan provided for a plebiscite in counties that wished to opt out of Home Rule, a fixed time period of exclusion and the holding of at least one general election during the exclusion period. After Redmond was informed, the exclusion period was set at six years, which would allow for a second general election to take place.[55] This

---

50   O'Leary and Maume, *Controversial Issues*, p. 35; *Cork Free Press*, 5 February 1914.
51   C. Reid, *The Lost Ireland of Stephen Gwynn* (Manchester, 2011), p. 118.
52   *Cork Free Press*, 20 February 1914; Warwick-Haller, 'Seeking conciliation', pp. 156–63.
53   M. J. Kelly, *The Fenian Ideal and Irish Nationalism* (Woodbridge, 2006), pp. 188–9.
54   *Cork Free Press*, 11, 12, 13, 19, 25, 26 February 1914.
55   O'Day, *Irish Home Rule*, p. 259.

solution, though unpalatable to Asquith, who had placed great store in 'Home Rule within Home Rule', was defended by him in a key speech to the Commons on 9 March. There were two scenarios that the cabinet had considered, he declared. On the one hand, if Home Rule were passed in the current form, then 'in Ulster the prospect of acute dissension and even of civil strife' was acute. On the other hand, if substantial alterations had been made, 'there is in Ireland, as a whole, at least an equally formidable outlook'.

Redmond made an effort to claw back some political ground by stating that the proposals were merely accepted 'as the basis of agreement and peace'. Carson rejected the proposals, stating that while exclusion was indeed a basis for negotiation, the introduction of a time limit was like a 'sentence of death with a stay of execution for six years'. The latter's reaction was undoubtedly a result of seeing his hopes of exclusion pending a federal settlement dashed.[56] Reaction from the AFIL was initially one of shock. The *Free Press* argued that the new proposals were 'as astounding as they are repulsive … the Catholics of the Excluded Counties … have been sold and betrayed by the men they supported and financed to baton and smother the policy of Conciliation, whose antithesis has brought this thing about'. Redmond, in their opinion, had ceased to be the leader of the nationalist movement.[57] A national conference was held in Cork on 14 March and passed a resolution calling on 'all genuine Irish Nationalists' to urge their parliamentary representatives to reject the exclusion measures. In response, Dillon and Redmond castigated O'Brien and the AFIL for conceding too much ground to unionists for the sake of Irish unity.[58]

---

56   R. Jenkins, *Asquith* (London, 1964), p. 302; O'Day, *Irish Home Rule*, p. 259; O'Leary and Maume, *Controversial Issues*, p. 38; Horgan, *Parnell to Pearse*, p. 253; Smith, 'Federalism, devolution and partition', pp. 508–9.

57   *Cork Free Press*, 10 March 1914.

58   *Ibid.*, 16, 17 March 1914; Bew, *Ideology and the Irish Question*, pp. 27–8; Schilling, 'William O'Brien', p. 163.

The Ulster question escalated at the end of March, when British Army regiments stationed at both Aldershot and the Curragh refused to be deployed to emplacements around Belfast. Over the next month the situation became radicalised, especially after UVF gun-running at Larne, County Antrim, on the evening of 24–5 April. The *Free Press* laid the blame at the door of Churchill, who had made an incendiary speech at Bradford on 14 March. In 'provocative and unrestrained' language, the first lord of the admiralty attacked Carson and the Ulster unionists for rejecting out of hand Asquith's 'final and reasonable offer to provide special treatment for Ulster'. If they continued to reject every government concession, then 'menace and brutality' would be put 'to the proof'. The paper argued 'that "the Ulster Bluff," "The wooden guns," and "The Carson circus" seem to have caused the Cabinet many anxious moments, and actually animated General Paget [the commander-in-chief of the army in Ireland] with "alarm"'.[59] In the midst of this crisis O'Brien made a powerful speech in the House of Commons on 1 April against exclusion and all the machinations that had brought this about. Tim Healy later recalled that it was one of O'Brien's 'most eloquent declarations. He used to say that something of the spirit of the old Hebrew prophets had inspired the speaker.' The *Free Press* congratulated him on 'a clear and succinct summary of the position and policy of the All-for-Ireland Party in these stirring times'.[60] At the final debate on the Home Rule bill on 25 May, however, O'Brien lacked verve, making incoherent arguments while denouncing the bill as a 'ghastly farce'. AFIL MPs held true to their March pledge and abstained from the final vote, which was carried 'with a certain element of tragic farce' by seventy-

---

59   *Cork Free Press*, 23, 24, 25, 26, 27, 28, 31 March 1914; Jalland, *Liberals and Ireland*, pp. 218–9.
60   S. O'Brien, 'William O'Brien as a parliamentarian', pp. 9–10, Sophie O'Brien papers, PR25/5, CCCA; *Cork Free Press*, 2, 4 April 1914.

seven votes.[61] The AFIL lost control of Cork county council in the elections in June, thus confirming the inevitability of 'anarchy and savage hatreds and the … collapse of any Home Rule worth having for the present generation'.[62]

The bill came before the Lords on 23 June, and the provisions of the Parliament Act meant that even if it was once more rejected it would become law subject to the calling of a general election. At this point O'Brien and the AFIL launched a final campaign to forestall exclusion. In a letter to *The Morning Post* he pleaded for a conference before 'death, damnation and disaster'.[63] Amendment of the Home Rule bill to exclude the entire nine counties of Ulster led to an impasse in the Lords. King George V, Asquith, the Master of Elibank (the Liberal chief whip) and other prominent cabinet members put pressure on all sides of the Irish question to meet in conference, with a view to ending the impasse. The fact that the initiative came from the king, whose sympathy to the cause of Ulster was well known, meant that any such conference would not, by definition, throw out exclusion.[64] Therefore the Buckingham Palace conference, which met from 21 to 24 July 1914, was derided by the *Cork Free Press* as plagiarism, but lacking any hope of success. Asquith's hopes for a compromise rested on securing Carson's support, and without backing from Bonar Law and the Tory leadership (who envisaged a general election in the near future) this was not forthcoming. Carson and Redmond clashed over Tyrone, rejecting Speaker James Lowther's suggestion that it be equally divided between nationalists and unionists. A settlement was not reached and the conference broke up.[65] A

---

61   *Cork Free Press*, 26 May 1914; Schilling, 'William O'Brien', pp. 165–6.
62   *Cork Free Press*, 1, 5 June 1914.
63   *Ibid.*, 27 June 1914; Schilling, 'William O'Brien', pp. 168–71.
64   Jenkins, *Asquith*, pp. 318–23; Gwynn, *History of Partition*, pp. 104–17; C. B. Shannon, *Arthur J. Balfour and Ireland* (Washington, 1988), p. 208.
65   *Cork Free Press*, 21, 22, 23, 24, 25 July 1914; O'Leary and Maume, *Controversial Issues*, p. 43; Smith, *The Tories and Ireland*, p. 197.

few days later, attempts by the Irish Volunteers to bring guns ashore at Howth, County Dublin, led to the 'Bachelors Walk massacre', which many feared signalled the start of a civil war in Ireland.[66] Few people, however, when reading the newspapers on the morning of 29 June, had taken in the significance of the news from the Balkan town of Sarajevo.[67]

In September 1914 the Home Rule bill was placed on the statute book, though with an amending act suspending its operation until the conclusion of the war. This brought to an end a series of the bitterest periods in British and Irish political history. Yet much of subsequent commentary on the events of 1910–14 erases the memory of the AFIL. Only in recent years have historians and others writing of the period acknowledged its presence and influence in the Home Rule crisis. Even so, they tend to concentrate on the personalities of O'Brien and Healy, as this essay has done. There is much more to be explored in relation to the composition and activity of the AFIL, and the conclusion of this essay will sketch out some avenues of further research.

A wealth of published material exists on the crisis over the third Home Rule bill and one of the problems associated with research in this area is the lack of proper contextualisation. It is useful, therefore, to think of the AFIL as two separate entities: a Cork-based agitative movement and a London-based clique with heavy leanings towards, but not much real influence on, Conservative Party politics. This is, however, only part of the story. The majority of AFIL MPs, including D. D. Sheehan, Eugene Crean and Patrick Guiney (and his brother

---

66   O'Leary and Maume, *Controversial Issues*, pp. 44–5; Bew, *Ideology and the Irish Question*, pp. 114–7; Miller, *Queen's Rebels*, pp. 106–8.
67   *Cork Free Press*, 29 June 1914. In *The Freeman's Journal* on 3 August, it was written that after Austria–Hungary had declared war on Serbia, 'no nation that … hopes to be free … can escape the fortunes of this conflict. All our fates are about to be decided.' Quoted in Finnan, *John Redmond*, p. 78.

John after 1913) formed a left wing of the AFIL, but still criticised much of the Liberal government's social platform. Both wings were, however, in unison on land purchase: they saw the Birrell Land Act of 1909 as the death knell for voluntary land purchase and constantly campaigned throughout this period for reform of the legislation. It is hard to see how both wings of the League could have been reconciled in a Home Rule parliament. Sheehan, Crean and the Guineys would have possibly aligned themselves with a rural labour movement; O'Brien would probably have led nationalist opposition to any government led by Redmond and Dillon. Furthermore, the AFIL's courting of groups as diverse as the Landowners' Convention and Sinn Féin only served to fragment it all the more. The one thing that may have united all sections was the Ulster question.

In the midst of the final passage of the Home Rule bill in March 1914, shortly before the Curragh mutiny, O'Brien attempted to organise a rally in Dublin against the exclusion of Ulster. He was contacted by John Scollan, the national director of the Irish-American Alliance (another branch of the AOH). The one major stumbling block was, inevitably, finance. Scollan enthusiastically projected that a number of bodies, including Sinn Féin, the Dublin Trades Council and the Irish Volunteers, would support the demonstration. He optimistically predicted that Arthur Griffith, Thomas J. Clarke, Sir Roger Casement, Countess Constance Markievicz, Jim Larkin and James Connolly would speak at such a meeting. O'Brien rejected the offer, perhaps in view of hostility towards his stance and his personal distaste for the work of men such as Larkin and Connolly.[68] What these two events suggest is that there were a number of individuals or small groups in pre-First World War Ireland whose political

---

68   John J. Scollan to William O'Brien, 25, 31 March 1914; William O'Brien to John J. Scollan, 3 April 1914, William O'Brien papers, Box AS, items 59, 60, 61, UC/WOB/PP/AS 59, 60, 61, Special Collections, Boole Library, University College Cork; O'Brien, *William O'Brien*, pp. 210–11.

views did not necessarily coincide with those of the two monolithic movements: Irish nationalism and Ulster unionism. From an AFIL point of view, it was the conduct of organisations allied to the former that gave it its *raison d'être*.

As was stated at the outset of this essay, the AFIL continues to exert fascination to many students of the Irish 'long nineteenth century'. This is undoubtedly due to the various strands encompassed under its umbrella. In effect, the AFIL constituted two separate groupings: a working-class and agrarian-based movement and a movement in favour of reforming the political landscape in Ireland. William O'Brien's sorties in favour of 'the three Cs' have been too readily dismissed by most historians, eager to travel from the turbulence of the 1910 elections to the Home Rule crisis of 1912–14. Just because we know the destination does not mean that the road was at all times clearly marked out. In the maelstrom that was the Home Rule crisis the AFIL's mere existence, actions and, more importantly, rhetoric have to be acknowledged. Its criticisms have to be tested and the assumptions underpinning its arguments have to be investigated thoroughly. Its social origins have to be examined and plans scrutinised. Why were so many plans for alternative Home Rule scenarios put forward? What were the outlooks of those who supported the AFIL? In searching for the answers to these and other questions, we can tease out the shifting perspectives of Irish nationalists and unionists (once we look behind the powerful polemic) during a fascinating, turbulent period of modern Irish history. 'Home Rule' was clearly a contested concept for Irish nationalists, and the AFIL's claims to be heard deserve further study.

8

The Murnaghan memos: Catholic concerns with the third Home Rule bill, 1912

Conor Mulvagh

So far from Home Rule meaning Rome Rule, my belief is that, under Home Rule, the influence of the clergy in political matters will continue to decline.

J. Annan Bryce, 1912[1]

In 1912 Herbert H. Asquith's Liberal government unveiled an ambitious programme of Home Rule for Ireland, which envisaged the transformation of the entire system of domestic and imperial governance in the British Isles.[2] One of the primary popular concerns

---

1 John Annan Bryce was Liberal MP for Inverness from 1906 to 1918. His brother James had been chief secretary for Ireland from December 1905 to January 1907 before being appointed British ambassador to Washington. This quotation appears in J. G. Swift MacNeill, *Home Rule and Religious Intolerance, A Refutation of Unionist Charges: a forgotten speech by Mr. Gladstone recalled* (London, 1912), p. 20.
2 In his speech in the House of Commons introducing this third Home Rule bill – two earlier such bills had been introduced (in 1886 and in 1893) but had been thrown out by the Commons and the Lords respectively – Prime Minister Herbert H. Asquith claimed that the system of Home Rule would eventually be extended to each of the constituent countries of the British Isles, stating that, 'I myself, while recognising to the full the priority and paramount urgency of the Irish claim have always presented the case for Irish Home Rule as the first step, and only the first step in a larger and more comprehensive policy.' *House of Commons Debates*, Fifth series,

about the creation of a Dublin parliament, with jurisdiction over the whole of the island, was that it would establish a discriminatory, Catholic institution. Regardless of the credibility of these fears in an era when the Home Rule leadership was comparatively conciliatory and inclusivist, opponents of Home Rule feared that the proposal would inevitably mean 'Rome rule'. As highlighted by the assurances of John Annan Bryce quoted above, however, the Catholic Church actually feared the diminution of its powers with the advent of Home Rule. Owing to their distinctive religious demographics, both Ireland and Scotland enjoyed the privilege of separate legislation in education and other matters from the English and Welsh system.[3] Thus, Catholicism in Ireland had fared comparatively better than it had in Britain in legislative terms. In education, in particular, the church enjoyed a favourable mix of autonomy in governance and state subvention in funding. Any measure as far-reaching as the Government of Ireland bill 1912, which threatened to alter this equilibrium, was inevitably going to be treated with caution by the Catholic hierarchy in general, and by the primate of All Ireland, Cardinal Archbishop Michael Logue of Armagh, in particular.

The extent of non-Catholic concerns with the Home Rule bill has been well documented, most recently by Daniel Jackson's study of opposition to Home Rule in Britain.[4] Loyalty, Ulster's religious and economic exceptionalism, and the maintenance of imperial unity in the face of the Liberals' early scheme for a federalised Britain and

---

vol. 36, 11 April 1912, col. 1403.

3   One other such area of distinctive legislation with a moral dimension to it was the question of licensed premises and their opening hours.

4   Jackson has documented how religion was a more dominant aspect of opposition to Home Rule in some cities than in others. For instance, sectarian rhetoric found a receptive audience in Glasgow and Liverpool whereas it was less effective in stirring up the crowd in more imperially minded centres such as Bolton or Portsmouth. D. M. Jackson, *Popular Opposition to Irish Home Rule in Edwardian Britain* (Liverpool, 2009).

Ireland were central concerns for opponents of Home Rule.[5] Before the question of partition dominated the debate, however, the fear that Protestants across the whole island of Ireland would be forced to exist within an uncompromisingly Catholic regime was arguably the most potent method of mobilising popular opposition to Home Rule on both sides of the Irish Sea. If religion was so central to the campaign against Home Rule, how then was the settlement to the Irish question proposed in 1912 received by the Catholic hierarchy in Ireland? Did the Irish Catholic bishops fear they would be subjected to punitive legislative constraints in an attempt to appease Protestant fears? How active were they in safeguarding or advancing their position in the Ireland of 1912? Finally, how did the Irish Party respond to the church's concerns? Focusing on a number of dossiers written by James A. Murnaghan, who was commissioned by the Catholic hierarchy to investigate the implications of the legislation for the church, this essay will undertake a critical analysis of the religious clauses of the bill. Furthermore, it will examine the private opinions of Ireland's most senior prelates, especially Cardinal Logue, whose letters in this period express a deep suspicion about Home Rule and an earnest commitment to safeguarding the church's role in education above all other concerns.

Voicing long-held doubts: Cardinal Logue's concerns with the third Home Rule bill

By the end of October 1912 the Home Rule bill was nearing the end of committee stages on its first of three passages through parliament. In the first half of 1912 opposition to the bill was still largely constitutional and confined to parliament. In September, however, the first manifestations of a more acute crisis arose through the dramatic

---

5   On the question of federalism, see J. Kendle, *Ireland and the Federal Solution: the debate over the United Kingdom Constitution, 1870–1921* (Kingston, 1989).

expression of regional opposition orchestrated by the Ulster Unionist Council in the signing of the Solemn League and Covenant.[6]

The provisions of the Parliament Act of 1911, coupled with the existence of a decisive Liberal–Irish Party parliamentary majority, meant that, on paper, Home Rule was a legislative fait accompli. As the bill progressed through the Commons, the increasing certainty of this encouraged a drift towards extra-constitutional paramilitarism on the part of the Conservative-Unionist opposition. It should have been evident to all that this was no time for the question of religion to be aired in the House of Commons. Despite the inadvisability of such a course, by early November 1912, Cardinal Logue had begun to express his personal concerns about the potential implications of the bill for the Catholic Church.

It was almost seven months after its introduction into the House of Commons when Cardinal Logue resolved to take action regarding the third Home Rule bill. On 5 November 1912, in a long letter to Patrick O'Donnell, bishop of Raphoe, Logue announced that it was now desirable for the hierarchy to make reasoned consideration of the bill but, justifying his inactivity up to that point, Logue admitted to his colleague that he had thought it 'hopeless to take action [previously], as the Irish Party seem averse to raise questions about anything which the Ministry introduce to assuage even the unreasonable prejudices of the Protestant party'.[7] For Logue, the establishment of a system

---

6   On 28 September 1912, 471,414 people signed the Ulster Solemn League and Covenant or (in the case of women) a companion 'Declaration'. Signatories of the Covenant pledged to 'stand by one another in defending for ourselves and our children our cherished position of equal citizenship in the United Kingdom and in using all means which may be found necessary to defeat the present conspiracy to set up a Home Rule parliament in Dublin.' The document signalled a departure from the principle of all-island resistance to Home Rule and was ostensibly aimed at the preservation of the union across a nine-county Ulster. Signatures of the Covenant and Declaration are now searchable online at http://applications.proni.gov.uk/UlsterCovenant/Search.aspx.
7   Michael Logue to Patrick O'Donnell, 5 November 1912, Cardinal Patrick O'Donnell papers, box 3, wallet I, folder D, Cardinal Tomás Ó Fiaich Memorial

of denominational education was one of his ultimate administrative aims and – prophesying a situation that would arise in Northern Ireland in the 1920s – he noted that such a desire was equally strong among episcopalian Protestants. Attempting to reason that a pan-Christian alliance existed in opposition to the desires of the Liberal government, Logue also claimed that Presbyterians were equally enthusiastic about establishing a denominational basis for education in Ireland. He pointed out that Presbyterians already practised a system of de facto denominational education in their own schools 'though they hypocritically claim the contrary'.[8]

Logue's perceived enemy was thus not the Protestant faiths wishing for the preservation of their ascendancy. The enemy was the chief secretary, Augustine Birrell. Birrell held the presidency of the Board of Education before his move to the Irish Office in 1907. There he had presided over an abortive attempt to overturn the system of state aid for denominational elementary schools in England that had been established by the Conservative Arthur Balfour's Education (England and Wales) Act of 1902.[9] In Logue's eyes, Birrell was a zealot. When he had come to the chief secretaryship, Birrell had attempted to reform intermediate education in Ireland in what Logue perceived as his 'Nonconformist mania for secularising secondary education'.[10] This passionate denunciation of the chief secretary can be seen as an indication of Logue's growing distemper in the course of writing to the bishop of Raphoe.

Among Logue's other concerns with the Home Rule bill was the fear that the ambiguity of clause three – relating to religious dis-

---

Library and Archive (OFMLA).

8   *Ibid.*

9   This has been covered in greater detail in C. Mulvagh, 'Rome Ruler? John Redmond, a Catholic voice in a Liberal chamber, 1906–1918' (MPhil thesis, Trinity College Dublin, 2008), pp. 18–26.

10   Logue to O'Donnell, 5 November 1912, O'Donnell papers, box 3, wallet I, folder D, OFMLA.

crimination – would not afford sufficient safeguards within the bill to uphold the *Ne Temere* decree in civil law.[11] In a manifestly negative frame of mind, the pessimistic cardinal went as far as to state that while he was as 'reluctant as anyone to embarrass the Irish Party in their difficult task … a few moves such as that of Mr Birrell regarding the secondary schools, would lead me to pray that the [Home Rule] Bill may never reach the statute book'.[12] That Cardinal Logue was prepared to countenance the failure of the bill indicated that, if it was in the church's interests, he had very few qualms indeed about embarrassing the Irish Party. The severity of this opinion can be only partly excused by the fact that it was stated privately, to another prelate, and not in public. Regardless of the intended audience, however, the comment faithfully represented the sentiments of the most senior member of the Catholic Church in Ireland, who was happy to see the failure of four decades of nationalist endeavours in the interests of Catholic education. The dogmatic nature of his views can be summed up by arguably the most revealing sentence of this very candid and revealing letter, in which Logue admitted: 'The temporal prosperity of the country is a grand end to aim at; but should it be secured only at the sacrifice of the eternal interests of our people, I would rather fall back on the days of persecution with all their poverty, misery and suffering.'[13] While many bishops' views had evolved towards firm commitment and active support for the Irish Party by 1912, Logue remained a committed sceptic.

Thus, finally, in November 1912, owing to a deep mistrust of both

---

11   The central element of the *Ne Temere* decree was that all marriages involving a Catholic – including mixed marriages – had to be performed by a Catholic priest or bishop. On the difference between *Ne Temere* in theory and practice, the latter extending to the raising of children, see E. de Bhaldraithe, 'Mixed marriages and Irish politics: the effect of "Ne Temere"', *Studies*, vol. 77, no. 307 (Autumn, 1988), p. 285.

12   Logue to O'Donnell, 5 November 1912, O'Donnell papers, box 3, wallet I, folder D, OFMLA.

13   *Ibid.*

the hidden dangers within the bill and the perceived inability of the Irish Party or an Irish parliament to remove them, Logue resolved that the bill should be sent for the consideration of what he dubbed 'a capable lawyer'.[14] He immediately indicated his preference for James A. Murnaghan, barrister on the north-western circuit and, since 1910, professor of Roman Law and Jurisprudence at the National University of Ireland.

Before continuing to discuss the choice of this lawyer, it should be pointed out that the present essay is not the first to have considered Logue's letter of 5 November 1912. David Miller's *Church, State and Nation in Ireland, 1898–1921*, published in 1973, makes reference to this letter, noting Logue's reference to 'Birrell's mania for denominational education'.[15] However, as Miller had available to him only the catalogue summary relating to this letter – the archive itself not having been opened to researchers for another twenty-five years – he could not have been aware of just how revealing the letter was of the cardinal's true sentiments on the Home Rule bill.[16] Whereas Miller had access to the Murnaghan memos themselves (as evidenced by the fact that a typescript copy of them is preserved in the John Redmond papers at the National Library of Ireland), the real importance of this episode in the ecclesiastical and political history of the period can be discerned only from the related correspondence, rather than the memos themselves.[17] Similarly, John Privilege has examined the letter, concluding that Logue's contention that he would 'sooner live under an imperial parliament than under a Home Rule parliament' did not necessarily

---

14   *Ibid.*

15   Miller was given permission to consult a calendar of material in the Armagh diocesan archives by Cardinal Conway in the early 1970s. At the time, the calendar was in the possession of Professor Tomás Ó Fiaich, Conway's successor to the primacy of All-Ireland in 1977. On the extent of Miller's access, see D. W. Miller, *Church, State and Nation in Ireland, 1898–1921* (Dublin, 1973), pp. ix–x.

16   The Cardinal Ó Fiaich Memorial Library and Archive was officially opened to the public only in 1999. See *The Irish Times*, 11 May 1999.

17   John Redmond papers, MS 15, 217/3, National Library of Ireland (NLI).

mean that he wished for the bill to fail.[18] As is shown here, however, the evidence suggests that Logue was more than prepared to jettison the bill in the interests of safeguarding the Catholic position.

Murnaghan: an unusual choice?

Returning to Logue's suggestion that the bill be sent for the consideration of 'a capable lawyer', in trying to establish a better understanding of why James Murnaghan was chosen for this most delicate of tasks, it is virtually impossible to arrive at a full picture of the motives that lay behind the Irish Catholic hierarchy's choice. Murnaghan's working relationship with the hierarchy seems to have stemmed from his appointment as draftsman to the University Commission, tasked with drawing up the statutes of the new National University following its establishment in 1908.[19] Archbishop William Walsh was a prominent member of this body and, according to Walsh's personal secretary and first biographer, Fr P. J. Walsh, the archbishop revelled in the work. Fr Walsh observed that his namesake's 'energy and endurance and legal acumen often caused surprise ... to the draftsmen, D. F. Brown, KC, and Mr James A. Murnaghan, BL'.[20] If this relationship is inverted, no less than Murnaghan appears to have been impressed with the archbishop's legal expertise, it would seem that Walsh was impressed with the commitment and skill of the young barrister. In the summer of 1912, before the Home Rule question was fully taken in hand by the bishops, a series of cordial letters passed between Archbishop Walsh and Murnaghan regarding

---

18 J. Privilege, *Michael Logue and the Catholic Church in Ireland, 1879–1925* (Manchester, 2008), p. 93.

19 In 1910, Murnaghan worked extensively with Archbishop Walsh on drafting the statutes of the university. For correspondence relating to this, see Murnaghan to Archbishop William Walsh, 18 February 1910, Walsh papers, box 382 I, folder 376/4 (laity), Dublin Diocesan Archives (DDA) and 14 June 1910, Walsh papers, Box 382 I, folder 376/3 (laity), DDA.

20 P. J. Walsh, *William J. Walsh: archbishop of Dublin* (Dublin, 1928), p. 564.

various historical legal cases.[21] Murnaghan's appointment to the chair of Roman Law and Jurisprudence at the university that he had played a part in establishing conferred upon him a status that compensated for his relative youth – he was only twenty-nine when he was awarded his professorship.

Despite his youth, there is a strong case to be made for the argument that James Murnaghan was simply the best man for the job in 1912. Ronan Keane has noted the scarcity of qualified Catholics suitable for promotion to the ranks of the judiciary as late as 1924. In 1912 the Irish legal profession was dominated by Protestants and unionists unacceptable to the Catholic hierarchy's needs. Even the Irish Party's own best legal mind, John G. Swift MacNeill, was a 'devout anglican'.[22] If Logue and his fellow prelates wished to appoint a member of the Irish Party as their legal advisor, and it will be argued presently that this was almost certainly not the case, then they had several qualified Catholic barristers at their disposal, notably John Pius Boland and Tom Kettle. Despite their qualifications, however, neither of these men was a practising lawyer. The hierarchy's choice of truly qualified legal experts who were also dependable and staunch Catholics thus boiled down to the law faculties in the newly created National University of Ireland.[23] Not only was Murnaghan chair of Roman Law and Jurisprudence at University College Dublin, but he was also the only legal academic in Ireland who had any prior history of advising the Catholic hierarchy through his work with Archbishop Walsh on the drafting of the university statutes.

---

21   See Murnaghan to Walsh, 11 June 1912, Walsh papers, box 384 I, folder 377/2 (laity), DDA, and 22 June 1912, Walsh papers, box 384 I, folder 377/1 (laity), DDA.
22   Quoting P. Maume, 'MacNeill, John Gordon Swift', in J. McGuire and J. Quinn (eds) *Dictionary of Irish Biography* (Cambridge, 2009), available online at http://dib. cambridge.org (accessed 20 July 2012).
23   It should by no means be assumed that all of these new appointees were Catholics. Indeed, J. G. Swift MacNeill was the first professor of Jurisprudence and Torts at University College Dublin; Maume, 'MacNeill, John Gordon Swift'.

There is, however, another aspect to Murnaghan's background which should not lightly be dismissed when analysing the hierarchy's choice of lawyer, namely the political dimension. The assertion here is not that James Murnaghan was himself a political animal – indeed his work before and after independence (when he advised the nascent Free State government in the drafting of the 1922 constitution before being appointed to the High, and later Supreme, Court) speaks of the ease with which he and other nationalist lawyers passed between the Home Rule and revolutionary eras. But while he may not have been political in his own right, it is possible that Cardinal Logue may have appointed him for political reasons. Having returned to farming in County Tyrone after more than two decades in America, James' father, George, became a prominent Ulster nationalist politician in the early twentieth century.[24] George Murnaghan represented one of those rare instances of maverick politicians (Laurence Ginnell being the most famous example), who managed to remain under the umbrella of the Irish Party while displaying a cavalier attitude to party discipline.[25] The reason why George Murnaghan's politics come into the equation here is that he had been a close ally of dissident nationalist T. M. Healy, who, up to 1910, had basked in the favour of Cardinal Logue. Healy had been by far the most loyal advocate of the clergy within nationalist politics up to that point.[26] Healy's clerical

---

24 Murnaghan sat for Mid-Tyrone from 1895 to 1910. See B. Hourican, 'Murnaghan, George', in Maguire and Quinn (eds), *Dictionary of Irish Biography*, http://dib.cambridge.org (accessed 20 July 2012).

25 Ginnell was notoriously unpredictable and independent. He was expelled from the Irish Party in 1909 following a row over the party finances, but before this he had launched something of a one-man crusade on the issue of cattle-grazing in the midlands in what became known as the 'ranch war'. Ginnell was the last Irish Party MP to be incarcerated by what was then a sympathetic Liberal administration. By 1917 Ginnell was firmly in the Sinn Féin camp. The best study of Ginnell's controversial political activities from 1906 to 1916 is M. Wheatley, *Nationalism and the Irish Party: provincial Ireland 1910–1916* (Oxford, 2005).

26 For a *longue durée* study of Healy's relationship with the Catholic hierarchy, see F. Callanan, *T. M. Healy* (Cork, 1996).

links were extremely valuable to him and the support of the clergy of Louth (at the behest of Cardinal Logue) was the decisive factor in the retention of Healy's seat. Since late 1900, Healy had been the *enfant terrible* of the Irish Party and, apart from a temporary détente in 1908–9, leader John Redmond and his colleagues spent much time counteracting Healyism in elections, at public meetings and in the press. Bridget Hourican explains that, despite being closely aligned to Tim Healy, George Murnaghan managed to escape Healyite purges of the Irish Party at the 1900 and 1906 general elections due to the support of Omagh's 'Healyite priests'.[27]

By 1910 there was a change in the electoral climate of Irish constituency politics brought about by the assertion of much stricter and more autocratic party discipline in Redmond's official Irish Party. This was exemplified by the management of the 1909 national convention of the Irish Party's constituency organisation, the United Irish League (UIL), which was stage-managed by the League's secretary, and rising star of the parliamentary party, Joseph Devlin, MP for West Belfast. The primary target of Devlin's purge was William O'Brien, MP for Cork city and, ironically, the founder of the UIL.[28]

---

27 Hourican notes that this was the term used by John Dillon to describe the Omagh clergy. Dillon, arguably the most powerful figure in Redmond's Irish Party, was an intense critic of Healy and was instrumental to his expulsion from the recently united party in 1901. Hourican, 'Murnaghan, George', in Maguire and Quinn (eds), *Dictionary of Irish Biography*, http://dib.cambridge.org (accessed 20 July 2012).

28 Good accounts of the 1909 UIL convention can be found in F. S. L. Lyons, *John Dillon: a biography* (London, 1968), pp. 303–4 and W. O'Brien, *An Olive Branch in Ireland and its History* (London, 1910), pp. 441–56. O'Brien devotes an entire chapter to the subject, entitled 'Molly Maguire, Imperatrix!': a derogatory reference to Devlin's Ancient Order of Hibernians (AOH), a lay Catholic fraternal organisation that was used to suppress and forcibly silence O'Brien and his supporters at the 1909 UIL convention which accordingly became known as the 'baton convention'. Devlin became president of the AOH in 1905 and was the only one of the Irish Party MPs elected after 1900 to enter the highest echelons of the party, eventually being earmarked as a successor to John Redmond for the chairmanship. See J. Loughlin, 'Devlin, Joseph' in Maguire and Quinn (eds), *Dictionary of Irish Biography*, http://dib. cambridge.org (accessed 18 June 2012).

Following the ousting of O'Brien and his allies, the official Irish Party was sufficiently confident to deal with vestigial maverick members and fielded an official candidate to run against George Murnaghan for his Mid-Tyrone seat in the January 1910 general election. Although the Irish Party candidate succeeded in polling more votes than Murnaghan, the victory of Redmondism was a pyrrhic one. The split in the nationalist vote allowed what should have been a firmly nationalist constituency to return a unionist member.[29] The Irish Party won back the seat in December 1910, but George Murnaghan never again stood or acted as a political representative.

The timing of George Murnaghan's last stand coincided closely with the elevation of his son James into the confidence of the Irish Catholic hierarchy. James Murnaghan may have been apolitical, but the bishops who began to take an interest in him were anything but. Logue ended his long alliance with Tim Healy in the spring/summer of 1910 when Healy finally entered into an unlikely alliance with the notoriously anti-clerical William O'Brien and joined O'Brien's new anti-Redmondite coalition, the All-for-Ireland League. George Murnaghan remained untainted by associations with Munster-based O'Brienism and, as such, stayed on the right side of Logue as a clerically inclined, anti-Redmondite, Ulster nationalist. These criteria were exactly what Logue was looking for in his search for an expert to cast a critical eye over a Home Rule bill that Redmondites appeared content to accept on any terms.[30] On balance, James Murnaghan's suitability derived from the fact that he was extremely rare in being

---

29 The unionist candidate, George Fitzgibbon Brunskill, polled 2,475 votes compared to 2,070 for the Irish Party candidate (John Valentine). George Murnaghan managed to secure only 1,244 votes. See B. M. Walker, *Parliamentary Election Results in Ireland, 1801–1922* (Dublin, 1978), p. 376.

30 By 1914 acceptance of the principle of partition among the Irish Party leadership (including Joseph Devlin) underlined just how far the party was willing to go to secure the passage of the Home Rule bill. On the final capitulation of Joseph Devlin to the principle of partition, see A. C. Hepburn, *Catholic Belfast and Nationalist Ireland in the Era of Joe Devlin, 1871–1934* (Oxford, 2008), pp. 148–9.

a Catholic with the requisite legal expertise to scrutinise the Home Rule bill, but the political stance of his father must have confirmed Logue's enthusiasm for the young professor.

The Murnaghan memos

Aware that the window for any changes to be introduced to the Home Rule bill was rapidly closing, Murnaghan set about his task quickly, producing the first memorandum for the consideration of the bishops within just two days. Working from the King's Inns Library and the National Library, he made extensive use of parliamentary papers and Hansard parliamentary debates in researching the issues at hand. He sent his memorandum (the first in a series of four) to Bishop O'Donnell, who brought it to the attention of Cardinal Logue.[31]

This first memorandum addressed the question of whether clause three of the Home Rule bill would 'leave the Irish Parliament power to abolish the Catholic disabilities of the Emancipation Act [1829]'. Of the four memoranda, this one dealt with issues which were, in Logue's words, 'not practically the most important'.[32] Murnaghan may simply have been getting an obvious and straightforward concern out of the way first while he gave fuller consideration to the more complex implications of the Home Rule bill, but it is revealing that the issue to which Murnaghan first devoted his attention was the prohibition on the involvement of the clergy and the prelates of Ireland in politics. Having devoted eight manuscript pages of foolscap to the vestigial disabilities of the clergy under the Catholic Emancipation Act, did he actually believe that the interest of the hierarchy in the bill was for their own entry into and involvement with electoral politics? Given

---

31 On Murnaghan's use of the King's Inns and National libraries, see Murnaghan to O'Donnell, 7 November 1912, O'Donnell papers, box 3, wallet I, folder D, OFMLA. For the letter enclosing the first of Murnaghan's memoranda, see Murnaghan to O'Donnell, 9 November 1912, O'Donnell papers, box 3, wallet I, folder D, OFMLA. 32 Logue to O'Donnell, 11 November 1912, O'Donnell papers, box 3, wallet I, folder D, OFMLA.

the content of the subsequent memos, the answer is almost certainly no, but, just as Cardinal Logue commented at the time, one is left wondering why such time and effort was devoted by Murnaghan to this rather trivial point.

In his next memorandum, Murnaghan moved away from the peripheral to the most central concern of the hierarchy with the bill. As evidenced by Logue's letter, the Liberal government's drive towards secularisation was a cause for grave concern, and the Catholic training colleges were the jewel in the crown of Catholic education on the island, from Logue's point of view. The idea that state grants might be removed from these institutions – clause three having specified that the state could not endow, either directly or indirectly, any religion – was a manifest threat to the material position of the Catholic Church in education.

The fear that grants would be terminated was by far the single greatest apprehension for Logue throughout the entire passage of the third Home Rule bill. It had already prompted him to enlist John Redmond to seek assurances from Augustine Birrell that there was no threat to funding, implicit or otherwise, in the clause in question. On foot of his inquiries, on 7 November, Birrell had provided Redmond with written assurances that the practice of granting funds to training colleges of all denominations was actually designed to promote equality of service between private denominational training colleges and the official training college at Marlborough Street in Dublin. According to Birrell, it was thus highly unlikely that the status quo would be altered by the proposed legislation.[33] Despite these written assurances, and their provenance, Logue remained sceptical.

Offering his personal interpretation of the situation, Murnaghan echoed what had been said by Birrell, namely that the grant was

---

33   Augustine Birrell to John Redmond, 7 November 1912, O'Donnell papers, box 3, wallet I, folder D, OFMLA.

almost certain to remain untouched. Stressing, however, the loose and imprecise nature of the Home Rule bill's wording, Murnaghan admitted that, from a strictly legalistic standpoint, it was 'difficult to say … to what extent the words "indirectly endow any religion" [could] be pushed'.[34] Mindful of the possibility that a future administration might be less sympathetic to Catholic interests, Murnaghan ventured a sub-clause drafted to dispel the ambiguity of the existing clause three. Doubting the necessity for such an addition, and perhaps mindful of the parliamentary ramifications of such a course of action, he concluded this second memorandum by stating that amendment on this issue, while useful, was not 'absolutely necessary'.[35]

Continuing on the theme of education, in the third memorandum, Murnaghan considered further the implications of clause three, in particular the prospect that government inspections of school premises would be inaugurated with a view to removing crucifixes and other religious symbols from classrooms even if no non-Catholic pupils were present. Turning to Logue's beloved training colleges, Murnaghan identified one potentially negative consequence of the clause, namely the prospect of non-Catholics being allowed to attend specifically Catholic training colleges. This was exactly the type of change to the composition of denominational training colleges that Logue feared. Murnaghan proposed the insertion of a sub-clause to clarify explicitly that: 'Nothing in this section shall … hinder any Training College or School from receiving public money, because it is founded or maintained by persons belonging to a particular church or denomination for the benefit solely of the members thereof.'[36] As David Miller pointed out in the 1970s, this clause was less about

---

34 Murnaghan, 'Memorandum continued', 14 November 1912, f. 3, O'Donnell papers, box 3, wallet I, folder D, OFMLA.
35 *Ibid.*
36 This proposed amendment is quoted in full and discussed in Miller, *Church, State and Nation*, p. 290.

safeguarding the existing rights of the church than about capitalising on the opportunity that the Home Rule bill presented to redefine the church's role and to extend its privileges under the law. Reflecting an apprehension about the secularisation of Irish politics such as that prophesied in the quotation from John Annan Bryce at the beginning of this essay, Logue and his colleagues were making efforts to be increasingly proactive in buttressing the church's role in education. The accuracy of Bryce's prediction would, however, be judged not by the desires of the hierarchy but by the receptiveness of nationalist politicians to such overtures.

Issues for in-house resolution: marriage and the Home Rule bill

Before moving on to the interactions between the church and the Irish Party at this time, it is important to consider one last question which provided the focus for the last of Murnaghan's four memoranda. In the context of the *Ne Temere* decree, which took effect at Easter of 1908 and stipulated conditions for the validity of marriage, it is surprising that marriage was considered only in memorandum number four.

Not only does this point to the absolute centrality of education among the Catholic hierarchy's concerns, but a passage from Logue to O'Donnell on the subject of marriage and the operability of *Ne Temere* also reveals a far more pragmatic cardinal than the one seen in the letter of 5 November. By 3 December Logue prosaically observed that 'the Church must enforce her own marriage laws by her own sanctions'.[37] Unlike education, where the protection and mainte-nance of state funding was a central pillar of policy, in marriage, state safeguards were deemed neither necessary nor particularly desirable in an area where the church felt confident in its ability to shepherd its own flock unassisted.

---

37   Logue to O'Donnell, 3 December 1912, O'Donnell papers, box 3, wallet I, folder D, OFMLA.

Reacting to Murnaghan: the tactics of amendment

The most important conclusion to be drawn from Murnaghan's memoranda is that, despite the level of apprehension seen in Cardinal Logue's letter of 5 November which had set in train this legal examination of the bill and its clauses, the hierarchy's chosen legal expert had found no substantive flaws in the bill, apart from its at-times imprecise language and a potential loophole affecting entry to the training colleges. Indeed, as David Miller has pointed out, Murnaghan had actually identified several potential opportunities for the extension of denominationalism through the establishment of a Home Rule parliament. In particular, Murnaghan noted that clause three would remove the prohibition on monks or nuns teaching in ordinary national schools and any similar proposals for secondary schools would also now be nullified.[38]

Despite submitting a largely satisfactory report on the bill, Murnaghan's observations on denominational training colleges had caused Logue some concern. Thus the memoranda and suggested amendments were forwarded to Redmond by Bishop O'Donnell at Logue's request. More conciliatory than Logue, O'Donnell acknowledged the poor timing of the enclosed information and, respecting the pressure that the Irish Party faced in the House, requested 'earnest attention' rather than any explicit action from Redmond and his party in this regard.[39]

Redmond's response to the episcopacy's requests did not disprove Logue's scepticism about the Irish Party's willingness and ability to act in the interest of the church. While regretful that he could not please his spiritual leaders, Redmond made it clear that he could not possibly introduce amendments on foot of Murnaghan's memoranda. First and foremost, the bishops had left it far too late in the day to

---

38 Miller, *Church, State and Nation*, p. 290.
39 O'Donnell to Redmond, 7 Dec. 1912, Redmond papers, MS 15,217/3, NLI.

suggest amendments. The committee stages of the bill had concluded many months previously and the route of amendment by consultation with the government was now firmly closed.[40] Three days later, in a second letter, Redmond admitted to O'Donnell that the idea of introducing 'Catholic' amendments in the House of Commons presented the danger of stirring up 'all the latent anti-Catholic feeling in England' in opposition to amendments manifestly instigated by the Catholic hierarchy.[41]

Redmond predicted that such a storm would 'in all probability wreck the Home Rule bill', a prospect that, it has already been shown, was not entirely against Cardinal Logue's principles. Redmond thus made clear that it was not worth the political risk to back the church at the expense of national self-government. Echoing Murnaghan, Redmond justified his stance with the assertion that the suggested amendments were unnecessary and that an Irish parliament would prove itself fully capable of safeguarding Catholic interests.[42] Redmond's refusal to represent episcopal interests does not appear to have soured relations with the bishops greatly – possibly owing to Bishop O'Donnell's close sympathy with the constitutional nationalist cause and his ability to act as a buffer between Redmond and the less conciliatory members of the hierarchy. To look at this saga from the opposite perspective, if Irish unionists were looking for evidence that Home Rule meant Rome rule, they would not find it here.

---

40 During the Henry Campbell-Bannerman and Asquith administrations, the Irish Party expressly preferred the route of private consultation as opposed to interrogation of the government. A particularly revealing letter in this regard is from the senior Irish nationalist and MP for Liverpool (Scotland) Division, T. P. O'Connor, who wrote to his party colleague, John Dillon, in 1908, mocking the efforts of Healy, O'Brien, and their followers in pressing an issue across the floor of the House while O'Connor sat tight in the knowledge that the party's views had already been privately communicated to the cabinet: T. P. O'Connor to John Dillon, 15 October 1908, Dillon papers, MS 6740/155, Trinity College Dublin.
41 Redmond to O'Donnell, 12 December 1912, O'Donnell papers, box 3, wallet I, folder D, OFMLA.
42 *Ibid.*

While Redmond was clearly eager to please the bishops, this was the crowning example of the *realpolitik* truth that he was also content to refuse politely to represent their interests when he saw disproportionate amounts of political capital at stake.[43]

Conclusion

Based on the assurances given by James Murnaghan about the overall soundness of the third Home Rule bill from a Catholic standpoint, it can be concluded that any fears harboured by the Catholic hierarchy about the bill were largely unsubstantiated. If anything, Cardinal Logue's greatest misgiving about the bill was that it did not give the proposed Irish legislature sufficient autonomy to advance further the status and privileges of the Catholic Church in Ireland. The most important question about the activities of Cardinal Logue and his episcopal colleagues at this point is why they left it so long to act upon their apprehensions about the contents of a piece of legislation that had been introduced as far back as April 1912. David Miller has suggested that 'rather intense discussion among the prelates was preventing prompt action [at this time]'.[44] One must, however, also consider that it was apathy rather than passion – along with a sense of fatalism over the difficulties that would be faced in introducing amendments – that lay at the root of this delay. Throughout the autumn of 1912 priests and others were bringing their concerns about the bill to the hierarchy. Despite this groundswell of concern, it took until November for Logue's evidently deep, yet theretofore unarticulated, misgivings about the secularism of the Liberals and the impotence of the Irish Party on this issue to be expressed on paper.[45]

---

43 Michael Wheatley has best summed up the conciliatory nature of Redmondism in these years as 'socially conservative, conciliatory, and imperialist'. See Wheatley, *Nationalism and the Irish Party*, p. 10.

44 Miller, *Church, State and Nation*, p. 290.

45 It was with his letter to the bishop of Raphoe on 5 November that Logue's transition into impassioned activity occurred.

Reflecting on the third Home Rule bill a century after the fact, its provisions are often eclipsed by the events that occurred in reaction to it. However, in looking at the bill simply as a piece of legislation, many scholars now ask whether it was, in fact, workable in its own right. In 1983 Patricia Jalland showed just how complex, unpalatable (from a nationalist perspective) and impractical the financial clauses of the bill were.[46] Most recently, Ronan Fanning's *Fatal Path* has questioned the entire bona fides of the Liberal government, which appears to have had no genuine intention of bringing the third Home Rule bill into operation.[47] It has similarly been shown here that one of the rising stars of the Irish legal profession also found flaws with the bill's contents, pointing to poor legal draftsmanship, hasty preparation and potential problems when it came to its actual implementation. Regarding clause three and religious safeguards, Murnaghan admitted, 'I find the greatest difficulty in interpreting the meaning … It bulks together many subject matters, and is evidently intended to have a very wide operation. How far the clause will be extended is very doubtful.'[48]

One does not need to err into the realms of counterfactualism to consider what sort of Ireland the Home Rule bill envisaged. The legislation and accompanying parliamentary debates dealt expansively with the shape of the proposed polity. This was, indeed, a subject that occupied the minds of many contemporaries.[49] The third Home

---

46   P. Jalland, 'Irish home-rule finance: a neglected dimension of the Irish question, 1910–14', *Irish Historical Studies*, vol. 23, no. 91 (May 1983), pp. 233–53.

47   R. Fanning, *Fatal Path: British Government and Irish Revolution, 1910–1922* (London, 2013).

48   Murnaghan, 'Memorandum continued' (accompanying Murnaghan to O'Donnell, 9 November 1912), O'Donnell papers, box 3, wallet I, folder D, OFMLA.

49   One important example of this in the context of education is Patrick Pearse's pamphlet *The Murder Machine* (Dublin, 1912), which anticipated the creation of an autonomous Irish education system distinct from that of the British model. The text of the original 1912 version is available online via University College Cork at http://www.ucc.ie/celt/published/E900007–001/index.html (accessed 22 November 2012).

Rule bill remains one of the great 'what ifs' of modern Irish history. According to its proponents – Liberals more so than nationalists – it laid out a coherent and workable solution to the Irish question. However, from a variety of angles, from finance to its failure to address Ulster's distinctiveness and – as has been shown here – its shaky and poorly drafted religious safeguards, the Home Rule bill represented a legislative landmine.

Just as the 1920 Government of Ireland Act facilitated the establishment of one-party sectarian rule in Northern Ireland, between the ambiguities and loopholes identified by James Murnaghan and the clear willingness of Logue to enshrine a system of denominationalism through a Home Rule parliament, the third Home Rule bill was not watertight when it came to the safeguarding of religious freedoms.[50] Whereas Cardinal Logue had initiated his inquiry into the bill in a state of apprehension, Murnaghan's memoranda largely put his concerns to bed. The cardinal, however, remained lukewarm in his enthusiasm for Home Rule. Drawing a line under this episode, and turning his attention to other matters,[51] Logue prophetically concluded: 'I suppose we must take the Bill with all its defects and shortcomings; that is if we get it, which is far from certain.'[52]

---

50   It should be noted that the ability of the churches to circumvent the religious safeguards written into both the 1914 and the 1920 Government of Ireland Acts was demonstrated in the latter instance by the resounding rejection of Lord Londonderry's scheme for developing a non-denominational state education system in Northern Ireland in the 1920s. In this case, a coalition of the Protestant churches combined to demand the establishment of a denominational system. A good summary of this can be found in N. C. Flemming, 'Lord Londonderry and education reform in 1920s Northern Ireland', *History Ireland*, vol. 9, no. 1 (Spring 2001), pp. 36–9.
51   Like the rest of Irish society, in 1913 the Catholic hierarchy turned its attention to partition.
52   Logue to O'Donnell, 14 December 1912, O'Donnell papers, box 3, wallet I, folder D, OFMLA.

9

'Resigned to take the bill with its defects': the Catholic Church and the third Home Rule bill

Daithí Ó Corráin

In its chronicle of events for 1912, *The Irish Catholic Directory* devoted just a single line to the introduction of the third Home Rule bill in the House of Commons.[1] This contrasted sharply with lengthy entries on the crusade against evil literature, intemperance, the sinking of *Titanic* and clerical obituaries. Even more striking was the silence of the Catholic hierarchy, which, as a body, did not issue any statement. This reticence should not, however, be regarded as episcopal disapproval. The bishops shared in the general air of expectancy that nationalist aspirations would be fulfilled by 1914: this was the product of the two general elections of 1910; the Parliament Act of 1911, which limited the capacity of the House of Lords to veto parliamentary measures; and the commitment of the Liberal Party under Herbert H. Asquith to introduce a third Home Rule bill. But for the hierarchy the possibility of Irish self-government presented both potential benefits and lurking dangers. Their responses to the bill and the deepening crisis of 1913 and 1914 were conditioned by two overarching factors.

---

1   *The Irish Catholic Directory* (ICD), 1913, p. 515.

The first was their level of confidence in the leadership of the Irish Party. The second applied chiefly to the Ulster bishops: the prospect of exclusion from an Irish parliament imperilled their religious and educational interests. By the onset of the First World War, the spectre of partition had stretched their trust in the Irish Party and support for a Home Rule settlement to breaking point.

The hierarchy's support for the Irish Parliamentary Party (IPP) was far from monolithic. There were clearly discernible divisions apropos Ireland's political representatives at Westminster. The sceptics included the two episcopal big beasts – Cardinal Michael Logue, archbishop of Armagh and primate of All Ireland, and Archbishop William J. Walsh of Dublin – along with Bishop Edward O'Dwyer of Limerick and the ailing Archbishop John Healy of Tuam. Logue's lack of enthusiasm for the Irish Party had its roots in the 1890s, when the party was divided into bitter Redmondite, Dillonite and Healyite factions. The cardinal had little confidence in Redmond and Dillon, even after the reunification of the party in 1900, believing them too secularist, and was drawn, like Walsh, to Timothy Healy's championing of Catholic interests. The active support of Logue and the clergy saw Healy consistently returned in North Louth; most notably he narrowly defeated the official Irish Party candidate in the election in January 1910 by eighty-four votes. By the December 1910 election, however, the politically pragmatic, if reticent, Logue had jettisoned Healy.[2] The cardinal's condemnation of the Ancient Order of Hibernians (AOH) further distanced him from the IPP. He was not their only critic. Bishop Abraham Brownrigg of Ossory, for example, privately viewed the AOH as a danger to the faith and

---

2   See J. Privilege, *Michael Logue and the Catholic Church in Ireland, 1879–1925* (Manchester, 2009), pp. 81–90; F. Callanan, 'Healy, Timothy Michael' in J. McGuire and J. Quinn (eds), *Dictionary of Irish Biography* (Cambridge, 2009), available online at http://dib.cambridge.org/viewReadPage.do?articleId=a3903 (accessed 12 October 2012).

public order.[3] But among the hierarchy Logue was by far the most publicly vocal opponent. During a visit to Carrickmore in 1908, he declared the AOH 'a pest, a cruel tyranny and an organised system of blackguardism'.[4]

The position of the archbishop of Dublin was somewhat different. By 1905 Walsh had largely withdrawn from politics. Even as Home Rule reached its zenith, the paucity of letters between him and John Redmond is striking. In March 1912, conscious of the damaging impression, at such a vital juncture, that the archbishop was 'out of sympathy with the methods and policy of the Irish Party', Redmond urged him to send a subscription to the Home Rule fund and sought an interview to discuss aspects of the bill.[5] He had to wait almost a fortnight for a brusque and dismissive reply: 'it is now some years since I made up my mind to have nothing more to do with Irish politics and that nothing in the world could now induce me to change my mind in the matter.'[6] Throughout this period the archbishop was afflicted by poor health and preoccupied in 1913 with Dublin's labour unrest, and in 1914 with ultimately unfruitful plans to build a cathedral on Ormond Quay.

The highly conservative Archbishop Healy may have sympathised with William O'Brien in private, and they were certainly friendly, but he made no public pleadings in favour of the All-for-Ireland League. From about 1909 he was in poor health and an auxiliary bishop was appointed in 1911.[7] Bishop O'Dwyer, a zealous champion of Catholic

---

3   Brownrigg to William Walsh, 4 April 1912, Walsh papers, 383/5, Dublin Diocesan Archives (DDA).

4   É. Phoenix, 'Nationalism in Tyrone, 1880–1972', in C. Dillon and H. A. Jefferies (eds), *Tyrone: history & society* (Dublin, 2000), pp. 770–1.

5   John Redmond to Walsh, 7 March 1912, Walsh papers, 377/1, DDA.

6   Walsh to Redmond, 20 March 1912, Walsh papers, 377/1, DDA.

7   P. Maume, 'Healy, John' in McGuire and Quinn, *Dictionary of Irish Biography*, http://dib.cambridge.org/viewReadPage.do?articleId=a3895 (accessed 12 October 2012); P. Maume, *The Long Gestation: Irish nationalist life, 1891–1918* (Dublin, 1999), p. 108.

education, was also in the sceptics' tent. Following his death, Bishop Michael Fogarty of Killaloe delivered a panegyric in September 1917, in which he suggested that O'Dwyer's dissatisfaction with the party 'arose from impatience on his part with what he considered their want of manly spirit in pressing the claims of Ireland'.[8] Distrustful of the party during the third Home Rule episode, O'Dwyer did, at least, curb his penchant for publicly criticising it.

A large episcopal middle ground – determined not to interfere in politics, supportive of the national cause and reliable subscribers to the parliamentary fund – separated the sceptics from the party loyalists. The partisans included younger prelates such as Charles McHugh, bishop of Derry, and the urbane Patrick O'Donnell of Raphoe. In an address of thanks to the priests of the diocese shortly after his inauguration in 1907, McHugh stated that priests did not cease to be Irishmen and that the laity looked on clergy as natural leaders and expected political leadership from them.[9] He was not shy about offering such advice. O'Donnell, a friend of McHugh since their student days in Maynooth and bishop of Raphoe since 1888, was the member of the hierarchy closest to the Irish Party leadership. Augustine Birrell, chief secretary from 1907 until 1916, described him as 'not in the least like either Logue or Walsh. He was frankly a Nationalist politician with a tinge of enthusiasm in his nature.'[10] A trustee of the party fund, O'Donnell was also an ardent supporter of the AOH and its national president, Joseph Devlin, who was elected nationalist MP for West Belfast in 1906. 'Wee Joe' reinvigorated the AOH, tied it to the Home Rule cause and gave it newfound respectability as a benefit society, but it remained avowedly sectarian

---

8   M. Fogarty, *The Great Bishop of Limerick: panegyric delivered by the Most Rev. Michael Fogarty, Bishop of Killaloe, at the month's mind of the dead prelate, in St John's Cathedral, Limerick, 18 September 1917* (Dublin, 1917), p. 16.
9   P. Donnelly, 'Bishop Charles McHugh of Derry diocese (1856–1926)', *Seanchas Ard Mhacha*, vol. 20, no. 2 (2005), p. 221.
10   A. Birrell, *Things Past Redress* (London, 1937), p. 209.

in outlook.[11] Since 1890 the bishop of Raphoe had also corresponded regularly with John Dillon.[12] Denis Kelly, bishop of the tiny diocese of Ross and the hierarchy's financial expert, also merits mention in this context, though he was not as bound to the party as McHugh and O'Donnell were.[13]

Home Rule is Rome rule

Cries that Home Rule would amount to Rome rule grew in intensity as Home Rule moved to the top of the political agenda. Religious tensions were exacerbated, particularly in Ulster, by the muscularity of the AOH and by two papal pronouncements: the *Ne Temere* decree, which came into effect in April 1908, and the *motu proprio*, a papal rescript, *Quantavis diligentia* of October 1911. They were a godsend to anti-Home Rule pamphleteers. In essence *Ne Temere* was a housekeeping measure, providing for the first time one uniform set of marriage regulations for all Catholics.[14] Under the canonical form, for a marriage to be valid it had to take place before a priest, who was a witness to that marriage. The decree did not, in fact, refer to the upbringing of children and generated little interest until the infamous McCann case in 1910.[15] Alexander McCann, a Catholic, married a Presbyterian woman in a Presbyterian church in Ballymena. The couple subsequently moved to the Falls Road. The marriage broke down and McCann left home with his two children in October 1910.

---

11   É. Phoenix, *Northern Nationalism: nationalistic politics, partition and the Catholic minority in Northern Ireland 1890–1940* (Belfast, 1994), pp. 4–5.

12   This continued until 1921. See correspondence in John Dillon papers, MSS 6764/1–121, Trinity College Dublin Archives (TCD).

13   The 1911 census recorded 44,011 Catholics in the eleven parishes comprising this diocese, ICD, 1915, p. 266.

14   On the evolution of the rules of the Catholic Church governing marriage, see W. Van Ommeren, 'Ne Temere', in *New Catholic Encyclopedia*, vol. 10 (second ed., Detroit, 2003), pp. 218–9.

15   See *The New legislation of the Catholic Church on Betrothals & Marriage: decree of the Sacred Congregation of the Council approved and confirmed by His Holiness Pope Pius X. Authorised translation* (Dublin, 1907), pp. 1–8.

Shortly after this he attempted to have the younger child baptised in the nearby St Paul's Catholic church but Mrs McCann apparently disrupted the ceremony. McCann then disappeared. This essentially private marital quarrel came to public attention under the shadow of *Ne Temere*. It was alleged that the marriage had ended when a priest informed the couple that their marriage was void and that they would need to remarry in a Catholic ceremony. This Mrs McCann refused to do, whereupon her husband departed with the children.[16] William Corkey, her Presbyterian minister, prepared a letter of appeal to the lord lieutenant on behalf of Mrs McCann, who pleaded:

> In my despair I am driven to apply to you, as the head of all authority in this country, for help. I am without money, and but for the charity of kind friends I would be starving. I want to get my children and to know if they are alive; and I have been told, kind sir, that if you directed your law officers to make inquiries they could soon get me my rights. Will you please do so, and help a poor heartbroken woman.

This emotive letter was published in *The Northern Whig* on 2 December 1910. It was accompanied by an editorial, 'Clerical kidnapping in Belfast', which warned starkly: 'To steal the children of a lawfully-married Presbyterian mother, and to turn them into Roman Catholics against her will – to tell her that she is a harlot and her children bastards – all that will come quite naturally after Home Rule.' This appeared just days before the general election and was used as propaganda against Joe Devlin in West Belfast. The McCann affair was debated in the House of Commons in February 1911 during a motion raised by the unionists. Seeking to defuse the issue,

---

16   See A. C. Hepburn, *Catholic Belfast and Nationalist Ireland in the Era of Joe Devlin, 1871–1934* (Oxford, 2008), pp. 129–30; M. Harris, *The Catholic Church and the Foundation of the Northern Irish State* (Cork, 1993), pp. 14–5; O. Rafferty, *Catholicism in Ulster, 1603–1983: an interpretative history* (Dublin, 1993), p. 180.

Devlin read statements from the priests in St Paul's. They insisted that they had never declared the marriage invalid. The nationalist MP claimed the affair was 'one of the most scandalous political dodges ever known'.[17] Nevertheless, the McCann case proved damaging. The situation was not helped by Cardinal Logue's Lenten pastoral in February 1911, which deemed anti-*Ne Temere* agitation as 'having been got up avowedly for the purpose of moving the civil authorities to fetter the action of the church and block the execution of her laws'.[18]

In this fraught atmosphere *Quantavis diligentia* further heightened anti-Catholic animosity by forbidding Catholics, under pain of excommunication, to compel ecclesiastics to attend civil tribunals. In Dublin the unionist paper *The Daily Express* seized on this as evidence of papal aggression and menacing Catholic power, and surmised that it would confer immunity from prosecution on Catholic clergy.[19] Daily reports and commentary on the papal rescript featured in *The Daily Express* from 21 December until the second week of January 1912. In a letter to the press, published on 30 December, Archbishop Walsh attempted to check what he later regarded as 'the lurid representation of the decree … based upon a total misconception' and stated that the exemption had lapsed in Ireland through long disuse.[20] He then became embroiled in a public quarrel with James Campbell, Unionist MP for Trinity and a prominent barrister, who asserted that the decree was indeed applicable in Ireland.[21] In *The Motu Proprio*

---

17 Hepburn, *Catholic Belfast*, p. 131.
18 ICD, 1912, p. 484; Lenten Pastoral 1911, Logue papers, Arch/9/9/5, Cardinal Tomás Ó Fiaich Memorial Library and Archive (OFMLA).
19 *The Daily Express*, 21 December 1911.
20 *Irish Independent, The Freeman's Journal*, 30 December 1911; W. J. Walsh, *The Motu Proprio 'Quantavis Diligentia' and its Critics* (Dublin, 1912), p. 7.
21 *The Daily Express*, 6 and 9 January 1912; P. Maume, 'Campbell, James Henry Mussen 1st Baron Glenavy', in McGuire and Quinn, *Dictionary of Irish Biography* (http://dib.cambridge.org/viewReadPage.do?articleId=a1422, accessed 12 October 2012).

'Quantavis Diligentia' and its Critics, a 110-page pamphlet published in early 1912, the archbishop refuted Campbell's claims, derided his qualifications 'as an interpreter of canonical documents' and drew attention to attempts to provoke outcry in the context of Home Rule.[22]

This did little to dispel the anxieties of the main Protestant churches as religious and political fears proved mutually reinforcing. At the root of this was a lack of confidence in an Irish government to maintain civil and religious liberties for all. The McCann case became a cause célèbre and was the subject of extensive protest. The General Synod of the Church of Ireland denounced *Ne Temere*. In his pamphlet *Rome and Marriage: an examination of the recent papal decree, 'Ne Temere'*, Dudley Fletcher, Church of Ireland rector of Coolbanagher, feared: 'If a papal decree on marriage can break up a home in Ireland under British law, what fair play or toleration could we expect under a Roman Catholic Parliament in Dublin, with an executive responsible thereto?'[23] The perils of mixed marriages prompted the General Assembly of the Presbyterian Church to appoint a committee on *Ne Temere* in 1911, which drew up a statement as to its nature and dangerous effects and sought to have the decree withdrawn.[24] The decree was also the subject of inter-church dialogue (together with national insurance, temperance and education) between the Church of Ireland and Presbyterian Church.[25] From 1908 intra-Protestant rapprochement was encouraged by the Lambeth conference, the decennial meeting of the Anglican church. Three years later the General Synod of the Church

---

22 Walsh, *Motu Proprio*, pp. viii, 28.
23 D. Fletcher, *Rome and Marriage: an examination of the recent papal decree, 'Ne Temere'* (Dublin, 1911), p. 8. On the Church of Ireland response to *Ne Temere* see A. Scholes, *The Church of Ireland and the Third Home Rule Bill* (Dublin, 2010), pp. 19–22.
24 *Minutes of the Proceedings of the General Assembly of the Presbyterian Church in Ireland*, vol. 12, June 1911, pp. 97, 108; June 1912, p. 377.
25 *Ibid.*, June 1912, p. 366.

of Ireland appointed a committee to this end; likewise the General Assembly established a Committee on Cooperation with other Evangelical Churches in Ireland.[26]

Quantavis diligentia and *Ne Temere* featured prominently and frequently in anti-Home Rule protests. At a convention in Belfast on 1 February 1912, over 40,000 Presbyterians feared that 'under Home Rule as foreshadowed, the parliament and executive alike are certain to be controlled by a majority subject to the direction of the authors of the *Ne Temere* and *Motu Proprio* decrees'.[27] As a subsequent resolution made clear, Presbyterian resistance to Home Rule could not be stated 'without fixing attention on the religious difficulty that lies at the heart of the question'.[28] Notably, fears of interference with religious liberty, denominationalisation of education and the endowment of the Catholic Church were all ranked ahead of the potential economic dangers of Home Rule. The convention had no confidence in any protections provided in the Home Rule measure: 'No safeguards which the wit of man could devise would prevent the Church of Rome from using the majority always at her command to further her designs. The security of the Protestant minority – their only security – is that they continue to be governed directly by the Imperial Parliament.'[29]

The same motif featured in a memorial from 131,351 adherents of the Presbyterian Church read at the General Assembly in 1913. A motion receiving the memorial and declaring the determined opposition of the church to Home Rule was overwhelmingly supported by 921 votes to only 43 against.[30] In 1914 Rev. James

---

26   I. Ellis, *Vision and Reality: a survey of twentieth-century Irish inter-church relations* (Belfast, 1992), pp. 3–7.
27   *The Irish Times*, 2 February 1912.
28   'Home Rule Statement prepared and issued in pursuance of a resolution of the Presbyterian Convention held at Belfast on 1st February 1912', p. 7.
29   *Ibid.*, p. 14.
30   *Minutes of the Proceedings*, vol. 12 (June 1913), pp. 635–6. The best-known

Bingham, the moderator of the General Assembly, described the Ulster Volunteer Force as 'a great and noble army of men … preparing to defend themselves and us from the dangers that threaten our citizenship, liberties and religion'.[31] Northern members of the Church of Ireland exhibited similarly trenchant opposition.[32] Yet in Dublin a meeting of southern unionists in January 1913 protested against the introduction of religious difference into party politics and disapproved of the identification of the Irish Protestant churches with a particular party.[33]

As might be expected, the Catholic bishops staunchly defended their position on confessional lines. They were not, however, insensitive to the political ramifications. Many bishops were all too aware of the easy political capital accruing to opponents of Home Rule, even if based on unionist misconceptions. Writing to Archbishop Walsh in early 1912, Cardinal Logue was 'sorry Your Grace is getting so much trouble with the Orange newspapers. It is almost useless to trouble about them. They want a pretext for a political cry, and no amount of explanation will stop them.'[34] In a revealing letter to the archbishop of Dublin, Bishop Brownrigg questioned the wisdom of the Holy See in imposing such legislation without consultation: 'It is said that the legislation is only tentative but that will not be taken into account by our enemies who can do any amount of injury to religion in the meantime.'[35] He believed that Walsh, with due deference to the Holy See, could not have adopted any other position in respect of the *motu proprio*. Archbishop Thomas Fennelly of Cashel believed that a

pro-Home Ruler was the Rev. J. B. Armour of Ballymoney.

31   R. F. G. Holmes, 'The General Assembly and politics', in R. F. G. Holmes and R. Buick Knox (eds), *The General Assembly of the Presbyterian Church in Ireland, 1840–1990* (Belfast, 1990), pp. 175–6.

32   See the essay by Andrew Scholes in this book.

33   *Irish Independent*, 25 January 1913.

34   Logue to Walsh, 7 January 1912, Walsh papers, 383/5, DDA.

35   Abraham Brownrigg to Walsh, 6 January 1912, Walsh papers, 383/5, DDA.

statement from Rome approving Walsh's publication (that the decree did not apply in Ireland) would quell the disquiet and safeguard the anticipated Home Rule bill.[36]

Curiously little was made at the time, or has been since, of the successful libel action taken by six priests and Robert Browne, bishop of Cloyne and uncle of famous photographer Father Frank Browne, SJ, against the proprietors of the Scottish newspaper the *Dundee Courier*, for alleging religious intolerance in Queenstown. In an article on 15 August 1911, the *Dundee Courier* charged that the priests and the bishop had abused their religious influence over the laity in 1909 to procure the indiscriminate dismissal of all Protestant shop assistants in the employment of Catholics and to ruin the business of a Catholic shopkeeper who had refused to discharge a Protestant employee.[37] In his address to the jury, Alexander Ure, KC, senior counsel for the plaintiffs and the lord advocate, claimed that as an example of disreputable journalism the case was, in his experience, without parallel and that 'political intent did not entitle a man to make a shameless and infamous attack upon other men's private character'.[38] Cardinal Logue believed that Browne, in winning his action, was not only 'defending his own character but the good name of the Bishops and priests of Ireland'.[39] In an effort to demonstrate that Protestants had nothing to fear under Home Rule, Bishop McHugh nominated David Hogg, a Protestant Home Ruler, for the Derry seat at Westminster in preference to Sir Shane Leslie, a Catholic convert. The bishop signed the nomination papers along with Samuel Patton, the Presbyterian chaplain to Derry prison.[40]

---

36   Fennelly to Walsh, 6 February 1912, Walsh papers, 383/5, DDA.
37   *Irish Independent*, 21 and 23 December 1911, 22 March 1912; ICD, 1912, pp. 512–3.
38   ICD, 1912, p. 513.
39   Logue to Walsh, 12 March 1912, Walsh papers, 383/5, DDA.
40   *The Irish Times*, 27 January 1913; Rafferty, *Catholicism in Ulster*, p. 188; F. J. Madden and T. Bradley, 'The diocese of Derry in the twentieth century,' in H. A.

Others such as Bishop Patrick Finegan of Kilmore expressed publicly the hope that Home Rule would be 'a solvent for the aimless, but bitter, hatreds that for too long have divided Irishmen'.[41]

As Home Rule drew closer the political necessity to reassure unionists that Irish self-government was not inimical to their interests became acute. To this end Jeremiah MacVeagh, MP for South Down, published two pamphlets in 1911. *Home Rule in a Nutshell: a pocket book for speakers and electors* contained, as its subtitle indicated, 'a brief exposition of the arguments for Home Rule, and answers to the objections raised'.[42] MacVeagh treated the religious dimension separately in *Religious Intolerance under Home Rule: some opinions of leading Irish Protestants*. This attempted to counter the so-called 'religious bogey' by inviting leading and representative Irish Protestants to state their views. The responses were then compiled and published. One of the most interesting came from the pen of Lord Pirrie, chairman of Harland & Wolff shipyard. Although a firm opponent of the first and second Home Rule bills, his attitude had softened greatly in the interim, and by 1911 he was a firm supporter of the Liberal government's plans for Home Rule:

> There is no fear that the impending inauguration of an Irish legislature will have, as one of its results, the religious persecution of Protestants … On the other hand, I confess with shame that in the past the spirit of religious intolerance has been and is even now, although in lesser degree, prevalent amongst a portion of the Unionist population of

Jefferies and C. Devlin (eds), *History of the Diocese of Derry from Earliest Times* (Dublin, 2000), p. 245.

41   *Anglo Celt*, 8 November 1913, cited in D. Gallogly, *The Diocese of Kilmore, 1800–1905* (Cavan, 1999), pp. 243–4.

42   J. MacVeagh, *Home Rule in a Nutshell: a pocket book for speakers and electors* (Dublin and London, 1911). The pamphlet was a response to the many manifestations of unionist electoral propaganda in Britain, for example *The Truth About Irish Home Rule (by one who knows)* (Dublin & Belfast, 1911).

Ulster. Happily the evidence that this unfortunate spirit is on the wane is indisputable.[43]

Both pamphlets were attacked in a unionist counterblast, *The Home Rule 'Nutshell' Examined by an Irish Unionist*, published by the Unionist Associations of Ireland. The recent papal decrees and examples of clerical interference in elections, such as that by Cardinal Logue in North Louth, were ventilated.[44] In an effort to neutralise fears of insidious Rome rule, Redmond published an article on nationalism and religion in *Reynolds's Newspaper*, listing occasions when the laity resisted Vatican intervention in Irish affairs.[45] This alarmed the Catholic hierarchy. In a letter to Walsh, Logue feared overcompensation by the Irish Party towards its rivals in religion by consenting to clauses in the Home Rule bill 'directly pointing to and restricting the actions of Catholics … We want no Catholic ascendancy; but we do not want Catholics logged and muzzled as if they were furious dogs.'[46] The bogey of religious intolerance proved impossible to quash.

Education

The sensitive area of education was the hierarchy's long-standing and key vested interest. There were three principal points of concern.

First, to ensure a Catholic ethos, Catholic control of all aspects of the educational infrastructure had to be maintained. This was jeopardised by the advance of secularist legislation. The abolition of school boards in England and Wales and the creation of local education authorities based on county councils under the 1902 Education

---

43   J. MacVeagh, *Religious Intolerance under Home Rule: some opinions of leading Irish Protestants* (London, 1911), p. 42.
44   *The Home Rule 'Nutshell' Examined by an Irish Unionist* (Dublin & Belfast, 1912), pp. 57–62.
45   Rafferty, *Catholicism in Ulster*, p. 189.
46   Logue to Walsh, 24 March 1912, Logue papers, Arch/9/3/3, OFMLA.

Act had set an unwelcome precedent. The Education bill of 1906, which was not carried into law, was even more alarming, with clause four proposing that the local authority would have absolute power as to the appointment of teachers.[47] School ethos was of signal import in Ulster as a means of sustaining a community that was both Catholic and nationalist or conversely Protestant and unionist.

The second point of concern was the tendency of the government to attach nondenominational strings to the grant of public money.

The third anxiety was simply the magnitude of that grant. Inadequate funding, especially in the expanding secondary-school sector, was a perennial grievance. When forwarding his subscription to the parliamentary fund in 1911, Bishop Joseph Hoare of Ardagh hoped 'the coming Home Rule Bill may satisfy our desires especially in the financial clauses'.[48] At a prize-giving ceremony in St Columb's college in June 1913, Bishop McHugh, the school's former president, contrasted the starved condition of secondary education in Ireland with the generous funding received in England and Scotland. He claimed it would require an annual grant of £120,000 to put Irish schools on an equal footing. The bishop urged that the financial relations between Ireland and London be settled on equitable terms *before* the passing of Home Rule, lest Irish schools remain underfunded.[49]

The Home Rule bill

In 1911 and 1912 finance rather than Ulster was considered the greatest obstacle facing Irish Home Rule.[50] The Primrose committee,

---

47   Redmond to O'Donnell, enclosing a confidential memorandum regarding the Education bill, 1906 and the Single School Areas bill, 1912, John Redmond papers, MS 15217/3, National Library of Ireland (NLI).

48   *The Weekly Freeman*, 22 April 1911 cited in D. W. Miller, *Church, State and Nation in Ireland, 1898–1921* (Dublin, 1973), p. 269.

49   ICD, 1914, p. 516.

50   P. Jalland, *The Liberals and Ireland: the Ulster question in British politics to 1914*

comprising experts without political associations, studied the financial relations between Britain and Ireland and investigated how sufficient revenue could be raised for Ireland to meet its needs. The balance between income and expenditure had deteriorated significantly in recent years. Between 1896 and 1911 Irish revenue had increased by 28 per cent, whereas government expenditure in Ireland had risen by 91 per cent, mainly due to land purchase and welfare benefits.[51] Bishop Denis Kelly was the Irish expert on the committee and he kept Redmond abreast of developments. The Primrose report on the fiscal arrangements of Home Rule favoured full fiscal autonomy, with the Imperial Exchequer assuming liability for all Irish pensions already granted. When the committee unanimously passed its report, Kelly wrote enthusiastically to Redmond that 'six months' thought and study have confirmed me in the view … that in the altered circumstances a bold and full measure of Home Rule has a better chance of success than a half-measure'.[52] In the event, the Primrose proposals were ignored, with only token concessions to fiscal autonomy in the Home Rule bill.

In the 1912 Lenten pastorals of the Irish bishops an unmistakable air of expectancy regarding the impending Home Rule bill jostled with warnings against immoral publications, excessive drinking and the dangers of socialism. That optimism gave way to resignation once the details of the bill were revealed. As feared, the financial provisions fell very far short of fiscal autonomy. Bishop Kelly would accept them, he told John Dillon, only 'with repugnance' because 'Ireland is not mistress in her own house'.[53] Imperial taxes would continue to be levied in Ireland and paid into the Imperial

---

(Brighton, 1980), p. 44.

51   *Ibid.*, p. 45.

52   Kelly to Redmond, 6 October 1911, Redmond papers, MS 15199/4, NLI.

53   Kelly to Dillon, 17 January 1912, Dillon papers, MS 6766/41, TCD.

Exchequer.[54] Under clause fifteen, the Irish parliament had power to impose independent taxes and to vary or discontinue imperial taxes. Such powers were, however, subject to a number of restrictive conditions. For example, there was no entitlement to impose new customs duties, and imperial customs and excise duties could only be varied by way of addition.[55] The cost of land purchase, old-age pensions, national insurance and the constabulary would initially remain imperial services. A 'transferred sum' would be paid into the Irish exchequer until such time as Irish revenue and expenditure balanced for three consecutive years. The clear implication was that the Irish parliament would be encouraged to tighten its belt. Though acknowledging that the 'hands of the Irish Party are tied', Cardinal Logue was disappointed at their lack of fight. 'I have always thought,' he wrote to Walsh, 'that the finance arrangement of Mr Gladstone's 1893 Bill would have left Ireland in poverty and misery. This bill is little if at all better.'[56]

With the financial facet practically immutable, the hierarchy turned its attention to the religious aspect of the bill, which was essentially contained in clause three. Logue, O'Donnell and Kelly were nominated to scrutinise the measure 'as far as it affects religious interests'.[57] In practice this meant educational interests. For the most part clause three replicated the provisions regarding religion in Gladstone's 1886 and 1893 Home Rule bills. The Irish parliament would have no power to make laws establishing or endowing any religion; impose any disability or confer any privilege or preference or advantage on account of religious belief; or impair the right of a child to attend a school receiving public money without attending religious

---

54 Government of Ireland. A bill [as amended in committee and on report] to amend the provision for the government of Ireland (2 & 3 Geo. 5 c. 14).
55 *Ibid.*, c. 15.
56 Logue to Walsh, 22 November 1912, Walsh papers, 383/5, DDA.
57 *Ibid.*

instruction. The furore over *Ne Temere* appears to have influenced the insertion of a sub-clause that religious belief or ceremony could not be made a condition of the validity of any marriage. An Irish parliament would have no authority to divert the property or, without consent, alter the constitution of any religious body without adequate compensation.[58] During the committee stage of the bill this provision was extended, under clause forty-two, to guarantee against appropriation of the property of Trinity College and Queen's University Belfast.[59]

Unsurprisingly, the potential impact on Catholic education dominated the bishops' consideration of the bill in November 1912. As Conor Mulvagh has discussed, Logue and O'Donnell sought the legal counsel of James Murnaghan, barrister and professor of Roman Law and Jurisprudence at University College Dublin. Tellingly, six of the eight questions put to him pertained to education.[60] Logue feared that the safeguards for Protestants embodied in the bill would limit Catholic freedom of action as 'so many fetters riveted to our limbs'.[61] The cardinal seemed underwhelmed by Murnaghan's opinion that clause three would leave the law as it stood, and there is an unmistakable note of resignation in his comment that 'that is the most we could hope for'.[62] Innately pessimistic, Logue was particularly fearful for the denominational status of teacher-training colleges in the light of Augustine Birrell's amendment that every school receiving public money should be open to all.[63] It was O'Donnell rather than Logue who communicated with Redmond; Kelly was in

---

58 Government of Ireland. A bill [as amended in committee and on report] to amend the provision for the government of Ireland (2 & 3 Geo. 5 c. 3).
59 *Ibid.*, c. 42.
60 See the paper by Conor Mulvagh in this book; Miller, *Church, State and Nation*, p. 289.
61 Logue to O'Donnell, 5 November 1912 cited in Privilege, *Michael Logue*, p. 93.
62 Logue to Walsh, 3 December 1912, Walsh papers, 383/5, DDA.
63 James Murnaghan to Walsh, 14 November 1912, Walsh papers, 377/1, DDA; Logue to Walsh, 12 December 1912, Walsh papers, 383/5, DDA.

Rome at this time. When Murnaghan's opinions belatedly reached Redmond in December 1912 he believed that it was too late for alterations. Moreover, the Irish Party leader maintained that 'some of the suggested amendments are of a character which would instantly arouse all the latent anti-Catholic feeling in England, and would create a storm around our heads which would in all probability wreck the Home Rule Bill'.[64] He did, however, offer reassurance about training colleges. If anything, Redmond's dismissive response demonstrates clearly the limits of episcopal authority and input. Logue was resigned to accept the bill, commenting bleakly: 'We were promised a generous measure of Home Rule. Now that the bill is through Committee it looks to me like a skeleton on which to hang restrictions.'[65]

The spectre of partition

By the beginning of 1913 these concerns appeared almost trivial as the Home Rule saga entered a new and ominous phase. In the House of Commons, on 1 January, Edward Carson, the effective leader of the Ulster unionists, unveiled a modified strategy with a resolution, which was defeated, to exclude the entire province of Ulster. For Redmond partition remained unthinkable, though he was willing to contemplate Home Rule within Home Rule, which in turn was anathema to the Ulster bishops. As tension rose in Ireland with the formation of unionist and nationalist paramilitary forces, the Irish Party was compelled to accept some form of separate treatment for Ulster. Rumours of compromise were deeply unsettling for northern nationalists. In a letter to Redmond on 9 October 1913 Bishop O'Donnell stressed the 'growing apprehension on the part of a good many Catholics and Nationalists in the North of Ireland in reference

---

64   Redmond to O'Donnell, 12 December 1912, Redmond papers, MS 15217/3, NLI.

65   Logue to Walsh, 12 December 1912, Walsh papers, 383/5, DDA.

to conference schemes'.[66] While he assured the nationalist leader that they would go to great lengths to meet unionist concerns, 'nothing could justify cutting this [nationalist] minority off from their claims under the Bill, and deliberately leaving them under a harrow that might be worse than what they have endured'.[67] Revealingly, he also emphasised fears of the detrimental impact that exclusion of the north-east would have on Catholic education.

In his Lenten pastoral in February 1914, Logue presciently forecast that 'this year is fraught with vital issues for the destinies of our dear country'.[68] As various exclusion schemes were mooted by the cabinet and unionist opposition mounted, the Ulster bishops grew increasingly apprehensive. It was inevitable that it should be so. Four dioceses – Armagh, Derry, Clogher and Kilmore – straddled the mooted six-county border, while two others – Dromore and Down and Connor – were situated entirely within the north-east corner. In February Bishop McHugh made clear his concern that the fate of northern Catholics was being marginalised at Westminster. As Phoenix has argued, the prelate's misgivings were a reflection of grass-roots feeling in Counties Tyrone, Fermanagh and Derry, and they could not be blithely dismissed.[69] Despite assurances from Joe Devlin that 'nothing will be done that will not have the sanction and support of all our friends in Ulster', the bishop, in consultation with O'Donnell, proposed a nationalist meeting in Derry.[70] As he explained to Redmond:

The Orange faction is never done crying out intolerance and publishing what they would suffer under H[ome] Rule, but there is not a word

---

66 O'Donnell to Redmond, 9 October 1913, Redmond papers, MS 15217/4, NLI.
67 *Ibid.*
68 *Irish Independent,* 23 February 1914.
69 Phoenix, *Northern Nationalism,* p. 11.
70 Devlin to McHugh, 19 February 1914 cited in Harris, *Catholic Church,* p. 48.

about what Catholics and Nationalists in Ulster would suffer if the Orangemen got control ... The great object of the meeting was to give the Liberal Party to understand that the Nationalists of the North have their rights as well as the Orangemen ... to see that there were two sides to the Ulster Question.[71]

The Irish Party leader appealed for the meeting to be called off and McHugh consented with great reluctance. Derry was the cause of further alarm in March when Redmond again prevailed on the bishop to cancel a proposed route march by Irish Volunteers, believing it 'a fatal mistake, also the best means of playing into [the] hands of Carson as almost certain to lead [to] terrible consequences and render our position here much more difficult'.[72] McHugh succeeded, but only after threatening to have the march denounced from the altar.[73] The political situation was beginning to spiral out of episcopal or party control.

Much depended, of course, on how exclusion was defined. Around mid-February O'Donnell appears to have met the IPP leadership in London. In the event of exclusion proving unavoidable, the prelate recommended the scheme proposed by Horace Plunkett: that Ulster should have the right to vote itself out after a period of not less than ten years.[74] David Lloyd George's county option favoured initial exclusion for any individual Ulster county for three years before coming under Home Rule. O'Donnell recognised the risks this posed: 'The perils to the party in the L.[loyd] G.[eorge] scheme are formidable. Even if we supposed the country willing in all the circumstances to accept or tolerate it, the party would not be safe without wide con-

71   McHugh to Redmond, 28 February 1914, Redmond papers, MS 15203/5, NLI.
72   Telegram Redmond to McHugh, 20 March 1914, Redmond papers, MS 15203/5, NLI.
73   McHugh to Redmond, 21 March 1914, Redmond papers, MS 15203/5, NLI.
74   *The Irish Times, Irish Independent*, 11 February 1914; Miller, *Church, State and Nation*, p. 297.

sultation amounting to a mandate.'[75] Redmond was forced to accept the scheme in early March, ostensibly as 'the price of peace'.[76] But winning acceptance for this formula was no easy task. He dispatched emissaries to elicit the support of prominent northern national- ists, including the Ulster bishops. Devlin met McHugh, O'Donnell and Tohill, the terminally ill bishop of Down and Connor,[77] with 'eminently satisfactory' results.[78] Given Logue's antipathy towards the AOH, Jeremiah MacVeagh and James Lardner, MP for North Monaghan, visited Ara Coeli, the cardinal's residence in Armagh. MacVeagh reported to Redmond that the cardinal recognised that the bill had to be saved: 'Of course he doesn't love the concessions but will not object.'[79] The bishops were prepared to rally behind the party as long as a unionist administration with possible control of educa- tion was not established in Belfast. Despite their endorsement, the bishops' private views were another matter. Logue confided to Walsh: 'I fear the concessions on the Home Rule Bill will be a bad business for us here in this part of the North. It will leave us more than ever under the heel of the Orangemen. Worst of all it will leave them free to tamper with our education.'[80] Bishop McKenna of Clogher hoped that southern unionists would not accept exclusion. He admitted to Michael O'Riordan, rector of the Irish College in Rome, his fear that if temporary exclusion was granted and worked reasonably well then it would almost certainly become permanent.[81] Asquith's doubling of the moratorium to six years merely intensified this anxiety.

Holding out for a clean break of six counties, Carson rejected the

---

75 O'Donnell to Redmond, 25 February 1914, Redmond papers, MS 15217/4, NLI.

76 D. Gwynn, *The Life of John Redmond* (London, 1932), p. 268.

77 He died on 4 July 1914 and was succeeded by Joseph MacRory in August 1915.

78 Gwynn, *Life of John Redmond*, p. 269.

79 MacVeagh to Redmond, n.d. [6 March 1914], Redmond papers, MS 15205/4, NLI.

80 Logue to Walsh, 13 March 1914, Walsh papers, 384/4, DDA.

81 Hepburn, *Catholic Belfast*, p. 152.

county option as it could guarantee him only four. As the political situation deteriorated rapidly with the Curragh incident, the UVF gun-running and increased enrolment in the Irish Volunteers, the threat of civil war grew progressively more real. This is captured by O'Donnell in a letter to Redmond in early May:

> A marked change for the worse has gradually come over the attitude and spirit of Ulster Unionists ... there is a bad 12th of July spirit even where it was not known for long years. I should not be surprised if it were worse in the included counties than in the N.E. In the N.W. the Unionists are constantly saying they will fight.[82]

Ultimately, the impasse over the geographical area to be excluded proved intractable, and the outbreak of the First World War merely postponed a resolution of the Ulster conundrum. In the spring and early summer the Ulster bishops were placed in an invidious position. They had deferred to Redmond's wishes while at the same time attempting to moderate the anxiety of the faithful. In Derry, for example, McHugh called for no public rejoicing when the Home Rule bill passed its third reading in May lest it be construed as provocation and spark disturbances.[83] Yet among the Ulster bishops a lurking fear intensified that they might be sacrificed in the interests of political expediency.

The death of Pope Pius X on 20 August 1914 and the election of his successor, Pope Benedict XV, preoccupied the hierarchy during the early weeks of the war. Logue spent six weeks in Rome at this time and had considerable difficulty negotiating a passage home, returning on 29 September.[84] Redmond's achievement in placing the

---

82 O'Donnell to Redmond, 9 May 1914, Redmond papers, MS 15217/4, NLI.
83 *The Derry Journal*, 25 May 1914.
84 Logue to Walsh, 12 September 1914, Walsh papers, 384/4, DDA; ICD, 1915, p. 538.

Home Rule bill on the statute book on 18 September was under-mined by its immediate suspension and Asquith's assurance that special provision would be made for Protestant Ulster. Messages of congratulation were forthcoming from the archbishop of Cashel and the bishops of Kerry, Elphin, Clonfert, Kildare and Leighlin, Raphoe and Portsmouth.[85] More telling is the number of prelates who did not write. No statement regarding Home Rule was made at the meeting of the Irish episcopal conference on 13 October 1914, but two resolutions touched on the war. The first declared that the supply of chaplains for Irish soldiers at the Front was inadequate. The second directed the clergy to remind the faithful of the sufferings of Catholic Belgium and to encourage them to subscribe to the Belgian relief fund.[86] A total of £27,000, or an average of £1,000 for every diocese, was raised by December 1914. Bishop Browne of Cloyne pressed for the contributions to be published in the press because of the belief that 'those who are opposed to us in religion or political sentiment parade what they have done, which is not much, and show a disposition to belittle, or suppress the publication of the generous contribution of our poor people'.[87]

Conclusion

The third Home Rule crisis demonstrated the limitations of the Catholic Church's political influence. The bishops were important figures, but they proved largely unable to shape the political process. The sense of hopefulness evident in 1912 quickly gave way to resignation and then to the dread among the northern bishops that their interests, especially in education, would suffer in any compromise with unionism. During the tribulations of 1914 the

---

85   ICD, 1915, p. 537.
86   *Ibid.*, pp. 540–1; Bishop Robert Browne to Walsh, 29 October 1914, Walsh papers, 384/4, DDA.
87   Browne to Walsh, 31 December 1914, Walsh papers, 384/4, DDA.

Ulster bishops moved from being disenchanted with Redmond's faltering policy to losing all faith in him. This was compounded by the formation of a coalition government in May 1915. Bishop Fogarty of Killaloe, hitherto a strong party supporter, deemed the 'coalition with Carson on top … a horrible scandal and intolerable slight on Irish sentiment'. In the same letter he pronounced Home Rule 'dead and buried' and suggested that Ireland was 'without a Nationalist Party'.[88] For his northern colleagues the *coup de grâce* was Lloyd George's ill-fated partition scheme in the summer of 1916. All bar O'Donnell publicly disavowed the proposals. Bishop Joseph MacRory of Down and Connor, McKenna and McHugh sent messages of support to an anti-exclusion meeting in Omagh, one of several in the north-west, on 7 June. For McKenna, partition was simply 'unthinkable' and 'repugnant to every patriotic Irishman no matter what his political views'.[89] The Irish Party leadership pinned its hopes on gaining acceptance for the proposals at a representative nationalist convention in St Mary's Hall, Belfast, on 23 June. Redmond sought Logue's views on the composition of the convention and requested a meeting with the Ulster bishops. Fearing 'a project to cut off Ulster except Cavan, Monaghan and Donegal', Logue arranged a meeting on 16 June in Dublin, where it would attract less attention.[90] The bishops insisted that a plebiscite be held in each excluded county at the end of the war, a proposal to which Redmond would not agree. The extent of the breach between the Ulster prelates and the party was captured in a frank letter from Bishop McHugh, writing from Dublin on 19 June, to Alderman James McCarron, which was published in *The Derry Journal*:

---

88   Fogarty to Redmond, 3 June 1915, Redmond papers, MS 15188/5, NLI.
89   *The Derry Journal*, 9 June 1916.
90   Logue to Bishop of Down and Connor, 7 June 1916, Logue papers, Arch/9/3/1/1, OFMLA; Logue to Redmond, 11 June 1916, Redmond papers, MS 15201/9, NLI.

As Irishmen, the bishops cannot but regard with feelings of deep regret the admission of the principle of a divided Ireland ... But what causes more alarm to the bishops than the voluntary surrender of the National ideal is the perilous position in which religion and Catholic education would be placed were those proposals, so imperfectly understood by the public, reduced to practice. If the provision is only temporary ... why is a New Executive to be established in Belfast with all the machinery of an independent body ... It is said that these are not the proposals of the Irish Party. I grant they are not. But I say to stand up in defence of them, to suggest the acceptance of them, is just as bad as to be branded with the dishonourable reputation of having fathered them.[91]

Despite episcopal repudiation of the Lloyd George proposals, Devlin's supporters ensured that they were approved at the Belfast convention. This pyrrhic victory inflicted irreparable damage on the Irish Party. The nightmare scenario of a local Ulster settlement led Logue to declare famously that it would be 'infinitely better to remain as we are for fifty years to come, under English rule, than to accept these proposals'.[92] His was a new spin on the well-worn three-word creed: Ulster says no.

---

91   *The Derry Journal*, 21 June 1916. On this episode see Phoenix, *Northern Nationalism*, pp. 28–33.
92   ICD, 1917, p. 517; *The Derry Journal*, 21 June 1916.

10

'Neither Whigs, Tories, nor party politicians'? The Church of Ireland and the Ulster crisis, 1910–14

Andrew Scholes

Alvin Jackson has warned that the 'great moral questions' raised by the third Home Rule bill crisis are 'incapable of definitive resolution' and are best left to 'priests and philosophers rather than the historian'.[1] Through their involvement in the events of this period, however, the priests – of all churches – themselves contributed to any moral complexity. In this context, if the historian has a job, it is to try to explain, where possible, the motives and actions of the 'priests' – which, for the purposes of this essay, belong to the Church of Ireland.

Church of Ireland opposition to the third Home Rule bill was unsurprising from an institution that had vociferously opposed the first and second bills (of 1886 and 1893 respectively), and which could, arguably, be seen as the Irish Unionist party at prayer, certainly among southern unionists. The Church of Ireland was, in 1911, the largest Protestant Church in Ireland, with its adherents making up thirteen per cent of the population, compared to the ten per cent who were Presbyterian. Significantly, the vast majority of Protestants in

---

1   A. Jackson, *Home Rule: an Irish history* (London, 2003), p. 141.

the three southern provinces were members of the Church of Ireland; in Ulster, the Church of Ireland was slightly outnumbered by the Presbyterian Church, with twenty-three per cent of the population as opposed to the twenty-six per cent who were Presbyterians.

Following the 1910 general elections, a Liberal government dependent upon the nationalist Irish Party for a parliamentary majority was returned to power. The constitutional safeguard against Irish Home Rule provided by the House of Lords was removed by the Parliament Act of 1911, and in 1912 the third Home Rule bill was introduced. In response, the Church of Ireland (to paraphrase A. T. Q. Stewart) mobilised to prevent the walls of Jericho falling.[2] Unsurprisingly, considering the demographic make-up of the church, this opposition was initially characterised by its all-Ireland nature. This essay will explore how – through the church's support for the 'Solemn League and Covenant' signed by unionists around Ulster in September 1912 and the Ulster Volunteer Force (UVF) – the 'Walls of Jericho' increasingly came to be identified with protecting Ulster, instead of all of Ireland, from Home Rule, and how the church in the north came to justify and defend its involvement in Ulster unionist militancy.

'Our church is the Church of Ireland': the 1912 General Synod

The General Synod, modelled on the Westminster parliament as it existed in 1870, is the supreme legislative authority of the Church of Ireland.[3] Composed of an upper house (the House of Bishops) and a lower house (the House of Representatives made up of two lay members for each clerical member), the General Synod's annual meetings at this time were usually given over to discussions or votes concerning matters pertaining solely to the church – amendments to

---

2   A. T. Q. Stewart, *The Ulster Crisis* (London, 1967), p. 25.
3   D. Ó Corráin, *Rendering to God and Caesar: the Irish churches and the two states in Ireland, 1949–73* (Manchester, 2006), p. 8; J. L. B. Deane, *Church of Ireland Handbook: a guide to the organisation of the Church* (Dublin, 1962), p. 146.

its constitution, changes in doctrine, articles, rites and rubrics, and consideration of the reports of the various committees and boards elected by the synod.[4] On 16 April 1912, however, the Church of Ireland held a specially convened General Synod to consider the impact of Home Rule upon Ireland in general and the church itself in particular – as it had done in 1886 and 1893 in response to the first and second Home Rule bills. The 1912 General Synod provides a valuable insight into what motivated the Church of Ireland, at this corporate, governmental level, to oppose the third Home Rule bill.

Before the meeting, a special sub-committee had been established to compose a series of resolutions to be voted upon at the General Synod, explaining the church's rejection of Home Rule. The sub-committee was carefully balanced between northern and southern sections of the church, including six bishops – the two archbishops, two bishops representing northern dioceses and two bishops representing southern dioceses.[5] The first resolution, moved by the archbishop of Dublin, Joseph Peacocke, affirmed the church's 'unswerving allegiance to the legislative Union'. He stressed the non-party-political nature of the church's stand – a point that had also been made by the primate, John Baptist Crozier, in his opening address to the synod. For Crozier, a native of Cavan, Home Rule was viewed through the lenses of a self-confessed 'patriotic' Irishman; for him, Ireland was as dear to the members of the Church of Ireland as to the 'so-called nationalists'.[6]

This rejection of Home Rule out of some deep-seated sense of Irish identity and a concern for all of Ireland reflected, in part, the Church of Ireland's self-perception as *the* Irish national church, as

---

4   *Ibid.*, p. 8.
5   Minutes of the House of Bishops, 16 January 1912, Representative Church Body library, Dublin (RCB); Minutes of the Standing Committee of the General Synod, 18 January 1912, RCB.
6   *Newsletter*, 17 April 1912; *Belfast Weekly Telegraph*, 20 April 1912.

the one church able to trace its historical lineage back to St Patrick and the ancient Irish church. In the words of one contributor to the Church of Ireland conference in Belfast in 1910, 'we are Irishmen, our Church is the Church of Ireland, and we are proud of the fact'.[7] The geographical distribution of the Church of Ireland contributed to this sense of Irishness, leading the archbishop of Dublin to claim in 1910 that the church's parochial system meant she occupied the whole country with her organisation.[8]

The result of the Church of Ireland's self-perception as the Irish church, and its demographic make-up, was the kind of all-Ireland brand of unionism espoused at the 1912 General Synod. The first resolution was a continuation of the rhetoric employed by many in the Church of Ireland since Home Rule had returned to the political agenda in 1910. At this stage of the third Home Rule crisis, there was no real desire among the Church of Ireland leadership or membership in Ulster to pursue some form of separate action for the province. This attitude was well summed up by Crozier, when, as bishop of Down, he told the 1910 Down diocesan synod that devotion to the union and loyalty to their fellow churchmen in the south of Ireland 'was not because they loved England only, but because they loved Ireland more'.[9]

The second resolution, moved by the provost of Trinity College, combined an economic and religious argument against Home Rule. The resolution proposed that Ireland's prosperity and industry was dependent upon the union and that Home Rule would 'unrest [sic]' Ireland's 'advance' by placing the progressive element in society under the unprogressive element. The resolution also stated that the property of the Church of Ireland, and Protestant civil and religious liberties, would not be safe under a parliament 'in which we should

---

7   *Newsletter*, 12 October 1910.
8   *Ibid.*
9   *Ibid.*, 4 November 1910.

be outnumbered by men who are dominated by traditions and aspirations wholly different from our own'.[10]

The supposed threat to Church of Ireland property was a commonly expressed fear. For John Henry Bernard, bishop of Ossory and Ferns, speaking in 1911, the chief danger of Home Rule was an 'act of spoliation', transferring Church of Ireland land and property to the Catholic Church. Bernard argued that Westminster had confirmed the Church of Ireland's rightful claim to its property when the church was disestablished. It would be a 'monstrous injustice' for this promise to be reversed by 'any local Parliament sitting in Dublin'.[11] Charles Frederick D'arcy, bishop of Down, articulated similar sentiments at his own diocesan synod a few weeks later, claiming the papal-directed intolerance he envisaged under Home Rule would see the Church of Ireland's 'prized possessions and financial resources' being placed in 'imminent danger', coming under threat from a government 'dominated by Roman influence'.[12]

Bernard and D'arcy's belief in a rapacious and ruthlessly acquisitive Catholic Church gives some idea of how widely held was the fear of the Catholic Church within the Church of Ireland. In 1911 the *Newsletter* described D'arcy as a theologian who 'held aloof from either extreme'; upon his death in 1938, *The Times* painted him as having been one 'to whom the via media seemed the way of truth and wisdom'.[13] Bernard, meanwhile, was distrusted by conservative laymen due to his advocacy of certain 'up-to-date' textbooks for the Divinity school; his elevation to the episcopacy in 1911 was opposed by an anti-ritualist grouping within the church.[14] However, clergy like D'arcy and Bernard believed, with the evangelicals, that the Catholic

---

10   *Ibid.*, 17 April 1912; *Weekly Telegraph*, 20 April 1912.
11   *The Irish Times*, 22 September 1911.
12   *Weekly Telegraph*, 4 November 1911.
13   *Newsletter*, 29 March 1911; *The Times*, 2 February 1938.
14   N. J. D. White, *John Henry Bernard, Archbishop of Dublin: Provost of Trinity College, Dublin. A short memoir* (Dublin, 1928), p. 11; *The Irish Times*, 29 July 1911.

Church posed a threat to Protestant civil and religious liberties. The religious argument against Home Rule represented the mainstream of Irish Protestant opinion and in the Church of Ireland was held by all shades of theological opinion and by those in the south and west as well as Ulster.

The alleged threat to Church of Ireland land and property under Home Rule was one aspect of the wider religious argument against Home Rule. The repeated cry was that Home Rule would mean 'Rome rule'; the fear was that by granting the majority Catholic population their desire for an Irish parliament, the civil and religious liberties of the Protestant minority would be threatened. By virtue of their position as 'spokesmen' of a church, clergy and bishops were well placed to articulate a belief in the supposed malevolent influence the Catholic Church would exercise in a Home Rule Ireland.

When the ecclesiastical concern over *Ne Temere* coincided with the political threat of Home Rule in the form of the McCann case, little encouragement was needed for Protestants to confirm their long-standing suspicions of the Catholic Church. Agnes McCann, who attended Townsend Street Presbyterian church in Belfast, and her husband, a Catholic, had been told by the local priest that their marriage was invalid in light of the *Ne Temere* decree. Mrs McCann refused to remarry in a Catholic ceremony, and eventually her husband left her, taking their two children with him.[15] Issued in 1907, *Ne Temere* declared marriage between a Catholic and non-Catholic to be valid only if the ceremony was carried out by a Catholic priest. Additionally, it was widely believed (albeit incorrectly) that the decree imposed a requirement that the children of such a mixed marriage must be raised as Catholics and therefore raised the spectre of demographic decline for Irish Protestants if the decree was enforced.

---

15   A. Megahey, 'God will defend the right', in D. G. Boyce and A. O'Day (eds), *Defenders of the Union* (London, 2001), p. 166.

The Protestant churches reacted swiftly to the McCann case. In January 1911 mass meetings were held in Dublin and Belfast to protest against *Ne Temere*; both were addressed by the great and good of Irish unionism, including the two Church of Ireland archbishops.[16] The reaction of the Church of Ireland to the McCann case provided a model for its later involvement in the Home Rule crisis. All levels of the church expressed opposition in various ways. The House of Bishops appointed a sub-committee to draft a resolution condemning *Ne Temere*, a resolution passed at the 1911 General Synod and subsequently reproduced in local papers and parish magazines.[17] In the local parish church, opposition to *Ne Temere* was expressed through sermons, or resolutions passed by general vestries. For example, in Holywood the decree was labelled an 'outrage upon morality, a menace to liberty, an insult to the Protestant churches, and as calculated to stir up social and domestic discord in this country'.[18] St Matthias' in Dublin copied its resolution to the lord lieutenant, prime minister, chief secretary and leader of the opposition.[19]

The third resolution at the 1912 General Synod was moved by D'arcy, the bishop of Down, and affirmed a desire to maintain Ireland's union with the imperial 'mother country'. D'arcy believed the best interests of Ireland would be served, not by having its own parliament, but instead by retaining the link with the imperial parliament that indirectly controlled so much of Britain's Empire.[20] This imperial argument against Home Rule was given sustenance before the General Synod by events such as Empire Day and the

---

16 *Weekly Telegraph*, 14 January 1911; *The Irish Times*, 31 January 1911.
17 Minutes of the House of Bishops, 17 November 1910, RCB; *The Irish Times*, 26 April 1911; see Donnybrook church magazine, April 1911, p. 246.25, RCB, for an example of a local church using the parish magazine to reproduce the House of Bishops' resolution against *Ne Temere*.
18 *County Down Spectator and Ulster Standard*, 28 April 1911.
19 St Matthias' Vestry minute book, 21 April 1911, p. 44.5.4, RCB.
20 *Newsletter*, 17 April 1912; *Weekly Telegraph*, 20 April 1912.

coronation of George V. Church services held to mark these events were often very well attended; Church of Ireland clergy sat on organising committees planning coronation day celebrations and select vestries passed resolutions affirming 'loyal devotion' to the new king.[21] Unionism was celebrated in general terms through the elevation of the British Empire's worth – in Enniskillen parish church the dean of Clogher claimed the coronation represented all that the British Empire stood for: 'belief in God; the glory of true liberty; the freedom of every man to worship according to the dictates of his conscience'. The coronation allowed them to 'rejoice' that they were 'loyal citizens' of this Empire.[22]

If the coronation confirmed, for the Church of Ireland, Ireland's imperial identity, it also served to reinforce the church's own self-perception as forming part of the British Empire. For John Henry Bernard, the coronation united the Irish church with other churches in the Anglican communion. Reflecting his high-church leanings, Bernard urged Archbishop Crozier not to sanction a coronation service that did not use the word 'altar', as this would differentiate the Irish coronation service from those in other Anglican churches. Bernard consciously used political language to enforce his point: 'I hope that you will not insist upon Home Rule in such a matter, for we all want to be Unionists in things ecclesiastical as in things civil.'[23]

Such enthusiastic celebration of imperial occasions was a common feature of the cultural and political landscape in Britain in the early twentieth century, and was shared by sister churches throughout the Empire, such as the Australian Anglican Church.[24] Events such as

---

21 Muckno Vestry minute book, 30 May 1911, MIC/151/D/2, Public Record Office of Northern Ireland (PRONI).
22 *Fermanagh Times*, 29 June 1911.
23 Bernard to Crozier, 9 April 1911, Peacocke papers, MIC/87, PRONI.
24 See R. Withycombe, 'Australian Anglicans and imperial identity, 1900–1914', *Journal of Religious History*, vol. 25, no. 3 (October 2001), p. 301.

Empire Day and the coronation may have reinforced the 'common bond of an "imagined community" inhabiting a vast and far flung empire', and provided the Church of Ireland with a sense of status borne from a belief that it – and Ireland – formed an integral part of the moral, spiritual and civilising force of the Empire.[25] A fear that this imperial identity would be lost in a Home Rule Ireland partly motivated the church's enthusiastic participation in Irish unionism. As Crozier put it in his opening address to the 1912 General Synod, Irishmen were 'freemen of the greatest Empire on which the sun has ever shone', but Home Rule would surrender this 'national greatness' and turn Ireland into a 'petty province of England … a paid tributary … an appendage or a colony of the imperial crown'.[26]

The resolutions presented to the General Synod received a warm welcome and appeared to reflect the mood of the church – 397 of the 402 members present voted in favour. Further evidence that the 1912 General Synod was representative of wider opinion in the church is shown by the fact that it was held after a large number of parishes had held their annual meetings (general vestries) and used these to pass their own resolutions against Home Rule. These resolutions tended to stress the representative nature of general vestries. For example, in Limavady the general vestry passed a resolution stating that the parish, 'representing over 1,000 persons', believed Home Rule would destroy 'civil and religious liberty, imperil the property of the church, bring about civil strife, and lead to the disruption of the Empire'.[27] The impression that general vestries were perceived as vehicles for articulating Protestant opposition to Home Rule was strengthened by the forwarding of resolutions to prominent politicians. St Thomas' in south Belfast received a handwritten letter from Edward Carson

---

25   J. English, 'Empire Day in Britain, 1904–1958', *Historical Journal,* vol. 49, no. 1 (2006), p. 249.
26   *Newsletter,* 17 April 1912; *Weekly Telegraph,* 20 April 1912.
27   *Newsletter,* 27 April 1912.

thanking the vestry for 'their emphatic protest against Home Rule'.[28]

The implicit assumption in the passing of the vestry and General Synod resolutions was that the structure of the Church of Ireland offered Irish Anglicans a 'vote' on Home Rule, otherwise denied to them by the government. An *Irish Times* editorial on the 1912 General Synod pointed out that the synod represented the Church of Ireland and therefore protested against Home Rule as it would harm the church's 'power for good'. The synod, however, *also* represented the views of half a million Irish people and, as a result, protested against Home Rule as it would 'arrest national progress and subordinate the progressive to the unprogressive elements of the community'.[29]

Like the Presbyterian anti-Home Rule convention, which had a Scottish and English nonconformist audience in mind, the Church of Ireland general and diocesan synods were intended to speak to an audience not solely confined to their own members.[30] The unionist press repeatedly stressed the representative nature of the general vestries, diocesan and general synods, and expressed a hope that 'English radicals' would be silenced by the arguments put forward. Following the 1912 General Synod, the *Newsletter* hoped those English Anglicans who supported Home Rule would instead listen to the 'earnest appeal of their brethren in Ireland'.[31]

Clearly, the anti-Home Rule tenor of the specially convened General Synod met with approval from the majority of synod members and the unionist press in Ireland. A vocal challenge to the dominant position was, however, mounted both at the synod

---

28   Vestry minute book, St Thomas', 18 April 1912, ,CR/1/36/D/4, PRONI; also see Vestry minute book, Trinity Church, 11 April 1912, CR/1/3/5/2, PRONI and Vestry minute book, Willowfield, 12 April 1912 (private possession), for examples of resolutions against Home Rule forwarded to Carson and Andrew Bonar Law.
29   *The Irish Times*, 17 April 1912.
30   G. Walker, 'The Irish Presbyterian anti-Home Rule convention of 1912', *Studies*, vol. 86, no. 341 (Spring 1997), pp. 71, 73–4.
31   *Newsletter*, 17 April 1912.

and in the letters page of *The Irish Times*. Opposition centred on James Owen Hannay, rector of Westport and the leading Home Rule clergyman in the Church of Ireland, and a coterie of southern laymen including Hutchinson Poe and Walter Kavanagh, who were in regular contact before the synod. In his speech to the 1912 General Synod, Hannay opposed the first resolution affirming allegiance to the union. Although he disliked the third Home Rule bill, he believed the synod's resolution was asking the church to oppose *any* Home Rule bill, a position from which he 'absolutely and totally dissented'. Walter Kavanagh used his speech at the synod to lament the turning of the synod hall into a 'political debating chamber'.[32] In the days following the General Synod, *The Irish Times* published a number of letters critical of the synod's political nature from churchmen anxious that the church adhere to strict neutrality. This correspondence tended to cast doubt on the jeremiads concerning the future of the Church of Ireland under Home Rule, or questioned the wisdom of discussing politics at the synod.[33]

The dissentient voices heard at the synod, while vocal and articulate, were not representative of the Church of Ireland as a whole. The overwhelming majorities recorded in support of the various resolutions suggest that substantial support for the opposing view was wishful thinking. The General Synod remained the main representative body for articulating the views of the Church of Ireland at a corporate level and would be expected to reflect divergences of opinion on participation in politics if they existed. A more representative position on the efficacy of the church's involvement in politics was given by the bishop of Kilmore when endorsing the first resolution at the 1912 General Synod. He claimed that as 'the tidal wave or the forest fire or the volcanic eruption did not mean politics to those who

---

32 *The Freeman's Journal*, 17 April 1912.
33 *The Irish Times*, 18, 19 April 1912.

were endangered by it ... so they felt with regard to the matter which brought them together that day'. Any grievance that did exist was on the 'side of the loyalists, both secular and clerical'.[34] This defence of the church's involvement in the Home Rule debate, as being somehow above the sordid nature of party politics, was emphasised in a letter to *The Irish Times* by a Dublin clergyman, Canon J. W. Tristam. He asserted that representatives at the 1912 General Synod had not acted in a party-political matter as they were 'neither Whigs, Tories, nor party politicians: but we may be allowed to judge and act when we consider our religion and liberties menaced'.[35]

The 1912 General Synod was seen as a potent demonstration of Church of Ireland, and more generally, Irish unionist opposition to Home Rule. The Church of Ireland, corporately, from archbishop to select vestry, had expressed opposition to Home Rule, for a mixture of religious, economic and imperial reasons; the church was pledged, in her own opinion, to a non-party-political stand in the interest of all of Ireland. The apparent unity within the Church of Ireland over opposition to Home Rule was, however, soon to be threatened by the Ulster Covenant and the formation of the Ulster Volunteer Force.

To shrink from no sacrifice: the Church of Ireland and Ulster Day

Ulster Day – 28 September 1912 – was the largest and most ambitious unionist demonstration of the entire Home Rule period. The *Church of Ireland Gazette* described the scene in Belfast on that day as 'unforgettable', claiming 'Belfast people are accustomed to flying the flag, but never before was anything like this seen'.[36] The events of the day were intended to demonstrate to the British government the unalterable determination of the great mass of Ulster Protestants to resist Home Rule. The day was to culminate with the signing of

---

34 *Newsletter*, 17 April 1912.
35 *The Irish Times*, 19 April 1912.
36 *Church of Ireland Gazette*, 4 October 1912.

a document, the 'Solemn League and Covenant', to which unionists around Ulster would put their name. The Covenant decried Home Rule as being disastrous to the material well-being of Ireland, subversive of religious liberty, a threat to citizenship and a danger to the unity of the Empire. As a result of these many dangers, the Covenant pledged its signatories, in humble reliance, to stand together in resisting Home Rule. The Covenant further promised that its signatories would refuse to recognise the authority of a Home Rule parliament.[37]

The Covenant certainly appealed to its target audience. 'Bowler-hatted stewards struggled to regulate the flow of men eager to sign', with ultimately 471,414 men and women signing the Covenant or the associated Women's Declaration.[38] Ulster Day was a marked unionist propaganda triumph, brilliantly planned by James Craig, who ensured that the tools of a nascent mass media were on hand to record the centrepiece event of the day – Carson's signing of the Covenant. This event, so important in Ulster unionist image-making and symbolism, was filmed for a wider British and country audience.[39] Its planners, however, hoped Ulster Day would be seen as more than a well-executed propaganda triumph. With its implicit threat of violence, the Covenant suggested Ulster unionists could not be persuaded or coerced into a Home Rule Ireland.

The Church of Ireland – and indeed the other Protestant churches – *mattered* to the Ulster unionist leadership in making Ulster Day a success. The Protestant churches were actively courted, with the result that Ulster Day would be marked by 'solemn religious services' in each 'convenient locality'.[40] The Ulster Unionist Council also established a clerical sub-committee to help plan events, composed

---

37 R. McNeill, *Ulster's Stand for Union* (London, 1922), pp. 105–6.
38 J. Bardon, *A History of Ulster* (Belfast, 2001), p. 438.
39 A. Jackson, 'Unionist myths, 1912–1985', *Past and Present*, no. 136 (1992), pp. 164–85.
40 Ulster Day committee minute book, 14 Aug. 1912, Ulster Unionist Council papers, D/1327/2/7, PRONI; *Weekly Telegraph*, 24 August 1912.

of, among others, the Dublin-born dean of Belfast, the Presbyterian moderator and the Methodist president. Organising committees were established in towns and cities around the province to decide such practical issues as where the Covenant should be signed and the arrangements for Ulster Day church services.

Church of Ireland clergy were often prominent figures on these organising committees, while many preached sermons, made speeches endorsing the Ulster Covenant and held Ulster Day services in their churches. In the weeks leading up to 28 September, the *Newsletter* published four lists outlining where Ulster Day services would be held. Of the 368 services advertised, forty-nine per cent were to be held in Church of Ireland churches, with thirty-five per cent in Presbyterian churches.[41] It is likely the Church of Ireland held more Ulster Day services as a result of its strength vis-à-vis the Presbyterian Church in the west of the province.

Clerical endorsement of Ulster Day confirmed the growing incorporation of unionism into the life of the parish church that had been ongoing since the Liberal Party returned to power in 1910. Clergy were keen to act as representatives of a political party, devoting time and energy to attending unionist meetings, making speeches, chairing various committees and generally providing an important leadership role 'on the ground'. Many clergy had campaigned for unionist candidates in the 1910 general elections. The involvement of the rector of Lisburn cathedral, Canon William Pounden, in the campaigns of James Craig and his brother Charles was indicative of the campaigning role played by Church of Ireland clergy in the 1910 election campaigns. Lisburn bordered two constituencies, East Down and South Antrim, contested by James Craig and Charles Craig respectively for the unionists. Pounden spoke at unionist association meetings, Orange Order gatherings and unionist rallies, extolling

---

41   *Newsletter*, 14, 17, 19, 23 September 1912.

the virtues of unionism and the Craig brothers, and lamenting the effect of Home Rule on Ireland.[42] The prominent role played by Church of Ireland clergy in 'grass-roots' unionism is illustrated by the fact that by 1912, forty-five of the 331 Unionist Clubs in Ireland had a Church of Ireland clergyman as either president or secretary. This compared with twenty-two clergy from other denominations holding similar posts.[43]

D'arcy was the first bishop to publicly support Ulster Day. D'arcy, the bishop of Down and Connor and Dromore, the most populous diocese in the Church of Ireland, wrote to the local press at the end of August, welcoming the intention to hold Ulster Day services and declaring that Ulster unionists should 'humble' themselves 'before God' and pray 'for the final overthrow of a policy which can bring nothing but strife and misery to our country'.[44]

D'arcy's call for prayer on Ulster Day was followed by a 'pastoral' issued by the five bishops of Ulster dioceses. The pastoral referred to the ongoing 'great crisis' in the religious and political history of 'our beloved native land'. Constancy and earnestness in prayer were, therefore, required so that God may 'overrule all things to the glory of His name and the greater good of His church and people'. To facilitate such prayer, special services of 'humiliation', confession of sin and intercession for Ireland's political leaders were announced for 22 September.[45] While such intercessory services were presented as an opportunity for the Church of Ireland in Ulster to wait upon God in prayer, in reality they represented a form of worship necessitated (in the bishops' opinion) by political circumstances. It is not surprising, therefore, that these services were used to rally the faithful and

---

42 See *Weekly Telegraph*, 1 January 1910; *Newsletter*, 28 January 1910; *Lisburn Standard*, 8, 29 January, 26 November, 2, 3 December, 1910.
43 Printed list of Unionist Clubs of Ireland, Ulster Unionist Council papers, D/1327/1/12, PRONI.
44 *Newsletter*, 26 August 1912.
45 *Church of Ireland Gazette*, 6 September 1912.

challenge the doubtful ahead of Ulster Day. D'arcy sent a public letter to the clergy in his diocese interpreting the 22 September services of intercession as an opportunity to prepare for Ulster Day, claiming 'there can surely be no better preparation for the great decision of the 28th than that the first day of that historic week should be thus set apart'.[46] The majority of clergy shared this interpretation of the intercessory services – for example, the dean of Dromore told his congregation on 22 September that Ulster Day was not merely a 'theatrical' gesture or bluff, but a sign that Protestants in Ulster would 'shrink from no sacrifices' in defending their 'civil and religious liberty'. In Newtownards, 'every loyal son' attending the parish church on 22 September was encouraged to sign the Covenant.[47]

In some ways it is not surprising that the Church of Ireland in Ulster supported Ulster Day. The Covenant expressed opposition to Home Rule for similar religious, imperial and economic reasons to those the Church of Ireland had recently articulated at its specially convened General Synod. The Covenant, however, went a step further, in pledging its signatories to resist Home Rule by any means possible, which appeared to imply some form of unconstitutional action. The bishop of Derry justified resistance to the state by arguing there was a limit to obedience: '"Bond servant, obey your master in all things", would be an utterly demoralising mandate unless checked and controlled by the influence of much higher laws.' Unionists should now 'appeal to a greater person than Caesar' and invoke 'the protection, the deliverance, the vindication of the King of Kings'.[48]

D'arcy resolved the dilemma of signing a document that appeared to pledge its signatories to resist the state if Home Rule became a reality by seeking advice from an old parishioner, Lord MacNaghten, a leading law lord who also happened to be an Ulster unionist.

---

46 *Ibid.*, 13 September 1912.
47 *Newtownards Chronicle*, 28 September 1912.
48 *Weekly Telegraph*, 28 September 1912.

MacNaghten told D'arcy that from a legal point of view, 'Ulster men are perfectly justified in signing the Covenant because the constitution is suspended'.[49] As a result of this advice, for D'arcy and those who followed his lead, resistance to the government was justifiable, as if, as MacNaghten claimed, the constitution was suspended, any attempt by the government to usurp Protestant civil and religious liberties was not lawful. MacNaghten's blessing, D'arcy later recalled, was of 'decisive importance' in encouraging the leading clergy in Down and Connor and Dromore to sign the Covenant.[50]

In addition to the extra-constitutional action implied by the Covenant, Ulster Day also seemed to suggest some form of separate treatment for the area – surely anathema to a church that had recently pledged opposition to Home Rule partly on the basis of its claim as the patriotic, all-Ireland church. In response, D'arcy claimed, in his Ulster Day sermon, that Ulster Day was intended to benefit Protestants in the south and west of Ireland and was not a 'selfish endeavour to keep privilege, or even security for ourselves'.[51] Archbishop Crozier took 2 Samuel 12:10 as the text for his Ulster Day sermon, a passage in which 'Joab speaks as a devoted patriot ready to do or die for the safety of his native land'. Crozier called for God to save Ireland from a 'patriotism' that allowed cattle houghing and murder – such behaviour 'prostituted' real patriotism. True, God-given patriotism was a readiness to 'suffer the loss of all things for their native land'. It was in this spirit that Ulster unionists had acted, calling on God to help them prevent the 'degradation of their native land and the dismemberment of the great Empire'. Those who signed the Covenant were 'brave men struggling for civil and religious

49 C. F. D'arcy, *Adventures of a Bishop* (London, 1934), pp. 189–90; also see Crozier's account of D'arcy's reasoning in Crozier to Davidson, 17 March 1914, Davidson papers, vol. 389/241–4, Lambeth Palace library (LPL).
50 D'arcy, *Adventures of a Bishop*, pp. 189–90.
51 *The Northern Whig*, 30 September 1912.

liberty'.[52] Thus, Crozier represented Ulster Day as a patriotic protest on behalf of all the people of Ireland against Home Rule.

Such arguments did not appear to convince southern bishops to sanction either services of intercession or religious services on 28 September in the southern provinces. Lord Bessborough, a southern layman, wrote to John Henry Bernard, the future archbishop of Dublin, agreeing with Bernard's opinion that it would be a mistake for the church to 'take any definite political step or unite itself in any way with any political party'.[53] Reasonably enough, Bernard believed Ulster Day entailed support for an exclusively *Ulster*-focused strategy. Similar sentiments were expressed by the bishop of Cork, who believed Ulster Day should not be observed by the Church of Ireland in the south as he was 'sure that the great majority of the laity in the south would strongly object to being in any way identified with the Ulster Movement'.[54] The archbishop of Dublin was able to confirm that '*All* the (southern) bishops are glad we are not taking action that would bring us into line with the Ulster movement and meeting on the 28th.'[55]

It is worth noting that this private opposition was not a signal of any weakening on the Home Rule issue. A number of southern bishops used their diocesan synod speeches, soon after Ulster Day, to lambast the government and criticise Home Rule.[56] Rather, their unease with Ulster Day was with what it foretold – that Ulster may indeed choose to go it alone, to get some form of exclusion from Home Rule for all or part of the province. The involvement of their

---

52 *Fermanagh Times*, 3 October 1912.

53 Lord Bessborough to Bernard, 31 August 1912, J. H. Bernard papers, MSS 52782/8–9, British Library (BL).

54 Peacocke to Bernard, 5 September 1912, Bernard papers, MSS 52782/13–4, BL.

55 *Ibid.*, 13 September 1912, Bernard papers, MSS 52782/15–6, BL.

56 See Peacocke's speech to the Dublin diocesan synod, *The Irish Times*, 15 October 1912 and the bishop of Meath's diocesan synod speech, Bernard papers, 25 October 1912, BL.

northern brethren in Ulster Day suggested to the southern bishops that the most populous part of the church was now pursuing a predominantly Ulster-focused opposition to Home Rule. The fear was that partition would rob southern church members of the support of their more numerous northern counterparts. If southern Protestants were abandoned, perhaps the prophecies of Protestant persecution under Home Rule, preached by the church, would come to fruition – a point made privately by the archbishop of Dublin to Bernard before Ulster Day:

> We have to consider the position of our clergy and people outside Ulster and the serious results that might follow, if, in consequence of our appearing in any way to identify the church and its people with the decision of the Belfast meeting, the ancient Hibernians and the Land League in revenge for the Belfast movement were to raise hostility against them throughout the 3 other provinces.[57]

The kind of private opposition shown by the southern bishops to the church's involvement in Ulster Day was repeated publicly by a small number of clergy in Ulster. Despite being a unionist and an Orangeman, John Frederick MacNeice, rector of St Nicholas' in Carrickfergus, refused to endorse the Covenant. Recognising the militancy implicit in the Covenant's terms, MacNeice held that the church must fight under 'Christ's banner, and in Christ's way, and need not borrow the weapons of the kingdoms of the world'.[58] He shrank from a policy that, in the last resort, entailed civil war. The rector

---

57 Peacocke to Bernard, 1 September 1912, Bernard papers, MSS 52782/10–12, BL.
58 J. F. MacNeice, *Carrickfergus and its Contacts: some chapters in the history of Ulster* (Carrickfergus, 1928), pp. 72–3. In 1914 MacNeice informed the archbishop of Canterbury: 'I am a Unionist. I am not a Volunteer. I am not a Covenantor.' John Frederick MacNeice to Randall Davidson, 1 April 1914, Davidson papers, vol. 389/309–12, LPL.

of Holy Trinity in Portrush also refused to endorse the Covenant, a stand that drew a private letter of support from Hannay. With characteristically colourful prose, Hannay lambasted his episcopal superiors, asserting that 'no man – were he fifty times a bishop – has a right to identify the cause of Christ with that of loyalist Herodians or nationalist Pharisees'.[59]

As with the political representatives of Ulster unionism, it is difficult to discern whether the Ulster bishops and clergy saw Ulster Day and the increase in militancy as a 'bluff' intended to defeat Home Rule for all of Ireland, or as a sign that preserving Ulster's place in the union was already the best unionists could hope for. What is clear, however, is that publicly the Church of Ireland in the north was committed to following whatever policy the Ulster unionist leadership decided to pursue in opposing Home Rule. As a result, bishops and clergy did not baulk when the UVF was established in 1913.

'That the God of Hosts would go forth with our armies': the Church of Ireland and the Ulster Volunteer Force

In July 1912 James Owen Hannay published a novel entitled *The Red Hand of Ulster*, using his pseudonym George Birmingham. The book was Hannay's attempt to satirise Irish unionist – and Church of Ireland – resistance to Home Rule.[60] It tells the story of an attempted revolution in Ulster, financed by a bored American businessman and led by an array of Irish unionists. Lord Kilmore, the narrator, is an almost bewildered observer of events, sucked into involvement in the putative rebellion by a domineering unionist hostess. The rebellious unionists are drilled by a retired colonel – who also happens to be a member of the Church of Ireland –

---

59 *The Northern Constitution*, 28 September 1912; James Owen Hannay to Revd T. Harvey, 30 September 1912, Hannay papers, MSS 3455/500a, Trinity College Dublin.
60 G. Birmingham, *The Red Hand of Ulster* (London, 1912).

using arms smuggled into Ulster aboard a boat called the *Finola*. Throughout the novel Birmingham used a Church of Ireland rector, called simply 'the Dean', to lampoon the involvement in unionist politics of the Church of Ireland hierarchy. The Dean explained that the 1912 General Synod appeared to be on the side of unionism only because unionism was always right. He argued that political questions involved differences of opinion among 'honest men': 'But all honest men are opposed to Home Rule, which is therefore not a political question.' His flying of the union flag from the church spire signalled the start of the rebellion. Inside the church, he held a service for those who would take part, rifles in hand.

Many Church of Ireland clergy evoked comparisons with Hannay's Dean, welcoming UVF contingents to church services, providing drilling areas in the form of church grounds, and taking an active part in the UVF as Volunteers. Around Ulster, clergy demonstrated their support for the Volunteers in a variety of practical ways – joining auxiliary sections of the UVF,[61] officiating at prize-giving ceremonies,[62] or taking part in fund-raising events.[63] In north Antrim, Rev. William Matchette of Ballintoy 'unreservedly' agreed to allow the UVF the use of his Model T Ford motor car, requesting only that he received 'reasonable compensation for loss or damage'. Matchette agreed to drive for the transport section of the UVF 'when necessary', although he preferred to have a driver assigned.[64] A number of clergy assisted in leading drill practices; others played an

---

61   The rector of Grange headed the nursing corps of his local UVF contingent, *The Ulster Gazette*, 11 October 1913; Rev. M. Hogg acted as a sanitary officer at an inspection of the Keady UVF ambulance corps, *The Ulster Gazette*, 28 March 1914.

62   Canon Clarke presented prizes to the UVF contingent in Dungonnell, *Ballymena Observer*, 20 March 1914.

63   Rev. T. McCreight and his wife won the croquet tournament but lost in the final of the lawn tennis at a UVF fund-raising fete in Ballynahinch, *The Down Recorder*, 3 January 1914.

64   North Antrim UVF papers, 10 January 1914, O'Neill papers, D/1238/3b, PRONI.

active role in the importation or storage of arms.[65] In July 1913 W. B. Stack was identified as a prime mover in the importation of arms into Fermanagh. The RIC county inspector reported:

> At a secret meeting of five delegates of the Ulster Volunteer Movement, held at Florencecourt, the Rev. Mr Stack, organiser, is said to have stated that a number of arms have been received into the County, via Bundoran and Ballyshannon, and brought up to Kesh and Irvinestown by small boats. This is being inquired into.[66]

Stack acted as camp adjutant at a UVF camp in Crom Castle in November, and accompanied Sir George Richardson as he inspected various battalions in Fermanagh.[67] J. Irvine Peacocke, rector of Bangor and a future bishop of Derry and Raphoe, was chaplain to the UVF battalion in Bangor and stored guns from gun-running in April 1914 in the cellar of his rectory.[68] In addition to such practical support for the UVF, clerical patronage was provided by allowing Volunteers to use parochial halls for drilling.[69]

Church of Ireland support for the UVF reflected a more widespread acceptance in church and society of militaristic organisations and hobbies. For example, the Church of Ireland at this time, quite independently of anything happening in the political arena, had a thriving rifle club. This was indicative of a wider enthusiasm in British churches

---

65   For example, Rev. J. G. Pooler, *The Down Recorder*, 3 January 1914; Rev. J. King Irvine, *Lisburn Standard*, 1 January 1914; Rev. A. W. McGarvey and Rev. J. W. Askins, county inspector reports, July 1913, confidential reports to Dublin Castle, CO/904/27/511, National Archives, Kew (NAK).

66   County inspector reports, July 1913, CO/904/27/511, NAK.

67   *Fermanagh Times*, 6 November 1913; 4 December 1913.

68   J. Irvine Peacocke, *Peacocke of Derry and Raphoe: an autobiographical sketch* (Dublin, n.d.), p. 33.

69   For example, at St Thomas' in Belfast, and Lisburn Cathedral; St Thomas' vestry minute book, 11 November 1913, CR/1/36/D/4, PRONI; *Lisburn Standard*, 1 November 1913.

for organisations with a militaristic ethos, such as the Boys' Brigade and Church Lads' Brigade.[70] Bishop D'arcy extolled the virtues of the Church of Ireland Young Men's Society (CIYMS) rifle club at the society's annual meeting in 1913. He believed that every man should be prepared to defend his country and that universal military training would be a great advantage to the 'manhood' of the United Kingdom.[71] Support for the UVF built on a wider culture of Christian militarism and reflected the 'muscular Christianity' that provided fertile ground in the rest of Britain for recruitment at the start of the First World War.[72]

Massed ranks of Volunteers became a familiar sight at Church of Ireland churches throughout 1913 and 1914, providing a potent symbol of the church's support, in Ulster, for the Volunteer movement. These services were often ecumenical affairs, involving clergy from the Church of Ireland and Presbyterian Church in a conscious display of Protestant unity, with acts of worship in Presbyterian and Church of Ireland UVF services following a familiar pattern, using similar hymns and Bible readings.[73] These 'united' services were a common feature of the Church of Ireland's opposition to the third Home Rule bill. Such cooperation built upon closer ties at a leadership level between the two churches; in 1910, for example, the Presbyterian moderator addressed the Church of Ireland conference in a speech that welcomed how the 'two churches were growing together'.[74] Archbishop Crozier, meanwhile, explained to the 1912 Presbyterian convention against Home Rule that the political crisis had 'welded together' the whole Protestant community in Ireland, with the result that an 'overwhelm-

---

70   J. Wolffe, *God and Greater Britain: religion and national life in Britain and Ireland, 1843–1945* (London, 1994), pp. 229–30.

71   *Weekly Telegraph*, 8 February 1913.

72   Wolffe, *God and Greater Britain*, p. 230.

73   Order of service for 1st Battalion South Down Regiment, 8 March 1914, in St Paul's Castlewellan; order of service for 1st Battalion South Down Regiment, 5 April 1914, in Clough Presbyterian church, Seaforde UVF papers, D/1263/4, PRONI.

74   *Newsletter*, 12 October 1910.

ing majority' of Church of Ireland members stand 'with the great mass of our Presbyterian brethren'.[75] At a more local level, the temperance Catch-my-Pal movement, founded by a Presbyterian clergyman, received widespread support within the Church of Ireland.

Such good relations probably aided cooperation between the two churches in opposing Home Rule, although it is possible that, in any case, the threat of Home Rule would have subsumed denominational identities under the overarching unity brought by unionism. The rector of Mary Magdalene (in south Belfast) summed up the neutral, nondenominational aspect of the church's cooperation by telling a united service attended by the Balmoral and Upper Malone Unionist Club that they were brought together on a 'sensible platform' of a 'common Protestantism and a common Unionism'.[76] Such an argument was re-iterated by the RIC county inspector of Antrim, who believed the Home Rule crisis and attendant drilling had 'welded the Protestant churches together by a community of interest and feeling which it would have taken at least a generation under other circumstances to bring about'.[77]

Clerical arguments in defence of the UVF reflected arguments utilised more widely by the Ulster unionist leadership to resolve the 'moral dilemma' of resisting the state: for them, the constitution had been suspended by the Parliament Act, which was the result of a corrupt bargain between liberals and nationalists; the government was not the lawful authority; and there was no mandate for Home Rule without a general election.[78] What clergy could do with more authority than politicians, however, was offer a theological justification for the UVF, and many set about constructing a moral,

---

75   *Ulster Gazette and Armagh Standard*, 3 February 1912.
76   *Weekly Telegraph*, 9 March 1912.
77   County inspector reports, July 1913, CO/904/27/511, NAK.
78   P. Buckland, *Irish Unionism II: Ulster unionism and the origins of Northern Ireland, 1886–1922* (Dublin, 1973), pp. 65–6.

'Christian' defence for Ulster unionist militancy against the criticisms of opponents who claimed loyalist resistance was illegal and reckless. In constructing some form of spiritual or scriptural basis for unionist opposition to Home Rule, a moral framework based on God's providential favour towards unionism was girded to the sometimes unconstitutional nature of Ulster unionist opposition to Home Rule.

In this vein, the bishop of Derry, George Chadwick, argued that it was absurd to claim Christianity taught 'servile obedience' to the government. A number of supposedly suitable examples were chosen to illustrate that the Bible did not enforce such obedience: Moses opposed the Pharaoh, Samuel dethroned King Saul and Elisha anointed Jehu king while Ahab still held power.[79] Chadwick claimed 'no man could really suppose the Christian religion forbade any violence under any circumstances whatever', and asserted that religious and political liberty were 'causes which no Christian should fail to defend'.[80]

The rector of Limavady, R. G. S. King, expressed a widely held confidence in God's favour towards militant Ulster unionism by claiming the UVF was bolstered by a belief 'that the God of Hosts would go forth with our armies'.[81] In a sermon preached to mark the first anniversary of Ulster Day, the dean of Dromore affirmed the righteousness of physical resistance, claiming that God 'will keep us in the struggle and give us deliverance' if the UVF was 'forced' into a civil war. They would fight because it was their 'religious duty' to resist wrong. The dean urged constant prayer and confession of sin in order to realise their strength came from God.[82] This widespread desire for prayer and intercession found expression in a series of prayer meetings held around Ulster throughout 1914.[83] Addressing one such

---

79 *Northern Constitution*, 14 June 1913.
80 *Ibid.*, 4 October 1913.
81 R. G. S. King, *Ulster's Refusal to Submit to a Roman Catholic Parliament, Stated and Justified* (Derry, 1914), p. 21.
82 *Lurgan Mail*, 4 October 1913.
83 For example, at Bangor, Portaferry and Portadown: see *Newsletter*, 9, 18, 21

meeting in Belfast, Rev. George Stephenson presented the old testament figure of Nehemiah as a 'man of prayer', whose faithfulness and patriotism unionists were encouraged to emulate. They must follow God with 'unquestioning devotion and obedience', whether God led them in the 'ways of pleasantness' or to civil war.[84]

Shortly after Ulster Day, a nationalist commentator claimed that 'An Orange sermon will incline [Irish unionists to view themselves] … as a sort of modern Israelites warring against the hosts of Canaan for the possession of the Promised Land.'[85] Certainly, clerical sermons and speeches provided a largely consistent narrative defending and justifying the UVF. This narrative provided clearly defined enemies to Ulster Protestants, in the guise of Irish nationalists, Liberal Party politicians, the papacy and the Catholic Church in Ireland; equally, potential heroes were provided by the leaders of Ulster unionism. Hopes of salvation from Home Rule were sustained by an interpretation of the Irish past in which the Ulster crisis was seen to fit seamlessly into earlier occasions of threats to Protestantism, such as the Siege of Derry and the Williamite war in Ireland. Unsurprisingly, clergymen looked further back, to the Bible, to find in many Old Testament characters examples for Irish Protestants to follow if they hoped to defeat Home Rule (Moses, Joshua and Nehemiah were particular favourites). What lay behind such an, at times, cavalier interpretation of the Bible was a belief that the ultimate source of deliverance lay in the providential blessing of a God benevolent towards Ulster unionism.

By cloaking the UVF with a degree of spiritual vitality, clergy reflected their own religiously motivated worldview and belief in a God who answered the politically motivated prayers of the penitent. In addition, to claim God was in full support of militancy may have

---

February 1914.

84 *Newsletter*, 10 March 1914.

85 F. C. Ormsby, 'Irish unionism', *Irish Review*, October 1912, p. 400.

encouraged support for the UVF among church members who were not convinced by arguments resting on conditional obedience to the state when faced with the apparent inevitability of armed resistance.

Alongside the moral justification lent to the UVF by clergy was a widely expressed desire for restraint on the part of Volunteers. Before Ulster Day a number of clergy had also been sensitive to the militancy implicit in the Covenant's terms. The archdeacon of Dromore encouraged his fellow clergy to sign it only after receiving assurances from James Craig that they could 'conscientiously' subscribe to it.[86] The dean of Belfast, while encouraging his congregation in Belfast cathedral to sign the Covenant, also called on them to pray that God would restrain 'reprehensible acts'. If they approached God in this manner, the dean assured them unionism would enjoy a 'bloodless victory'.[87] Canon Pounden believed the holding of Ulster Day services guaranteed a peaceful demonstration and that the Covenant did not inevitably entail armed resistance.[88] It is possible to see in the pacific interpretation of Ulster Day constructed by a number of clergy a framework with which to justify support for the UVF upon its formation in 1913. For its clerical apologists, the UVF, like the Covenant, would bring stability, strength and unity, and would work to restrain angry passions. At a service in Belfast cathedral attended by 1,300 Volunteers, Rev. T. Collins acknowledged the threat of civil war and the readiness of every Volunteer to sacrifice 'even life itself'. He maintained, however, the importance of discipline and 'implicit obedience to those in authority'. The Covenant and UVF had, he continued, produced a 'quiet' and 'self-possessed' spirit in Ulster, and instead of 'outbreaks of disorder, you have a calm, deliberate preparation'.[89]

---

86   E. D. Atkinson, 'The Covenant', in S. King and S. McMahon (eds.), *Hope and History: eyewitness accounts of life in twentieth-century Ulster* (Belfast, 1996), pp. 33–4.
87   *Newsletter*, 23 September 1912.
88   Lisburn cathedral magazine, September 1912.
89   *Newsletter*, 2 February 1914.

The attitude of Crozier and D'arcy, the leading Ulster-based bishops, towards the Volunteers was a mixture of justification accompanied by calls for restraint. D'arcy became a regular feature at ceremonies to consecrate the colours of UVF regiments, offering prayer or blessing.[90] According to Wilfrid Spender, Crozier was consulted before the Larne gun-running and subsequently attended 'Family Prayers sitting on benches filled temporarily with rifles instead of Bibles'.[91] Writing privately to the archbishop of Canterbury, Crozier emphasised the widespread support for the UVF by pointing to the actions of his own wife, who, as a member of the UVF nursing corps, had recently attended some first-aid classes in Gosford castle. Crozier explained 'these ladies would have been hunting, or playing golf otherwise!'[92]

Alongside such overt support for the Volunteers, both bishops publicly stated a belief that the UVF brought order and stability. D'arcy claimed in a letter to *The Times* that the most 'extraordinary result' of the UVF was its influence in 'controlling passions and preventing riot'.[93] In March 1914 Crozier urged a congregation of over 700 Volunteers to avoid provoking those who differed from them 'even though those men wished to throw Ireland back into the filth of the Slough of Despond'. They needed to be obedient to their leaders and remember that 'defence and not defiance was their motto'.[94]

These calls for restraint suggested that, unlike the Dean in *The Red Hand of Ulster*, the majority of Church of Ireland clergy were not prepared to provoke a rebellion. The calls for restraint can be read in two ways. On the one hand, they may have reflected a conservative,

---

90 *Newtownards Chronicle*, 7 February 1914; *Lisburn Standard*, 6 March, 17 April 1914; *Ballymena Observer*, 8 May 1914.
91 Wilfrid Spender to C. Brett Ingram, 1959, Spender papers, D/1295/2/6, PRONI.
92 Crozier to Davidson, Easter day 1914, Davidson papers, vol. 389/319–26, LPL.
93 *The Times*, 23 April 1914.
94 *Newsletter*, 23 March 1914.

top-down view of the UVF in which the force was only to act at the bidding of the Ulster unionist leadership. Through military rigour, discipline would be established and uncontrolled rioting, with its attendant political damage, prevented.[95] The supposed propaganda value of the UVF motivated clergy to both support the force and urge restraint, as outbreaks of disorder would be detrimental to the Ulster unionist case in England. In this view, gun-running was the crowning glory to the 'defence, not defiance' strategy, ensuring that the government would drop Home Rule or be forced into calling a general election.

It is, however, possible that, on the other hand, clerical calls for restraint reflected a genuine fear regarding the volatility of the rank and file. The fear of disorder drove a number of churches to take out insurance policies against damage caused by 'civil commotion', such as that taken out by Down parish church 'in view of possible riots in connection with the forcing of Home Rule upon the loyalists of Ulster'.[96] If it was feared churches could be damaged by political violence, it is not surprising that clergy exerted what influence they had to 'restrain angry passions'.

At various points in 1914, Crozier and D'arcy privately informed the archbishop of Canterbury of the volatility of the Volunteers and what appeared to them as the real possibility of violence in Ulster.[97] Such private unease, allied to the repeated requests for order from clergy and the civil-commotion insurance policies, could be interpreted as recognition that the UVF was not the malleable tool of the Ulster unionist – or indeed clerical – leadership.

---

95   C. Townshend, *Political Violence in Ireland: government and resistance since 1848* (Oxford, 1983), p. 249.
96   Down vestry minute book, 12 June 1914, , CR/33/DB/2, PRONI.
97   Crozier to Davidson, 4 April 1914, Davidson papers, vol. 389/309–12, LPL; D'arcy to Davidson, 3 May 1914, Davidson papers, vol. 389/327, LPL.

Conclusion

The Church of Ireland's widespread opposition to Home Rule is understandable in the light of the fact that the church's interests were seen to be under genuine threat. There is no doubt that the Church of Ireland sincerely believed Home Rule would prove detrimental both to it as a church, and to Ireland as a whole; as a result, public support for unionism was articulated both at the corporate, governmental level of the General Synod and at the local level of the parish pulpit and general vestry. As expressed at the 1912 General Synod, the Church of Ireland's proud boast that it was *the* Irish national church, and, as such, would pursue an all-Ireland, non-party-political opposition to Home Rule, was to prove premature. Instead, it was the all-Ireland nature of the church's composition that was to prove internally divisive, as the Ulster crisis produced competing views on an Irish settlement within the church.

In supporting Ulster Day and the UVF, the church in Ulster was tied to the increasingly exclusivist strategy adopted by Carson and Craig. At an episcopal level, the exclusion of all or part of the province was a position accepted by D'arcy; Crozier found himself in a more difficult position. He supported the UVF, but rejected Ulster being permanently excluded from Home Rule – a result of his strong belief that to do so would weaken the Church of Ireland and put at risk what he described as the church's 'real stake' in the rest of the country.[98] The position of the majority of southern bishops was best expressed by the bishop of Killaloe at the start of the Great War, who rather provocatively argued that it was a Christian's duty to 'accept and obey' an act of parliament.[99] Following the outbreak of the war, the position of the Church of Ireland in the south was to be most forcefully represented by John Henry Bernard, archbishop of Dublin,

---

98 Crozier to Davidson, 5 August 1914, Davidson papers, vol. 390/72–82, LPL.
99 *Church of Ireland Gazette*, 7 August 1914.

who, fearing partition, came to pursue some form of reconciliation with Redmondite nationalism.

If the Ulster crisis risked fracturing the show of unity expressed at the 1912 General Synod, Ulster unionist militancy also posed problems to otherwise sympathetic clergy and laity in Ulster. In answering the 'great moral questions' posed by the Ulster crisis – namely how to justify pledging to resist the lawfully instituted authorities or the lending of moral and spiritual authority to illegal drilling and importation of arms – clergy resorted to legal arguments based on constitutional theory and, more appropriately, theological arguments resting on conveniently chosen biblical texts or a prayerful expectation that God was on their side. Like Hannay's Dean, many Church of Ireland clergy and bishops in Ulster played a leading role in legitimising and encouraging Ulster unionist militancy. The reality of the church's role in the UVF was, however, more complex than in Hannay's satire. Many clergy – perhaps optimistically, or with a degree of wishful thinking – viewed the UVF as a top-down organisation, which acted as a safety valve for the rank and file and was never actually intended to take up arms.

The ambiguities and complexities in the Volunteers' position as 'loyal rebels' were illustrated by the different armies attending church services around Ulster in 1914. In St Mark's, Newtownards, the year began with the UVF being anointed by Crozier, the leading Anglican churchman in Ireland, and ended with the 12th battalion of the Royal Irish Rifles, camped near Newtownards, attending morning worship.[100] The 'Red hand of Ulster' was not waved in 1914, but this was small consolation, as the potential battlefield of Ulster was replaced by the all-too-real and bloody battlefields of Gallipoli and the Western Front.

---

100 *Newtownards Chronicle*, 24 January & 14 December 1914.

11

Irish Presbyterians and the Ulster Covenant

Laurence Kirkpatrick

The relationship between religion and politics goes back a long way, arguably to Moses' confrontation with pharaoh regarding the release of Israelites from his control,[1] and the experience of Irish Presbyterians also has a long history. While the earliest Presbyterians arrived in Ireland in the late sixteenth century, meaningful numbers of Scottish Presbyterians made the short journey from Ayrshire to Antrim and Down from 1603 with encouragement from the new Stuart monarchy. The 'Plantation of Ulster' scheme accelerated this process and produced the patchwork quilt pattern of settlement that is still a feature of modern Northern Ireland. The Presbyterian Church system came to Ulster with a Scottish army in 1642, following the 1641 uprising. The vanguard of General Munroe's ten Scottish regiments arrived in Carrickfergus from 3 April 1642 and the 'Army Presbytery' was founded shortly afterwards, on Friday 10 June 1642, by five army chaplains and four elders.

The General Assembly of the Presbyterian Church in Ireland was formed in Rosemary Street church, Belfast, on 10 July 1840 by the amalgamation of two Presbyterian bodies: the Seceders, comprising

---

1   Exodus 5:1–2.

141 congregations, and the larger General Synod, comprising 292 congregations. This new body had a membership of 650,000 individuals, or 12.6 per cent of the population of Ireland. The ethos of Presbyterianism, to this day, is democracy. The church is governed by elders, with a local minister (a 'teaching elder' elected by the congregation) chairing a kirk session comprising elders also elected by the congregation. The General Assembly (the supreme court of the church) meets annually in June and is chaired by a moderator (elected annually as a *primus inter pares* by representatives of all the congregations).

Coming from Scotland, though originating in John Calvin's Geneva, Presbyterianism intruded into Ulster in a significant manner in the early seventeenth century. Throughout their history Irish Presbyterians have understood themselves as a people caught between two other groupings on the island: the indigenous Irish who have maintained their Catholic religion, and the ruling Protestants with their Anglicanism. On the stage of Irish history, throughout various scenes and acts, the Presbyterians have often displayed a stubborn independence of mind, sometimes feeling more Irish than British, and at others more British than Irish.

The privileged position of the Church of Ireland, the Anglican Church in Ireland, had long irked Presbyterians. Although not as disadvantaged as Catholics, Presbyterians had resented their status as second-class citizens under the penal laws, especially the Test Act (of 1704) by which they could not take up public appointments unless they agreed to take communion in the Church of Ireland. Similarly, Anglican clergy did not recognise Presbyterian ordination, and therefore Presbyterian marriages were, in the eyes of the established church, invalid and the children of such marriages illegitimate. Throughout the discomforts and grievances of the eighteenth century, many Irish Presbyterians despaired of experiencing peace and prosperity in Ireland, and in their thousands they emigrated to America.

The Protestant ascendancy, while always wanting to keep the Presbyterians in a second-class compartment, felt that it could always count on Presbyterian support in a real crisis, that it could engineer a pan-Protestant alliance against the common Catholic majority. In 1798 this assumption was severely tested when a significant number of liberal Presbyterians opted to rebel against the status quo. The most famous Presbyterian martyrs from that period were James Orr, Henry Joy McCracken and Rev. James Porter. The resultant Act of Union (of 1800) was designed to tie Ireland to Britain and raise Irish living standards, and thereby hopefully to incubate attitudes of loyalty.

While Presbyterians undoubtedly benefited through the rise of industrial Belfast, where they predominated, they were never totally united and deep fissures within the church were exposed by the Home Rule crises of the late nineteenth century – when Prime Minister William Ewart Gladstone introduced the first and second Irish Home Rule bills (in 1886 and 1893 respectively) in the House of Commons – and early twentieth century – when Prime Minister Herbert H. Asquith introduced the third (in 1912).

Nothing melds Irish Presbyterian identity better than the unofficial badge of the church, the burning bush.[2] First used on *The Banner of Ulster*, a Presbyterian newspaper, in June 1842, the original burning bush, in addition to an open Bible, featured several Irish symbols: an Irish wolfhound, a Celtic tower, intertwined thistle and shamrock. As Irish nationalism became more vociferous in the latter half of the nineteenth century, the Irish symbols within Presbyterianism disappeared, and it is lamented in some quarters today that even the open Bible has disappeared in modern adaptations. Growing ultramontanism within Irish Catholicism and evangelicalism within Irish Presbyterianism further increased the chasm between the two sides.

While a majority of Irish Presbyterians have consistently displayed

---

2   Exodus 3:1–22.

loyalty to Britain, there has always been a robust minority view that supports Irish interests over those of Britain. Irish nationalist John Mitchel was the son of an Irish Presbyterian minister, yet he achieved fame as a Young Irelander.[3] He founded *The United Irishman* news-paper in 1848, and was tried for 'treason felony' and sentenced to hard labour, firstly in Bermuda, then Van Diemen's Land (Tasmania), before escaping to America and subsequently being elected as MP for Tipperary shortly before his death in 1875.

Land

A majority of Irish Presbyterians were tenant farmers and so, naturally, they joined with their Catholic neighbours in pressing for an improvement to their rights in the aftermath of the Irish famine of the 1840s. Many Presbyterian ministers supported their parishioners in advocating the 'Ulster custom' of allowing farmers to be reimbursed for improvements made to their holdings. Rev. Nathaniel McAuley Brown of Drumachose was a champion of the tenant farmer and is credited with designing the formula 'the three F's': fair rent, fixity of tenure and free sale of a tenant's interest in a holding.[4]

In 1847 the General Assembly expressed support for the 'Ulster custom' to be recognised in law. Although having only the status of custom, and therefore lacking legal status, it was nonetheless widely recognised that it contributed significantly to good landlord–tenant relations and social stability. When the Tenant Right League was established in 1850, Presbyterians and Catholics were largely united in advocating reform of land tenancies.[5] The northern delegation was

---

3   Rev. John Mitchel was minister of Scriggan congregation (1805–19), First Derry congregation (1819–23) and Newry congregation (1823–40).

4   Rev. Nathaniel McAuley Brown was minister of Drumachose congregation 1845–1907 and moderator of the General Assembly in 1891. He was awarded a DD degree by Presbyterian Theological Faculty Ireland in 1885.

5   The Tenant Right League was formed in Dublin in 1850 by Charles Gavan Duffy and Frederick Lucas as a vehicle to secure reforms in the Irish land system.

led by ten Presbyterian ministers and four Catholic priests, and in the 1852 election fifty Tenant Right candidates won seats in Westminster and sat as the independent Irish Party. However, in the following years it proved impossible to keep the land question free from other issues and, ultimately, the question of Home Rule became a wedge that divided Presbyterians and Catholics.

In December 1868, at the commencement of the first of his four terms as British prime minister, Gladstone declared that his mission was to pacify Ireland, and certainly he made some progress. The twin achievements of his administration in Ireland were the Irish Church Act (of 1869) and the Irish Land Act (of 1870). Irish Presbyterians warmly applauded these measures. Decades of discrimination could not be forgotten, and most Presbyterians were quietly satisfied to see the Church of Ireland disestablished and eagerly accepted their own government compensation award of £585,750 in lieu of a cessation of *regium donum* payments.[6]

Presbyterians had consistently supported tenant rights in Ireland, and Gladstone received solid Presbyterian support for the Land Act of 1870, by which he attempted to provide more security for Irish tenants by legislating that landlords must pay their tenants compensation for improvements made to their holding. The formation in 1879 of the Irish National Land League, however, with Charles Stewart Parnell as president, was a bridge too far for many Presbyterians, who were increasingly faced with a choice between submergence under a tsunami of Irish Catholic nationalism and forging a bulwark with Irish Anglicans in a common Protestant and unionist resistance.[7]

---

6   *Regium donum*, literally 'king's money', was an annual government grant to Irish Presbyterians in lieu of recognition of their key role in society. The first payment was made in 1672.
7   The Irish National Land League was founded on October 1879 in Castlebar and encouraged a proactive policy to secure fairer rents and, ultimately, secure a transfer of land ownership.

Politics

Irish Presbyterians are unevenly dispersed across the island, with over ninety per cent in the north-east, largely reflecting their seventeenth-century plantation pattern. Despite outnumbering Anglicans in Ulster, Presbyterians boasted a remarkably meagre parliamentary representation. Between 1832 and 1857 there were only five Presbyterian MPs, compared to twenty-five Anglicans.[8] Presbyterian representation rose to twelve between 1857 and 1885, possibly due to the foundation in the 1850s of the Presbyterian Representation Society. Presbyterianism has a remarkable propensity for fragmentation and the Irish variety is no different. Irish Presbyterians were not united politically, with a pro-Tory faction, led for many years by Rev. Henry Cooke, and a more rural, pro-Liberal faction. This political fragmentation was evident in numerous nineteenth-century elections with Presbyterian votes divided between Conservative and Liberal candidates. This trait had important implications in that it was only the topics of Church of Ireland disestablishment and land reform that pushed Presbyterians into potential alliance with Catholics, but, conversely, their natural fear of growing Catholic influence pulled them into alliance with Anglicans in a common Protestant cause. This tension manifested itself constantly in the latter half of the nineteenth century and it is a fact that Catholic voters proved the more consistently coherent supporters of Irish Liberal candidates.

This situation was volatile. Once the Land League policies were activated, Catholics had a viable alternative for which to vote and this, allied with a Presbyterian anti-Home Rule shift towards Conservatism, resulted in a virtual collapse of Liberal support. The resultant pan-Protestant versus nationalist political blocs are evidenced by the 1885 election results in Ulster, which resulted in a

---

8   The five Presbyterian MPs were Leonard Dobbin (Armagh 1832–7), William Kirk (Newry 1852–9 and 1868–71), Samuel Greer (County Londonderry 1857–9), James Gibson (Belfast 1837) and John Boyd (Coleraine 1843–52 and 1857–62).

return of eighteen nationalists, sixteen Conservatives and no Liberals. Irish Presbyterianism was moving from a more radical and liberal late eighteenth-century position to a distinctly conservative and reactionary stance in the late nineteenth century. Having shed the yoke of Anglican ascendancy in 1870, Presbyterians were distinctly unwilling to embrace a Catholic ascendancy.

An understanding of these mechanisms clarifies much of what happened within Irish Presbyterianism during the third Home Rule crisis. It is significant that in numerous Assembly debates the Presbyterian Church consistently pronounced itself overwhelmingly anti-Home Rule but at the same time requested the London parliament to act to address persistent tenant grievances. It must ever be remembered, though, that not all Irish Presbyterians supported union with Britain. Wealthy Belfast merchant, and Presbyterian, Joseph Biggar served as nominal joint treasurer of the executive of the Irish National Land League and president of the Belfast Home Rule Association in the 1870s. He was elected as Home Rule MP for Cavan in 1874 and reputedly converted to Catholicism in 1877. Another example is Presbyterian minister Rev. Isaac Nelson, who famously described the 1859 revival as a 'year of delusion' and became the nationalist MP for Mayo in 1880.[9]

The first Home Rule bill (1886)

Irish Presbyterians were shocked by the seventy-five-year-old Gladstone's political conversion to Home Rule. They had welcomed his Land Acts of 1870 and 1881, but this was an altogether more serious matter. The annual meeting of the General Assembly of the

---

9   Rev. Isaac Nelson was minister of First Comber congregation (1838–42), Donegal Street congregation, Belfast (1842–80), and Nationalist MP for County Mayo (1880–88). Nelson Memorial Church in Belfast was built as a memorial by his sister, Mary Nelson, in 1894. The 1859 revival originated in Connor Presbyterian congregation and spread throughout Ulster. About 100,000 professed to have experienced a religious conversion.

church was normally held in June, but so critical was this issue that a Special Assembly was convened to discuss Gladstone's proposal on 9 March 1886 in May Street church, Belfast. It was attended by 259 ministers and 152 elders. Moderator Rev. James Whigham of Ballinasloe opened with a declaration that the Assembly was meeting 'to consider the present serious state of the country and the duty of the General Assembly in relation thereto'. The official minutes of this meeting comprise a mere three pages and record the fact that six resolutions were unanimously passed after almost nine hours of debate, which raised three main concerns. Firstly, the Assembly deplored 'the disturbed and lawless state of many parts of the country'. Secondly, the land issue was identified as the long-standing principal cause of Ireland's woes:

> sympathising deeply as we do with those classes of our fellow-countrymen who have suffered so much through the prevailing depression, we are strongly of opinion that the permanent settlement of the land question will be best secured by a wise and comprehensive measure which … shall give material relief to the agricultural classes from their heavy burdens …

Thirdly, Presbyterians opposed the creation of an Irish parliament as the legislation contained insufficient safeguards for minority religious groups. The resolutions were seconded by elder and businessman Thomas Sinclair of Belfast, aged forty-eight, who would later become the author of the Ulster Covenant signed by unionists around Ulster in September 1912.[10]

The only protesting voice at this Special Assembly was that of Rev. Matthew Macauley of McKelvey's Grove congregation, and he does not appear in the official minutes of the meeting. He was not noticed by the moderator and therefore denied an opportunity to

---

10   General Assembly minutes, 1886, pp. 12–4, Union Theological College Library.

speak.[11] His independence of mind was not to the taste of his fellow Presbyterians and, despite his making several attempts to address the assembly after the vote was taken, his voice was drowned by numerous shouts of 'No'.[12]

The next month, on 8 April 1886, Gladstone introduced his Government of Ireland bill. This was far short of a proposal for Irish independence. During a three-hour speech he proposed the establishment of an Irish parliament, comprising twenty-eight peers and seventy-five MPs, which would be responsible for specified Irish affairs such as education, agriculture and transport, with the imperial parliament retaining control of main affairs such as foreign policy, customs and excise, army, navy and police. This devolution measure was debated over fourteen nights before it was defeated by ninety-three dissident Liberal MPs, who were prepared to vote against Gladstone's policy. The final vote was 343 to 313 and the proposal thus fell at the first hurdle.

The Presbyterian Assembly met as usual in the summer and on 16 June debated the issue of Home Rule, and again passed resolutions stating that the land question was most pressing and deploring recent disturbances in Belfast. In fact, riots had started in the shipyards and continued throughout the summer, resulting in at least thirty-two fatalities and over 370 injuries. Macauley spoke on this occasion, warning that 'the country and the church were in the presence of a very serious crisis'.[13]

The second Home Rule bill (1893)

Gladstone's fourth premiership lasted from 1892 to 1894, during which time he was head of a minority Liberal government and able

---

11   Rev. Dr Matthew Macauley was minister of McKelvey's Grove congregation 1843–7 and 1848–86. He died in 1907.

12   *The Belfast Evening Telegraph*, 10 March 1886.

13   *The Belfast Newsletter*, 17 June 1886.

to form an administration only with the support of Irish MPs. Even before the general election it was no secret that Gladstone would, if elected, introduce a new Home Rule bill for Ireland. Thomas Sinclair organised a massive anti-Home Rule convention in the Botanic Gardens, Belfast, on 17 June 1892. Of the £20,000 collected to defray the costs of this convention, £3,000 was spent in constructing a massive temporary hall measuring 244 feet by 150 feet and covering 33,000 square feet. A total of 12,300 delegates attended, representing a broad cross-section of Ulster people. It was reported in *The Northern Whig* that 5,000 of the delegates were tenant farmers and a further 2,500 were farm labourers. The occasion was dignified and respectable and indeed conciliatory towards Catholics, with a large platform banner proclaiming *Erin go bragh* (Ireland for ever). The Anglican archbishop of Armagh, Rev. Brent Knox, opened proceedings with prayer and ex-Presbyterian moderator Rev. Dr Nathaniel Brown read Psalm 46. Numerous resolutions were passed in opposition to Home Rule, after which Dr Brown closed proceedings by pronouncing the benediction. Sinclair continued to orchestrate a careful amalgamation of all religious and political opinions in opposition to Home Rule.

The second Home Rule bill was introduced at Westminster on 13 February 1893 and, as in 1886, the Irish Presbyterians, at the instigation of their 'Committee on the State of the Country', held a Special Assembly in Belfast in March. A total of 403 ministers and 254 elders crammed into May Street church to debate the issue. Presbyterians at the local level were clearly agitated at this renewed prospect of Home Rule, and a massive 278 identical memorials from congregations were presented, asking the assembly to:

> use all legitimate means to oppose and defeat the measure now before Parliament, which proposes the establishment of a national legislature and executive for Ireland, and also urgently to press upon the Legislature of the United Kingdom that, while unalterably hostile to the creation of

a Dublin Parliament and in favour of a good Local Government Bill, they consider the time has come for the abolition of dual ownership in Irish land and for the making of every tenant the proprietor, on equitable terms, of the land he tills.[14]

Rev. James Brown Armour of Ballymoney unsuccessfully proposed an amendment to the effect that Home Rule should be embraced by the Presbyterian Church with the proviso that there would be protection for minorities.[15] In his speech Armour raised the theologically uncomfortable issue of the possibility that God wanted Home Rule for Ireland and that the Presbyterians were now 'alarmed because God was answering their prayers, though not in the way they wanted'. Armour's cousin, Rev. Dr James Dougherty, a professor at Magee College, Londonderry, tried to speak in favour of this amendment but was shouted down. After five hours of debate the amendment was lost on a show of hands, only one being raised in its favour. Professor Dougherty appealed in vain that abstentions were not recorded, but the assembly rose en masse and spontaneously sang a verse of the national anthem.

On 9 June 1893 the General Assembly reaffirmed the opinion of the March Special Assembly by a vote of 304 to 11. Significantly, however, there were 341 abstentions, and perhaps the critical distinguishing factor with this second bill, when compared to the first, was that it made provision for Irish political representation in London.

The bill passed its third reading in the Commons on 1 September by thirty-four votes. It was, however, heavily defeated in the Lords on 9 September, by 419 votes to 41.

Before the close of the century several attempts were made

---

14 General Assembly minutes, 1893, p. 469, Union Theological College Library.
15 Rev. James Brown Armour was minister of Trinity congregation, Ballymoney (1869–1925) and, unquestionably, the best-known Presbyterian minister in support of Home Rule.

to alleviate the land problem, with acts passed in 1885, 1887 and 1896, and such steps received strong Presbyterian support. The chief secretary, Lord Ashbourne, introduced his Land Act in 1885, under the terms of which the government advanced £5 million for Irish land purchase. For the first time tenants were granted the entire purchase price for their holding and could repay the total amount over forty-nine years at four per cent interest. Some 25,000 tenants purchased their farms in this way, but the weakness of the scheme was that it was not compulsory: landlords were not obliged to sell land. In 1891 the Conservative chief secretary, Arthur Balfour, made a further £33 million available for land purchase, and over the course of the following twelve years an additional 47,000 tenants bought their farms. Millions of pounds were made available for tenants to purchase land, with strong approval from Irish Presbyterians.

Presbyterians in the early twentieth century

Irish Presbyterians were in buoyant mood at the dawn of the twentieth century. At the suggestion of Dublin Presbyterians, a Twentieth Century Thanksgiving Fund was launched at the 1898 General Assembly, with a projected financial target of £100,000, this money 'to be used as an instrument of spiritual adventure', with a 70:30 home:overseas expenditure policy. The major tangible outcome of the Thanksgiving Fund was the purchase of the Fisherwick Place church building in Belfast for £16,000, with the congregation moving to its current location on the Malone Road, and the opening on 5 June 1905 of the imposing Church House headquarters building with its double-balconied 1,600-seat Assembly Hall on the former church site – a tangible monument to Presbyterian strength. Interestingly, the new Fisherwick congregation bought its Malone Road site from a Major Frederick Crawford, later famous as the chief architect of the gun-running operation in 1914 for the anti-Home Rule Ulster Volunteer Force (UVF), when rifles and ammunition were landed at various Irish ports.[16] In 1900 there were forty-nine Presbyterian congregations in Belfast, and the number was increasing at a rate of one per year to accommodate the burgeoning city population, which expanded from 250,000 in 1890 to 350,000 in 1900.

The population of Ireland in 1901 was 4,456,546, of whom some 10 per cent (443,494) were Presbyterian. Roman Catholics and Anglicans comprised 74 per cent and 13 per cent respectively. As had always been the case, the vast majority of the Presbyterians (426,177, or 96.1 per cent) were concentrated in Ulster. They were dispersed lightly around the other provinces as follows: Leinster 11,735 (2.64 per cent), Munster 3,312 (0.75 per cent) and Connaught 2,270 (0.51 per cent). The church was led by 658 ministers, serving a total of 565 congregations and spread throughout thirty-six presbyteries.

Land reform continued, again with Presbyterian support. The Wyndham Land Act (of 1903) enabled 200,000 tenants to purchase their land by making £100 million available, loans being repayable over sixty-eight years, with bonus payments to landlords willing to sell whole estates. The Birrell Land Act (of 1909) introduced compulsory purchase and 61,000 tenants benefited, making the total number of farms that had been purchased under the new legislation 390,000. The Irish Party had split disastrously in 1890 when Parnell, by then its leader, had been cited as co-respondent in the O'Shea divorce case. Pro-union governments ruled at Westminster until 1906, and it is certain that the Conservative motive in advancing Land Acts was undoubtedly fuelled by a desire to further neutralise demands for Home Rule.

The 1906 general election saw the Conservatives ousted and a Liberal administration return to power with a massive majority. Not every Liberal MP, however, was in favour of reasserting Gladstone's

---

16 Major Frederick Crawford (1861–1952), a Methodist, was descended from Scottish Presbyterian stock. His ancestor, Rev. Thomas Crawford, a Presbyterian, came from Ayrshire to Donegore, County Antrim, in 1655.

policy of Irish Home Rule as a priority for the new administration. The consensus that emerged was one of gradual, step-by-step movement towards Home Rule as an aspiration of party policy. While this dismayed Irish nationalists, it laid the basis of a warning to Irish unionists, including the majority of Irish Presbyterians.

Presbyterian fears that Home Rule would mean Rome rule was fuelled by the application of the papal *Ne temere* decree in Belfast. Pope Pius X (1903–14) issued this decree on 10 August 1907 and it became effective at Easter, 19 April 1908. *Ne temere*, from the Latin 'not rashly', was a modification of the *Tametsi* decree of the Council of Trent, which had forbidden clandestinely celebrated marriages.[17] In this new matrimonial decree, the pope declared that marriages involving a Catholic were invalid unless performed by a Catholic priest or bishop. This ruling had a devastating effect upon one young couple, Alexander and Agnes McCann (née Barclay).

Alexander was a Catholic and Agnes a Presbyterian, and they were married on 16 May 1908 in High Street Presbyterian church, Antrim, by Rev. Robert Gilmour, who also baptised their first child.[18] The couple later moved to the Falls Road area of Belfast, where a second child was born in August 1910. In early 1910 a local priest visited the McCann home and informed the couple that their marriage was not valid under the *Ne temere* decree. The priest insisted that their marriage ceremony should be repeated in the Catholic chapel but Agnes refused. Understandably, this situation brought new strains into their relationship, which deteriorated rapidly. Alexander attempted to have his second child baptised in St Paul's Catholic church, and Agnes was expelled upon trying to disrupt this ceremony.

In October 1910, when Agnes was absent from the home,

---

17   Council of Trent 1563, chapter 1, session 24, available online at http://history. hanover.edu/texts/trent/ct24.html (accessed 30 December 2013).

18   Rev. Robert Murray McCheyne Gilmour was minister of Wellington Street congregation, Ballymena (1886–1929).

Alexander removed their two young children and subsequently refused to reveal their whereabouts to his wife. This case became a cause célèbre in Belfast and beyond. Agnes' minister, Rev. William Corkey, of Townsend Street Presbyterian church, publicised the case of this poor Presbyterian woman wandering the streets of Belfast seeking her children, the youngest of whom was only two months old, at a meeting of the Knox Club in Edinburgh on 21 February 1911, the same day on which Asquith introduced the Parliament bill in the House of Commons. The case horrified Presbyterians and others alike, and there were public demonstrations in Belfast, Dublin and Edinburgh in support of Agnes. The matter was also raised at Westminster in February 1911. The Ulster Women's Unionist Council (UWUC) also expressed outrage and in January 1912 obtained over 100,000 signatures on a petition of support for Agnes McCann. However, she never saw her children again and only recently has it been established that they were taken to Canada. Shelter and care were provided for Agnes by a retired missionary family.

Understandably, the McCann case was exploited by unionist politicians as an example of what Home Rule would mean for Protestants in Ireland: 'Home Rule is Rome rule.'[19] Irish Presbyterians, who had suffered Anglican insinuations as to the legality of their marriages for years, were particularly sensitive to the implications of the McCann case. It was not widely reported that West Belfast MP Joseph Devlin obtained statements from all three priests attached to St Paul's church, in which each denied informing Agnes McCann that her marriage was invalid. Devlin went on to allege that the McCann marriage was stormy and that the 'McCann scandal' was released into the public domain by unscrupulous unionist politicians just five days before the December 1910 general election in the hope of embarrassing and unseating him. As events transpired he retained

---

19   Credited to Quaker MP John Bright (1811–89).

his seat with a majority of 463 over the Liberal Unionist candidate, J. Boyd Carpenter. Interestingly, a joint Catholic–Presbyterian Service of Reconciliation was held in Townsend Presbyterian church in November 2010, the hundredth anniversary of that sad event.

David Lloyd George's infamous 1909 budget indirectly precipitated a new Ulster crisis. The Liberal majority in the Commons was opposed by the Tory majority in the Lords and, following two general elections in 1910, the Liberals retained power, but only with support from Irish nationalist MPs. This fact, coupled with the passing of the Parliament Act of 1911, by which the Lords' veto was reduced to a delaying power of two years upon any legislation passing in the Commons for three successive sessions, ensured that Irish matters once more rose to the top of the British political agenda.

Presbyterians, like others, anticipated, and began to make preparations for, the forthcoming struggle and they had representation in high places. Captain James Craig was a member of Belmont Presbyterian church in Belfast. The sixth son of a wealthy whiskey millionaire, he had served in the Boer War with the Royal Irish Rifles and entered parliament in 1906 as MP for East Down. He was to be Irish unionist leader Sir Edward Carson's right-hand man and chief organiser of Ulster resistance to Home Rule. Craig also served as the first prime minister of Northern Ireland from June 1921 until his death in November 1940.

Presbyterian Andrew Bonar Law was elected leader of the Conservative Party on 13 November 1911, despite never having sat in cabinet. His father was a Presbyterian minister, the Rev. James Law, who had been born in Portrush in 1822 and emigrated to New Brunswick in 1845. Bonar Law was raised by an aunt in Glasgow and visited Ulster regularly when his father returned there in 1877. Throughout the Home Rule crisis, Bonar Law showed himself to understand the Irish Presbyterian psyche better than most British politicians did. He was to hold the double distinction of being the only foreign-born British prime minister and the shortest-serving prime minister of the twentieth century. He was born on 16 September 1858 in New Brunswick and served for 211 days as prime minister from 23 October 1923.

Dawn of the third Home Rule bill

Asquith had entered parliament in 1886 and therefore personally witnessed the fiery Irish debates of that year and of 1893. Now, in 1911, as prime minister of a government beholden to Irish nationalist MPs to remain in power, he clearly saw that the Irish question must be faced again. There was one important difference this time: the veto power of the Tory-dominated House of Lords was now reduced to that of a temporary delay, and it was this fact which sharpened everyone's focus.

As early as January 1910, on the eve of the first general election of that year, eleven former Presbyterian moderators published a manifesto, 'To the Electors of Great Britain', in which they railed against the idea of creating an Irish parliament.[20] They warned specifically that such a parliament would be under (Roman Catholic) 'clerical control' and that British government safeguards on this matter were wholly inadequate. Royal assent was granted to the Parliament Act on 18 August 1911, and this removal of a former safety net marks the commencement of a frenetic period of political activity culminating in the commencement of the First World War.

Carson agreed to become leader of the Ulster unionists in February 1910, when former leader Walter Long accepted a parliamentary seat in London. Some unionist leaders certainly were thinking ahead as to various scenarios which might now unfold. In November 1910 – the forthcoming general election would be in December – the Ulster Unionist Council formed a small select committee to plan

---

20   *The Witness*, 14 January 1910.

and oversee the importation of thousands of arms and ammunition with which to resist Home Rule by unconstitutional means if necessary. In April 1911 James Craig wrote to Major Frederick Crawford, secretary of the Ulster Reform Club, encouraging him to obtain suitable weapons. Craig was increasingly active in planning to publicise plans for opposing Home Rule. He organised a rally at his home, Craigavon, on the eastern outskirts of Belfast, on 23 September 1911. A crowd estimated at 50,000, and composed of Unionist Club and Orange Lodge members, heard Carson warn that unionists must prepare to assume the responsibility of government if Home Rule passed in parliament.

As in 1892, Irish Presbyterians organised a Belfast convention as a means of demonstrating their opposition to Home Rule. Again, as in 1892, the man behind the 1912 Convention was Thomas Sinclair. Over 50,000 people attended, with the main rally located in the Presbyterian Assembly Hall on 1 February and overflow rallies in ten locations around the city. The Presbyterian faithful in attendance listened to anti-Home Rule speeches by over 100 individuals. It is surely an indication of the seriousness with which the impending crisis was viewed that this convention did not actually have official denominational sanction, a fact that encouraged Rev. J. B. Armour to attack it with considerable vehemence. No board or committee of the church asked for such a rally, the assumption being that virtually every Presbyterian would be in agreement with its import. Armour suggested that no official sanction was sought because Sinclair knew that he could not secure a request from four Presbyteries for such a meeting.

As proof of the nationalist aggression that could be expected under a Dublin administration, a Mr Farrington, a Presbyterian farmer and member of Galway congregation, was paraded on the platform in the Assembly Hall. This man, it was claimed, was a victim of religious intolerance and a boycott. His life was endangered to the extent that while attending worship an armed policeman had to sit beside him in his pew. The proceedings ended with cries of 'No Home Rule' and the singing of the national anthem.

The Methodist Church followed a similar pattern, with five convention meetings on 14 March, and the Church of Ireland convened a Special Meeting of the General Synod on 16 April. Clearly, popular Protestant resistance to Home Rule included all the main churches.

The depth of popular resentment was further evidenced in the week following the Presbyterians' Belfast convention by the occupation of the Ulster Hall by a group of anti-Home Rule demonstrators on 8 February 1912, thus denying its use to Winston Churchill, who had been invited to speak in Belfast to the Ulster Liberal Association. Churchill suffered the ignominy of delivering his pro-Home Rule speech in a rain-sodden Celtic Park and leaving immediately by a deviant route for the Larne boat to avoid confrontation by more anti-Home Rule demonstrators.

The largest public demonstration against Home Rule was held on Easter Tuesday, 9 April 1912, at the Balmoral Showgrounds of the Agricultural Society. Over seventy English, Scottish and Welsh MPs were in attendance to witness 100,000 men march past the platform in military style. Bonar Law raised the loudest cheer on that day when he linked the present crisis with Ulster Protestant's past in a clear and emotive reference to the siege of Derry in 1689:

Once again you hold the pass, the pass for the Empire. You are a besieged city. The timid have left you; your Lundys have betrayed you; but you have closed your gates. The Government have erected by their Parliament Act a boom against you to shut you off from the help of the British people. You will burst that boom.[21]

---

21 *The Belfast Newsletter*, 10 April 1912.

As a resolution against Home Rule was passed, the largest union flag in existence, measuring forty-eight feet by twenty-five feet, was hoisted upon a ninety-foot flag pole. The proceedings were started with public prayers, led by Church of Ireland Primate Dr Crozier and Presbyterian moderator Rev. John Macmillan. Both the Anglican and Presbyterian Churches were honoured and pleased to be showcased in this manner.

Asquith introduced the Home Rule bill in the Commons only two days later, on the same day the ill-fated *Titanic* sailed from Queenstown (now Cobh). The proposal was modest. The new Irish parliament was to have two chambers; a forty-member Senate, initially nominated by the cabinet, and a 164-member Commons elected on a provincial basis as follows: 59 Ulster, 41 Leinster, 37 Munster, 25 Connaught, plus two representatives for Dublin University. It was an uncomfortable fact for the Presbyterians that their co-religionists in Scotland and England did not largely support them, their religious consciousness rather leading them to support Home Rule as a measure of justice for the majority of the Irish people.

The 1912 General Assembly was a muted affair with only one simple statement by the State of the Country Committee on political affairs:

> With regard to the question of Home Rule the Committee consider that the views of the vast majority of the Presbyterians in Ireland received sufficient expression at the Presbyterian Convention held in Belfast on 1 February last, and do not consider it necessary for the General Assembly to make any pronouncement on the subject at present.[22]

This announcement was proposed by leading Presbyterian elder and anti-Home Ruler Thomas Sinclair, and seconded by pro-Home Ruler Rev. James Armour – harmony indeed! This apparent tranquillity was,

---

22   General Assembly minutes, 1912, p. 350, Union Theological College Library.

however, somewhat artificial, being the product of an irregular midnight meeting at which a former moderator, Dr John McIlveen, used all his diplomatic skills to persuade the State of the Country Committee to cut all strident pro-union statements from its report, and Armour similarly to withdraw his equally outspoken anti-union amendment. This episode illustrates that a significant proportion of Presbyterians desired to avoid a potentially damaging division within their church. Ultimately, neither side was satisfied with this compromise, each fearing that it would be misrepresented by others.

Community tension rose in the following weeks and boiled over in the summer. The annual Sunday School excursion from Whitehouse Presbyterian church on the outskirts of north Belfast was a train journey to Castledawson in mid-Ulster on 29 June 1912. The party of fifty children had its own band and carried union flags and banners bearing scripture texts. An Ancient Order of Hibernians parade, comprising about 250 men, was provoked by the waving union flags and attacked the Sunday School party. Local Protestants intervened and serious fighting ensued. The next morning in church, Rev. Robert Barron urged his congregation not to talk about the incident but it was too late; local newspapers published full details of the 'Castledawson outrage' and serious reprisals were taken against Roman Catholics, most notably in the Belfast shipyards on 1 July. As a result of this affray, twenty-seven Hibernians and seven Protestants were brought to trial at the Winter Assizes in Londonderry. All the Hibernians were sentenced to three months' hard labour, and all seven Protestants were acquitted. The sentences of hard labour were reduced to half upon receipt in Dublin Castle of a plea for mercy signed by a large number of Castledawson residents representing a cross-section of the community. Tension mounted, however, throughout the summer and erupted again on 14 September at a Celtic–Linfield football match at Celtic Park, attended by 10,000 supporters. A display of rival slogans and chanting progressed to fighting at half-time, which spilt into surrounding streets and after which over sixty supporters required hospital treatment.

The Ulster Covenant

Even before the summer rioting had started in Belfast, Carson and Craig were giving attention as to how they could focus popular Protestant resentment against Home Rule. Naked sectarian aggression was always worryingly near the surface in Ulster society and troubled all the church leaders. Carson, however, aspired to lead a disciplined opposition, and he did not want Protestant anti-Home Rule sentiment to be portrayed as bigoted or anti-Catholic. The plan to compose an 'Ulster Covenant' emerged quite naturally, primarily as a means of focusing and tempering Protestant ire. Initial progress was made when Ulster businessman and secretary of the Belfast Unionist Club, Boughey Montgomery, son of Anglican clergyman Rev. Thomas Montgomery of Dromore, spotted James Craig doodling with pencil and paper in the Constitutional Club in London. In conversation Craig admitted that he was attempting to compose something like an oath for his supporters in Ulster. Montgomery advised that he consult the wording of the historic Scottish covenants, the club librarian produced the Scottish text and the idea of an 'Ulster Covenant' was born. The 1643 Solemn League and Covenant was a religious covenant and civil league between England and Scotland against their common enemy at that time, Charles I, who was deemed a threat to the reformed religion and civil liberty in both nations. To Ulster unionists, Home Rule posed a similar threat to religion and civil liberty in Ireland, so the symbolism of a covenant was perfect for their cause. The Ulster Covenant is, in many ways, the 'birth certificate of Northern Ireland', and as such its importance cannot be overemphasised.

A special committee was appointed in Belfast to devise an appropriate wording. Most of the credit for the resultant document goes to Presbyterian Thomas Sinclair, though his original proposal was reduced by almost half in the final form used on Ulster Day, 28 September 1912. It has subsequently been remarked that the Covenant represents 'the traditional Presbyterian technique of reminding God whose side He was on'.[23] Sinclair's full text was preserved as a resolution of the Ulster Unionist Council. Significantly, Carson and Craig consulted privately with the main Protestant churches upon the wording of their covenant before proceeding with their plan for widespread public signing by supporters. Soundings were taken from the leaders of the Presbyterian, Church of Ireland, Methodist and Congregational Churches. The Presbyterians, on the advice of leading Belfast solicitor and Presbyterian Alexander McDowell, insisted that the proposed document could be construed as committing the prospective signatories to oppose Home Rule for an unlimited duration. The Presbyterian Church insisted that, before its congregations could be encouraged to sign the Covenant, the wording should be clarified as referring only to the present crisis. Accordingly the phrases 'throughout this our time of threatened calamity' and 'the present conspiracy' were inserted. The Presbyterians did not want to give a blank cheque to political leaders in the sense of an open-ended commitment to follow the path of resistance, whatever the circumstances.

Insufficient attention has been directed by historians to the social and gender aspects of the Ulster Covenant. On 17 August it was announced in the press that 28 September had been designated 'Ulster Day' and that arrangements would be made for supporters to sign the Ulster Covenant. The definitive wording of the Covenant was finally unanimously approved by the Standing Committee at Craigavon on Thursday 19 September. A 'Women's Declaration' was also devised, though it has received scant attention from later historians. Women in Edwardian society were certainly second-class citizens after men and

---

23   J. Lee, *The Modernization of Irish society, 1848–1918* (Dublin, 1973), p. 133.

it is interesting to note their parallel organisations in the Home Rule cause. The Ulster Unionist Council (male) was formed in 1905 and the Ulster Women's Unionist Council (UWUC) in 1911; the Orange Order (male) was founded in 1795 and the Association of Loyal Orange Women in 1911. The Women's Declaration is further evidence of a gendered division of activities for the same cause. The declaration's wording was shorter than that of the Covenant and was agreed at a Women's Council meeting on 17 September 1912; unlike the Covenant, it was to be circulated for signatures only within Ulster. There are remarkably few women in extant pictures of Ulster Day, especially in relation to the iconic image of Carson signing the Covenant upon a table decked with a union flag in the entrance to Belfast City Hall. Perhaps this is largely explained by the fact that the Women's Declaration was being signed at the same time in the nearby Ulster Hall.

Analysis of the wording of the Covenant reveals that the signatories protested against Home Rule on four main grounds: economic, religious, civil liberty and Empire cohesion. The main economic fear was that Belfast, the only industrial city in Ireland, would inevitably suffer under a restrictive Dublin-favoured administration. Belfast's growth and prosperity were heralded as evidence that the union worked. In the nineteenth century Belfast was largely a Presbyterian city, but the religious balance was shifting, with an ever-increasing proportion of Belfast citizens professing to be Catholics. The increasing identification of Roman Catholicism with Irish nationalism in the latter half of the nineteenth century sounded alarms for Presbyterians and Anglicans alike, and throughout the Home Rule crisis these two churches worked more closely together than ever before. Civil liberty was perceived to be under threat in that a united Ireland would immediately condemn all Protestants to a minority status and 'clerical control' in Dublin would erode Protestant lifestyle choices. The British Empire would also suffer a serious fracture if Ireland obtained Home Rule.

The thrust of the Covenant's words are simple and direct, and have an almost soldierly quality, a pledge to act in whatever manner thought necessary to maintain the status quo. God is mentioned twice: 'relying on the God whom our fathers in days of stress and trial confidently trusted' and 'in sure confidence that God will defend the right'. While the minutes of the UWUC simply record that 'the wording of the Declaration was unanimously approved', having been 'prepared by the Advisory Committee and recommended by them for adoption by the Executive Committee',[24] it is known from correspondence between UWUC honorary secretary Edith Wheeler and Dawson Bates, secretary of the Ulster Unionist Council, that it was the men who had the final say in drafting the declaration.[25]

Analysis of the wording of the Women's Declaration reveals the generally accepted gender roles of that age in which women would not be seen as active participants in resistance. The women, in addition to pledging their loyalty to the king, simply expressed a 'desire to associate ourselves with the men of Ulster in their uncompromising opposition to the Home Rule Bill now before Parliament'. The same basic role was enacted when many of the men enlisted in the newly formed Ulster Volunteer Force; the women enlisted as nurses and in noncombatant administrative support roles. Similar roles were mirrored in the churches; while the Presbyterian Church had many female missionaries serving in India and China (such leadership roles were acceptable in a 'foreign land'), it was only in 1908 that the first Irish Presbyterian deaconesses were trained for service within Irish congregations, and the first women minister, Ruth Patterson, was ordained in 1976. Of course, women were not able to vote for parliament on equal terms with men until 1928.

24   Ulster Women's Unionist Council Executive Council minutes, 17 September 1912, D.1098, Public Record Office of Northern Ireland (PRONI).
25   Edith Wheeler to Dawson Bates, D.1098/2/3, PRONI. Dawson Bates was an Ulster-born solicitor and first Minister of Home Affairs in Sir James Craig's government.

In 1881 only eighteen per cent of Ulster men were qualified to vote – only four per cent of the total population. Franchise changes in 1884 saw the overall proportion of male voters rise to sixty-four per cent. While Emmeline Pankhurst founded the Women's Social and Political Union in 1898 to agitate for voting rights for women, it is noteworthy that devout Presbyterian Isabella Tod had formed the first suffrage society in Ireland, The Belfast Northern Ireland Society for Women's Suffrage, twenty-seven years earlier, in 1871. She was also a leading voice against Home Rule. On 3 February 1912, only two days after the Presbyterian convention, suffragette Christabel Pankhurst addressed a full Opera House in Belfast, but it seems that the signatories of the Women's Declaration were content to forgo suffrage claims and maintain a passive stance on this subject until the Home Rule crisis passed. Sir Edward Carson promised in September 1913 that women would be permitted to vote in Ulster and also be represented on every committee of the Central Authority. Craig certainly supported this stance, but unionist leaders were divided and Carson would not allow this issue to split the anti-Home Rule campaign. As a direct result, militant suffragette action erupted on 10 April 1914, when windows were broken in the Old Town Hall and Carson himself was harangued publicly by two suffragettes who accused him of 'betraying the women of Ulster'. Within a six-month period there were eleven arson attacks, mainly upon unionist-owned properties. Abbeylands House was burnt, as was the teahouse at Bellevue Zoo and the manicured grass of Cavehill Bowling and Tennis Club was vandalised. Thirteen women were imprisoned, and bolder suffragettes voiced the not unreasonable opinion that this was outrageous when Sir Edward Carson and his followers had imported rifles and ammunition without punishment.

In February 1918 the parliamentary vote was granted to women over thirty years old with certain property qualifications, and in the general election of that year Constance Markievicz became the first female MP elected to the House of Commons.[26] The Representation of the People Act in 1928 granted the vote to all women over the age of twenty-one on the same terms as men.

Ulster Day

A carefully choreographed series of evening and weekend rallies, commencing in Enniskillen on 18 September 1912, swept across Ulster towards Belfast and heightened the air of expectancy. At an eve-of-signing rally in the Ulster Hall on 27 September, Carson was presented with a yellow silk banner which, it was claimed, had been carried into battle by the forces of William III at the Battle of the Boyne in 1690. An Ulster Day committee, comprising representatives of the Unionist Council, Orange Order and Unionist Clubs, made detailed arrangements to maximise the news impact on the day and also facilitate the practical issue of enabling as many supporters as possible to sign copies of the Covenant on 28 September. The Presbyterian moderator, Rev. Henry Montgomery, appointed the previous Sunday, 22 September, as a 'Day of Humiliation' before God, when he asked all Presbyterians to seek God's deliverance.[27]

Ulster Day began with religious services. Many Presbyterian ministers were members of their local organising committees, which agreed where community church services should be held and where the Covenant should be signed. In doing so they were displaying open cooperation with Orange Order and Unionist Club representatives – a united leadership for the ordinary Protestants to follow. *The Witness* published lists of centres where religious services would be

---

26 Countess de Markievicz was the first woman elected to Westminster, for the constituency of Dublin St Patrick's, in December 1918, though she did not take her seat. Viscountess Nancy Astor was elected in 1919 and was the first female MP to take her seat. She replaced her husband as MP for Plymouth Sutton when he was raised to the peerage.

27 *The Witness*, 13 September 1912. Special prayers offered in church services emphasised the seriousness of the political situation.

held and also where the Covenant could be signed. Across Ulster, church services were very well attended, with the largest congregations, naturally, in Belfast. Ulster Day services started at 11a.m. and several large Presbyterian churches in Belfast were packed: Fitzroy Avenue, Fisherwick, Belmont, Elmwood and Duncairn. Interestingly the political leaders did not favour any denomination by attending any church building. Unionist leaders attended worship in the Ulster Hall, where 1906 moderator Rev. Dr William McKean preached upon the text 'Keep that which is committed to Thy trust'.[28] These services closed with the hymn that was becoming the battle cry of the campaign, 'O God our Help in Ages Past'. *The Belfast Newsletter* remarked, 'Ulster on Saturday morning was a province at prayer.'

The signing of the Ulster Covenant is forever etched in popular consciousness by the memorable photograph of a determined Carson signing in the foyer of Belfast City Hall, but people signed in halls all over Ulster on that day. It was not permitted that anyone would sign the Covenant in a church sanctuary, but in all, eighty-six Presbyterian halls were used to sign and ninety-seven Church of Ireland halls were utilised in this way. The uniqueness of this occasion, linking politics and religion, was reported by *The Belfast Newsletter*:

A church should never be turned into a place for the discussion or advocacy of party politics and the pulpit is not the rostrum from which to expound political views but there are some questions which transcend the domain of ordinary politics, and Home Rule is one of these. It affects Protestantism too deeply to be ignored, and touches upon the interests of religion itself. One of the striking features of the present fight is the way in which men who under normal conditions would take little part in political matters have come forward and shown praiseworthy activity in the contest – amongst these being ministers who had never formerly

---

28   I Timothy 6:20.

appeared upon a political platform, but who have felt compelled in obedience to the dictates of their consciences and the claims of their religion to do their utmost in defence of the Unionist cause.[29]

In fact 345 Presbyterian ministers signed the Ulster Covenant, or 63 per cent of all ministers of the Irish Presbyterian church. This compares with 392 (74 per cent) of Church of Ireland and 61 (42 per cent) of Methodist ministers. The first page signed at Belfast City Hall is headed by Edward Carson, followed by Lord Londonderry, but, significantly, the third signatory is Presbyterian moderator Rev. Henry Montgomery. The sixth of the ten first-page signatories is Rev. Charles Lowe, general secretary of the Irish Presbyterian church.

As in 1886 and 1893, not all Presbyterians concurred with the above-mentioned sentiments. Visiting Presbyterian evangelist William P. Nicholson was conducting a mission in the moderator's Shankill Road Mission in September 1912 and cancelled his evening rally on Ulster Day. Nicholson, a hero in working-class religious circles, made no comment on the political matters of the day, preferring to keep religion separate. Other Presbyterian ministers made their objections more obvious. Rev. Armour disparagingly termed the day 'Protestant fool's day'.[30] Rev. Robert Hamilton declared that he could not discern the will of God in acting against Home Rule and was subsequently lambasted in *The Witness*.[31] Rev. John Waddell in First Bangor church refused permission for the Covenant to be signed in his church hall and suffered the subsequent odium of a significant proportion of his congregation. He resigned in 1914 and moved to Egremont Presbyterian church in Liverpool. It says much about Irish

---

29   *The Belfast Newsletter*, 18 September 1912.
30   Letter from Rev. James B. Armour to his son, William Stavely Armour, August 1912, D.1792/A3/3/25, PRONI.
31   *The Witness*, 25 October 1912. Rev. Robert Hamilton was minister of Burt congregation (1880–85) and Railway Street congregation, Lisburn (1885–1930), and moderator in 1924.

Presbyterianism, however, that he returned in 1920 to become minister in the influential Belfast congregation of Fisherwick and was elected moderator in 1937. In December 1912 several notable literary figures, including William Butler Yeats, George Bernard Shaw and Arthur Conan Doyle, protested in London with the Protestant Home Rule Association regarding the 'bigotry and intolerance' of Irish Protestants who opposed Home Rule.[32]

Partition

In total, 218,206 men signed the Ulster Covenant and 228,991 women signed the Women's Declaration in Ulster (an additional 19,162 men and 5,055 women signed elsewhere). It is a curious fact that, following Ulster Day, the signed Covenant sheets were returned to the old Belfast Town Hall where the signatures were counted and the result hailed as an overwhelming rejection of Home Rule, yet nothing more was done with the sheets. They were not, for example, presented at the door of 10 Downing Street, and it seems that there was no follow-through strategy as far as the Covenant was concerned. The point of the entire exercise was a tangible demonstration of an overwhelming and united Protestant opposition to government intention. It was, in effect, an end in itself, acting in September 1912 as a communal safety valve that galvanised Protestant determination. The original sheets were deposited with the Public Record Office of Northern Ireland (PRONI) in 1959 though the original first page bearing Carson's signature was displayed upon a wall within the Official Unionist Party offices in Glengall Street, Belfast.[33] This page has been missing, presumed destroyed, since a series of bomb attacks upon the building in the 1970s.

Events moved apace following Ulster Day. The clock was ticking

---

32   *The Witness*, 6 December 1912.
33   Ulster Covenant digital records are available online at http://www.proni.gov.uk/index/search_the_archives/ulster_covenant.htm.

on the Home Rule bill and it was obvious that, under the terms of the Parliament Act, the bill would become law in 1914. In January 1913 the Ulster Volunteer Force was formed: 100,000 men pledged to follow Carson and Craig upon a path of active resistance to Home Rule. The 1913 General Assembly was another opportunity for Presbyterians to debate the developing situation. By a vote of 921 to 43 the assembly passed a memorial 'that the opposition of the Church to Home Rule continues as determined and unyielding as in the years 1886 and 1893, and records its firm conviction that the present Home Rule Bill is a measure that would inflict incalculable injury on our country and our Church'.[34] Armour tried unsuccessfully to move an amendment simply re-affirming the unanimous decision of the 1912 Assembly, but it lost heavily on a show of hands. The die was cast.

The unionist leaders continued to follow through on their pledge to resist Home Rule, and by September 1913 a Provisional Government was ready to assume power at an opportune time. Presbyterian fervour was further excited by the fact that June 1913 marked the tercentenary of Irish Presbyterianism. By October 1913 Asquith, recognising at last that the unionists were not bluffing, broached the possibility of partition as a possible compromise solution. Further escalation in the situation was marked by the formation in November 1913 of the Irish Volunteers and their importation of weapons at Howth on 26 July 1914. The 'Curragh incident' in March 1914 revealed the unreliability to the government of using the army to crush the Ulster unionists, and the following month the stakes were ratcheted up even more by the UVF importation of 30,000 rifles and three million rounds of ammunition at Larne, Bangor and Donaghadee.[35]

---

34   General Assembly minutes, 1913, p. 636, Union Theological College Library.
35   Asquith was informed on 21 March 1914 that fifty-seven officers at the Curragh, east of Dublin, would prefer to accept dismissal from the army rather than proceed north against Ulster unionists.

One notable Presbyterian contribution to the gun-running events of 24–5 April was that of Rev. William Marshall (1888–1959), Presbyterian minister in Aughnacloy and 'Half-Company Officer' of the South Tyrone UVF. He joined other car owners who drove to Larne, and loaded rifles and ammunition before returning to his manse at Aughnacloy, where he concealed them until they could be distributed in accordance with further orders. Writing afterwards, he reported how his clandestine activity was almost discovered when he met two policemen that night while carrying a full box of ammunition, but he was not challenged regarding his burden. Marshall was more famous as 'the Bard of Tyrone', publishing four collections of poems between the 1920s and 1940s. *The Witness* announced the success of the gun-smuggling operation with the headline 'Great Volunteer Coup'.[36]

The Presbyterian Church made no official comment upon these events. The active support and participation of Presbyterian Church leaders in the events of Ulster Day drew it, with the entire unionist community, into the vortex of these succeeding events. Presbyterian support for the UVF was inevitable given the Ulster Covenant pledge to oppose Home Rule by any means necessary. So determined were the vast majority of Presbyterians to oppose Home Rule that there were very few voices raising concerns at these increasingly militaristic activities. Along with Church of Ireland clergy, Presbyterian ministers provided a moral basis for the resistance movement, and fostered the theological notion that God was on the side of unionism, as immortalised by the slogan on the UVF badge: 'for God and Ulster'.

As the pressure towards civil war grew, Presbyterians and other church leaders feared an uncontrollable outpouring of violence. Services for Ulster Volunteers, at which company colours were dedicated, indicate that ministers were following a precarious policy of supporting the UVF but at the same time consistently urging restraint and

---

36   *The Witness*, 1 May 1914.

faith in God. The Irish problem was a Gordian knot for politicians and church leaders alike. It was clear that it was impossible to give everyone what they wanted, and the option of some form of partition, 'Home Rule within Home Rule', emerged as a potential compromise. An initial proposal by Asquith that the four counties with clear Protestant majorities (Antrim, Down, Londonderry and Armagh) should be excluded from the bill for a period of six years was rejected by Carson as merely 'a sentence of death with a stay of execution'. Various partition options were floated, based on the permanent or temporary exclusion of four, six or nine Ulster counties, but none proved entirely satisfactory and Ireland lurched on towards civil war. It was the outbreak of European war that changed the entire situation. The progress of the Home Rule bill was inexorable and it passed the Commons for the third and final time on 25 May 1914, requiring then only the king's signature to become law. As Ireland stuttered towards internal conflict, the assassination of Archduke Franz Ferdinand in Sarajevo on 28 June, and the British declaration of war upon Germany on 4 August, resulted in the passing of the Government of Ireland Act on 18 September but also in its immediate postponement until after the war. This external factor altered everything in Ireland.

The eventual partition of Ireland in 1920 created problems for everyone, including the Presbyterian Church in Ireland. The church claimed to be an all-Ireland institution, albeit with an overwhelming concentration in the north-eastern counties. Partition meant that 50,000 Irish Presbyterians were to be abandoned to what the majority of Presbyterians had sworn would never happen. There is no doubt that some Presbyterians felt totally betrayed by partition – and blamed their fellow co-religionists:

I sometimes visited a manse in County Donegal where on the mantelpiece on the study was a framed copy of the Ulster Covenant. It had been torn in two and written across it were the words, 'The broken covenant'. At first sight, the writing looked like a dark stain. It had been written in the minister's own blood. He had been a unionist and had been appointed with another to represent the unionists of Donegal at a meeting with Carson at the City Hall in Belfast. Instead of being treated sympathetically, he and his companion were called upon to resign. They refused and were evicted. No longer was it 'Ulster Will Fight and Ulster Will Be Right'. Donegal, Monaghan and Cavan were to be sacrificed. The night he returned home saw the torn and blood-stained covenant placed on the study mantelpiece where it remained until the day he died.[37]

There is no doubt that the majority of Irish Presbyterians supported Britain in the war, and forty-four ministers served as chaplains during the conflict, with Rev. John M. Simms serving as the principal chaplain in the British Army. Events in 1916 further illustrated diverging opinions in Ireland, with nationalists and unionists each revering their respective blood sacrifices, the Easter Rising and Somme. The 1917 Irish Convention represented a final attempt to reconcile all opinions in Ireland, but it failed to achieve reconciliation. The members of the Irish Presbyterian General Assembly sounded a strident tone, that 'under no circumstances, will we consent to come under the rule of a Dublin parliament'.[38]

Partition changed Ireland and the Presbyterian Church. The wealth, power centre and demographics of the church were thereafter, more strongly than ever, Belfast based, and the 'southern Presbyterians' were weak and dependent upon northern largesse. In the immediate years after partition Presbyterian numbers in the South dwindled rapidly:

---

37 J. M. Barkley, *Blackmouth and Dissenter* (Belfast, 1991), p. 152.
38 General Assembly minutes, 1917, p. 390, Union Theological College Library.

With the acceptance of the Treaty and the formation of a Provisional Government, it was hoped that peace would be brought about in the Southern area of Ireland, where upwards of 50,000 members of our Church reside. These hopes were doomed to failure ... The withdrawal of all Imperial Forces from Southern Ireland and the desertion of law-abiding citizens, both Roman Catholic and Protestant, who have now no protection for life or property, is one of the darkest stains in the annals of British administration ... We learn with regret that the trend of events in Southern Ireland is leading to the gradual withdrawal of many Protestant families in that area. In one Presbytery the membership has been reduced by 45% in the last seven years.[39]

The Presbyterian Church played a full role in the emerging province of Northern Ireland. The Presbyterian Theological College in Botanic Avenue was vacated by the church and the Northern Ireland Parliament met there from 1921–32 while the new parliament building at Stormont was constructed. Two Presbyterian ministers served as ministers during the Stormont regime: Rev. Robert Moore as Minister of Agriculture (1948–60) and Rev. Professor Robert Corky as Minister of Education (1943–4). The Presbyterian Church in Ireland continues to play a significant role within Ireland, though it has never lost its original planter distribution pattern. Today, membership totals 241,677 with a provincial breakdown as follows: Ulster (236,826 people, 98 per cent of total), Leinster (3,933 people, 1.6 per cent of total), Connacht (727 people, 0.3 per cent of total) and Munster (191 people, 0.1 per cent of total).[40]

---

39 *Ibid.*, 1922, p. 103.
40 *Ibid.*, 2012, p. 280. Of the 236,826 Presbyterians living in Ulster, 8,344 live in Counties Donegal, Monaghan and Cavan.

12

'Grotesque proceedings'? Localised responses to the Home Rule question in Ulster

Jonathan Bardon

Winston Churchill, first lord of the Admiralty, agreed to speak in favour of Home Rule in Belfast on 8 February 1912. He was to regret that decision. The Irish chief secretary, Augustine Birrell, who would have to provide security cover for the visit, was horrified that Churchill had chosen the Ulster Hall, where his father Randolph had warned loyalists in 1886 that Home Rule could come upon them like 'a thief in the night'. 'My own belief,' Birrell wrote on 28 January, 'is that if you hold a mid-day meeting in a tent, *no* blood will be shed. But the *moral* is: Leave Ireland alone in future.' As Rev. J. B. Armour, Presbyterian minister of Ballymoney, informed his son, the 'Unionist Council is threatening to raise a riot and commit murder if Winston dares speak in the Ulster Hall'. Reading police reports about 'great quantities of bolts and rivets having been abstracted from the yards' by shipwrights, Birrell ordered north five battalions of infantry, two companies of cavalry and police reinforcements. And a tent it would be: the organisers had a marquee rushed over from Scotland to be erected in the new venue, Celtic Park in west Belfast.

The visit was a miserable experience from start to finish. On the night ferry from Stranraer, suffragettes tramped round and round the deck, shouting 'Votes for women!' outside the cabin where Winston and his wife Clementine were trying to sleep. After facing a hostile reception as they disembarked at Larne, the couple drove to Belfast and got into the Grand Central Hotel only with difficulty: outside loyalists had gathered to demonstrate. They almost overturned their car a few hours later when they prepared to leave for Celtic Park.

Heavy rain flooded the football ground as the first lord entered the marquee. There he was joined by Lord Pirrie, managing director of Harland and Wolff shipyard; the Rev. Armour of Ballymoney; Joseph Devlin, MP for West Belfast; and John Redmond, MP, leader of the Irish Party. To their disappointment, the tent was only three-quarters full. The sole interruption was made by suffragettes, one of them crying out to Churchill, 'Will you give the suffrage to women?'

For five hours 10,000 loyalists endured downpours in Royal Avenue, waiting to give Churchill a hostile reception on his return to the hotel. But on urgent police advice the first lord changed his plans: he travelled by a circuitous route back to Larne before those who were standing in the rain in the city centre knew what was happening. They did at least have the satisfaction of reflecting that they had forced Churchill to leave Belfast, as one wag put it, 'like a thief in the night'.[1]

Churchill had learned at first hand the intensity of feeling in Ulster. It was a lesson he never forgot. He was not alone in being taken aback by the impassioned reaction there. In the ensuing months of 1912 politicians on the other side of the Irish Sea were to be reminded again that society in the north of Ireland was dangerously fractured, bitterly divided to a degree quite beyond the experience of any other part of the United Kingdom.

It was widely assumed across the Irish Sea that the 'Ulster problem'

---

1   J. R. B. McMinn, *Against the Tide: J. B. Armour, Irish Presbyterian minister and home ruler* (Belfast, 1985), p. 104; R. Jenkins, *Churchill* (London, 2001), pp. 234–5.

was unique, quite without parallel in the rest of Europe. But was it? Actually in 1912 many places could be found on the European mainland with inhabitants fiercely sundered by similar clashing aspirations. By 1912 modern nationalism, speeding along rapidly extending railway lines, posed a deadly threat to multinational states, in particular to the sprawling dynastic empires of Austria–Hungary, Russia and Turkey. Dreams of imperial glory were conflicting abrasively with mounting demands for national self-determination. Some, like the Greeks and Romanians, had already won their independence. For others, such as the Poles, national self-determination in 1912 seemed but a dream.

The prospect of national liberation revealed a grave difficulty: nationalities were rarely neatly divided from each other. Often impelled by raw and aggressive racism, peoples in their struggle for freedom competed with each other for the same territory. For example, the Czechs laid claim to Slovakia, on the grounds that it was part of the state originally created by King Wenceslas (the one who looked out); but Magyars also claimed Slovakia as an integral part of the lands of King Stephen, the first Christian monarch of Hungary. Few thought of asking the Slovaks what they themselves wanted.

In short, there was hardly a people in 1912 who had obtained national self-determination, or were still campaigning for it, who did not have a minority within the territory won or claimed, objecting strongly to the majority view. Ireland was no exception to this. Just as Hungarian, Romanian and German speakers were not neatly divided from each other in Transylvania, so nationalists and unionists – as near as makes no difference, Catholics and Protestants – were not neatly divided from each other in Ulster. For example, in 1912 there were more Catholic nationalists in Belfast, where they then formed only a quarter of that city's population, than there were in Fermanagh where they formed a majority. In 1912 it never occurred to either loyalists or nationalists in Ireland that their colliding ambitions could be compared with those festering so dangerously in central and eastern Europe.

Once the Parliament Act was on the statute book in 1911 it seemed that the very last obstruction to Home Rule had been removed. If the Home Rule bill promised was introduced early in 1912 and, as would be expected, the Lords rejected it, the very latest that Ireland would get a parliament of her own would be some time in the year 1914.

Euphoria swept through the ranks of the Irish Party at Westminster. Back home, nationalists all over the island rejoiced, even though Home Rule would give Ireland devolved powers no greater than those nowadays enjoyed by the Scottish Parliament in Holyrood. They eagerly anticipated the dawn of a new age in Ireland, the imminent arrival of a long-yearned-for freedom, democratically sanctioned by a majority of the elected representatives of the entire United Kingdom.

The Protestants of Ulster, in contrast, stared at the future in horror. Home Rule to them was a deadly threat to their liberty. They felt sure that a Dublin parliament would weigh down the prosperous north-east with crippling taxes to subsidise impoverished peasants in the south and west. They feared that Home Rule would be Rome rule, that the Catholic Church would come to dominate the country's institutions, schools in particular. International Catholicism was seen as a dark conspiracy, its power growing inexorably, perpetually endangering Protestant liberties. The promulgation of the *Ne Temere* papal decree in 1907, which many honestly, if incorrectly, believed laid down that Catholics marrying Protestants must bring up their children as Catholics, had recently aroused Protestant fury. Before the decree around thirty per cent of Presbyterian ministers favoured Home Rule; after it, the percentage dropped to about four.[2]

In addition, unionists were certain that nationalists would never be satisfied with mere devolution; that – once they had their Home Rule parliament up and running in Dublin – they would, from that

---

2   K. Dunn, 'A short history of mixed marriage in Ireland', in P. McLaughlin (ed.), *Mixed Emotions: real stories of mixed marriage* (Belfast, 2012), p. 77.

position of increased strength, press on to make a complete break with Britain, thereby casting the loyal people of the north out of the United Kingdom altogether.

The importance that Ulster unionists attached to the economic arguments against Home Rule must not be overlooked. Today the private sector in Northern Ireland is extremely fragile. It was so different in 1912: the north-east of Ireland was then one of the planet's most dynamic corners. Ulster was the world centre of the linen industry. Back in 1894 H. O. Lanyon, president of the Belfast Chamber of Commerce, had made this estimation:

> I find the length of yarn produced in the year amounts to about 644,000,000 miles, making a thread which would encircle the world 25,000 times. If it could be used for a telephone wire it would give us six lines to the sun and about 380 besides to the moon. The exports of linen in 1894 measured about 156,000,000 yards, which would make a girdle for the earth at the Equator three yards wide, or cover an area of 32,000 acres, or it would reach from end to end of the County of Down, one mile wide.[3]

Output was even greater by 1912. Entire towns, such as Gilford, Sion Mills, Killyleagh and Drumaness, were devoted exclusively to processing flax into linen, though it was in Belfast, by passing down the canyon of the Crumlin Road, flanked by tall forbidding mills, or by looking up at the great ornate warehouses in Donegall Square and Bedford Street, that the global dominance Ulster had in this textile industry was made most obvious.

At the beginning of the twentieth century Belfast was, after London and Liverpool, the port of third importance in the United Kingdom, then the greatest trading state on earth; and in 1912 it had the world's biggest linen mill, ropeworks, tobacco factory, spiral-guided gasometer,

---

3   *Belfast Directory*, 1896; J. Bardon, *A History of Ulster* (Belfast, 1992), p. 390.

tea machinery and fan-making works, aerated-waters factory, dry dock, handkerchief factory and shipyard (launching vessels which were the largest human-made moving objects on earth). In short, Ulster was by no means an obscure corner of the United Kingdom. Indeed, its very prosperity – then ascribed, of course, to the beneficial power of the Protestant work ethic – gave unionists confidence that they had the power to face down Home Rule.

By the beginning of 1912 they were ready. This had taken quite a bit of time. Their leader, Colonel Edward Saunderson, described by his friend J. Mackay Wilson as being 'absolutely devoid of business capacity', had died in 1906. His replacement, Walter Long, dismissed by David Lloyd George as an 'amiable Wiltshire Orangeman', was hardly an improvement on Saunderson; he deigned to attend a golfing dinner at Portrush but failed to appear at the annual meetings of the Ulster Unionist Council (UUC) in 1908 and 1909.[4]

That UUC had been formed back in 1905 by men who rightly predicted that their Conservative allies would soon be put out of office, opening the door for the Liberals and their nationalist friends. The Orange Order, which for several decades had been cold-shouldered by moneyed and landed Protestants, was enjoying a spectacular revival, thanks in no small measure to the MP for East Down, Captain James Craig, who impressively augmented the number of brethren by indefatigably addressing lodge after lodge.

Walter Long, perhaps taking heed of a friend's warning against 'sinking yourself in the Irish stew', gave up his Dublin seat in 1910 and got elected in a London constituency.[5] Sir Edward Carson took his place. MP for Trinity College Dublin, the man who had brought down Oscar Wilde, a former solicitor general, Carson quickly proved

---

4   A. Jackson, *The Ulster Party: Irish unionists in the House of Commons, 1884–1911* (Oxford, 1989), pp. 58, 286; Bardon, *History of Ulster*, p. 426; A. Jackson, *Colonel Edward Saunderson* (Oxford, 1995), p. 112.
5   Jackson, *Ulster Party*, p. 296.

himself the leader Ulster unionists had yearned for. No man in Ireland, with the possible exception of the trade union leader Jim Larkin, could sway an audience with such skill. Carson's tall frame commanded respect and the grim set of his lower jaw seemed to show northerners that he would not yield in championing their cause.

On 23 September 1911 Carson crossed the Irish Sea to address 50,000 men who gathered to meet their new leader in the extensive grounds of 'Craigavon', Captain Craig's home in east Belfast. 'With the help of God,' Carson assured them, 'you and I joined together will yet defeat the most nefarious conspiracy that has ever been hatched against a free people.' By now dynamically led and efficiently organised, the Ulster unionists could nevertheless not hope to succeed on their own. It was vital to forge a closer alliance with the Conservative Party.

A good many bridges between Ulster unionists and British Conservatives were in urgent need of repair. When he was chief secretary, George Wyndham had found 'the parochialism of the Ulster right-wing ... beyond belief', and had remarked: 'My contact with the Ulster members is like catching an "itch" from park pests.'[6] But exclusion from office after 1905 for years on end had been a chilling and sobering experience for Conservatives. And just like Ulster unionists, Conservatives were in urgent need of a dynamic leader who could hold them together. In November 1911 they found such a man – Andrew Bonar Law. Though he had been born in Canada and lived most of his life in Scotland, his father was an Ulster Presbyterian minister who had been born in Coleraine and then had retired there. Bonar Law quickly proved an unflinching friend of loyalist Ulster.

A fresh bonding of Ulster unionists and Conservatives on the other side of the Irish Sea was overdue. Early in the spring of 1912 the UUC prepared a great demonstration against Home Rule in

---

6   *Ibid.*, p. 128; A. T. Q. Stewart, *The Ulster Crisis* (London, 1967), p. 48.

south Belfast, with Bonar Law as the keynote speaker. The city's tram service was suspended as seventy special trains brought in demonstrators from all over Ulster to the agricultural show grounds at Balmoral. No fewer than seventy English, Scottish and Welsh Conservative MPs had come over to take part. More than 100,000 men marched in military formation past the platforms. After prayers and the singing of the ninetieth Psalm, a resolution against Home Rule was passed with a rousing acclamation; immediately afterwards, from a ninety-foot flagstaff rising from a tower in the centre of the grounds, the largest Union Jack ever woven was broken and unfurled.

As Bonar Law stepped forward to speak, he knew that a reference to the Siege of Derry would strike a chord in the hearts of his listeners:

> Once more you hold the pass, the pass for the Empire. You are a besieged city. The timid have left you: your Lundys have betrayed you; but you have closed the gates. The Government have erected by their Parliament Act a boom against you to shut you off from the help of the British people. You will burst that boom.[7]

This formidable display of loyalist strength was an outward and visible sign, an open declaration that the Conservative Party had made a fateful decision – it had unequivocally committed itself to giving unswerving support to all that the Ulster unionists intended to do to oppose Home Rule. Banishing all doubts, Bonar Law echoed Bismarck's 'blood and iron' speech to the Reichstag at a great unionist rally at Blenheim Palace in July. 'There are things stronger than parliamentary majorities,' he told his listeners. 'I can imagine no length of resistance to which Ulster can go in which I should not be prepared to support them.'[8]

---

7   Stewart, *Ulster Crisis*, p. 55.
8   Stewart, *Ulster Crisis*, pp. 54–7; A. Parkinson, *Friends in High Places: Ulster's resistance to Irish Home Rule, 1912–14* (Belfast, 2012).

On 11 April Asquith had introduced the Home Rule bill in the Commons. In nationalist Ulster feelings of elation were short-lived. In June a Liberal backbencher, Thomas C. Agar-Robartes, put forward an amendment to the bill, commenting that 'I have never heard that orange bitters will mix with Irish whiskey.'[9] This amendment proposed to exclude the four Ulster counties (Antrim, Down, Londonderry and Armagh) with a Protestant majority from the bill's operation. Though it was defeated, the idea that all or part of Ulster would be excluded from the operation of Home Rule was to gain favour at Westminster.

This was a matter of deep concern for Joseph Devlin. 'Wee Joe' had succeeded in wresting control of the Irish Party machine from the bishop of Down and Connor, Bishop Henry Henry (what were his parents thinking when they named him?). Devlin had left school at twelve to work as a bottle-washer in a pub, and had won the North Kilkenny seat in 1902. Acting as general secretary of the United Irish League from 1903, he won West Belfast by a margin of sixteen votes in 1906. Proving himself to be an eloquent and colourful figure in the House of Commons, he became known there as the 'Pocket Demosthenes'.

The politics of this single-identity ghetto fiefdom in west Belfast was narrow. Devlin took over control of the Ancient Order of Hibernians (AOH) – an overtly sectarian body, a Catholic mirror image of the Orange Order, directly descended from the Defenders of the late eighteenth century and the Ribbonmen of the nineteenth. This was a high-risk strategy: the hierarchy's ban on the Order had only been removed in 1904 and Cardinal Michael Logue continued to describe the AOH as 'an organised system of blackguardism'. In the words of Éamon Phoenix, 'Devlin failed palpably to comprehend the exaggerated image of an insidious Catholic power which his reinvigorated

---

9   Stewart, *Ulster Crisis*, p. 59.

AOH conjured up in the minds of Ulster Protestants.'[10] Devlin argued that if the Order was brought under the umbrella of the Irish Party it could be better controlled and a source of strength. In that he was right: the AOH was more deeply rooted in Ulster than the United Irish League could ever hope to be. In a speech he had made in 1906, Devlin declared that the AOH had a great mission to perform, 'but let that mission be performed in a spirit of holy toleration' – in the north of Ireland that was a big ask. He became national president and grand master of its ruling body, the Board of Erin. By 1911 there were no fewer than 433 divisions of the AOH in Ulster.[11] Certainly the unity northern nationalists displayed in 1912 was impressive.

Carson and Bonar Law had metaphorically published the banns of marriage between the Ulster unionists and Conservatives. What next should be done to halt Home Rule in its tracks? The Ulster Unionist Council now set about organising a rolling programme to demonstrate to the world, and the British public in particular, the determination of northern Protestants to resist all attempts to impose on them the authority of a Dublin parliament. Captain Craig and his team worked ceaselessly to make sure that this display of unionist strength would be so impressive that the world's press could not ignore it. They were also acutely conscious of the need to depict their movement as respectable, law abiding, disciplined and dignified. These organisers knew their own province. Elizabethan conquest and Jacobean plantation had sent shock waves reverberating down the centuries. Acrid memories of previous dispossessions and massacres passed down from one generation to another. Here fierce emotions sustained by ancient hatreds lurked just below the surface. Already there were alarming indications that those passions might not stay there.

---

10   É. Phoenix, *Northern Nationalism: nationalist politics, partition and the Catholic minority in Northern Ireland* (Belfast, 1994), pp. 2–6.
11   A. Morgan, *Labour and Partition: the Belfast working class 1905–23* (London, 1991), pp. 39–41; *The Irish News*, 7 May 1912.

On Thursday 27 June 1912 there was an attack on pupils of the Sacred Heart convent in Lisburn – eighty girls aged between five and thirteen, looked after by three nuns. The sisters had hired two motor brakes to take them to and from the beach at Ballyhornan near Ardglass. On the outward journey, which began at 7.30 a.m., the children were subjected to 'insulting epithets' and a volley of stones in Young Street but, though one nun was struck by a stone on her leg, the children got to their destination without serious injury. A much larger mob gathered at the Ballynahinch Road in Lisburn to await the return of the excursionists. The children were assailed with 'mud, stones, sticks and filth'; the nuns put up their umbrellas in a vain attempt to ward off the missiles, 'and in consequence were singled out for special rough treatment'. The most concentrated attack was on a car carrying several priests who had accompanied the children, subjected to showers of stones from Young Street to the Union bridge, 'whilst the yelling of the mob was audible far and wide'.[12]

Two days later, on Saturday 29 June 1912, nationalists held what was billed as a 'Great Ulster Home Rule meeting' at Maghera in County Londonderry. The attendance of some Protestant members of the Liberal Party enabled *The Irish News* to sport the headline the following Monday: 'Creeds combine to make vigorous demand for self-government'. Special trains running from Coleraine, Ballycastle, Cookstown, Ballymoney and Antrim helped to bring the numbers attending to around 10,000. Just before one o'clock the procession was marshalled in the town square. Here were gathered members of the Irish Party, the United Irish League, the AOH and the Liberal Party, all of them Home Rulers. The speeches were notably mode-rate: one said that they 'sought peace and security, loyalty to the King and Empire, that they wanted to manage their own domestic affairs at home, subject to the supremacy of the Imperial Parliament (Hear,

---

12 *The Irish News*, 27 June 1912.

hear). They wanted neither separation from England nor a separation of Ulster (Cheers).' Resolutions were carried with acclamation: the fourth directly concerned itself with the amendment, put before the House of Commons eighteen days earlier to exclude the four most Protestant counties from the bill's operation. It read:

> That made up as we are of men from that portion of Ulster which it was proposed to exclude from the provisions of the Home Rule Bill, we protest against anything that would tend to differentiate us from the rest of Irishmen. We are one in name and in fame with our fellow countrymen in the other parts of the country.[13]

It was not the Maghera meeting itself but what happened immediately afterwards that made Saturday 29 June 1912 a notorious day in Ulster's history. Whitehouse Presbyterian church in north Belfast organised its Sunday school outing that day to Castledawson, a County Londonderry village near Lough Neagh. Around 500 children left Belfast by train under the supervision of adults, including Rev. Mr Barron. At the close of what had been a pleasant day out in a field lent by the local bleachworks, the children paraded back through the village to the railway station with their flute band, holding aloft banners bearing texts from scripture and a union flag. Coming in the opposite direction were four divisions of the AOH, about 200 men, described as being 'all fully grown ... apparently of the labouring type'. They, of course, were returning from the meeting in Maghera, some seven miles away from Castledawson. As the two parties passed, one Hibernian grabbed the union flag from a child, and suddenly the children and the adults with them were assaulted by Hibernians who, a Welsh observer later reported, were 'under the influence of drink ... more like wild beasts than men'. Unionist

---

13   *Ibid.*, 1 July 1912.

accounts included descriptions of women stabbed 'promiscuously' with ceremonial AOH pikes, flags and banners being torn, and the faces of many children being cut. The police rushed to the scene and, once they presented their weapons, the Hibernians fled. But the terrified children had been scattered, some hiding under bushes, and it took hours to get them all back to the station.

Though it gave extensive coverage to the Home Rule meeting in Maghera, *The Irish News* made no mention at all of the assault at Castledawson. But *The Northern Whig* carried the headline 'Nationalist outrage – women and children stabbed', and gave a vivid description of the children's ordeal.[14] That Monday, 1 July, Protestant workers at the Castledawson bleach green came out on strike because, they alleged, one of the employees was a Hibernian involved in the attack. Next day violence erupted in Belfast, beginning in Workman Clark's shipbuilding yards. As *The Irish News* reported:

> The trouble originated in the North Yard, where a party of young men took it into their heads, after the breakfast hour, to single out such of their fellow-workers as were suspected of leaning towards Catholicism in religion or Nationalism in politics, and subject these obnoxious individuals to abuse and maltreatment ... inside of a very few minutes turmoil was spreading through the departments ... none who was supposed to answer in any way to the widely applied epithets of 'Fenian' or 'Papist' – accompanied by characteristic language – escaped the attention of the marauding gang. Several were attacked and beaten in a brutal and cowardly manner ...[15]

These men took the offensive, rallying to the cry 'Remember Castledawson', and then proceeded to the Milewater wharf, seeking

---

14 *The Northern Whig*, 1, 2 July 1912; *Belfast Newsletter*, 1, 2 July 1912; Morgan, *Labour and Partition*, pp. 126–7; McMinn, *Against the Tide*, pp. 111–12.
15 *The Irish News*, 3 July 1912.

more victims. 'Any who were found were knocked down, beaten and kicked.' Some Protestant foremen, seeing the attackers approach, smuggled Catholic workers out in the nick of time. In the afternoon, the loyalist shipwrights swept into Workman Clark's south yard and soon succeeded in clearing out all the Catholic employees there, numbering 300–400. Those Catholics who decided to stand their ground or simply did not move out fast enough were struck with angle irons and the like.

Those who rushed out of the gates were subjected to further assaults until their tormenters were driven off by police wielding batons. Around 7 p.m. a large crowd gathered at the Northern Counties railway terminus, intent on attacking a labour parade. Organised by James Connolly of the Transport Workers' Union, and D. R. Campbell of the Belfast Trades Council, this had begun at the Customs House steps with speeches by the two men. There Campbell and Connolly made strong appeals that all workers should put sectarianism aside and work in unity and harmony for the betterment of their conditions. But hearing that 'an unruly gathering' had assembled, the speakers abandoned a planned march with their 'non-sectarian brass band' and urged their hearers to go home immediately.[16]

The expulsions resumed next day, 4 July, spreading all over Queen's Island. During 'dinner hour' Catholics who had not already fled were singled out in the dining hall, dragged off and 'pretty severely maltreated'. At the bottom of one boat 'a couple of unfortunates who, it transpired, belonged to the same religious category as their assailants, were soundly beaten, on the grounds that they were "sympathisers" with the minority'. The violence continued because a considerable number of those driven out had not received their pay and could only get it by returning to the shipyards. On 5 July shipwrights broke in to the Sirocco engineering works at Bridge End. Having made a

16 *Ibid.*; Morgan, *Labour and Partition*, pp. 128–9.

successful rush at the gate, they swept forward, demanding that any 'Catholic workers should be cast forth'. Around forty men, employed in this, the largest fan-making and tea machinery works in the world, were driven out. The expulsions spread to Anderson's felt works and the Linfield flax mill and across the city in the weeks that followed.

At Westminster Devlin told fellow MPs that, from a message he had received that morning, over 2,000 Catholic workmen had been driven from their employment, and there was uproar when he asserted that Sir George Clark had encouraged the expulsions from the Workman Clark yards. Charles Craig, brother of Captain James, said that Clark had only returned from Switzerland that morning and anyway, he continued, shouting above the uproar, the trouble in the shipyards 'had been a small disturbance at Belfast altogether compared to the brutal and inhuman conduct with regard to the Sunday school excursion at Castledawson'. Joe Devlin weakened an otherwise strong case by denying what the Hibernians had perpetrated in Castledawson.[17]

Belfast was not the only place affected. Catholics were driven out of their places of work in Carrickfergus and on 7 July Catholics were fired on at Maghery on the southern shore of Lough Neagh. A feis was being held at Maghery to raise money for a new Catholic church in Loughgall. Nationalists from Armagh city, accompanied by the Armagh Irish Pipers' Band, proceeded by brakes and cars to the feis. At the request of the police they took a circuitous route. But on the return journey around a hundred loyalists had gathered at Tullyroan corner to vent their displeasure. As the motor vehicles ran this gauntlet, shots were fired at the nationalists from a nearby hill. Fortunately the bullets failed to strike their targets.[18]

Back in Belfast the approach of the annual holiday, known as the 'Twelfth Fortnight', provided some respite. The expelled workers

17 *The Irish News*, 5, 6 July 1912; Morgan, *Labour and Partition*, p. 132.
18 *The Irish News*, 8 July 1912.

sent a deputation to London to see both Redmond and Birrell. Both played down the gravity of the expulsions. Disappointed though they were, expelled Catholics agreed to attempt to get back their jobs at the end of the holiday, on Tuesday 23 July at Harland and Wolff, the 'big yard', and on Friday 26 at Workman Clark, the 'wee yard'. At breakfast time around 2,000 loyalist workers surged out of both yards to attack those trying to return. The police were swept aside. On Sunday 28 July a committee of Catholic clergy and laymen launched a relief fund on behalf – as *The Irish News* put it – of 'the Wounded soldiers of the Home Rule struggle'. A parish priest in Banbridge, John Rooney, wrote a long letter to *The Irish News* on 5 August, urging this Vigilance Committee to widen its appeal beyond Ulster:

> The support of the thousands of persons who are now on the verge of starvation through the brutal intolerance and inhuman violence of their fellow-workers would require that collections be started immediately in every parish throughout the length and breadth of Ireland ... it may be necessary to appeal for aid to our co-religionists in Great Britain, the United States, and the English Colonies. Strong men compelled to be idle through fear of their lives, their wives and children in dire want through loss of their earnings, and the maimed and wounded lying on their beds of pain in the Mater Infirmorum Hospital are sad and melancholy facts ...[19]

Harland and Wolff did at least punish 500 men working on the SS *Daro*, known as the 'Orange Boat', by laying them off. The military commander in Belfast, Count Gleichen, Queen Victoria's nephew, felt he had no choice but to respond to a request from the RIC to send in more troops. Devlin actually offered the army a map to guide the soldiers and to indicate likely flashpoints on Queen's Island. And

---

19 *Ibid.*, 9 July, 5, 6 August 1912.

so British troops were on active service in Belfast for much of the summer of 1912, patrolling the Queen's Road in particular with fixed bayonets. The soldiers were not withdrawn until 16 September.

Some of those who had been to the fore in driving Catholics out of the yards were brought before the courts. Carson, holidaying at a spa in Germany, got to hear about them. More concerned about those charged than their Catholic victims, Carson wrote to Craig on 21 August from Bad Homburg: 'I am very distressed about the men who are being prosecuted for the rows in the shipyards. Do you think they or their families ought to be assisted in any way? You know how much I feel about others suffering when I don't, and they received great provocation.'[20]

The danger of sudden intercommunal strife remained constant. For example, on 14 September, during a football match at Celtic Park between Linfield and Celtic, fighting broke out at half-time. Quickly the ground was engulfed by rival hordes of supporters engaging each other with fists, bottles, knives and revolvers, until the Blues supporters were driven back into their Protestant enclaves.

At that very moment on the other side of Europe the world was being given a grim demonstration of what could happen in an all-out conflict in a deeply divided society. That autumn of 1912 the Balkan wars began to rage, characterised by merciless ethnic slaughter on a biblical scale. By June 1913 no fewer than 200,000 combatants had fallen, in addition to tens of thousands of unarmed men, women and children savagely cut down, mutilated or raped, simply – as they would say in Ulster – for being 'the other sort'.[21]

Meanwhile in Belfast the organisers were redoubling their efforts to ensure that the climax of their campaign, 'Ulster Day', would not be besmirched by undignified, unseemly behaviour. It had been

---

20   Morgan, *Labour and Partition*, p. 137.
21   M. Glenny, *The Balkans 1804–1999: nationalism, war and the Great Powers* (London, 1999), pp. 229, 244.

agreed some time before that the solemnity of the occasion could best be sealed by getting their followers to enter a binding oath to resist Home Rule. At his London club, Captain Craig was advised by a friend: 'You couldn't do better than take the old Scotch covenant. It is a fine old document, full of grand phrases, and thoroughly characteristic of the Ulster tone of mind at this day.'[22] The phrasing of the 1580 covenant actually proved too archaic but it was retained as a template. The final text of the Ulster Covenant was composed by Thomas Sinclair, one of a commission of five appointed to frame a constitution for a provisional government of Ulster.

Craig's meticulously planned campaign kicked off on 18 September at Enniskillen, where Carson was met at the railway station by two squadrons of mounted volunteers and escorted to Portora Hill. There he reviewed 40,000 members of Unionist Clubs marching past him in military order. Next day Sir Edward read out the text of Ulster's Solemn League and Covenant to journalists who had gathered in the grounds of Craig's home. Signatories would pledge themselves 'to stand by one another in defending for ourselves and our children our cherished position of equal citizenship in the United Kingdom, and in using all means which may be found necessary to defeat the present conspiracy to set up a Home Rule Parliament in Ireland'.

That evening, 19 September, Carson rushed to Lisburn to view a great procession of men carrying dummy wooden rifles and flaming torches and marching to bands playing such well-known loyal anthems as 'The Protestant Boys' and 'Boyne Water'. Over the following days at least a dozen more meetings ensued, with Carson being joined by such Conservative dignitaries as Lord Salisbury, Lord Willoughby de Broke, F. E. Smith, Lord Charles Beresford and Lord Hugh Cecil. At every meeting a single resolution was carried: 'We will not have Home Rule.'

---

22   Stewart, *Ulster Crisis*, p. 61.

All of this was leading up to 'Ulster Day', Saturday 28 September, when across the northern province men were invited to sign the Covenant and their womenfolk a matching Women's Declaration. That day, declared a public holiday, dawned bright and clear and defied the forecast by remaining almost cloudless. At 9.25 a.m. a guard of 2,500 men recruited from the Unionist Clubs of Belfast gathered at the City Hall; at 10 a.m. the first relief of 500 men wearing bowler hats and white armlets, and carrying white staves, began the day-long task of marshalling the crowds and protecting the flowerbeds. The Portland stone of the City Hall gleamed in the sun; formally opened six years before, this was one of the most sumptuous municipal centres in the United Kingdom, a fitting pivot of the resistance to Home Rule. To most of its citizens Belfast's prosperity depended on it remaining an integral part of the United Kingdom. Now they prepared to give fervent expression to their feeling.

Just before 11 a.m. Bedford Street was packed with spectators as Carson stepped into the Ulster Hall. Craig reminded everyone in the packed hall that there should be no applause as this was a religious service. The congregation sang 'O God, our help in ages past', and after prayers and lessons had been read, the Rev. Dr William McKean rose to deliver his sermon, taking as his text II Timothy 6:20: 'Keep that which is committed to thy trust'. 'We are plain, blunt men who love peace and industry,' the former Presbyterian moderator declared. 'The Irish question is at bottom a war against Protestantism; it is an attempt to establish a Roman Catholic ascendancy in Ireland to begin the disintegration of the Empire by securing a second parliament in Dublin.'

All over Ulster similar services were being held in Protestant churches. From the Ulster Hall Sir Edward walked bareheaded into Bedford Street towards Donegall Square. Captain Anketell Moutray proudly carried before him King William's flag, a yellow banner decorated with a star and a red cross, said to have been borne at the

Boyne. The guard of honour that had escorted Carson – splendid with military medals, specially embroidered sashes, and white staves – stood to attention on either side of the Queen Victoria memorial statue as the lord mayor, R. J. McMordie, MP, the councillors in their scarlet and ermine robes, the civic mace bearers and other city dignitaries greeted Carson.

Carson entered the vestibule and advanced towards a circular table directly under the dome rising 173 feet above him. He took up the silver square-sided pen made by Sharman D. Neill of 22 Donegall Place and presented to him the evening before. It bore the inscription: 'With this pen I, Edward Carson, signed Ulster's Solemn League and Covenant, in the City Hall, Belfast, on Ulster Day, Saturday 28th September, 1912'. When he re-emerged the reverential hum in the vast crowd outside changed to tempestuous cheering as he made his way bowing and waving down Donegall Place to Royal Avenue, where he was to be the guest of the Ulster Reform Club for luncheon. Behind him the stewards struggled to regulate the flow of men eager to sign the Covenant in the City Hall. A double row of desks stretching right round the building made it possible for 550 to sign simultaneously. Some cut themselves and signed in their own blood – though Major Frederick Crawford of gun-running fame lied when he declared he had done so. Every signatory was given a handsome parchment paper copy of the Covenant to take home.

All over Ulster men and women were signing the Covenant or the declaration. At Castle Upton in County Antrim, Lord Templetown signed the Covenant on an old drum of the Templepatrick Infantry. At Baronscourt the Duke of Abercorn inscribed his signature under an old oak tree.

At 2.30 p.m. a procession of bands from every Protestant corner of Belfast converged on the City Hall. As each contingent arrived the bandsmen halted at a prearranged position in Donegall Square, all continuing to play different tunes, creating, in the opinion of *The*

Northern Whig, 'a fine post-impressionist effect about it that should have pleased admirers of the new style of music'.[23] J. L. Garvin, reporting for the *Pall Mall Gazette*, wrote:

> Seen from the topmost mast outside gallery of the dome, the square below, and the streets striking away from it were black with people. Through the mass, with drums and fifes, sashes and banners, the clubs marched all day. The streets surged with cheering, but still no policemen, still no shouts of rage or insult …[24]

Signatures were still being affixed in the City Hall after 11 p.m.

Huge crowds sang 'Rule Britannia' and 'God save the King' as Carson and the unionist leaders walked round the corner from the Ulster Reform Club in Royal Avenue to the Ulster Club in Castle Place. Trams had to be diverted and jarveys were forced to take their horses away from the Bank Buildings to a place of safety. At 8.30 p.m. a brass band advanced towards the Ulster Club playing 'See the Conquering Hero Comes', its staff major and spear carriers almost having to carve a way through the surging mass. A searchlight from the Olde Castle restaurant played on the scene and deafening cheers greeted Carson when he came out of the club and, with twenty other dignitaries, climbed into a waiting motor brake designed for twelve passengers. Lord Londonderry, swept off his feet, temporarily got lost in the crowd. The vehicle was pulled down High Street by hundreds of willing hands. 'With a roaring hurricane of cheers punctuated on every side by the steady rattle of revolver shots,' Garvin wrote, 'onward swept this whole city in motion with a tumult that was mad.'

Another enormous crowd was waiting at the Belfast Steamship Company's shed in Donegall Quay; many clung to perilous perches

---

23   *The Northern Whig*, 30 September 1912.
24   *Pall Mall Gazette*, 30 September 1912.

on cranes and lampposts. Sir Edward was saluted by a fusillade of shots and prolonged cheering. After making a short speech, he was welcomed aboard the SS *Patriotic* by Captain John Paisley, and from the upper deck, the *Belfast Newsletter* reported, he shouted out: 'I have very little voice left. I ask you while I am away in England and Scotland and fighting your battle in the Imperial Parliament to keep the old flag flying. (Cheers). And "No Surrender!" (Loud Cheers).' As the vessel steamed into the Victoria channel, bonfires in Great Patrick Street sprang to life, a huge fire on the Cave Hill threw a brilliant glare over the sky, fifty other bonfires blazed from hills and headlands round Belfast Lough, and salvoes of rockets shot up into the air.

All over Ulster people were still signing the Covenant. Altogether 471,414 men and women who could prove Ulster birth either signed the Covenant or the declaration.[25]

Ulster Day was denounced as 'a silly masquerade' by *The Irish News* and as 'an impressive farce' by *The Freeman's Journal*, while the *Manchester Guardian* contrasted 'the anarchic hectoring of the ascendancy party and the loyal patient reliance of the Ulster Nationalists upon English justice and firmness'. Garvin, however, now knew this was no game of bluff and blackmail: 'No one for a moment could have mistaken the concentrated will and courage of those people.'[26] The next two years seemed to reveal the truth of his judgement.

Northern nationalists attempted to treat Saturday 28 September 1912 as part of a normal autumn weekend. Meetings that Sunday organised by the United Irish League had probably been arranged long beforehand. The biggest was held at Newtownhamilton in south Armagh after last mass, 'almost the entire congregation assembling outside the church to hear the address', we are assured. Dr Charles

---

25 *Belfast Newsletter*, 30 September 1912; Stewart, *Ulster crisis*, pp. 62, 66–7; Bardon, *History of Ulster*, pp. 437–9.
26 *The Irish News, The Freeman's Journal* and *Manchester Guardian*, 30 September 1912. For Garvin see Stewart, *Ulster Crisis*, p. 65.

O'Neill, MP for South Armagh, singled out Lord Londonderry, the man who had signed the Covenant immediately after Carson in Belfast City Hall, for special scorn:

> Lord Londonderry had very little to do with Ireland, except to extract rack rents from his starving tenantry, who were mainly Protestants. (Hear, hear.) He also derived a huge income from collieries in the North of England, at Durham, Cumberland, and other places. His sweated workers thus enabled him to propagate all the hollow mockery he was now engaged in, and to carry on his campaign of vilification of Ireland and the Home Rule cause. (Hear, hear).[27]

The Irish News tried not to be exultant when it reported that a widow named Eliza Watterson, a resident of Church Street, Downpatrick, had dropped dead immediately after subscribing her name to the Women's Declaration. Its headlines were: 'Carson's Covenant comedy, concluded'; 'a silly masquerade in Belfast'; 'Grotesque proceedings'; 'City Hall utilised as political playground'; '"Religious" rantings'; 'Unionist Clubmen "the Supers" in gigantic farce'; 'Noisy night scenes'; and 'Revolver shots and fireworks attend "Ulster king's" departure'.

It gave a very full account of Ulster Day if only to mock the whole proceedings:

> At last the curtain has been rung down on the Ulster day farce, and … wound up its fantastic career in a paroxysm of flag-waving and noise, emblematic of the whole grotesque scheme from start to finish. The stage lost an actor manager when the law and politics claimed Sir Edward Carson. His unfailing instinct for theatrical effect was never better exemplified than on Saturday in his state 'progress' from the Ulster Hall to the City Hall … he had set himself a part which was a mixture

---

27   *The Irish News*, 30 September 1912.

of Cromwell and King William III, with just a suggestion of Charles I on the way to execution; but he rather spoiled the effect by introducing a melodramatic swagger reminiscent of Sidney Carton's farewell.[28]

What is clear is that northern nationalists refused to regard this demonstration of unionist strength, this determination to ignore the decisions of a Dublin parliament, as a deadly threat to Home Rule in their province. When Redmond dismissed Carson's speeches as bluff and blackmail, he was undoubtedly being advised by Joseph Devlin. Devlin had this strong belief that a substantial number of Ulster Protestants supported Home Rule or that they could be persuaded to see its merits in the end. Above all, nationalists were sure that Asquith could and would deliver. They were not to be frightened by men marching with dummy rifles.

The spirits of nationalists in Ulster were raised spectacularly by a by-election victory in the Londonderry City seat at the end of January 1913. The city was so polarised at this juncture that the turnout was extraordinarily high – 98.25 per cent. The unionists had held the seat for thirteen years but on this occasion the Irish Party candidate, David Hogg, was elected by a majority of fifty-seven votes. As the result was announced snow was falling thickly from a lowering sky. As nationalists cheered jubilantly and unionists jeered and groaned, shots were fired, and loyalists began to throw volleys of snowballs, loaded with as much mud as possible. Nationalists broke through the police cordon. Armed police came to attention and charged to separate the mobs. That evening, *The Irish News* reported:

Bonfires were lighted in the Nationalist centres, arches were erected, flags and other emblems displayed; the windows were illuminated by rows of candles, and portraits of famous Nationalist leaders and Gladstone ...

28 *Ibid.*

> This only embittered the Unionists ... A number of their supporters came over Carlisle Bridge at ten o'clock in a riotous mood. The police stationed in the Square met them at the double, and the mob ran helter-skelter.[29]

Hogg's victory gave the nationalists an overall majority in the nine counties of the historic province of Ulster. This gave Redmond a false sense of security. The 1911 census showed that over fifty-seven per cent of the inhabitants of Ulster were Protestant. The point often made by Devlin, that a great many Protestants were Home Rulers, seemed to be proved. Actually it proved that the redistribution of seats in Ulster was long overdue – eastern Ulster, greater Belfast in particular, was seriously under-represented.

Of course there were Ulster Protestants who gave strong support to Home Rule. The night before the by-election, the principal speaker urging voters to cast their ballots for Hogg was Swift MacNeill, MP. As reported, he said:

> He as a Protestant wanted Derry, with all its traditions, to be in the front line. He wanted a vote from Derry to consummate Ireland's achievements ... He was a Protestant, the son of an Irish Protestant clergyman, and the grandson of an Irish Protestant clergyman and as strong a Protestant as anyone.[30]

A covenant in favour of Home Rule was drawn up by Rev. Armour of Ballymoney, and Ulster Protestants were invited to affix their signatures to it. Armour had once declared that the 'principle of Home Rule is a Presbyterian principle' and denounced his fellow ministers' 'senseless fear of Romanism'. He scoffed at loyalist threats of resistance as 'the result of a bad attack of *delirium tremens*'. When

---

29   *Ibid.*, 1 February 1913.
30   *Ibid.*, 29 January 1913.

the threats began to materialise, Armour described Carson as 'a sheer mountebank, the greatest enemy of Protestantism in my opinion existing, inflaming men to violence'.[31] Amongst those who signed this anti-covenant were Sir Roger Casement, recently knighted for his consular services in exposing brutality and enslavement in the Belgian Congo and the Amazon basin, and still a moderate Home Ruler; and Captain Jack White of Ballymena, a man with a distinguished service record who would go on to help form the Citizen Army in Dublin. The significant fact, however, is that only around 3,000 signatures were collected for this anti-covenant, and a great many of those who signed were not really Irish nationalists; they were old-style Liberals opposed to the Conservative and Unionist Party and resentful of the residual arbitrary power of landlords and Church of Ireland clergy. Armour of Ballymoney clearly fell into that category.

If unionist spirits were cast down by Hogg's victory in the Londonderry by-election, they were raised again by the Ulster Unionist Council's decision at its AGM in January 1913 to unite volunteers who had been marching and drilling – many of them for more than a year – into a single body, the Ulster Volunteer Force (UVF).

Perhaps even more than the tramp of drilling Ulster Volunteers, northern nationalists feared the ever-growing threat that Ulster or part of it would be excluded from Home Rule. The likelihood of partition had lurched into the foreground when, in December 1912, the standing committee of the UUC, as quietly as it could, decided to set to one side its opposition to Home Rule for all Ireland. Henceforth that opposition would be limited to the nine northern counties of the historic province. This was confirmed on 1 January 1913, when Carson put forward a resolution in the House of Commons to exclude the whole province of Ulster from the operation of Home Rule when it was enacted.

---

31   McMinn, *Against the Tide*, pp. xli, li–lii, lvi.

For as long as he could Devlin resisted demands from his own followers to form a Catholic Defence Force. Redmond, too, would not sanction a nationalist volunteer force. However, the pressure to create a counterweight to the UVF in the end proved too strong. Significantly it was a northerner, Eoin MacNeill, who spearheaded the launch of the Irish Volunteers at Dublin's Rotunda in November 1913.

During the twelve months between the summer of 1913 and the summer of 1914, Ulster – indeed, Ireland as a whole – was careering down the road to civil war. The gun had returned centre-stage to Irish politics. Even before corps of loyalists who had taken to drilling had been brought together to form the UVF, militant separatism was revitalising. The Irish Republican Brotherhood, almost defunct at the beginning of the century, recruited a new generation of activists.

Since one extreme is liable to produce another, it is not surprising that Ulster tended to spawn those who most strongly believed that freedom was most reliably produced from the barrel of a gun. Immediately after the meeting in the Rotunda in November 1913, Tom Clarke, the Dungannon dynamiter who had served a long penal servitude sentence, wrote to Joe McGarrity, the Tyrone-born Clan na Gael leader in Philadelphia:

> Joe, it is worth living in Ireland these times – there is an awakening – ...
> about 4,000 enrolled that night ... 'tis good to be in Ireland these times
> ... Wait till they get their fist clutching the steel barrel of a business rifle
> and then Irish instincts and Irish manhood can be relied upon.[32]

At the beginning of December 1913 the funds of the Irish Volunteers stood at £8 7s 6d, this at a time when the UVF had over £1 million pledged to it and £70,000 invested in a hazardous enterprise to bring

---

32   F. X. Martin, 'MacNeill and the foundation of the Irish Volunteers', in F. X. Martin and F. J. Byrne (eds), *The Scholar Revolutionary: Eoin MacNeill and the making of the new Ireland* (Shannon, 1973), pp. 174–5.

guns to Ulster. But the Irish Volunteers soon grew to match and even surpass the Ulster Volunteers in numbers if not in resources. By the beginning of 1914, while Asquith was still trying to persuade Redmond to accept at least the temporary exclusion of some Ulster counties from Home Rule, northern nationalists were becoming ever more anxious. After the near-mutiny of cavalry officers at the Curragh camp in March 1914, the inspector general of the RIC observed that northern Home Rulers were 'getting restive under the strain of the political crisis'.

Then on the night of 24–5 April 1914 came the landing of 24,600 rifles and 5 million rounds of ammunition at Larne, Bangor and Donaghadee – 216 tons in all. The UVF was now armed to the teeth. In response nationalists rushed forward to swell the ranks of the Irish Volunteers. By May, of 129,000 Irish Volunteers, 41,000 were enrolled in Ulster. In Belfast Irish Volunteers marched and paraded along the Lower Falls while, separated by just a few short, narrow streets (the very ones torched in August 1969), Ulster Volunteers drilled up and down the Shankill Road and Peter's Hill. A bloody conflict seemed impossible to avoid. Colonel Maurice Moore, organiser of Irish Volunteers in Tyrone, Derry and Donegal, declared in June 1914, 'any government that attempts gerrymandering the nationalist counties out of Ireland must render an account to us'.[33] Soon after Carson addressed the UVF at Larne, making public his melancholy: 'I see no hopes of peace … I see nothing at present but darkness and shadows … we must be ready … the fate of our country cannot be delayed for many weeks … we shall have once more to assert the manhood of our race.'[34]

He meant Ireland. Of course, it was not in Ulster but in Flanders, Gallipoli and beyond that the manhood of Carson's race would be asserted. Civil war in Ireland was averted, or at least postponed, by a very much more terrible internecine conflict on the European mainland.

---

33 Phoenix, *Northern Nationalism*, p. 14.
34 Stewart, *The Ulster Crisis*, p. 223.

13

The Ulster Volunteer Force, 1913–14

Timothy Bowman

This article will consider the Ulster Volunteer Force (UVF) in what could be termed its 'classical period' of 1913–14, at the height of the third Home Rule crisis, from the formation of the force in January 1913 until the passage of the third Home Rule bill in September 1914.[1] The UVF was built on the foundations of existing Orange Lodges, Unionist Clubs and the Enniskillen Horse.[2] Its formation was more rapid in some areas of Ulster than others (and it was formed in all of the historic nine counties of Ulster) and local issues also impacted on arming, equipment, training and membership, meaning that the force took on a rather 'patchwork' appearance. UVF personnel in different areas also took very varying attitudes as to what their duties would be in the event of an outbreak of civil unrest. At its height in the summer of 1914, the UVF may have been able to call on as many as 110,000 members. It can, at one level, be viewed as a military force and, indeed, men were trained and armed, and contingency plans drawn up for likely conflict in the event of Home Rule being passed. However, the

---

1   Much of this paper is based on my *Carson's Army: the Ulster Volunteer Force, 1910–22* (Manchester, 2007).
2   The Enniskillen Horse was formed in September 1912, as was the Young Citizen Volunteers (YCV) in Belfast. The YCV were incorporated into the UVF in spring 1914, but they have been excluded from specific mention here as they were originally formed as a 'non-sectarian' and 'non-political' force.

UVF should also be seen as fulfilling a crucial propaganda role. It was UVF personnel who provided enthusiastic and disciplined crowds for many of the Unionist rallies, addressed by Sir Edward Carson and other leading politicians, which so impressed sympathetic journalists from Great Britain throughout 1913 and 1914.

It is tempting to portray the UVF as both the first fascist army and one of the earliest paramilitary forces in Europe in the twentieth century. The late Professor F. X. Martin of University College Dublin raised the question, 'Was the Ulster Volunteer Force the first fascist army in modern times?'[3] Ideologically, of course, the UVF had little in common with fascism; no new economic programme, no dreams of regaining lost provinces and essentially endorsing the mainstream conservative policies of the Unionist party. It would be very misguided to categorise UVF attitudes to Catholics as similar to Nazi attitudes to Jews. Whatever sectarian views an element within the UVF may have held about their Catholic neighbours, one looks in vain in the local press for any speeches by unionist leaders where Catholics are demonised as some form of *untermensch*. Indeed, there is some evidence of Catholic membership of the UVF, notably in Lisburn, County Antrim.[4] However, in terms of fascism simply as a mass movement with impressive parades, propaganda campaigns and rallies, there is clearly a resonance with the UVF.

Paramilitarism, which, as a mass movement, had been largely confined to Ireland before the First World War, became a European phenomena immediately after the war.[5] However, the conditions that

---

3   F. X. Martin, '1916: myth, fact and mystery', *Studia Hibernica*, vol. 7 (1967), p. 56.
4   UVF Order 74, 18 July 1914, O'Neill papers, D.1238/178, Public Record Office of Northern Ireland (PRONI); *Fermanagh Times*, 4 September 1913.
5   Richard Bessel, *Germany after the First World War* (Oxford, 1993); Julia Eichenberg, 'The dark side of independence: paramilitary violence in Ireland and Poland after the First World War', *Contemporary European History*, vol. 19 (2010); Robert Gerwarth and John Horne, *War in Peace: paramilitary violence in Europe after the Great War* (Oxford, 2012); Timothy Wilson, *Frontiers of Violence: conflict and Identity in Ulster and Upper Silesia, 1918–1922* (Oxford, 2010).

bred paramilitarism in Europe in 1919, dependent as they were on the after-effects of the First World War, were very different from those that had given birth to paramilitarism in Ireland in 1913. Rather than seeing the UVF as a predecessor to fascism and paramilitarism in inter-war Europe it would be more accurate to locate it within what can be termed an Irish Protestant volunteering tradition. This can be traced back to the plantations of the late sixteenth and early seventeenth centuries and later manifested itself in the Laggan Army of the 1640s, the Irish Volunteers (1775–92), Irish Yeomanry (1796–1834), Ulster Volunteer Force (1913–14), Ulster Special Constabulary (1920–70), Ulster Defence Regiment (1970–92) and post-1966 Loyalist paramilitary groups.[6] The formation of the UVF also built on the experience of militant Ulster unionists during the first and second Home Rule crises. Drilling certainly took place at Richhill, County Armagh, in 1886, when a local solicitor drilled around thirty men in the demesne and Temperance Hall. The government's failed attempt to prosecute those participating in this drilling seriously curtailed the Liberal administration's ability to act against the more widespread drilling of 1913–14.[7] In County Fermanagh in 1893 small

---

6   Allan Blackstock, *An Ascendancy Army: the Irish yeomanry 1796–1834* (Dublin, 1998); David Boulton, *The UVF 1966–73* (Dublin, 1973); Steve Bruce, *The Red Hand: Protestant paramilitaries in Northern Ireland* (Oxford, 1992); Michael Farrell, *Arming the Protestants: the formation of the Ulster Special Constabulary and the Royal Ulster Constabulary 1920–27* (London, 1983); Arthur Hezlet, *The 'B' Specials: a history of the Ulster Special Constabulary* (London, 1972); Kevin McKenny, *The Laggan army in Ireland 1640–1685* (Dublin, 2005); D. W. Miller, 'Non-professional soldiery, *c.*1600–1800' in Thomas Bartlett and Keith Jeffery (eds), *A Military History of Ireland* (Cambridge, 1996); John Potter, *A Testimony to Courage: the regimental history of the Ulster Defence Regiment* (Barnsley, 2001); Chris Ryder, *The Ulster Defence Regiment: an instrument of peace?* (London, 1991); D. H. Smyth, 'The Volunteer movement in Ulster: background and development, 1745–85', unpublished PhD thesis, Queen's University Belfast, 1974; Stephen Small, *Political Thought in Ireland 1776–1798: republicanism, patriotism and radicalism* (Oxford, 2002), pp. 83–112; I. S. Wood, *God, Guns and Ulster: a history of loyalist paramilitaries* (London, 2003).

7   '1886–1913 Arms importation + distribution', memorandum from George Hazlett, sessional crown solicitor, Lurgan to chief secretary, 11 June 1886, CO

groups of men were drilling at Castle Irvine, Ballinamallard, Killadeas, Maghera[lough] and Carrickreagh. Most of this drilling appears to have been organised by Major Gerard Irvine, a major landowner, and the RIC believed that no more than 200 men were being drilled, armed with nothing more than dummy guns. The local district inspector of the RIC felt that prosecution of Irvine would serve no useful purpose as it would simply serve to publicise his activities and political views.[8] The year 1893 also saw the formation of the Young Ulster movement under the leadership of Fred Crawford, who was later to become famous for organising the large-scale UVF gun-running of 1914. This movement was a small, secret society, whose members had to own a Martini rifle, Winchester rifle or a .45 revolver. Crawford also claimed to have established several rifle clubs and revived the North of Ireland Rifle Club's range to allow unionists to practise shooting. It appears that the Young Ulster movement petered out as Crawford became worried that his arrest was increasingly likely, and, of course, the second Home Rule bill was defeated in the House of Lords.[9]

The UVF, when formed in January 1913, aimed to provide a focus for existing militant activity by Ulster unionists and also to fully mobilise the 'unorganised unionism' that had been witnessed in September 1912 with the signing of the Ulster Covenant by almost 220,000 men.[10] It drew on existing military activity (usually nothing more demanding than basic drill) that was being carried out by Orange Lodges and Unionist Clubs. By December 1910 Orange Lodges were undertaking military preparations, and by April 1911 the RIC were

---

904/28/1, British National Archives (BNA); and 'Prosecution for illegal drilling in June 1886', CO 904/182, BNA.

8   All details on this 1893 drilling are taken from '1886–1913 arms importation + distribution', reports by chief inspector, Fermanagh, 22 September 1893, District Inspector P. R. Slacker, 21 July 1893 and District Inspector G. A. Gambell, 18 March 1893, CO 904/28/1, BNA. Also the *Donegal Vindicator*, 12 May 1893.

9   F. H. Crawford, *Guns for Ulster* (Belfast, 1947), pp. 10–11.

10   *Northern Whig*, 30 September 1912.

reporting that lodges in County Fermanagh were starting to drill. By the end of 1911, the police had firm evidence that Orange Lodges in County Armagh had started to obtain rifles from Birmingham.[11] The Unionist Clubs, which had originally been formed in 1893 and had been in abeyance since 1896, were reformed by Viscount Templetown in April 1911 under instructions from the Ulster Unionist Council. By mid-August 1912 there were 316 clubs, all but ten of them in the nine counties of Ulster.[12] The establishment of Unionist Clubs occurred, however, in an *ad hoc* manner, which may partly be explained by Alvin Jackson's view that unionism was able to manifest itself through pre-existing organisations in some areas.[13] While the county inspector for Tyrone in February 1911 noted a marked lack of enthusiasm in the county, his counterpart in Antrim noted that clubs had been reformed in most of the towns there and the commissioner in Belfast also noted that a number of clubs were being reformed or established in the city.[14]

Of course, the Unionist Clubs were not simply established as the basis for a military organisation. They had a propaganda role and were associated with particular parliamentary constituencies in Great Britain where they were expected to promote the Irish unionist cause at the next general election. Clubs also had a social aspect, hosting concerts for their members and, certainly in some Belfast areas, providing club rooms and bars. Nevertheless, by autumn 1912 most clubs had established drill classes and some also rifle clubs, though some senior

11   Report from Belfast detective department, RIC, 4 April 1911, CO 904/28/2, BNA; letter from Colonel R. H. Wallace to Masters of Orange Lodges, December 1910 (precise date unknown), CO 904/182, BNA; report by District Inspector J. McMahon, 6 April 1911, CO 904/182, BNA. Also the *Northern Whig*, 1 December 1911; *The Irish Times*, 7 December 1911; '1886–1913 Arms importation + distribution', report by Inspector E. S. Cary, 11 December 1911, CO 904/28/1, BNA.
12   'Minutes re. Unionist clubs', minutes of special meetings 15 December 1911, 23 August 1912, and AGM 29 February 1912, D.1327/1/1, PRONI.
13   Alvin Jackson, 'Unionist politics and Protestant society in Edwardian Ireland', *Historical Journal*, vol. 33, no. 4 (1990), pp. 839–66.
14   Report of inspector general, RIC to under secretary, Dublin Castle, March 1911; Report by county inspector for Tyrone to inspector general, CO 904/83, BNA.

police officers still felt that the drill being carried out was more for propaganda than strictly military purposes.[15]

The UVF also sought to bring some other military formations under the definite control of the Ulster unionist leadership. This was most noticeable in the case of the Enniskillen Horse. This regiment was formed by the maverick local newspaper proprietor and editor, William Copeland Trimble, of the *Impartial Reporter*, to provide an escort to Sir Edward Carson when he visited Enniskillen on 18 September 1912 to launch his series of public meetings, which would culminate at Belfast City Hall on Ulster Day, 28 September 1912. Trimble knew that the unionist demonstration, held in sparsely populated and majority-Catholic County Fermanagh, would not mobilise a massive crowd, compared to other, majority-Protestant areas of Ulster. On 3 September 1912 he issued a circular letter calling on his fellow unionists to form a mounted escort for Sir Edward Carson stating:

> Other places may have their meetings. Enniskillen must have one great distinctive feature of its own … This Escort will be the greatest feature of the day … As the Enniskillen meeting will be the first to be addressed by Sir Edward Carson in this campaign, unusual importance attaches to it, and newspapers will be represented from all parts of the globe. It is, therefore, all the more incumbent on us that our mounted escort be no childish affair with clumsy men and unmanageable horses, but a fine turn out of smart soldierly-looking men, well-groomed horses, and all showing the effects of organisation and discipline.[16]

---

15 'Minutes of special meeting', 23 August 1912, D.1327/1/1, PRONI; AGM, 5 March 1913, 'Minutes re. Unionist clubs'; 'Minutes', 23 April 1913, D.1327/1/2, PRONI; 'Minutes of the meetings of the Executive Committee of the Unionist Clubs Council', *Belfast Newsletter*, 6 March 1913; 'Minute book of Fortwilliam Unionist Club', D.1327/1/9, PRONI; 'Drilling by Orangemen and Unionist Clubs', 8 February 1913, CO 904/27/1, BNA.

16 'Miscellaneous papers regarding "drilling" by civilians in Ulster', circular letter from W. C. Trimble, 3 September 1912, WO 141/26, BNA.

As a result of Trimble's initiative, 200 mounted men paraded in Enniskillen on 18 September.[17]

While what might now be recognised as the first unit of the UVF was on parade in Enniskillen as early as September 1912, the term 'Ulster Volunteer Force' appears to have been used publicly for the first time by Colonel Sharman-Crawford, while addressing the Bangor Unionist Club on 22 December 1912, when he spoke of the arrangements for recruiting the new organisation.[18] UVF County Committees, normally consisting of senior local unionists and retired army officers, were formed in December 1912 and were responsible for administering the force and appointing officers at county level, but recruitment was patchy and subject to considerable local variations. A. P. Jenkins, the president of Lisburn Unionist Club, started enrolling men for the UVF in Lisburn and Dunmurray in January 1913, and had recruited 270 men by the end of the month, although recruiting continued until March 1914 when the Lisburn Battalion numbered 967 men.[19] In equally unionist Newtownards recruitment for the UVF did not begin until the end of February 1913, and until the summer of that year recruitment remained sluggish, a fillip being provided by Carson's visit to the town in July.[20] In South County Londonderry there seems to have been a significant delay in organising the UVF in some rural areas and as late as January 1914 the local unionist press was referring to a number of units as 'recently organised'.[21]

Throughout 1913 there were a series of demarcation disputes

---

17 'Enniskillen Horse', report by chief inspector, 4 October 1912, CO 904/27/1, BNA; *Fermanagh Times*, 19 June 1913; W. C. Trimble, *The History of Enniskillen with references to some Manors in Co. Fermanagh and other local subjects* (Enniskillen, 1919–21), vol. II, p. 1068.
18 *Northern Whig*, 23 December 1912.
19 'Membership roll of Lisburn Battalion, UVF', D845/1, PRONI; report by C.I. Vere Gregory, 26 January 1913, CO 904/27/2/I, BNA.
20 Trevor McCavery, *Newtown: A history of Newtownards* (Belfast, 1994), pp. 179–80.
21 *Mid Ulster Mail*, 10 January 1914.

between Unionist Clubs and the UVF. In March 1913 Lieutenant Colonel J. C. Madden of Clones Unionist Club 'suggested the advisability of distributing six rifles to each Club for instructional purposes'.[22] Madden may have believed that drilling under the aegis of the Unionist Club was a sensible precaution for unionists in the predominantly Catholic County Monaghan, or he may have been offended that Lieutenant Colonel Sir John Leslie had been appointed to command the Monaghan Regiment of the UVF. As late as April 1913 Unionist Clubs in the north-west wanted to hold a drill competition, but this was banned by the executive committee of the Unionist Clubs, who felt that a less overtly militarised demonstration would be more appropriate, presumably as military displays were now felt to be within the purview of the UVF.[23] In Newry there were obvious tensions between the Unionist Club and the County Committee of the UVF over the appointment of local UVF commanders, tensions that came to a head in September 1913 when the Club asserted its right to appoint all local commanders.[24] The problems manifest in Newry were seen elsewhere and in September 1913 Sir Edward Carson sent a circular letter to all Unionist Clubs calling on all of their eligible members to join the UVF. In October 1913 this call was echoed by Colonel R. H. Wallace, who made a similar plea to all Orangemen in the province of Ulster.[25] Nevertheless, as late as 3 October 1913, when Carson addressed a unionist demonstration at Raphoe, County Donegal, the local unionist press remained confused

---

22 Minutes of AGM, 5 March 1913, 'Minutes re. Unionist Clubs', D1327/1/1, PRONI.
23 Minutes, 23 April 1913, 'Minutes of the meetings of the Executive Committee of the Unionist Clubs Council', D1327/1/2, PRONI.
24 Letter from J. A. Orr to Captain Roger Hall, 1 October 1913, D1540/3/12, PRONI, cited in Patrick Buckland, *Irish Unionism 1885–1923: a documentary history* (Belfast, 1973), p. 232.
25 Entry for 10 September 1913, 'Minute Book of Fortwilliam Unionist Club' D1327/1/9, and letter from Colonel R. H. Wallace to Lord Bangor, 21 October 1913, D1889/1/2/3, PRONI.

about whether they were witnessing a parade by the Ulster Volunteers or by the 'drill sections' of the local Unionist Clubs.[26]

The UVF relied on the gentry, clergy, small professional classes and businessmen of Ulster for the majority of their officer corps. For example, in the 5th Tyrone Regiment the commanding officer was Thomas MacGregor Greer, a landed proprietor, the adjutant was John Byers, a solicitor, and the company commanders were Thomas Hegan (a farmer), William Leeper and Hugh Duff (both mill owners), Viscount Charlemont and Thomas Greer (both landed proprietors), Rev. C. A. B. Millington (one of three clergymen holding a rank in this battalion) and William Weir (a publican).[27] There were, however, some regional variations. The landed gentry seem to have been most important in organising and commanding the UVF in Cavan and Monaghan, though much less so in Donegal, the other Ulster county where Protestants were in a small minority, and Lord Leitrim faced some intimidation for his role in training and arming Ulster Volunteers there.[28] By contrast, in Seaforde, County Down, Major William George Forde, JP DL, the major landowner in the village, was happy to serve in the ranks of the local UVF company, which was commanded by Alexander McMeekin, his coachman.[29] Desmond Murphy believes that in Counties Donegal and Londonderry the gentry and Protestant clergymen were practically obliged to take command of UVF units, as local businessmen were concerned that they would be boycotted

---

26 *Derry Standard*, 3 October 1913.

27 This is based on a return in D.1132/6/7A, PRONI, detailing those attending the Baronscourt camp.

28 Terence Dooley, *The Plight of Monaghan Protestants, 1912–1926* (Dublin, 2000), p. 22 and *The Decline of the Big House in Ireland: a study of Irish landed families, 1860–1960* (Dublin, 2001), pp. 223–4; letter from Gerald Madden to Jack Madden, 26 December 1913, Madden papers, D.3465/J/37/55, PRONI; RIC County Inspector's report for Donegal for August 1913, CO 904/90, BNA; *The Donegal Independent*, 1 November 1913.

29 All details taken from D.1263/3, PRONI, enrolment register for Seaforde company.

if they accepted leadership roles. Clergymen were also important in providing the officer corps for UVF units in Fermanagh, providing five of the officers in the 1st Fermanagh Regiment.[30]

In theory officers were elected by the rank and file of the force: squads of twelve men would each elect their squad leader; two squads were to form a section with the men again electing their section leader; two sections were to form a half company, again electing a half company commander. Colonel Repington, the military correspondent of *The Times*, suggested that the system extended to the higher ranks of the UVF. He noted that company commanders were elected by the section leaders and they would then elect the commanding officer of their battalion, who would be appointed subject to the approval of UVF headquarters. Commanding officers might, or might not, be given the power to appoint their own second in commands and adjutants.[31] This system of election was similar to that used in Rifle Volunteer units in Great Britain between 1859 and the mid-1880s.[32]

William Copeland Trimble, commander of the Enniskillen Horse, remembered his election, stating, 'No local military gentleman would undertake the command; and sitting in the saddle at Castlecoole gate, troop by troop the men themselves elected Mr. Trimble as Commander.'[33] However, not all battalion commanding officers implemented the democratic system. E. C. Herdman, who was an officer in the North Irish Horse and chairman of the North Tyrone Unionist Association, and who seems to have assumed command of the Sion Mills Volunteers on the basis that he was part owner of the extensive

---

30   Desmond Murphy, *Derry, Donegal and Modern Ulster 1790–1921* (Derry, 1981), pp. 196–7; Adjutant's roll of 1st Fermanagh Regiment, D.1267/1, PRONI.

31   H. S. Morrison, *Modern Ulster: its character, customs, politics and industries* (London, 1920), p. 155; *The Times*, 18 March 1914.

32   I. F. W. Beckett, *Riflemen Form: a study of the Rifle Volunteer movement 1859–1908* (Aldershot, 1982), p. 175; Hugh Cunningham, *The Volunteer Force: a social and political history, 1859–1908* (Hamden, 1975), pp. 53–4.

33   Trimble, *The History of Enniskillen,* vol. II, p. 1068.

linen mills in the town, wrote to his section leaders stating that they should simply appoint 'smart young men' as their squad leaders.[34] In the Tyrone Regiment, UVF personnel were informed that instructors (i.e. men with some military experience) should not be elected as section commanders. They could be elected as company commanders but it was felt that they would be most valuable as colour sergeants. This attitude may have reflected a certain degree of snobbery in the UVF, as most former soldiers were employed in low status jobs, whereas there seems to have been a sense that UVF officers, if not gentlemen, should be drawn from at least the middle class.[35] Elsewhere UVF headquarters confirmed some officers' appointments in the autumn of 1913, apparently taking the view that having established themselves as local unionist leaders no further election to UVF command was needed. This was certainly the case for Captain Hon. Arthur O'Neill, MP, who commanded the North Antrim Regiment, and A. P. Jenkins who was appointed to command the Lisburn battalion of the UVF largely on the basis that he was president of the town's Unionist Club.[36]

The UVF could draw on a number of British Army officers to command or train its units, although other historians have vastly over-estimated the numbers so employed.[37] While most Edwardian army officers were unionist in their politics, comparatively few were prepared to throw in their lot with the UVF.[38] Overall, 132 serving or former

---

34   Battalion Orders for 1st (North) Tyrone Regiment, D.1414/30, PRONI. For details on Herdman see his obituary in *The Times*, 11 February 1949.

35   Lowry papers, typescript, 'Organisation of Section and Companies', D.1132/6/1, PRONI.

36   Letters from J. S. Reade, honorary secretary, County Antrim Committee to Captain Hon. Arthur O'Neill, 2 September 1913, and 10 October 1913, O'Neill papers, D.1238/9AK and 9AL, PRONI; Jenkins papers, letter from J. S. Reade to A. P. Jenkins, 17 October 1913, D.845/3, PRONI; *Lisburn Standard*, 29 November 1913.

37   A. T. Q. Stewart, *The Narrow Ground: the roots of conflict in Ulster* (London, 1967), p. 168.

38   On unionist sympathies amongst British Army officers see: I. F. W. Beckett (ed.), *The Army and the Curragh Incident 1914* (London, 1986); Timothy Bowman

officers, including cadet members of Officer Training Corps units, have been positively identified as being involved as officers in the UVF.[39] These officers essentially divided into two groups. One consisted of officers who were domiciled in Ulster and who had either retired from the regular army or were serving officers in the part-time Special Reserve. The other group consisted of professionals who were brought to Ulster by the unionist leadership, either to fill important staff and command positions, or to take up commands in the Belfast regiments.

Those British Army officers who took up UVF commands because they were already domiciled in Ulster were a rather varied group. Many were aristocrats or gentry who, like many of their counterparts in Great Britain, had spent a short period of time in the army before returning to Ulster to manage their estates. Good examples of this group are Viscounts Acheson and Northland, who had both retired from the army as mere lieutenants, but ended up commanding an entire UVF battalion each in the Tyrone Regiment due to their business interests and landholdings in the area. Others had spent their entire careers in the army, often rising to high rank and had retired to their estates after decades of service. Good examples of this group are Major General W. T. Adair, who had major landed interests around Ballymena and commanded the whole of the UVF in County Antrim, Colonel Oliver Nugent, who inherited the Farren Connel estate in County Cavan and commanded the Cavan Regiment, and the elderly

---

and Mark Connelly, *The Edwardian Army: recruiting, training and deploying the British Army, 1902–1914* (Oxford, 2012), pp. 170–5.

39 This figure has been principally calculated from 'Nominal Roll of Officers recently serving with UVF who have been recalled to Army Service', Richardson papers, D.1498/7, PRONI; 'HQ Irish Command report on Ulster Volunteer Force', *c.* September 1913, Mottistone papers, MSS 22/f.171, Nuffield College, Oxford; Carson papers, 'Return of Officers on Reserve or Special Reserve serving as Commanders + Staff officers with the Ulster Volunteer Force', *c.* June 1914, D.1507/A/10/10, PRONI; returns of officers involved in drilling civilians in Ulster, 1912–14, WO 141/26, BNA; *Hart's Army Lists*, 1903–1914; reports in the *Belfast Evening Telegraph, Belfast Newsletter* and *Northern Whig* for 1913–14.

Major General W. E. Montgomery, who commanded the UVF company in Greyabbey, County Down. Finally, there were gentry, professionals or businessmen whose entire British Army service had been spent in part-time units in Ireland, whether the pre-1908 militia, post-1908 Special Reserve, or the North Irish Horse. Amongst this group were to be found Major F. H. Crawford, who had served in the Donegal Artillery Militia, and Captain James Craig MP, who had served in the 4th Royal Irish Rifles (North Down Militia).

Those professionals who were brought to Ireland by the unionist leadership and British League for the Support of Ulster and the Union were a much smaller group, around fifteen officers in total, and were concentrated in the UVF headquarters and Belfast regiments, it having proved difficult to obtain a sufficient number of local officers to command UVF units in Belfast. Just as Sir Edward Carson did not qualify as an Ulsterman by birth or domicile (and was, therefore, theoretically ineligible to sign the Ulster Covenant of 1912), so the retired Indian Army officer, Lieutenant General Sir George Richardson, brought in to be the GOC of the UVF and to command the self-styled 'Covenantors', appears to have had no Ulster connections. The unionist leadership's first choice for this role had been Field Marshal Lord Roberts, the most famous Anglo-Irish soldier of his day but, while he sympathised with the UVF, Roberts was devoting all of his energies to the work of the National Service League, promoting the need for a conscript army in Britain. Richardson was offered command of the UVF on Robert's recommendation.[40]

The regular officers who came to serve with the UVF under the auspices of the British League for the Support of Ulster and the Union contained some idiosyncratic characters. Colonel J. H. Patterson was a well-known figure in Edwardian Britain, following the publication of his imperialist epic, *The Man-eaters of Tsavo*, in which he described

---

40 Hew Strachan, *The Politics of the British Army* (Oxford, 1997), p. 112.

how he managed to stalk and kill two lions who were killing labourers working on the Mombasa to Uganda railway. He was appointed to command the West Belfast Regiment and went on to have a colourful Great War record, commanding the Zionist Mule Corps at Gallipoli and the Jewish Brigade of the Royal Fusiliers.[41] F. P. (Percy) Crozier had a chequered military past, with service in the ranks in the Boer War and, as a commissioned officer, in the Manchester Regiment and West African Frontier Force. This led to alcoholism and his decision to resign his commission in 1909, having issued a number of dishonoured cheques. Having signed 'the pledge', he served in the Canadian Militia before joining the UVF. He also had a colourful war record, commanding the 9th Royal Irish Rifles on the Somme before being appointed to command a brigade. After the Great War he served as a Major General in the Lithuanian army before returning to Ireland to command the Auxiliary Division of the RIC in 1920-1.[42]

Michael Foy has claimed that the headquarters staff of the UVF 'had entirely adequate military credentials' and without doubt the UVF did manage to attract some well-qualified, long-serving regular British Army officers.[43] On the technical side, Lieutenant Colonel Robert Davis, a retired officer of the Indian Medical Service, was well qualified to be the secretary of the UVF medical board, and Major F. H. Crawford, a former Royal Artillery (Militia) officer, was equally qualified to be the director of ordnance. Colonel G. W. Hacket Pain,

41   Diary of Lady Lilian Spender, entry for 10 June 1914, D.1633/2/19, PRONI; J. H. Patterson, *The Man-eaters of Tsavo* (London, 1907); Patrick Streeter, *Mad for Zion: a biography of Colonel J. H. Patterson* (Harlow, 2004); J. H. Patterson, *With the Zionists in Gallipoli* (London, 1916); J. H. Patterson, *With the Judians in the Palestine Campaign* (London, 1922); Martin Watts, *The Jewish Legion and the First World War* (Basingstoke, 2004).
42   F. P. Crozier, *A Brass Hat in No Man's Land*, pp. 32-4; D. Starret, 'Batman', p. 14, 79/35/1, Imperial War Museum; personal file of Brigadier General F. P. Crozier, WO 374/16997, BNA.
43   M. Foy, 'The Ulster Volunteer Force' (PhD thesis, Queen's University Belfast, 1986), p. 71.

the chief staff officer, and Captain Wilfrid Spender, the assistant quartermaster general (QMG), brought appropriate command and staff experience with them, Hacket Pain having had considerable combat experience in both the Sudan and South Africa and having held the post of assistant adjutant general in the Egyptian army in 1897.[44] Spender was one of the relatively few officers of the British Army to hold the coveted 'psc' distinction after his name in the *Army List*, denoting that he had been selected for and passed through the Staff College course. This was no mean feat, especially given the tough competition amongst Royal Artillery officers for the small number of Staff College places allocated to this corps. He was not really to live up to these high expectations, however, entering the Great War as a captain and ending it as a lieutenant colonel, slow progress in a war where promotion was unusually fast. This should not distract us from the fact that he was perfectly competent to carry out the duties entrusted to him at UVF headquarters – which, as effectively QMG and secretary to the Provisional Government and three of its sub-committees, were, if not onerous, certainly diverse and complicated.[45]

Other men serving on the UVF headquarters staff had more flimsy military credentials. Major T. V. P. McCammon, who was appointed 'I[n] C[harge] Administration', was certainly a brave man and good commanding officer. He achieved the lieutenant colonelcy of the 5th Royal Irish Rifles at the age of thirty-eight, young for a Special Reserve unit, and was killed in action in April 1917 while

---

44 *Kelly's Handbook to the Titled, Landed and Official Classes* (London, 1914), p. 1128; obituary notice in *The green 'un* [regimental journal of the Worcestershire Regiment], April 1924, p. 5; obituary in *The Times*, 15 January 1924.
45 On Spender see I. L. Maxwell, 'The life of Sir Wilfrid Spender, 1876–1960' (PhD thesis, Queen's University Belfast, 1991). On the prestige of the Staff College in this period see Brian Bond, *The Victorian army and the Staff College 1854–1914* (London, 1972), p. 153 and I. F. W. Beckett, '"Selection by disparagement": Lord Esher, the general staff and the politics of command, 1904–14' in David French and Brian Holden Reid (eds), *The British general staff: reform and innovation, 1890–1939* (London, 2002), p. 43.

commanding the 2nd Hampshire Regiment.[46] But he was not viewed as a satisfactory staff officer when temporarily holding the position of Assistant Adjutant QMG in the 36th (Ulster) Division.[47] H. O. Davis, who had retired from the army as a mere lieutenant, seems to have been poorly qualified to hold the post of 'S[enior] O[fficer] for Instructors'.[48] What skills Lloyd Campbell, who had never held any military rank, had to be appointed 'Director of Intelligence' are completely unclear, and there is certainly no paper trail which suggests that he discharged these functions to any degree.[49] Indeed, the intelligence gathered by the UVF seems to have been gained through local initiatives or happy coincidence rather than through anything organised at UVF headquarters level.

Material on the rank and file of the UVF is rather sparse, particularly for Belfast, which, with its large, urbanised, Protestant population, accounted for one-quarter of the membership of the force. Detailed enrolment records survive for only a small minority of units. To the extent that any inference can be drawn from such a limited sample, they suggest that the UVF should be regarded as reflecting accurately the society from which it was drawn.[50] Joost Augusteijn's and Peter Hart's important works on the Irish Republican Army in the 1917–

46   Personal file of Lieutenant Colonel T. V. P. McCammon, WO 339/46427, BNA.

47   Personal file of Lord Craigavon, undated memorandum [July 1915], WO 339/3792, BNA.

48   Ulster Unionist Council (UUC) papers, 'Headquarters' Staff Enrolment Forms', D.1327/4/12, PRONI; O'Neill papers, UVF order 16, 11 November 1913, D.1238/115, PRONI.

49   UUC papers, 'Headquarters' Staff Enrolment Forms', D.1327/4/12, PRONI.

50   See especially, RIC report on Enniskillen Horse, CO 904/27, BNA; Adjutant's roll of 1st Fermanagh Regiment, D.1267/1, PRONI; enrolment register of Seaforde Company, D.1263/3, PRONI. A few UVF units' lists of members and addresses, but not occupations, survive: see PRONI, D. 845/1, for the Lisburn Battalion and D.3054/4/2 for Derry City UVF; the archive for 1st North Antrim Regiment held at Mid-Antrim Museum. The author is cross-tabulating these lists with the 1911 census returns to build up a larger sample of the UVF as a whole. It is hoped that the fruits of this research will be published in 2015.

23 period suggest that it was drawn disproportionately from skilled working-class and lower middle-class groups,[51] whereas, by contrast, in the 1st Fermanagh Regiment of the UVF fifty-seven per cent of men were farmers or farmers' sons, with twenty-five per cent labourers and just six per cent skilled workers and two per cent shop assistants or clerks.[52]

Of course there was considerable variation in the social structure of different UVF units. Lilian Spender highlighted the low social status of members of one unit:

> The West Belfast Regiment is the poorest of all, I mean its men are of a lower class than the others, as they are all in Devlin's constituency, which is the slummiest in the city. Many of the men looked just the type you see loafing about public houses, and were no better dressed, but they marched every bit as well as the others, and looked just as keen and determined.[53]

By contrast the Young Citizen Volunteers, after their incorporation into the UVF in spring 1914, remained as a self-conscious 'class corps' and, indeed, this unit was one of the few UVF units to wear a uniform. In the case of the Young Citizen Volunteers this was a grey uniform closely modelled on that of the 5th Scottish Rifles, an exclusive Territorial Force unit recruited from the middle class in Glasgow. A contemporary noted of the Young Citizen Volunteers:

> This was a body composed largely of young business men … In general type it closely resembled units of the standing of the London Scottish or

---

51 Joost Augusteijn, *From public defiance to guerilla warfare: the experience of ordinary volunteers in the Irish War of Independence 1916–1921* (Dublin, 1996), pp. 354–9 and Peter Hart, *The IRA at war 1916–23* (Oxford, 2003 edition), pp. 110–40.

52 These figures have been calculated from the Adjutant's roll of 1st Fermanagh Regiment, D.1267/1, PRONI.

53 Lilian Spender diary, entry for 6 May 1914, D.1633/2/19, PRONI.

the Artists' Rifles; and a very large number of its members subsequently obtained commissions [in the British Army during the Great War].[54.]

In theory those being recruited for the UVF had to be aged between seventeen and sixty-five. In many areas, however, particularly those where unionists were in a minority, this regulation seems to have been more honoured in the breach than the observance. Jack Sears, a retired NCO and UVF county instructor, noted that in Bellagh, County Fermanagh, of sixteen UVF members present at one drill five were boys.[55] At the other extreme, *The Times*' military correspondent, reviewing a parade of the North Belfast Regiment, remarked: 'I noticed, too, some of those quite old men who join the Volunteers for sentiment's sake.'[56] The oldest member of the Derry City Regiment appears to have been David McCauley, who was seventy-seven years old in 1914. A number of men, however, were simply noted as 'aged', and may have been even older.[57]

Details on the ages of all 3,428 men who served in the Derry City Regiment of the UVF survive. These show that seventeen per cent were aged between sixteen and nineteen years old, thirty per cent, twenty to twenty-nine, twenty-three per cent thirty to thirty-nine and ten per cent fifty to fifty-nine.[58] As with the IRA of 1917–23, therefore, the bulk of UVF members appear to have been in the twenty to twenty-nine age bracket. The proportion over twenty-nine was, however, much higher in the UVF than in the IRA; indeed the over-forty group, which was tiny in the IRA, was a significant percentage of the

---

54   Ramsay Colles, *The History of Ulster from the Earliest Times to the Present Day* (London, 1920), p. 249.

55   Charles Falls papers, notebook of John Sears, entries for 26 January, 12 February and 18 March 1914, D.1390/19/1, PRONI.

56   *The Times*, 16 April 1914.

57   J. M. Harvey papers, enrolment register for Derry City Regiment, D.3054/4/2, PRONI.

58   J. M. Harvey papers, roll book of the Derry City Regiment, D.3054/4/12, PRONI.

UVF. If, as Peter Hart has argued, membership of the IRA was partly the result of a rebellion of youth, then membership of the UVF seems to have been more likely the result of a mid-life crisis.[59]

The training provided for the UVF was very patchy and depended on the availability of sufficient instructors. It seems that most UVF units carried out one evening of drill per week, with occasional parades. Camps of instruction were set up for UVF officers and NCOs from autumn 1913 and for entire UVF regiments from Easter 1914. There was wide variation depending on the availability of instructors, suitability of accommodation and the number of rifles available. Jack Sears noted that in August and September 1913, drilling in County Fermanagh ranged from the poor to exemplary and that it had already ceased in some areas.[60] By December 1913 the City of Derry Regiment was deemed to be carrying out only 'very elementary' work, due to a shortage of officers and instructors.[61] As late as February 1914 the commander of 'A' Company, 2nd North Antrim Regiment, admitted that out of his seventy-three 'effectives', 'only a small proportion of them have had any musketry practice or would know anything about a rifle'.[62] As the crisis worsened there is some evidence that training became more intensive. At Crom, County Fermanagh, by early March 1914, for example, drill was taking place on Tuesday and Saturdays, with shooting practice on Thursdays.[63] It seems to have been early 1914 before training changed from drill to anything more advanced such as practice attacks and skirmishing.[64]

59   Peter Hart, 'Youth culture and the Cork IRA', in David Fitzpatrick (ed.), *Revolution? Ireland 1917–1923* (Dublin, 1990).
60   Charles Falls papers, John Sears's notebook, references for August and September 1913, D.1390/19/1, PRONI.
61   O'Neill papers, UVF order 15, 14 February 1914, D.1238/100, PRONI.
62   Hamilton papers, return for 'A' Company, 2nd North Antrim Regiment, 14 February 1914, D.1518/3/9, PRONI.
63   Charles Falls papers, John Sears's notebook, entry for 8 March 1914, D.1390/19/1, PRONI.
64   Charles Falls papers, John Sears's notebook, entries for 20 and 21 March 1914,

There were high absentee rates in a number of UVF units, as was the experience for many Territorial Force units in Great Britain, and this adversely affected training. In no. 1 section, 'J' Company of the 4th (Dungannon) Battalion, Tyrone Regiment, of fifty-nine members in November 1913 the average drill attendance was only thirty-two, with only nine men attending all drills and eight none at all.[65] In 'A' Company of the 2nd North Antrim Regiment, the CO reported seventy-three 'effectives' and fifty-eight 'non-effectives' in February 1914, continuing: 'A large proportion of the above [non-effectives] have never attended any drills + it is questionable whether these men intend to turn out in any capacity.'[66] Jack Sears was rather blasé about the poor parade attendance in the 1st Fermanagh Regiment. When inspecting the supposedly forty-eight strong 'B' company on 30 July 1913, he noted, 'The attendance (19) was fairly good considering busy time of year causing many men to be late.'[67] Seasonal factors also influenced drill attendance at other times of the year; a poor turnout at Enniskillen of just forty-two men out of a unit of 133 was thought to be due to the proximity of Christmas, and across County Fermanagh as a whole, drills were poorly attended during the harvest season.[68]

Absenteeism was a more widespread problem than the few detailed rolls which survive suggest. By March 1914 George Young, commanding a battalion of the Central Antrim Regiment, reported that he had 950 'effectives' but 1,100 non-effectives, 'many being unknown to him or any other commander'.[69] It seems likely that

---

D.1390/19/1, PRONI.

65   R. T. G. Lowry papers, note headed 'No. 1 Section, 'J' Company Dungannon Battalion', D.1132/6/17, PRONI.

66   Hamilton papers, return for 'A' Company, 2nd North Antrim Regiment, 14 February 1914, D.1518/3/9, PRONI.

67   Charles Falls papers, John Sears's notebook, entry for 30 July 1913, D.1390/19/1, PRONI.

68   Charles Falls papers, John Sears's notebook, entries for 30 August and 17 December 1913, D.1390/19/1, PRONI.

69   Memorandum by CO, Central Antrim Regiment, 1 March 1914, O'Neill

UVF attendance at parades was better than that for routine drills, but it is difficult to be certain in this respect as the unionist press tended to over-estimate the numbers on parade. Certainly at a parade in January 1914 the 10,000-strong East Belfast Regiment was reported as mustering just 3,000 to 4,000.[70] Between March and June 1914 most UVF units appear to have stopped recruiting and started to dismiss those who were deemed to be 'non-effective'.[71]

It seems likely that the turn-out for drills deteriorated over time as, under efficient instructors, men could have been taught the basics of company drill in three months. After this period, if not instructed in field craft or provided with rifle practice, it is easy to understand how enthusiasm would have waned. It also seems likely that drill was difficult to organise in rural areas, especially in winter when men would have had to walk long distances in cold and wet conditions to attend. Various mock battles and field days were carried out in spring and summer 1914, which were of some training value, but were organised primarily to provide publicity for the UVF and boost morale within the force.

Rifle practice was very difficult to organise as it was April 1914 before most UVF units received a significant amount of firearms. The first mention of a company of the Fermanagh Regiment using rifles is in January 1914 when it was noted that the Colebrook 'club' had eighteen Mauser rifles.[72] The issue of passing men as 'effective' without them having undergone rifle drill was addressed by Major General Adair who stated, 'So long as the authorities keep us short of arms men may at the discretion of Batt[alio]n. Com[man]d[an]t.

papers, D.1238/8, PRONI.

70 *Northern Whig*, 29 January 1914.

71 Lyle papers, circular letters issued by Lieutenant Colonel H. J. Lyle, March 1914 and circular letters issued by General W. T. Adair, May 1914, D.1518/3/8, PRONI.

72 Charles Falls papers, John Sears's notebook, entry for 28 January 1914, D.1390/19/1, PRONI.

be passed in drill without arms; but the use of even broomsticks when drilling, especially in extended order, is most desirable.'[73]

Finding experienced drill instructors was a great problem for many UVF units, especially as not all former or serving soldiers automatically made good instructors. In Tempo, County Fermanagh, the local UVF had been poorly drilled, despite the fact that their instructor was a member of the North Irish Horse. In Aughnaskew the instructor was 'an old man' whose only military experience had been around forty years previously, serving in the militia. The result of this was that by November 1913 the number of men who had passed the basic drill test in County Fermanagh was very low, with just 198 in the 1st Fermanagh Regiment, 79 in the 2nd Fermanagh Regiment, and 279 in the 3rd Fermanagh Regiment.[74]

The success of UVF training was, to some degree, dependent on the premises available; this was particularly the case in autumn and winter and in areas where unionists were a small minority of the population and did not want to drill in public. In County Fermanagh Jack Sears noted that at Kinowley the hall was 'very small for drill purposes' while at Crom, 'Drill is carried out in riding school where practically any movement with these men could be carried out.'[75] It seems likely that drill was easy to arrange in Belfast, where factories and warehouses were available and in various outbuildings that supportive landowners would provide, but otherwise could be impossible to perform properly in rural areas, where only a small church or Orange hall would be available. How to carry out drilling in private was a constant worry for the UVF. General W. T. Adair wrote to units in County Antrim in March 1914 stating:

---

73 Adair to regimental commandant, 14 February 1914, O'Neill papers, D.1238/9, PRONI.
74 Charles Falls papers, John Sears's notebook, entries for 19 August, 19 and 29 September 1913, D.1390/19/1, PRONI.
75 Charles Falls papers, John Sears's notebook, entries for 13 September 1913, D.1390/19/1, PRONI.

the Police are not to be allowed to enter any private demesnes where U.V. Forces are assembled, force being used if necessary ... in the event of the Police unduly interfering with any movements of the U.V.F., on duty, or going and coming from any such Camps or exercise, the police are to be warned that if they persist in such interference force will be used to prevent the same.[76]

One test of the military efficiency of UVF units was how quickly they could have turned out in the event of an emergency. Curiously, such exercises were not supported by UVF headquarters, an order of May 1914 noting, 'The General Officer Commanding deprecates such Mobilizations being carried out more than once, except where grave defects have been experienced the first time, as he considers it is an unnecessary hardship on the men, and in some cases a serious loss to employers.'[77] Detailed figures for the Pomeroy UVF during practice alerts were certainly not encouraging. At this trial mobilisation on 13 February 1914, the first man did not arrive until sixty-nine minutes after the warning was sent out at 5.06 p.m., while 204 minutes after the warning had been sent out only fifty-seven per cent of the unit had arrived.[78]

A large number of camps of instruction were organised, which were designed to teach UVF officers and NCOs their duties. Only in July 1914 were camps for whole battalions being formed, as in the case of that for the 2nd North Londonderry Regiment which was at Magilligan for three days.[79] The Tyrone Regiment camp was the earliest held, from 4–11 October 1913 at Baronscourt demesne. These camps varied considerably in size. The North Down Regiment

---

76   O'Neill papers, memorandum by Adair, 5 March 1914, D.1238/7, PRONI.
77   UVF Order 52, 23 May 1914, O'Neill papers, D.1238/150, PRONI.
78   Lowry papers, returns re. trial mobilisation of No.1 Section, 'J' Company, 4th Tyrone Regiment, D.1132/6/17, PRONI.
79   *Northern Whig*, 24 July 1914.

camp at Clandeboye at Easter 1914 had about 300 men, whereas the North Antrim Regiment camp at Lissanoure had just 116.[80] Attempts were made to run the camps in a thoroughly soldierly manner. At the camp held at Lissanoure Castle in April 1914 for the 1st and 2nd North Antrim Regiments no dogs or alcohol were allowed, and it was made clear that the camp would be organised under military discipline. Those attending were also requested not to interfere with the game or damage any trees or shrubs.[81]

It seems questionable how useful these camps were. They were, in most cases, shorter than the Territorial Force's recommended two-week camp, but other problems were more apparent. UVF HQ made only small grants towards their running costs (a grant of only £75 was made towards the Baronscourt camp) and this meant that additional finance was required. It was felt that employers would provide employees in UVF command roles with a week's leave on full pay so that they could attend the camp; in situations where this did not happen men were left in the position of both giving up their annual holiday and being considerably out of pocket for the privilege of attending one of the camps of instruction.[82] When a number of camps were held over Easter 1914, these not surprisingly saw a serious shortage of both instructors and equipment, and it says much for the lack of logistical support in the UVF that catering had to be entrusted to private firms.[83]

---

80   Letter from Lieutenant Colonel T. V. P. McCammon to Captain Hon. Arthur O'Neill, 27 March 1914, O'Neill papers, D.1238/65, PRONI; 'North Antrim Regiment: numbers who completed the 3 days course of instruction in camp at Lissanoure', O'Neill papers, D.1238/79, PRONI.
81   Printed booklet, 'Ulster Volunteer Force, North Antrim Regiment, Lissanoure camp', O'Neill papers, D.1238/68; letter from McCammon to O'Neill, 27 March 1914, O'Neill papers, D.1238/65, PRONI.
82   Circular to officers commanding companies, undated but probably August 1913, Lowry papers, D.1132/6/1, PRONI.
83   Letter from McCammon to O'Neill, 27 March 1914, O'Neill papers, D.1238/65, PRONI; letter from Director, Bloomfield Bakery to Captain Hon. Arthur O'Neill, 11 April 1914, O'Neill papers, D.1238/44, PRONI.

Despite these shortcomings many UVF personnel seem to have been impressed by the military training offered at the camps. At the Cavan Regiment camp in March 1914 Colonel Oliver Nugent, in his final address, compared the men favourably to regular soldiers and, offering a vote of thanks, Sergeant John Armstrong (presumably a retired NCO) spoke of the 'gentlemanly style' of training, continuing, 'Not an unkind word was ever made use of by any officer to any individual.'[84]

Closely linked to training was, of course, the issue of the supply of firearms to the UVF. Calculating the total number of firearms available to the force is simply impossible and this is shown by the disparity in figures offered by other historians. A. T. Q. Stewart has provided an incredibly precise figure, stating that in July 1914 the force had 37,048 rifles, while Josephine Howie has suggested a figure of 60,000 rifles by early May 1914.[85] The major gun-running coup of April 1914 brought in 20,000 rifles, but there were many other small-scale gun-running endeavours. In 1917, when there were fears that the IRA would raid UVF arsenals for arms, 54,130 military rifles of various patterns were placed under the care of the British military authorities, although it is clear that many rifles still remained in private hands after this point.[86] Nevertheless, many UVF commanders appear to have been unwilling to provide detailed returns of the numbers of rifles they possessed to UVF headquarters, fearful that they would be asked to surrender some of them to less well-armed units. The RIC was not a particularly effective detective force in any case, and the very lax firearms legislation in existence meant that, along with the Customs Service and Royal Navy, they were reluctant to stop and search suspected arms shipments. Before the Firearms Act of 1920 was introduced, there were a very

---

84   *Irish Post*, 21 March 1914.
85   Stewart, *The Ulster Crisis*, p. 248 and Josephine Howie, 'Militarising a society: The Ulster Volunteer Force, 1913–14' in Yonah Alexander and Alan O'Day (eds), *Ireland's Terrorist Dilemma* (Lancaster, 1986), p. 221.
86   'Return of rifles in possession of Ulster Volunteer Force', 28 February 1917, CO 904/29/2, BNA.

large number of revolvers, rifles and shotguns in private hands, in most cases not covered by any sort of licence. It seems likely that, in the event of a civil war, practically every member of the UVF could have been provided with a firearm of some sort.

The military rifles purchased by the UVF were of a variety of designs, calibres and vintages, the arsenal consisting of Lee Metford, Martini Henry, Martini Enfield, Mauser, Steyr and Vetterli rifles. As Charles Townshend has stated, this would have created a 'logistical nightmare' in any conflict and this seems to have been the case given the unwillingness of UVF units to agree to any sensible redistribution of arms.[87] Most rifles were of the single shot variety and a large minority were Vetterli rifles, which were purchased from the bargain basement of the international arms market, having been withdrawn from service in the Italian army in 1887.[88] Brigadier General Count Gleichen was utterly dismissive of the military value of these Italian rifles, noting 'they were not good, but weedy + weak + only cost 5 francs apiece, including belt and bayonet!'[89] It was probably the poor quality of these rifles that made the redistribution of arms throughout the UVF, as suggested by Colonel Hacket Pain, impossible, as no county committee wanted to risk their units being re-equipped solely with these Italian rifles, while their more highly prized British, German and Austrian rifles were sent elsewhere.

The distribution of rifles, as suggested by the numbers given over to the British authorities in 1917, does seem to have been based on political rather than military considerations. UVF units in Antrim, Down and Belfast in a strong position to lobby UVF headquarters,

---

87   Charles Townshend, *Political Violence in Ireland: government and resistance since 1848* (Oxford, 1988), p. 255.

88   John Whittam, *The Politics of the Italian Army, 1861–1918* (London, 1977), p. 194.

89   Report by Brigadier General Count Gleichen, 'The Ulster Volunteer Force', 14 March 1914, Mottistone papers, MSS 22/f.193–4, Nuffield College, Oxford. See also Count Gleichen, *A Guardsman's Memories* (London, 1932), p. 366.

received a disproportionately high number of modern Lee Enfield magazine rifles, all eleven machine guns and very few of the despised Italian rifles. By contrast, the bulk of the UVF arsenal in Armagh, Fermanagh and Londonderry consisted of Italian rifles, with almost forty per cent of the rifles in Monaghan also being Italian. From a military point of view, therefore, the units that were in the most danger were, in general, the worst equipped.

What exactly the UVF would have done, in the event of the Home Rule bill being enacted, is open to considerable conjecture. UVF headquarters did not function like a normal army headquarters and many command decisions would quickly have devolved onto unit or county commanders. At a province-wide level Colonel Hacket Pain attempted to introduce some emergency planning in May 1914, asking regimental commanders how many special service units they could form for service outside their own districts.[90] The answer in many areas was naught. Captain Hon. Arthur O'Neill, for example, commander of the North Antrim Regiment, utterly rejected the scheme, noting that as his district contained a considerable number of nationalists and no help from Belfast could be guaranteed, he felt that he could not spare any men for service elsewhere.[91]

More secretive contingency planning did take place. At a meeting in December 1913 in London, between the Ulster unionist leadership and UVF staff, there was a curious mix of indecision and prevarication. If arms were to be seized by the government the view was taken that organised resistance should take place but with 'No shooting'. It seems that a series of more detailed contingency plans were drawn up by Captain Wilfrid Spender in early 1914, although it is unclear the extent to which these were discussed, much less approved.[92] The 'Headquarters Defence Scheme' put its emphasis on maintaining communications

---

90 Memorandum by Hacket Pain, 7 May 1914, O'Neill papers, D.1238/88, PRONI.
91 Letter from O'Neill to Adair, 24 July 1914, O'Neill papers, D.1238/181, PRONI.
92 Maxwell, 'The Life of Sir Wilfrid Spender', p. 60.

and rapidly concentrating UVF units in an emergency: the role of the UVF was to be as a police rather than a military force, enabling the Ulster Provisional Government to assert its authority.[93] The lack of comprehensive contingency planning was probably an attempt to disguise the divisions within the UVF leadership over how they should react to military action by crown forces. James Craig thought that the UVF should risk everything in one 'stand up fight' with crown forces, while Fred Crawford felt that guerrilla warfare was the obvious response.[94] Lord Dunleath, a senior figure in the County Down UVF, stated, 'I do not believe that our men are prepared to go into action against any part of His Majesty's Forces.'[95]

It seems that some local units did carry out detailed contingency planning. The Central Antrim Regiment noted that UVF members were over-awed by nationalists in Cushendun and Cushendall, and plans were made to send two companies from Ballymena to these areas in the event of the Provisional Government being established.[96] Elsewhere there was clearly little agreement over what actions should be taken in the event of Home Rule being introduced. In County Cavan, the local UVF commander, Colonel Oliver Nugent, was wary of Belfast headquarters and stated that, in the event of conflict, his men would merely act as a police force in Cavan protecting Protestant lives and property.[97] Envisaging an entirely different scenario, Sergeant John Armstrong, speaking at the Cavan Regiment camp, was reported as saying:

93 'Headquarters Defence Scheme', undated but early 1914, Spender papers, D.1295/2/8, PRONI.
94 Memorandum by Craig, 26/7/1913, cited in Josephine Howie, 'Militarising a society', pp. 222–3; Craigavon papers, D.1415/B/34, PRONI; F. H. Crawford, 'The arming of Ulster', p. 27.
95 Letter from Lord Dunleath to Carson, 9 March 1914, Carson papers, D.1507/A/11/17, PRONI.
96 Memorandum by CO, Central Antrim Regiment, 1 March 1914, O'Neill papers, D.1238/8, PRONI.
97 Farren Connel papers, 'CVF Scheme', c. June 1914, D.3835/E/10/1, PRONI.

He wanted the commanding officer never to lose sight of the fact that no matter when they were called on, either by night or by day, to mobilise at a few moments' notice, they would be with him any place he required them to fall in (hear, hear) and till the last man dropped would stand by him, and would cheerfully obey his orders and all orders issued by him through their superior officers in charge of their respective districts.[98]

The UVF developed through 1913 and 1914 as something of a 'Frankenstein's monster' for the Ulster unionist leadership. Initially seen as useful in calming extremists and providing disciplined crowds for unionist demonstrations, it soon took on a life of its own. Had Home Rule been declared, the unionist leadership would have been committed to a military response, if only because they would have had little option but to support the local actions of individual UVF units. Following the Curragh 'incident' of March 1914, however, it seems unlikely that British troops could have been relied on to disarm the UVF. The RIC, small in number and also politically unreliable, would not have been able to act unaided. The Irish Volunteers, often seen as a political counterweight to the UVF, were a militarily insignificant force in the summer of 1914, poorly armed and badly trained. It seems likely, therefore, that the UVF would have been able to enforce the writ of the Ulster Provisional Government throughout most, if not all, of Ulster had not the First World War changed the political environment in Ireland entirely.

---

98 *Irish Post*, 21 March 1914.

The persistence of Liberal Unionism in Irish politics, 1886–1912

Ian Cawood

Political historians on both sides of the Irish Sea have largely overlooked an anniversary, even though 9 May 2012 marked 100 years since the formation of the modern Conservative and Unionist Party. It is an event forgotten because the reason for the party's creation, the threat of Home Rule for Ireland, had just moved a step closer on the day of its formation, when the second reading of the third Home Rule bill was passed by a majority of 101 in the Commons (two earlier Home Rule bills had been introduced – in 1886 and in 1893 – by Prime Minister William Ewart Gladstone, but neither had passed into law). Until recently, those scholars interested in British unionism have tended to view the issue from an Irish perspective, or more particularly, from an Ulster one. The largest number of studies published recently on British attitudes towards Ireland and on British support for the union in the late nineteenth and early twentieth centuries, have tended to focus on the personalities, ideologies and events on the island of Ireland. D. George Boyce and Alan O'Day have largely regarded Liberal Unionists as mere 'dissident Liberals', ciphers for Conservative opposition to devolution, not worthy of the attention that they give the Ulster unionist movement.[1] James

---

1   D. G. Boyce, *The Irish Question and British Politics, 1868–1986* (second edition,

Loughlin has been savage in his condemnation of the 'racism' (as he perceives it) of the English unionists, though he is frequently weak on the complexities of the British political narrative at this time.[2] Frank Thompson and Graham Walker have also written studies that briefly address the Liberal Unionists' role in 1886, but they are all more interested in the rise of Edward Carson's Ulster Unionist Party (UUP), which dominated the politics of Northern Ireland in the twentieth century, despite the fact that there was no connection between T. W. Russell's Ulster Liberal Unionists and Colonel Edward Saunderson's Ulster Loyal Anti-Repeal Union, from which the UUP evolved.[3] As Ian McBride wrote over fifteen years ago, 'much less research has been done on … the neglected strand of Unionism, represented by the Liberals'.[4]

At Westminster, unionist Liberals and the Conservatives had

Basingstoke, 1996); A. O'Day, *Irish Home Rule, 1867–1921* (Manchester, 1998); D. G. Boyce and A. O'Day (eds), *The Ulster Crisis, 1885–1921* (Basingstoke, 2006); P. Bull, '"Irish Protestants feel this betrayal deeply …".: home rule, Rome rule and nonconformity', in D. G. Boyce and R. Swift (eds), *Problems and Perspectives in Irish History since 1800: essays in honour of Patrick Buckland* (Dublin, 2004); D. G. Boyce and A. O'Day (eds.), *Defenders of the Union: a survey of British and Irish unionism since 1801* (London, 2001). Despite the title of the last, the Liberal Unionist Party is dismissed in two pages, pp. 105–6.

2   J. Loughlin, *Gladstone, Home Rule and the Ulster Question, 1882–1893* (London, 1986); J. Loughlin, 'Joseph Chamberlain, English nationalism and the Ulster Question', *History*, vol. 77, pp. 202–19; J. Loughlin, *The British Monarchy and Ireland, 1800 to the Present* (Cambridge, 2007). See also G. K. Peatling, 'Victorian Imperial theorist? Goldwin Smith and Ireland', in P. Gray (ed.), *Victoria's Ireland? Irishness and Britishness, 1837–1901* (Dublin, 2004). For an effective counter to these views, see P. Mandler, '"Race" and "nation" in Mid-Victorian thought', in S. Collini, R. Whatmore and B. Young (eds), *History, Religion and Culture: British intellectual history, 1750–1950* (Cambridge, 2000), pp. 242–4.

3   F. Thompson, *The End of Liberal Ulster: land agitation and land reform* (Belfast, 2001); G. Walker, *A History of the Ulster Unionist Party: protest, pragmatism and pessimism* (Manchester, 2004); G. Walker, 'Thomas Sinclair, Presbyterian Liberal Unionist', in R. English and G. Walker (eds), *Unionism in Modern Ireland: new perspectives on politics and culture* (Basingstoke, 1996), pp. 19–40. For a recent, more nuanced view of Irish unionism, see A. Jackson, *Ireland 1798–1998: war, peace and beyond* (second edition, Chichester, 2010), pp. 212–41.

4   I. McBride, 'Ulster and the British problem', in English and Walker (eds), *Unionism in Modern Ireland*, p. 13.

formed a pact before the first Home Rule bill's defeat in the Commons on 8 June 1886, under the terms of which they refused to put up rival candidates in any forthcoming election. The Liberal Unionist Party, however, was not founded until the summer of 1886, after the electoral defeat of Gladstone's government by the united action of the unionist factions. Most contemporaries had expected the Liberal leader – who was seventy-six – to retire after this event, and the leadership of the party to be resumed by the Marquess of Hartington – leader of the seventy-eight unionist Liberals who had retained their seats – who would then drop the policy of Home Rule. Gladstone, however, did not retire and so the unionists were forced, somewhat reluctantly, to form themselves into a political party and to enter into a tentative and limited 'compact' with the minority Conservative government of Lord Salisbury. Despite their historic reputation as a short-lived party of antediluvian Whigs, unable to come to terms with the new political environment of mass electorates, the new party, after an initial period of indecision, began to pioneer new techniques of political propaganda and organised a highly effective administration of local associations, agents and canvassers.[5]

Despite unionism's association with sectarian politics, John Bew has convincingly demonstrated that liberal unionism had a strong tradition in and around Belfast throughout the nineteenth century.[6] Despite having failed to win a single seat in the 1885 general election, in March 1886 the Irish Liberals organised a convention in St George's Hall, Belfast, after Randolph Churchill's speech at the Ulster Hall and Hartington's speech to the Eighty Club. Around 700 people attended, both Catholic and Protestant, and adopted the resolution of the leading Liberal businessman, Thomas Sinclair, that the union

---

5   For a full history of the Liberal Unionist party see I. Cawood, *The Liberal Unionist party, 1886–1912: a history* (London, 2012).
6   J. Bew, *The Glory of Being Britons: civic unionism in nineteenth-century Belfast* (Dublin, 2009).

should be maintained, as to do otherwise would be 'an abandonment of past Liberal policy in premature despair of its efficiency and as in our judgement fraught with danger to the industrial, social and moral welfare of the country'; he argued that 'an extended system of local self-government' should be adopted instead.[7] The historian W. E. H. Lecky, hitherto a favourite academic of the nationalists, attacked the idea of a separate parliament in a series of letters to *The Times* and spoke against the new policy in March.[8] His support, together with that of Daniel O'Connell's son and that of Catholic intellectuals such as Thomas Maguire, the first Catholic to become a Fellow of Trinity College Dublin, was crucial in enabling the Irish Liberal Unionists to present themselves as immune from sectarian Protestantism and representative of the whole community of the United Kingdom.[9] A further Liberal demonstration against the bill was held on 30 April at the Ulster Hall, at which it was resolved that a committee should be formed.[10] An Ulster Liberal Unionist Committee finally met on 4 June 1886, publicly condemning the violence that was breaking out across Belfast at that time and calling for restraint from all sides.[11] The membership comprised the majority of Belfast Liberals but was clearly limited in its organisation, as it later admitted that 'West Belfast was lost in 1886 merely by bad management and careless registration.'[12] In the general election of July they ran eight

---

7   *The Ulster Liberal Unionist Association: a sketch of its history, 1885–1914* (Belfast, 1914), pp. 15–6.

8   T. H. Ford, *A. V. Dicey: the man and his times* (Chichester, 1985), p. 165.

9   J. Biggs-Davison and G. Chowdharay-Best, *The Cross of St Patrick: the Catholic unionist tradition in Ireland* (Bourne End, 1984), pp. 213–16; G. Douglas, *Autobiography and Memoirs* (vol. 2), (London, 1906), p. 433; See also W. E. H. Lecky, *An Irish Historian on Home Rule for Ireland* (London, 1889).

10   *Ulster Liberal Unionist Association*, p. 19. Christopher Harvie comments that 'constitutional logic carried the universities'; C. Harvie 'Ideology and Home Rule: James Bryce, A. V. Dicey and Ireland, 1880–1887', *English Historical Review*, vol. 91 (1976), p. 312.

11   *The Times*, 5 June 1886.

12   I. Budge and C. O'Leary, *Belfast: Approach to Crisis: a study of Belfast politics,*

candidates in Ireland (five in the north and three in the south). First, they hoped to win the support of Roman Catholic unionists in areas where the Catholics would never vote Conservative because of that party's alliance with Orangeism, as typified by Colonel Saunderson, MP for North Armagh, and his Irish Loyal and Patriotic Union (ILPU).[13] Second, they hoped to win the support of tenant farmers, as their candidates were clearly identified as opposing the landlord influence, and the founder of the Ulster Tenants Defence League, T. W. Russell, was standing as a Liberal Unionist. Third, they hoped to appeal to working-class voters by exposing the consequence of separation: the imposition of protectionist economic policies from a nationalist government.[14] Their relationship with the local Conservatives was, as a result of these issues, very difficult, and 1886 saw constant bickering in the pages of *The Northern Whig* as to the allocation of candidatures.[15] The battle for the unionist leadership in Ulster was fought in these years between Saunderson's ILPU and the Liberal Unionist Association which was supported by tenant farmers and Belfast businessmen.

The Irish Liberal Unionists were considered as distinct a faction as Joseph Chamberlain's Radical Unionists by the *Pall Mall Gazette* in September 1887, and it was admitted by the official party organ in as early as July 1887 that Lea and Russell differed from the rest of the party in the level of their discontent with the first Irish land bill that Balfour introduced in 1887.[16] In much the same way that Chamberlain tried to push through as much of the 'unauthorised

---

1613–1970 (Basingstoke, 1973), p. 105; *The Liberal Unionist*, vol. 74, March 1892.

13   A. Jackson, *Colonel Saunderson: land and loyalty in Victorian Ireland* (Oxford, 1995); N. C. Fleming, 'The landed elite: power and Ulster unionism' in Boyce and O'Day (eds), *The Ulster Crisis*, pp. 92–3.

14   'Working man and Home Rule', *Northern Whig*, 10 May 1886.

15   This spread into municipal politics with Liberal Unionists (successfully) putting up candidates against Conservatives in the November 1887 municipal election; Budge and O'Leary, *Belfast: Approach to Crisis*, pp. 121–2.

16   *Pall Mall Gazette*, 14 September 1887; *The Liberal Unionist*, 18, 27 July 1887.

programme' of 1885 as the Conservatives would stomach, Russell was clearly determined to promote the cause of the tenant farmers he represented, regardless of the problems this caused within the unionist alliance.[17] Rather pathetically, Hartington complained, 'I am afraid the Ulster members will get us into trouble. The government will not agree to the inclusion of the rent revision clauses.'[18] Russell sent a letter to *The Times*, announcing his resignation from the party when the Conservatives in the Lords attempted to remove the rent-revision amendments he had included during the debate in the Commons.[19] Russell had influential allies in the Catholic community, such as the poet Aubrey de Vere, who championed the reforming unionist cause in the *National Review* and *Edinburgh Review*.[20]

Russell was also supported by an efficient organisation, in contrast to most of the Liberal Unionist Party in its earliest days. As well as the Tenants' Association, a number of branches of the Women's Liberal Unionist Association (WLUA) had been established after 1888 in Leinster, Connacht and Munster. Despite the best efforts of the chief organiser, Isabella Tod, membership although 'very numerous' was not always 'earnest' or even motivated by purely political impulses. A Tipperary nationalist, in his account of a WLUA public meeting in Clonmel on 7 September 1889, asserted that the meeting, in an area where 'no other Loyalist Association of any kind exists', was largely

---

17 The Ulster Association's honorary secretary, Thomas Harrison, noted the Ulster Liberal Unionist Association's (LUA's) work 'in connection with [W. S. Caine's] London Liberal Union and the Birmingham Radical Union'. T. Harrison, 'Liberal Unionist work 4: the Ulster Liberal Unionist Association', *The Liberal Unionist*, vol. 35, December 1888.

18 Hartington to James, 10 July 1887, Henry James papers, M45/282, Hereford Record Office. In fact, Balfour agreed, on the grounds that Russell's demands were 'essential if Ulster is to be retained'. Balfour's memorandum on proposed legislation as it affects the Land bill, 8 April 1887, quoted in J. Loughlin, 'T. W. Russell, the tenant–farmer interest and progressive unionism in Ulster, 1886–1900', *Éire–Ireland*, vol. 25 (1990), p. 49.

19 The peers backed down and Russell's announcement was withdrawn.

20 Biggs-Davison and Chowdharay-Best, *The Cross of St Patrick*, pp. 194–8.

attended by those who were seeking to make more personal alliances; 'it was a great day for mothers with marriageable daughters.'[21] The WLUA probably had greater influence in England as, before the 1892 election, 'a band of Irish ladies' had travelled the country 'to press upon English voters the claims of the Irish loyalists'.[22] This work, together with that of the Nonconformist Unionist Association, which paid both Russell and Tod to speak at election campaigns in England to persuade voters that 'the whole body of Protestant opinion in Ireland [was] against Home Rule', was arguably crucial in retaining many of the votes of nonconformists for the unionists in 1892 and thus preventing Gladstone from gaining an overall majority for his party.[23]

Under Arthur Balfour's secretaryship some significant agrarian measures were obtained for Ireland, but a Land Purchase Act, which made thirty-three million pounds available through the Congested Districts Board, took until 1891 to get past the obstinacy of Whig and Conservative Irish landlords. That it did so in time for the 1892 election gave Russell the opportunity to expand his power-base, and three of the Liberal Unionists' seats were won with ease; the two sitting MPs increasing their majorities fourfold, in marked contrast to Liberal Unionist performance elsewhere, and H. O. Arnold-Forster captured West Belfast. With the nationalists at each others' throats over Charles Stewart Parnell's adultery, Russell cannily persuaded William Kenny QC ('a Roman Catholic Liberal Unionist and a leading member of the Irish bar') to stand for Dublin St Stephen's Green.[24] Here, two nationalist candidates, divided on Parnell's leadership, handed him the victory by fifteen votes. Although Kenny's election took advantage of the nationalist split, it proved the *Northern*

---

21   Quoted in *The Liberal Unionist*, vol. 44, September 1889.
22   *The Liberal Unionist*, vol. 78, July 1892.
23   *Ibid.*, vol. 35, December 1888.
24   *Ibid.*, vol. 74, March 1892.

Whig right when it wrote that support for the union 'is shared by the most respectable Catholics'.[25] The victory of the Irish Liberal Unionists, as with that of Chamberlain's Radical Unionists in the English West Midlands, increased the influence that Russell's group could have over the unionist alliance in general and the new Liberal Unionist Party leadership in particular.[26]

Unlike the Conservatives, the Liberal Unionists believed that a nuanced combination of coercion and reform could improve the Irish character so that some degree of self-government would be possible in the distant future. As Lecky put it in a letter to *The Times* in January 1886:

> What is now wanting for Ireland is a restoration of the liberty of the people, of that first and most fundamental condition of liberty, a state of society in which men may pursue their lawful business and fulfil their lawful contracts without danger or molestation.[27]

Of course, many Liberal Unionists differentiated between the humble Irish cottager and the 'Fenian' terrorist. Since 1882, and the murder of Cavendish and Burke and the Maamtrasna massacre, many Liberals had accepted that there must be no concessions to violence and threats of disorder, otherwise the rule of law itself might be in jeopardy. As George Trevelyan had put it in 1883, when chief secretary for Ireland, if British rule was abandoned in Ireland, 'we should have a mutual massacre'.[28] The cowardly use of violence by nationalists against the defenceless was a constant theme in Liberal Unionist propaganda, as were the consequences of a nationalist government. There was also the

---

25   *Northern Whig*, 29 November 1887.
26   For the wider context of the 1892 election see I. Cawood, 'The 1892 General Election and the eclipse of the Liberal Unionists', *Parliamentary History*, vol. 29 (2010), pp. 331–57.
27   *The Times*, 13 January 1886.
28   Quoted in P. O'Farrell, *England and Ireland since 1800* (Oxford, 1975), p. 177.

belief that there was no strong popular support for agrarian unrest, despite Gladstone and the nationalists' claims, as only two per cent to four per cent of the tenant farmers joined the 'Plan of Campaign', and that intimidation and corruption explained the massive nationalist majorities in rural Ireland.[29] Such genuinely liberal concerns as to the motives and behaviour of the nationalists explain the majority of the Liberal Unionist Party's willingness to accept coercion in 1887, and *The Liberal Unionist* continuously fed this attitude with its 'Latest outrages in Ireland' feature, which ran for every one of the paper's eighty issues. Chamberlain consistently argued that, far from oppressing the average Irishman, the Crimes Act was a guarantee of freedom from intimidation. In this way, coercion was, in the words of a letter writer to *The Baptist Magazine*, both 'just and Christian'.[30]

It was only in September 1890 that the party officially sanctioned mention of the risk of 'civil war' in Ulster if Home Rule was forced upon the country.[31] To many, such as A. V. Dicey, the Liberal Unionists' chief ideologue, such talk was provocative and the very purpose of Liberal Unionism was to ensure the supremacy of the law over party-political concerns.[32] To threaten to break the law when it did not suit a political group's interests would be to lower oneself to the moral standards of Parnell and the nationalists.[33] Instead, the party preferred to emphasise the positive benefits from an inclusive and united British identity, which appealed alike to lowland Scots, Ulster tenant farmers, Cornish Wesleyans and Birmingham radicals. As a

---

29   E. Biagini, *British Democracy and Irish Nationalism 1876–1906* (Cambridge, 2007), p. 242.

30   *The Baptist Magazine*, May 1886.

31   E. Dawson, 'Shadow of the sword', *The Liberal Unionist*, vol. 56, September 1890.

32   A. V. Dicey, *A Leap in the Dark* (London, 1893), pp. 181–2.

33   As Phillip Gell, secretary to the Delegates of the Oxford University Press, wrote to Alfred Milner, the Liberal Unionists saw themselves as 'the party of law and order'; Gell to Milner, 4 August 1887, Milner papers, MS 4, Bodleian library, Oxford.

Catholic unionist announced at a unionist meeting at Leinster Hall on 11 November 1886:

> The Unionists … believed in … union between all classes and sections of the community; union between Catholics and Protestants; union between the rich and the poor; union between landlords and tenants; and union between Great Britain and Ireland.[34]

The Liberal Unionist Party resorted to appeals based on Protestant distrust of clericalism only when their electoral oblivion appeared to beckon in the early 1890s. With the Irish episcopacy's direct intervention in nationalist politics in the condemnation of Parnell, Henry James warned the Liberal Unionist Club in April 1891 that 'if the government of Ireland is given to the Irish people, it will, in fact be given into the hands of the Roman Catholic priesthood'.[35] The following month, the party newspaper included a number of anti-clerical statements and began a series of articles entitled 'The clerical conspiracy in Ireland'.[36] Such policies were risky – ideologically, as Liberalism had traditionally attempted to appeal across sectarian lines, and electorally, as many unionists in southern Ireland were Catholic.[37] It is, however, possible, as Graham Walker has suggested, even to see this argument as consistent with traditional liberal principles.[38] Lewis McIver, a confirmed radical, was faced with a tough challenge in South Edinburgh in 1892 and turned to religion

---

34   *The Irish Times*, 30 November 1887; see J. Stapleton, 'Political thought and national identity, 1850–1950', in Collini, Whatmore and Young (eds), *History, Religion and Culture*, p. 252.
35   *The Liberal Unionist*, vol. 64, May 1891.
36   *Ibid.*, vol. 65, June 1891.
37   Biggs-Davison and Chowdharay-Best, *The Cross of St Patrick*, pp. 245–82. On the selection of William Kenny to fight Dublin St Stephen's Green, it was noted that 'Mr Kenny belongs, as very many of the most zealous Unionists in the city of Dublin do, to the Roman Catholic Church.' *The Liberal Unionist*, vol. 70, November 1891.
38   Walker, 'Thomas Sinclair', pp. 31–2.

in his speeches, accusing the Liberals of tolerating 'the priest in politics'. He denied accusations that he was 'endeavouring to stir up religious animosity', preferring to brandish 'the true Liberal's feeling for religious freedom, religious tolerance, of respect for every man's religious opinions sincerely held', and to use the names of John Bright and Charles Spurgeon freely.[39]

The party was, however, keen to distance itself from accusations that it was playing the Orange card, as Churchill had done with such violent consequences in 1886. The only recent study of the Orange–unionist alliance in Scotland states that 'a discreet public distance was [usually] maintained'.[40] Asked to take the position of president of the Irish Unionist Alliance when the ILPU was re-founded on a broader political basis in 1891, Hartington expressed reluctance as 'I thought the thing had an Orange appearance which would not be acceptable to some of my friends in Ireland'.[41] Instead, the party leadership chose to warn of a potential rebellion in Ulster in order to bring the different unionist traditions in Ireland together and encouraged the holding of anti-Home Rule demonstrations in and around Belfast as the 1892 general election approached. These culminated in the Ulster Convention of 17 June, held in a specially erected building at the Botanic Gardens. This was reported by *The Tory* as having included 12,330 Ulstermen from all classes, amongst whom there were 730 clergymen, 443 magistrates

---

39 *The Liberal Unionist*, vol. 75, April 1892; Bright and Spurgeon were prominent Liberal thinkers in the second half of the nineteenth century, who discussed the relationship between religion and politics in some depth.

40 E. W. McFarland, 'The Orangeman's unionist vision', in C. M. MacDonald (ed.), *Unionist Scotland 1800–1997* (Edinburgh, 1998), p. 43. As Robert Colls has argued, the Orangeman's identity was distinct from that of the tolerant Englishman, to whom Liberal Unionism appealed; R. Colls, 'Englishness and the political culture', in R. Colls and P. Dodd (eds), *Englishness: Politics and culture, 1880–1920* (London, 1986), p. 40.

41 Hartington to Wolmer, 30 January 1892, Selborne papers, Selborne MS II (4) 170, Bodleian library, Oxford.

and 915 professionals. As Jonathan Bardon comments, this was a carefully choreographed demonstration of respectable resistance: 'Unionist leaders were determined to erase the memory of the vicious rioting that had so besmirched the opposition to Home Rule in 1886.'[42] It was emphasised that it comprised 'descendants of Scotch Covenanters ... descendants of leaders of Volunteers ... descendants of United Irishmen ... sons of old fighters for Catholic Emancipation ... advocates of ... the rights of the tillers of the soil' and that 'Orangemen are only one element in this movement.' Even those Orangemen present, as a result of their involvement with more liberal-minded unionists, demonstrated 'a calmness and moderation of spirit which is new in their history'.[43] Thomas Sinclair made a speech threatening resistance to any Home Rule parliament, but his rhetoric was notably non-violent:

> We will have nothing to do with a Dublin parliament. If it be ever set up we shall simply ignore its existence. Its acts will be but as waste paper; the police will find our barracks preoccupied with our own constabulary; its judges will sit in empty court-houses. The early efforts of its executive will be spent in devising means to deal with passive resistance to its taxation.[44]

The convention itself passed off without any riot or violent incident, a deliberate contrast with the ethnic cleansing of areas of Belfast in June 1886. There were, it was said, all creeds present at the event: 'Episcopalians, Presbyterians, Roman Catholics, Methodists, Unitarians, Independents, Baptists, Jews and Friends'.[45] Peter Gibbon

---

42 J. Bardon, *A History of Ulster* (second edition, Belfast, 2005), pp. 409–10.
43 I. Tod, *The Liberal Unionist*, vol. 76, May 1892.
44 Quoted in R. Colles, *The History of Ulster from the Earliest Times to the Present Day* (vol. 4), (London, 1919), p. 222.
45 *The Liberal Unionist*, vol. 78, July 1892. Another 100,000 unionists processed peacefully past Balfour in Belfast during the debate on the second bill on 4 April 1893.

goes as far as to suggest that this event, organised by the Liberal Unionists, marked the birth of 'the Ulsterman'.[46] Over 200 Unionist Clubs were subsequently formed across Ireland under the leadership of Lord Templetown to promote Liberal Unionist opposition to the second Home Rule bill.[47]

The Liberal Unionists were just about able to hold the majority of their seats in the 1892 election and then to take advantage of the failure of the second Home Rule bill and Lord Rosebery's shambolic Liberal administration of 1894–5 to return to nearly their original numbers when they won seventy-one seats in 1895. Their cross-class, cross-denominational appeal, which was crucial to the unionist landslide in 1895, was based on their claim to be the true inheritors of the Liberal tradition. Looking back in 1912, the Earl of Selborne, Liberal Unionist whip between 1888 and 1892, stated his belief that the Liberal Unionists were 'the natural heirs of mid-Victorian Liberalism'. He convincingly asserted that the Liberal Unionists had maintained the principles of constitutionalism, the defence of minorities and the benefit of the nation as a whole rather than self-interest.[48] It was the Gladstonians who had abandoned their principles in 1886 by surrendering to the forces of disorder in Ireland and threatening to abandon the religious and ethnic minorities to sectarian government by the Catholic, southern Irish majority.[49]

---

46   P. Gibbon, *The Origins of Ulster Unionism: the formation of popular Protestant politics in nineteenth-century Ireland* (Manchester, 1976), p. 136. Hennessy disagrees, asserting that the Ulster unionist enjoyed 'a multitude of identities and allegiances'; T. Hennessy, 'Ulster unionist territorial and national identities 1886–1893: province, island, kingdom and empire', *Irish Political Studies*, vol. 8 (1993), p. 23. There was also a convention held at Leinster Hall in Dublin on 23 June 1892, but this received far less attention; *The Irish Times*, 24 June 1892.

47   P. Buckland, *Irish Unionism: Ulster unionism and the origins of Northern Ireland* (Dublin, 1973), pp. 16–7.

48   D. G. Boyce (ed.), *The Crisis of British Unionism: Lord Selborne's domestic political papers, 1885–1933* (Gloucester, 1987), p. 83.

49   See in particular A. Froude, *The Two Chiefs of Dunboy: an Irish romance of the last century* (London, 1889); H. Paul, *The Life of Froude* (New York, 1905), p. 110.

Hence the Liberal Unionist Party could call on a convincing array of influential Liberal supporters such as Millicent Fawcett, Herbert Spencer, John Bright, Leonard Courtney and T. H. Huxley.

During the period of opposition T. W. Russell again came into conflict with the landlord influence in the party over land reform, and actually had to resign from it to get his way in 1894.[50] He withdrew this resignation, but, as Chamberlain told Balfour, 'the relations between the landlord and Orange party and the tenant and Liberal Unionist sections are very much strained'.[51] William Kenny also criticised Chamberlain when he resorted to anti-Catholic rhetoric in October 1894, aware as he was of the damage that such language could do among his middle-class Catholic electorate.[52] When the unionist coalition was being formally arranged in July 1895, Chamberlain pressed for Russell to receive a junior office, but Russell would accept only if his demands for land reform were acceded to. He was clearly distrusted by the Conservatives who blocked the attempt of the editor of the *Impartial Reporter*, W. C. Trimble, to fight Enniskillen as a Liberal Unionist in 1895.

In 1895 the Liberal Unionists entered a coalition government with Salisbury's Conservative Party, but unwisely failed to secure any agreement of policy and so, as the junior partner to the Conservatives, who held an overall majority, they found themselves increasingly isolated and abandoned by their leaders. Russell, now secretary to the Local Government Board, persevered with his demands, however, aiding Kenny in his triumphant retention of St Stephen's Green in the 1895 general election. The Irish Liberal Unionists then won a fifth seat when W. E. H. Lecky was elected for

---

50   Loughlin, 'T. W. Russell', p. 55.
51   Chamberlain to Balfour, 25 May 1894, Balfour papers, Add. MSS 49773, British Library.
52   W. Kenny to H. de F. Montgomery, 29 October 1894, quoted in Biagini, *British Democracy*, p. 253.

Dublin University in December 1895, both of which results demonstrated the continuing commitment of the Irish branch of the party to non-sectarian solutions to Ireland's problems and its commitment to the maintenance of law and order.[53] The Irish Liberal Unionists subsequently passed a resolution at their annual meeting in 1897 demanding democratic local government and a land purchase bill. The Land bill, introduced in 1897, was opposed by some moderate Liberal Unionists, such as Walter Morrison, on the grounds that it was interfering with the liberal principle of the sanctity of property.[54] Russell had to threaten resignation for a third time to overcome Conservative and moderate Liberal Unionist opposition to the bill and had to swallow a series of amendments. The act that emerged did, however, achieve Russell's principal aim: protection for tenants' rights and improvements.[55]

Fulfilling the pledge to local-government reform proved even more difficult as the moderate Liberal Unionists opposed any scheme, for fear of its being monopolised by the National League, while Chamberlain's pet project of 'provincial councils' for Ireland was regarded with horror by Russell and his faction. The Irish Local Government Act was eventually introduced by the Irish chief secretary, Gerald Balfour, in February 1898 and was perhaps the greatest triumph for progressive unionism in the period. Although Gerald Balfour is usually credited with 'killing Home Rule by kindness', there is a case to be argued that the pressure that the Russellites brought to bear on the cabinet was decisive. Russell attempted to resist the growing anti-Catholic bigotry in his constituency, South Tyrone, and voted in favour of a Catholic university for Ireland,

---

53   Loughlin, 'T. W. Russell', pp. 56–7.
54   W. Morrison to Devonshire, 26 July 1895, Devonshire papers, DP 340.2693, Chatsworth House (CH).
55   Loughlin, 'T. W. Russell', p. 58. The Act was eventually consolidated by the 1903 Wyndham Act, affording a buy-out of Irish landowners far more expensive than that proposed by Gladstone in 1886.

which prompted other loyalists to oppose him with an Independent Unionist candidate in 1900.[56]

Russell triumphed, but he eventually resigned from the party in 1902 in frustration over loyalist refusal to accept George Wyndham's proposals for land purchase. He proceeded to field independent 'Russellite' candidates against Saunderson's Ulster unionists at two by-elections, East Down (February 1902) and North Fermanagh (March 1903), and won both these, added to which was his crowning achievement, the Land Purchase Act of 1903, which finally enabled the tenant farmers of Ireland to buy their land. Alvin Jackson has written that 'between 1900 and 1906 the most serious political challenge to the [unionist] leadership came ... from within Ulster constituencies from independent Unionists'.[57] Russell's extraordinary career continued when he retained his seat as an Independent Unionist in 1906, and then won a by-election in 1911 with Liberal support, after which he was appointed undersecretary for the Department of Agriculture and Technical Instruction for Ireland under Herbert H. Asquith.[58]

The achievements of the Ulster Liberal Unionists were in marked contrast to the lack of reform elsewhere in Britain, and the unease that many Liberal Unionists felt was made far worse by the introduction of the 1902 Education Act, which appeared to them mainly to benefit Anglican schools. A wave of influential backbench figures rejoined Sir Henry Campbell-Bannerman's Liberal Party, which had been carefully avoiding the Home Rule question for years.[59] Joseph Chamberlain, the colonial secretary and leader of a rump of Radical

---

56 *Northern Whig*, 3 October 1900.
57 A. Jackson, *The Ulster Party: Irish unionists in House of Commons, 1844–1911* (Oxford, 1989), p. 267.
58 N. Whyte, *Science, Colonialism and Ireland* (Cork, 1999), p. 97.
59 Chamberlain wrote to Devonshire, 'our best friends are leaving us by scores and hundreds never to return'. J. Chamberlain to Devonshire, 22 September 1902, Devonshire papers, DP 340.2998, CH.

Unionists, attempted to counter this creeping decline by adopting an aggressive policy of 'Imperial protection', despite a lack of cabinet support and the opposition of Hartington, now Duke of Devonshire.[60] The former governor of Ceylon, West Ridgeway, commented at the time that the Liberal Unionist Party had been 'strangled by its own parent'.[61] In this way, the two unionist parties split into Free Trade and Tariff Reform factions and went down to a catastrophic defeat in the 1906 election, in which the Liberal Unionists were reduced to twenty-six seats.

At this point, with both Liberal and Conservative Unionists belonging to rival clubs and associations over the tariff issue, it becomes impossible to speak of a Liberal Unionist Party in any meaningful sense. Its continuance until 1912 was largely to suit individual MPs, not least Austen Chamberlain, who used the label to appeal to their local electorates, and both the Liberal Unionist Council and Club both waned in these years. The Radical Unionists, both Liberal and Conservative, who had followed Joseph Chamberlain in 1903, now strove to take control of their local party organisations and, in the struggle between the local Tory elites and this younger generation of male and female activists, the distinction between Liberal Unionist and Conservative became increasingly unimportant.[62]

With the threat of Home Rule raised once again in the aftermath of the Parliament Act of 1911, the decision was taken by the new Conservative leader, Andrew Bonar Law, and Austen Chamberlain to 'fuse' the two wings of unionism.[63] On 21 March it was announced

---

60   See R. A. Rempel, *Unionists Divided: Arthur Balfour, Joseph Chamberlain and the unionist free traders* (Newton Abbot, 1972) for a detailed account of the divisions between the 'Tariff Reformers' and 'Free Traders'.

61   J. W. Ridgeway, 'The Liberal Unionist party', *Nineteenth Century and After*, vol. 342 (August 1905), p. 197.

62   See D. Thackeray, 'Home and politics: women and Conservative activism in early twentieth century Britain', *Journal of British Studies*, vol. 49 (2010), pp. 826–48.

63   The decision was first announced in the interim report of the unionist Committee on Organisation in April 1911, which Balfour had appointed, and Arthur

in *The Times* that 'the expediency of amalgamating the headquarters organisation of the Conservative and Liberal Unionist parties is again under consideration'.[64] The only places where any resistance to fusion was voiced were in Birmingham, where Conservative and Liberal Unionists had remained rivals throughout the previous two decades and, surprisingly, in Ulster. As a result, complete amalgamation was postponed for an 'interim period' (of an unspecified duration), during which constituencies were allowed to maintain 'separate organisations'.[65] On 9 May therefore, two 'special' conferences of the National Conservative Union and the Liberal Unionist Council were held and the resolutions were carefully phrased to limit the proposed fusion to 'the amalgamation of the *central* organisations of the two wings of the Unionist Party'. The achievement of 'fusion' was therefore the combination of the National Conservative Association and the Liberal Unionist Association into the National Unionist Association of Conservative and Liberal Unionist Organisations (NUACLUO).[66]

Although the Ulster Liberal Unionist Association continued until the 1920s, its attempt to maintain a liberal identity within the unionist movement in Ireland became increasingly eclipsed by the growing extremism and highly provocative tactics of the Ulster unionists. The unionists, rid of Russell's awkward radicalism after 1902 and without the intellectual leadership of W. E. H. Lecky, who died in October 1903, had split over the Irish Reform Association's proposals for devolution, endorsed by George Wyndham's undersecretary Anthony MacDonnell in 1904.[67] The northern unionists deserted the Irish Unionist Alliance and formed the Ulster Unionist Council (UUC) in

Steel-Maitland, the newly appointed head of the committee, was given responsibility for achieving the task. *The Times*, 14 April 1911.
64   *The Times*, 21 March 1912.
65   *Ibid.*, 20 April 1912.
66   *Ibid.*, 10 May 1912.
67   A. Jackson, *Home Rule: an Irish history 1800–2000* (Oxford, 2003), pp. 108–9.

1905 under Walter Long's leadership, which was implicitly pledged to resist Home Rule through violent, as well as legislative, means. As Jackson concludes, 'by the time of the third Home Rule bill, Unionism was to all intents and purposes an Ulster phenomenon'.[68] It had also lost much of its liberal identity as Ireland increasingly polarised, politically and culturally.[69] Edward Carson himself had originally been elected as a Liberal Unionist for Dublin University,[70] and he and Thomas Sinclair had collaborated in the creation of the Ulster Solemn League and Covenant, in which Graham Walker detects a lingering liberal influence.[71] But Carson was increasingly forced to abandon his preference for maintenance of the complete union between Britain and Ireland, under pressure from both Bonar Law and his own deputy, James Craig.[72]

Liberal Unionist discomfiture with Ulster unionist identity was made clear in January 1912 when A. V. Dicey wrote to *The Times* demanding that Winston Churchill, then first lord of the Admiralty, should be allowed to speak at Ulster Hall, and that the UUC should restrain the Ulster Volunteer Force, whose members were threatening Churchill with violence.[73] Sinclair organised a further peaceful convention, this time of Presbyterian unionists, to emphasise the connection between Ulstermen and Scots and thus deny that Ireland could ever be a nation.[74] Sinclair had, however, been in poor health for many years and when he died on 14 February 1914 the idea of Liberal Unionism in Ireland, with its key policies of

---

68   Jackson, *Ireland 1798–1998*, p. 229; Jackson, *The Ulster Party*, p. 104.

69   See D. M. Jackson, *Popular Opposition to Irish Home Rule in Edwardian Britain* (Liverpool, 2009), chap. 4, pp. 133–63.

70   A. T. Q. Stewart, *Edward Carson* (Dublin, 1981), p. 20.

71   Walker, 'Thomas Sinclair', p. 35.

72   Walker, *History of the Ulster Unionist Party*, pp. 30–7.

73   J. Hostettler, *Sir Edward Carson: a dream too far* (Chichester, 1997), p. 172.

74   For the Ulster Liberal Unionist position in the third Home Rule crisis, see T. Sinclair, 'The position of Ulster', in S. Rosenbaum (ed.) *Against Home Rule* (London, 1912), pp. 170–81.

'impartial government, the promotion of business, land purchase and agricultural reform', died with him.[75]

Alvin Jackson describes the 'death of Irish Unionism' thus:

A once widely … spread movement had effectively withdrawn to the north-east … of the island; a socially and culturally diversified movement had been … simplified, stripped of the advocacy of Trinity intellectuals and the more … tangible support of southern land and Dublin commerce … The leaders of the [Ulster Unionist] movement … were willing to sacrifice territory, partners and principles in order to protect their own Unionist arcadia.[76]

Liberal Unionism failed as a national party, due to mistreatment by its own leadership, and Irish Liberal Unionism never recovered from Russell's resignation. Nevertheless, the core belief of Liberal Unionism – that religious and political toleration were best protected and the social and economic interests of all were best served in a parliament of the whole United Kingdom – remained a potent weapon in the British political arguments between unionists and nationalists throughout the years of the Home Rule crisis. The best evidence that it did is that this belief remains an article of faith in all the three main British political parties to this day.

---

75   Walker, 'Thomas Sinclair', pp. 36–7.
76   Jackson, *Ireland 1798–1988*, p. 240.

15

The role of the leaders: Asquith, Churchill, Balfour, Bonar Law, Carson and Redmond

Martin Mansergh

The late historian Eric Hobsbawm once described the business of historians as being to 'remember what others forget'.[1] The third Home Rule bill, though not the crisis around it, has been well and truly forgotten, and it is quite possible to attend whole conferences commemorating the centenary of the Ulster Covenant without hearing a single reference to the content of the bill.

While centenaries are more significant than fiftieth anniversaries, it is most unlikely such a conference as gave rise to this book could have been organised fifty years ago without raising suspicions of all sorts of agendas. It is worth exploring for a moment how, paradoxically, the events of 1912–14 appeared more distant then than they do today, despite the fact that people who had played a part in them, Winston Churchill in particular, were still politically active into the 1950s. At that time most British politicians and historians regarded the Irish question as solved. Robert Blake, in his biography of Andrew

---

1   Tribute in *The Guardian*, 2 October 2012, extract from E. Hobsbawm, *The Age of Extremes* (London, 1994).

Bonar Law, written in 1955 and entitled *The Unknown Prime Minister* (from an unkind quip of Herbert H. Asquith's following Bonar Law's funeral, about how appropriate it was that 'the Unknown Prime Minister' had been buried in Westminster Abbey, close to the tomb of the Unknown Soldier), apologised for devoting so much space to the Home Rule crisis. Blake described it as a great struggle that had vanished into the realm of 'old unhappy far-off things and battles long ago', adding that in England such quarrels had become 'as remote as those curious disputes with which Gibbon so agreeably entertains us in his chapters on the early Christian Church'.[2] Harold Macmillan, when he met Éamon de Valera as taoiseach in Downing Street on 18 March 1958, kept changing the subject, when de Valera repeatedly tried to raise the issue of partition. He commented in his diary: 'The revolutionary fire is gone, and he cannot understand why we are so bored with Ireland and so glad to be rid of her, after all these weary centuries.' Having met Taoiseach Seán Lemass on 20 March 1963, Macmillan reflected that, despite having dominated parliament for nearly a century, Ireland had ceased to be of any interest; there was now 'peace – perfect peace. No one ever speaks or cares about Ireland.' His negativity arose from factors such as his perception of Lemass' armed role in the War of Independence, war-time neutrality, Ireland's departure from the Commonwealth, and its church-led social conservatism, with the result that 'the Irish "rebels" now enjoy the most conservative, clericalist and reactionary government in Europe', the population having shrunk to under three million.[3]

On the Irish side of the Irish Sea, the third Home Rule bill had been disowned by nationalists and republicans, as it always had been by Ulster unionists, and was only of interest in its role as a catalyst

2   R. Blake, *The Unknown Prime Minister: the life and times of Andrew Bonar Law 1858–1923* (London, 1955), pp. 120–1.
3   *The Macmillan Diaries, Volume II: prime minister and after, 1957–66* edited with an introduction by P. Catterall (London, 2012), pp. 104, 550.

for revolution and partition. As Donal McCartney put it dismissively, writing of the period in the 1967 edition of *The Course of Irish History*, 'what still made the loudest noise, on the political surface, however, was home rule'.[4] Even Stephen Gwynn, when writing on Irish Party leader John Redmond in 1919, could describe the pre-war crisis as 'a state of things not far off in time, but divided from us of today by the marks of a vast upheaval'.[5] My father, Nicholas Mansergh, gave a Thomas Davis lecture on Redmond in 1956, which was quite critical, but I remember him saying to me that, in the context of the series, Redmond was not a topic with which many historians in Irish universities were keen to engage.[6]

The difference today, of course, is that we know that the 1920–1 settlement was not final, and that the whole problem in relation to Northern Ireland, also fundamentally involving British–Irish relations, boiled over in the late 1960s. After a twenty-five-year conflict, and in the perspective of the peace process, it is instructive to look back at the key events a century ago which eventually culminated in partition and the formation of the Irish Free State and Northern Ireland, civil war in the south, and some involuntary movement of population both north and south, none of which could have been anticipated in 1912.

This is the context for reflections on political leadership, concentrated on the 1912–14 period. There are two broad ways of looking at the Home Rule crisis: as an opportunity for an historic compromise and peaceful evolution missed, or simply, notwithstanding different and sometimes tragic vicissitudes, as an affirmation of the origins of how we arrived at where we are today, separate statehood on the one

---

4   T. W. Moody & F. X. Martin (eds), *The Course of Irish History* (Cork, 1967), p. 304.

5   S. Gwynn, *John Redmond's Last Years* (London, 1919), p. 106.

6   C. C. O'Brien (ed.), *The Shaping of Modern Ireland* (London, 1960), pp. 38–49, reprinted in D. Mansergh (ed.), *Nationalism and Independence: Selected Irish papers by Nicholas Mansergh* (Cork, 1997), pp. 23–31.

hand and vindication of the union on the other, and as something to be commemorated and celebrated, preferably without triumphalism. Perhaps, for those of us who value highly our independent statehood, we should be grateful in a perverse sort of way to people like Edward Carson and Walter Long, who made it possible by their adamant resistance to Home Rule until far too late. Eoin MacNeill and Patrick Pearse expressed this idea long before Peter Hart.[7]

I should like to consider each of the leaders under three headings: their basic political position, their tactics, and, finally, outcomes.

Asquith

Asquith, prime minister of the last Liberal administration in Britain from 1908 to 1916 (from 1915, a wartime coalition), was a very skilled and sophisticated political leader. He was relatively relaxed, writing letters at cabinet meetings to a much younger woman he admired, apt to go off on long walks with attractive ladies-in-waiting when staying for the weekend at a royal palace, and enjoying rounds of bridge. 'Wait and see' was, according to his wife Margot, issued as a warning to the opposition on one occasion and, like a lot of attributed mottos, not meant to be taken as a guiding principle. All the same, as Stephen Gwynn observed, 'Mr Asquith was the last of mankind to make a quixotic stand for principle, and the most disposed to pride himself on a practical recognition of realities.' His official biographers admitted that he undoubtedly failed to reckon with the Irish temperament, 'which regarded settlements of the British type as either surrenders or betrayal'.[8]

While the Liberal Party had a huge respect for the memory of

---

7 R. D. Edwards, *Patrick Pearse: the triumph of failure* (London, 1977), pp. 177–9; P. Hart, 'Walter Long: Irish revolutionary', in M. Dungan (ed.), *Speaking Ill of the Dead* (Dublin, 2007), pp. 106–22.

8 M. Asquith, *The Autobiography of Margot Asquith* (London, 1962), p. 306; Gwynn, *John Redmond's Last Years*, p. 87; J. A. Spender and C. Asquith, *Life of Herbert Henry Asquith, Lord Oxford and Asquith* (vol. 2), (London, 1934), p. 15.

William Ewart Gladstone, his espousal of Home Rule had split the party and put the Conservatives in power for the best part of twenty years. Following their victory at the polls in 1906, the Liberals were in no hurry to return to the subject until the elections of 1910 forced them to do so. Indeed, one of the weaknesses of their position was that Home Rule was always the deal for Irish Party support. Gladstone was a lot better than Asquith at dressing up political opportunism or necessity as a matter of high moral principle.

Asquith had outmanoeuvred the Conservatives over the House of Lords. Indeed, one of his biggest achievements, and an important late contribution of the Irish Party to British democracy, was the reduction of the House of Lords' power of veto. Henceforth, the franchise, rather than the extent of property ownership, would be the determining principle in deciding who would wield power.

Asquith was a Liberal imperialist. Home Rule could, as Cecil Rhodes perceived when giving financial support to Charles Stewart Parnell on the understanding that this would promote his favoured policy of imperial federation, just as easily be complementary to empire as destructive of it.[9] It also had the advantage of taking pressure off the House of Commons. In his opening speech on 11 April 1912, Asquith presented the legislation as settling the controversy between the two countries since the union. There was no question of separation. The powers being granted were delegated powers: 'We maintain in this Bill unimpaired, and beyond the level of challenge or question, the supremacy absolute and sovereign of the Imperial Parliament.' His emphasis had always been on the grant of local powers or, as Lord Grey put it, the analogy was with Quebec or Ontario, not the dominion of Canada as was and would be the case in 1886 and 1921. Asquith challenged the opposition for their answer

---

9   E. Byrne, 'Irish Home Rule: stepping stone to imperial federation', *History Ireland*, vol. 20, no. 1 (January/February 2012), pp. 25–7.

to the demand of Ireland, 'beyond the naked veto of an irreconcilable minority and the promise of a freer and more copious outflow to Ireland of Imperial doles?' (This was a typically Liberal criticism of the Conservative policy from the 1890s of generously grant-aiding Ireland.) All over the Empire, the problem of reconciling local autonomy with imperial unity had been addressed.[10]

Asquith, who sat in Gladstone's last cabinet, was well aware of the Ulster difficulty, but was not inclined or in a position, given his dependence on nationalist support, to make concessions up front. While surprised that arming and drilling would be supported by the opposition, he did not believe in the threat of civil war. The only later statement of principle he made was at Ladybank on 25 October 1913, in response to the unionist resistance, in which he set out three requirements:

- There must be established a subordinate Irish legislature with an executive responsible to it;
- 'Nothing must be done to erect a permanent and insuperable bar to Irish unity' (a very flexible requirement, incidentally);
- Ireland should not have to wait till there was a complete scheme of decentralisation, i.e. Home Rule all round.

Blake describes the speech as being of 'Delphic obscurity'.[11]

As far as tactics were concerned, Asquith was well aware that the objective of the Conservative Party in Britain was to force a general election before Home Rule could be enacted, as part of its campaign against the Parliament Act. Confident in his own ability to manoeuvre, he seems to have been convinced that he could place the opposi-

---

10   Spender and Asquith, *Life of Herbert Henry Asquith*, p. 163.
11   Gwynn, *John Redmond's Last Years*, p. 85; Blake, *Unknown Prime Minister*, p. 163.

tion in a false position and that if given enough rope they would hang themselves. His room for manoeuvre was limited by what nationalists could accept, given that he depended on them for a parliamentary majority with which to govern. He had to manage very carefully relations with the monarch, George V, whom the opposition were trying to entice into a constitutionally dubious interventionist role.

By the summer of 1914, with Home Rule about to pass into law, there was still an impasse, even if differences had been narrowed down. The threatened use of even limited force in Ulster against unionists lost all credibility after the Curragh mutiny. The unionist-nationalist stand-off, each with armed or semi-armed Volunteers at their back, was put off by the advent of the First World War and (in theory) by the ensuing burying of political differences for the duration.

In terms of outcomes, success had been denied. Home Rule for Ireland on whatever terms should have been a great Liberal achievement. Though placed on the statute book, despite unionist protests, it was stillborn. For the most part, Asquith had chosen not to confront either his opposition or his generals. The creation of rival armed paramilitary forces in Ireland had been the result.

His administration was represented in Ireland by Augustine Birrell, who also practised a softly-softly approach. One of the interpretations of the 1916 rebellion, borne out for example in Desmond FitzGerald's memoir, is that Ireland and Britain were becoming ever more closely entwined and that a dramatic gesture was required to keep the separatist flame alive.[12]

There is an interesting parallel of a kind to the Ulster crisis: the situation in Algeria in the late 1950s and early 1960s. Algeria admittedly was a much more recent colony, having been conquered in 1830. The French Algerians, too, denied there was any such thing as an Algerian nation, and they sought union with France or, failing that,

---

12   D. FitzGerald, *Memoirs of Desmond FitzGerald* (London, 1968), pp. 80–1.

partition. The French army was mobilised and not disposed to obey the Fourth Republic. They assisted Charles de Gaulle to come to power to avoid civil war, but he subsequently faced them down. His advantage was that he, too, unlike Asquith, was a general, with more prestige than any other. The price of a solution, however, was the complete abandonment of the French Algerian community, which, unusually, had to be completely repatriated post-independence. It is not really a model for the much more deeply embedded Irish situation, but nor was Northern Ireland a suitable model for French Algeria, as de Gaulle, with his McCartan grandmother and deep Catholic faith, was well aware.[13]

In 1916 Asquith reversed policy, replacing Birrell with Sir John Maxwell, with disastrous results. Birrell, before departing, had written: 'It is not an Irish rebellion, and it would be a pity if *ex post facto* it became one.' By early 1920 Asquith was advocating dominion status, what was euphemistically called dominion Home Rule, long before David Lloyd George came round to the idea, on the grounds that parallel Sinn Féin institutions of government derived their legitimacy not from sporadic terrorism, but from the support of the great bulk of the Irish people.[14]

Churchill

The one minister in Asquith's cabinet with some predisposition to strong-arm methods was the young Winston Churchill. He showed some courage in visiting Belfast in 1912, carrying the opposite message to that of Lord Randolph Churchill in 1886. Winston, driven by unionist protests from the Ulster Hall to west Belfast, appealed to Ulster for the reconciliation of races, for forgiveness of ancient wrongs, and for the unity and consolidation of the British

---

13   M. Winock, *L'agonie de la IVème République. 13 mai 1958* (Paris, 2006).

14   Spender and Asquith, *Life of Herbert Henry Asquith*, pp. 214–5, 329–36; Gwynn, *John Redmond's Last Years*, p. 104.

Empire. While he soon favoured partition and the separate treatment of the Ulster Protestant community and had discussions with Bonar Law in Balmoral on these lines in 1913, he was always instinctively pugnacious in dealing with challenges to authority. If there were a revolt, he argued that sea and railway communications with Ulster would be cut off. In the spring of 1914, as first lord of the Admiralty, he ordered the third battle squadron from the Mediterranean to be stationed off the island of Arran in south-west Scotland, though after the fiasco of the Curragh mutiny he had to countermand that. On 14 March 1914 in Bradford, in a speech that greatly pleased nationalists, he said that if Ulster rejected the offer (i.e. exclusion for a period), 'it can only be because they prefer shooting to voting and the bullet to the ballot'. Bloodshed was lamentable, but there were worse things. If the law could not prevail, if the veto of violence was to replace the veto of privilege, 'let us go forward and put these grave matters to a proof'.[15]

It is interesting that at this stage of his career Churchill was as willing to bully the unionists as he was later to try to bully nationalists. It suggests a more robust approach in the event of unreasonable resistance was possible.

Churchill's overall record on Ireland was erratic, and his vision of a submissive and cooperative Ireland that in part was autonomous but firmly within the Empire was never to be realised. Ulster consent, as he would have called it, later became the guiding principle for him. In his 1912 Belfast speech, he had stated:

The separation of Ireland from Great Britain is absolutely impossible. The interests and affairs of the two islands are eternally interwoven. The whole tendency of things, the whole irresistible drift of things is towards a more intimate association. The economic dependence of Ireland on

---

15   Gwynn, *John Redmond's Last Years*, p. 104.

England is absolute … The two nations are bound together till the end of time by the natural force of circumstances.[16]

That would explain why he later found it very hard to stomach de Valera and Irish republican separatism.

Balfour

Arthur Balfour stepped down as Conservative Party leader in 1911, under growing internal party pressure ('Balfour must go'). Under his leadership, the Tory Party had lost the two elections of 1910 and the battle over the House of Lords veto. In his last two decades after relinquishing the party leadership, he made important marks in international affairs, and in Britain was the leading elder statesman of the age.

He had made his reputation as chief secretary in Ireland under his uncle Lord Salisbury's administration from 1886 to 1891. His brother Gerald, chief secretary in the late 1890s, was also effective and the period from 1886 to 1905 – including the Balfour administration from 1902 to 1905 – saw important reforms in local government and land purchase as well as an active regional policy. According to Sir Henry Robinson, a leading Dublin Castle civil servant up to 1922, the phrase 'killing Home Rule by kindness', just like 'wait and see', was a selective quotation used by opponents and commentators to caricature Conservative policy. Gerald Balfour said 'that he did not conceive it would be possible to kill Home Rule by kindness, but he hoped to do all he could to ameliorate the lot of the people'.[17] The revival of Home Rule was, nevertheless, unwelcome, as unionists for a long time

---

16 Paul Bew, 'The strange death of Liberal England: William Flavelle Moneypenny's *The two Irish nations*', in J. Horne & E. Madigan (eds), *Towards Commemoration: Ireland in War and Revolution 1912–1923* (Dublin, 2013).

17 The Rt Hon. Sir Henry Robinson Bart, KCB, *Memories: wise and otherwise* (London, 1924), p. 114.

thought they had buried it through a generous reform policy of which they were proud. Arthur Balfour's view was that Home Rule for Ireland would not work, that it would set up a lopsided constitutional framework and that an Irish parliament would inevitably clash with the Westminster one. Even Grattan's parliament, representing only a small minority of the inhabitants, found its position of subordination intolerable and used a moment of national disaster (the British defeat by the French and the Americans at Yorktown in 1781) to assert and win recognition of its legislative independence.[18]

Balfour fully backed his successor Bonar Law, and did not at any stage rein him in. In response to Churchill, he asserted that a crisis in which it was justifiable to resist the government occurred once every two or three centuries, the last one no doubt being in 1688–9, known in Britain as the 'Glorious Revolution'. In the attempts to pressure King George V to stall the Home Rule bill, one option put forward by Balfour was that either he or another ex-prime minister, Lord Rosebery, should form an interim government and dissolve parliament.[19] In general, he carried too much baggage from earlier times, and was not seen as a constructive influence.

In later times, after the formation of the Irish Free State, Balfour claimed vindication for the view that there had been no middle way between union and separation.[20] The 1926 Balfour Declaration, codified in the Statute of Westminster in 1931, provided the legal framework that enabled the Irish Free State to break free of the restrictions of the Treaty signed in 1921 and move towards complete sovereignty and independence, even though this was contested unsuccessfully for a time by the British.

---

18   A. J. Balfour, 'A note on Home Rule', in S. Rosenbaum (ed.) *Against Home Rule: the case for the union*, with Introduction by Sir Edward Carson and Preface by A. Bonar Law, (first published London, 1912, reprinted Dallas, 1970), pp. 197–8.

19   K. Young, *Arthur James Balfour: the happy life of the politician, prime minister, statesman and philosopher 1848–1930* (London, 1963), pp. 334–6, 339.

20   N. Mansergh, *The Commonwealth Experience* (London, 1969), pp. 193–4.

Bonar Law

Bonar Law was always something of a dark horse, from the time he won the Conservative leadership contest of 1911. His father, a Presbyterian minister in Canada, was born in Ulster and retired there, where his son, a Glasgow businessman and MP, regularly visited him. Bonar Law felt very strongly about Ulster being subjected to a Dublin government, because Home Rule would inflict intolerable injustice on the unionist minority. On the basis of nationalist hostility to the Boer War, he feared the attitude of the Irish government in a great war. Given the remarkable increase in prosperity resulting from land purchase, there was, he believed, no need for Home Rule.

The Home Rule crisis took place in the context of a political background of all-out, no-holds-barred opposition as exemplified by the House of Lords' rejection of the 1909 'People's budget'. Bonar Law rapidly moved to a position where he gave blank-cheque support to Ulster resistance to Home Rule. In his famous Blenheim speech of 29 July 1912, he said, 'I can imagine no lengths of resistance to which Ulster can go in which I would not be prepared to support them.'[21] Anticipating de Valera post-Treaty, he remarked 'there are things stronger than parliamentary majorities'. His rhetoric was wildly over the top, accusing the Asquith government of being 'a revolutionary Committee which has seized upon despotic power by fraud'. Asquith responded by accusing him of furnishing for the future 'a complete grammar of anarchy'.[22] On a later occasion, Bonar Law even stated Ulster would prefer foreign rule to nationalist rule, which Churchill interpreted as a threat to secede to imperial Germany, Captain Craig saying more explicitly that Ulster might need another William to save them.[23] Bonar Law supported the Curragh mutiny and

21 R. J. Q. Adams, *Bonar Law* (London, 1999), p. 109.
22 *The Times*, 6 October 1912.
23 W. Hünseler, *Das Deutsche Kaiserreich und die Irische Frage 1900–1914* (Frankfurt am Main, 1978), pp. 199–202.

the Larne gun-running. He strongly disliked Asquith's insistence on putting the Home Rule bill on the statute book after the outbreak of war, even though his friend Lord Beaverbrook argued that 'it was merely to fill in a post-dated cheque which had little prospect of being honoured'.[24]

If Bonar Law genuinely cared about Ulster, he was much more indifferent to the question of Home Rule for the rest of Ireland, something to which his fellow leader in the House of Lords, and southern Irish landowner, Lord Lansdowne, was totally opposed.

It was one of those dangerous instances where strong party prejudice appeared to coincide with party interest. All the manoeuvres and scenarios involving the king were designed to force a general election and to cancel out the relative neutering of the House of Lords. In one respect, Bonar Law temporarily modified his position, in that he would no longer endorse physical resistance to Home Rule if, in the meantime, the electorate endorsed it. Ulster unionists remained pledged to continue resisting Home Rule in all circumstances. The situation was deadlocked right up to the outbreak of the First World War. As events in 1917 in Russia showed, imperial Germany liked to exploit and fan internal divisions in other countries to destabilise its enemies, and it is no surprise that German guns were supplied to both sides in 1914. Lord Haldane, lord chancellor and previously war secretary, claimed that the Germans had stopped the traffic on the Kiel Canal to let the *Fanny* with its arms shipment for Larne evade the British navy.[25] It is an ongoing question whether some of the leaders of imperial Germany were misled until too late as to Britain's likely position, as being too preoccupied to participate in war.[26] The opposite was the case, the First World War being the *deus ex machina* that relieved the acute domestic crisis.

---

24 Lord Beaverbrook, *Politicians and the War 1914–1916* (London, 1959), p. 44.
25 Lord Haldane, *Lord Haldane's Autobiography* (London, 1931), p. 269.
26 Hünseler, *Das Deutsche Kaiserreich*, pp. 231–64.

With the war, Bonar Law's style of politics changed, and in the end he was influential in the fall of Asquith and, ultimately, Lloyd George. For a long time he was self-effacing after 1918, by being willing to serve under Lloyd George even though he was leader of much the largest party in coalition, a party which had a majority on its own. He took the view that once on the statute book, Home Rule, provided it did not involve the coercion of Ulster, could go through. He did not disapprove of the Truce in 1921, and supported the Treaty, with reservations only about Lloyd George's apparent attempts in November 1921 to put pressure on Craig. Bonar Law's support was vital in enabling Lloyd George to survive as long as he did. What has been little noted by historians was his pressure for a firmer attitude to the Provisional Government and insistence on an immediate restoration of law and order following the assassination of Sir Henry Wilson. In a House of Commons speech, Bonar Law said he had supported the Treaty on the basis that the men who had signed it were willing to take risks, but that he would not have supported it now. Interestingly, this, he claimed, was not because of anarchy in Ireland, or the murder of Sir Henry Wilson; he had been wrong in believing that those who signed the Treaty accepted that Ulster could never be brought in except by their consent.[27] One could argue therefore that the British pressure that finally triggered the Civil War was partly in reaction to the covert campaign led by Collins and Mulcahy to attack Northern Ireland, perhaps in an attempt to find common ground with some of the anti-Treaty forces.

Carson

Easily the most charismatic unionist leader to this day remains Sir Edward Carson, whose histrionic abilities pulled together the unionist community in its hour of need. He gloried in the drama of

---

27   Blake, *Unknown Prime Minister*, pp. 440–2.

unconstitutional action, and he, not Pearse, was the first to declare a Provisional Government. He was, of course, a southern unionist and initially thought Ulster could be used to defeat Home Rule for the whole of Ireland. The Covenant spoke of 'using all means which may be found necessary to defeat the present conspiracy to set up a Home Rule Parliament in Ireland'. *The Irish Times*, organ of southern unionist opinion, in its editorial of 28 September 1912, backed the Covenant and Carson to the hilt, saying that 'the back of the great conspiracy is already broken', relying on the veto of unionist Ulster. Evidently the unionist veto trumped Irish democracy. Carson's reckless rhetoric, whatever its intent, often had consequences in terms of sectarian outbreaks in the workplace.

By the end of 1913 Carson realised that southern unionists were too dependent on the goodwill of their Catholic neighbours to participate in all-out resistance, and he was prepared to contemplate exclusion of the greater part of Ulster.[28] He found, however, right up to and including July 1916, post-rebellion, the aristocratic and gentry leadership of southern unionists was not willing to concede defeat in any part of Ireland.

Nevertheless, while securing the exclusion of six Ulster counties, Carson, unlike the leadership of his party, was deeply unhappy with the Treaty and regarded his political career as a failure. He even claimed to have been a naive victim of British party manoeuvres, a claim most of his former colleagues treated with scorn.[29]

When Carson died in 1935, though praised to the heights in Belfast, he was much criticised by *The Irish Times* for his pre-war tactics, which had opened the door to armed violence and led to partition.[30]

---

28 G. Lewis, *Carson: the man who divided Ireland* (London and New York, 2005), pp. 127–8.
29 H. Montgomery Hyde, *The Life of Sir Edward Carson. Lord Carson of Duncairn* (second edition, London, 1976), pp. 462–7, 491.
30 'Carson of Duncairn', *The Irish Times*, 23 October 1935.

Arguably, the outcome by the 1930s represented a massive miscalculation by Carson and his allies. George V, at least, was ready to admit this when he told his prime minister, Ramsay MacDonald, in 1930: 'What fools we were not to have accepted Gladstone's Home Rule Bill. The Empire would not have had the Free State giving us so much trouble and pulling us to pieces.'[31] Even today, it is possible to find, amongst one or two who have been involved for a lifetime in unionism at a high level, the occasional regret at the consequences of partition. They concede that such intense resistance to Home Rule might have been a mistake, even if Home Rule had led on to dominion status, which might have been embraced without the bitterness of conflict.

It should be added that some of Carson's inflammatory rhetoric helped drive Catholic workers out of the shipyards in 1920. In the House of Commons he could be much more reasoned. In his opening speech on the third Home Rule bill on 11 April 1912, he argued: 'There is no middle course possible. If Ireland and England are not to be one Ireland must be treated like Canada or Australia.' In 1928 he admitted privately that the Free State might as well be a republic.[32] Unfortunately such insights did not guide Carson's public conduct. Perhaps, as was suggested earlier, the citizens in the Republic of Ireland may have cause, in a perverse sort of way, to be grateful to Carson for his part in smashing the compromise of Home Rule and paving the way for independent statehood.

Redmond

John Redmond has arguably been the subject of both critical caricature and uncritical hero-worship. As a Parnellite, Redmond inherited some of the constitutional ambiguity of that party's original

---

31 K. Rose, *King George V* (London, 1983), p. 242.
32 Montgomery Hyde, *The Life of Sir Edward Carson*, p. 486.

fundamental position. As Dermot Meleady notes in his first volume of Redmond's life, apropos of the centenary celebration of 1798, in a platform speech in 1898 Redmond speculated about foreign allies that would rally to Ireland's cause 'if ever the day should come – and which of us would not be glad to see it, when in the complications of the world Ireland would once again have the opportunity of striking a blow for liberty'.[33] Needless to say, when the 1916 Rising took place, with the proclamation invoking 'gallant allies in Europe', Redmond was horrified.

As leader of a united party, he succeeded, when holding the balance of power, in putting Home Rule back on the agenda and eventually onto the statute book. That did mean that there would definitely be some form of self-government for a large part of Ireland, post-war, which advanced the situation. Both Carson's and Redmond's ability to compromise was limited by the fact that they could not simply throw overboard their respective supporters where they were minorities, in Redmond's case in Ulster, in Carson's case in the rest of Ireland. Enthusiasm for Home Rule was dampened not so much by the limited powers of a domestic parliament, some of which could be extended, as by the realisation that even this would come only at the price of partition. Interestingly, Gwynn claims that the Irish MPs lost popularity once they came to be paid a salary by the state from 1911, instead of being supported by voluntary contributions from their constituents.[34] *Plus ça change …*

Ironically for a constitutional leader, Redmond ended up as a political leader of a paramilitary organisation, the Irish Volunteers mainstream, simply because each position, nationalist and unionist, wanted the backing of armed force in order to impress the government. The government, the army and the police persistently bore

---

33   D. Meleady, *Redmond: the Parnellite* (Cork, 2008), p. 299.
34   Gwynn, *John Redmond's Last Years*, p. 52.

down much more heavily on the nationalist than on the unionist side, provoking the Labour MP J. H. Thomas to complain that the army seemed to have no problem putting down striking miners and railwaymen: 'Was the Army to be used against all movements except those under the patronage of the Tory Party?'[35]

Redmond, like de Valera after him, could accept temporary exclusion, or an autonomous parliament for the six counties subordinate to Dublin, but that was as far as he could go. For many of his followers, he was too comfortable at Westminster and with a Home Rule Ireland playing a full part in the British Empire. Conceivably, by accepting partition earlier he might have obtained marginal gains in territory, but only at the price of betraying Joseph Devlin, the effective leader of northern nationalism.

As war became imminent, Margot Asquith wrote to Redmond telling him he had the opportunity of his life, if he would go to the House of Commons and 'in a great speech offer all his soldiers to the Government or, if he preferred, to the King', as it appeared to her that it 'might strengthen the claim of Ireland upon the gratitude of the British people'. He replied that he hoped to see the prime minister the following day and be able to follow her advice.[36] On 3 August he made a speech that went down very well, offering the Irish Volunteers to defend Ireland, a gesture fully in line with the Grattan tradition, which he explicitly invoked. On 18 September the Home Rule bill, with a Suspensory Act postponing its implementation, went onto the statute book. Perhaps there was some understanding with Asquith about what was to follow, once this was done.

There is no more dangerous moment for a political leader than the moment of triumph. Two days later, at Woodenbridge, Redmond called on the Volunteers to go wherever the firing line extended,

---

35   *Ibid.*, p. 108.
36   Asquith, *Autobiography of Margot Asquith*, pp. 284–5.

which promptly led to a split. This act of generosity, regarding which Stephen Gwynn claimed Redmond did not consult his party, won no dividends for the Irish cause.[37] Once the war developed into a bloody stalemate and speculation about conscription intensified from 1915, events began to pass him by. Unlike John Dillon, Redmond misjudged the 1916 rebellion and appeared to condone at least some of the executions that followed it. The Irish Convention, which he sought, failed to recapture the initiative and, with the virtual elimination of the Irish Party after his death, his political career was branded a failure. None of his successors (or predecessors) achieved completely their more ambitious constitutional goals. It was a sad end to forty years of endeavour that had advanced the position to the extent that the principle of some form of limited self-government for Ireland was now established, but in practice only as far as twenty-six counties were concerned. The issues still open were timing, the question of boundary adjustments and the future governmental arrangements of the excluded areas of Ulster vis-à-vis London and Dublin.

Conclusions

Failure of leadership is shown, first, by the dangerous impasse reached in the summer of 1914, with an entirely uncertain denouement in the absence of war, and second, by the subsequent unsatisfactory and uneasy settlement which was reached only after several years of violence, an outcome that would have to be revisited many decades later after an even worse and more prolonged period of violence in Northern Ireland. There was little realisation at first amongst those who supported and those who resisted Home Rule that any outcome beyond the status quo would, in all probability, involve partition.

Partition was politically and economically damaging to both parts of Ireland and to both traditions in Ireland, but Irish democracy could

---

37   Gwynn, *John Redmond's Last Years*, pp. 129–36, 154–5.

not simply be brushed aside. The problem was that democracy was understood by both sides only in majoritarian terms. In the negotiations leading up to the Good Friday Agreement of 1998, the British Labour government formed under Tony Blair had a large majority, so that looking to the opposition for all-out support, 1912–14 style, was not a realistic option for unionists. If, as A. T. Q. Stewart wrote, the Home Rule crisis was in some respects 'the last ditch stand of the Ascendancy', which was, of course, spread across Ireland rather than just concentrated in Ulster, the stand was a failure.[38] If the purpose was to retrieve and ring-fence six Ulster counties from the effects of Irish democracy, it succeeded in winning them another half-century unencumbered, but at a high long-term price. Southern unionists, who blocked any deal because of their closeness at leadership level to the British establishment, grossly overestimated the strength of their position. As Mikhail Gorbachev warned the East German Politburo on the fortieth anniversary of the GDR in the autumn of 1989, 'life punishes those who move too late' – a dictum that applies to all those who failed, deliberately or otherwise, to pin down a settlement before August 1914.

---

38 A. T. Q. Stewart, *The Ulster Crisis: resistance to Home Rule 1912–14* (London, 1969), p. 44.

16

The centenary commemoration of the third Home Rule crisis

Gabriel Doherty

With the benefit of historical hindsight we can all see things which we would wish had been done differently or not at all. But it is also true that no one who looked to the future over the past centuries could have imagined the strength of the bonds that are now in place between the governments and the people of our two nations, the spirit of partnership that we now enjoy, and the lasting rapport between us.

Excerpt from a speech given by Queen Elizabeth II
during a dinner at Dublin Castle, 18 May 2011[1]

At the time of the state visit of Queen Elizabeth II to Ireland in May 2011 little attempt was made publicly by either the British or Irish governments to suggest that it was expressly or directly related to the then imminent 'decade of commemorations' for the series of interconnected events in the period 1912–23 that defined so much of the political, cultural and social landscape of modern Ireland, north

---

1   See http://www.dublincastle.ie/HistoryEducation/TheVisitofHerMajestyQueen ElizabethII/FullTextofTheQueensSpeech/ for the full text (accessed 26 January 2013).

and south.[2] The remarkably warm tenor of the proceedings, however, certainly provided a very favourable tail-wind for the process, and is the best starting place for a consideration of the manner and significance of the remembrance of the first significant development of that decade, that is, the Home Rule crisis of 1912–14. It is, of course, more than a little premature to draw any definitive conclusions about the nature of that commemoration, given that at the time of writing we are little more than six months into a controversy that lasted for well over two years. It is to be hoped, however, that this necessarily brief historical interim result will assist in the production of a full set of accounts, when the proper time comes to file such a return.

The mutual acknowledgement of historical (if not equal) wrong-doing in the relationship between Ireland and Britain, and the hope for future reconciliation between the two peoples, were the principal tropes of the speech given by Queen Elizabeth II quoted above. These were, of course, highly relevant in the context of the public discussion over the meaning and significance of the crisis of 1912–14, given that the impassioned debates, and momentous events, of those years touched on so many aspects of Anglo-Irish relations, not least their history. The continuing salience of the 'Ulster question' in that broader relationship was also adverted to in the queen's speech when she referred to the loosening of a 'knot of history' as a result of the formation of the power-sharing Northern Ireland Executive in May 2007. The re-formation of that Executive two days before her visit, with Peter Robinson of the Democratic Unionist Party and Martin McGuinness of Sinn Féin as first minister and deputy first minister respectively, was another encouraging portent for the decade of commemoration, for if figures with such utterly divergent political

---

2   It seems that the principal factor that determined the timing of the event was the fact that the fourteen-year term in office of President Mary McAleese – who had done so much to promote better relations between the United Kingdom and Ireland – was entering its final six months.

views could coalesce (albeit involuntarily) and agree on difficult matters of contemporary governance, then there seemed to be a genuine prospect of a productive period of reflection on the origins of the modern 'state' of Northern Ireland. (The party political dimension to the commemoration within Northern Ireland is considered in more detail below.)

It was not just in the six-county area that political events in the period before 2012 conspired to produce an atmosphere conducive to considered retrospection. In Britain the general election of May 2010 had produced a coalition of the Conservative and Liberal parties. The fact that these parties had been diametrically opposed to each other during the struggle over Home Rule for Ireland, but had now, a century later, been able to forge a working (if, at times, strained) relationship was a striking historical counterpoint and one that boded well for British engagement with the issues at stake. Then there was the even more striking outcome of the general election in the Republic in March 2011. This saw Fine Gael emerge as the largest party for the first time in the history of the state as a result of an unprecedented fall in the Fianna Fáil vote, and as the dominant partner in the coalition with the Labour Party that was formed immediately after the election. Such a political earthquake was likewise favourable to public debates south of the border on events of 'historic' significance.

The remainder of this essay is given over to the public discourse that attended the commemoration of the Home Rule crisis during the course of 2012, and has two parts. The first consists of a discursive chronicle of the principal forms of commemoration of the events and personalities of the crisis, and is sub-divided into sections corresponding to those forms – ceremonial, textual, visual and so on. The second discusses the political debates that occurred during the year regarding the commemoration of the crisis, in Northern Ireland, in the Republic and in Britain. For reasons of space other significant and interesting dimensions of the commemoration of the Home

Rule crisis, notably the 'public historiography' of the events and personalities of the 1912–14 period, have had to be excluded from this book, although I hope to discuss them in another place.

FORMS

Ceremonial

The anniversary of the signing of the Solemn League and Covenant on Saturday 28 September 1912 was, by some distance, the most discussed single event of the early stages of the Home Rule crisis to be marked in 2012 – much more so than the formal introduction of the third Home Rule bill itself to parliament. Here my attention is focused in particular on the large-scale parade that was organised in Belfast on Saturday 29 September 2012 to mark the event, before I go on to discuss other 'ceremonial' elements of the commemoration process.

Before briefly discussing the logistics of the parade, it is interesting to note that some months before the parade a new organisation, the Unionist Centenary Committee (UCC), had come into being. This body was formally launched in Craigavon House in April 2011, following a consultation process that had been taking place for some time within the unionist community in Northern Ireland regarding the correct approach to be adopted towards the commemorations.[3] Its membership was a who's who (or rather what's what) of the principal unionist organisations – including political parties (the Democratic Unionist Party (DUP) and Ulster Unionist Party (UUP), for example), loyal orders (such as the Grand Lodge of the Orange Order and

---

3   Details of the consultation process, formal foundation and other activities associated with the committee can be obtained from its website http://www.unionistcentenaries.com/news.php (accessed 28 January 2013), which went live on the same date as the organisation itself was publicly announced (9 April 2011). The 'mission statement' of the body is available online at http://www.unionistcentenaries.com/dynamic_news.php?id=31 (accessed 28 January 2013). For press coverage of the launch of the committee see *The Belfast Newsletter*, 9 April 2011.

the Apprentice Boys of Derry), commemoration groups (such as the Somme Association) and miscellaneous other groups.[4] The fact that such a coalition of at-times contending forces could form in the first instance was a powerful statement of the emotional capital invested in the 1912–14 period by the unionist community and the UCC was to prove itself a more than adequate vehicle through which much of the commemorative energies of that community were channelled during the year.

The 'Balmoral Review' of 18–19 May 2012 was held under the UCC banner to commemorate the assembly of nearly 200,000 unionists on Easter Tuesday 1912 in one of the first mass demonstrations against the third Home Rule bill (whose first reading at Westminster was at that time imminent). As it happened the original venue (the Royal Ulster Agricultural Showgrounds at Balmoral) was unavailable, so the gathering took place in Ormeau Park in Belfast (even though the event retained the 'Balmoral' moniker) and the date also differed slightly from that of the original rally. Its stated purpose was to give 'people a better understanding of the Home Rule crises [note the plural] from a unionist perspective' and, in so doing, hopefully 'reduce any tensions there may be as we as a community commence a decade of centenaries'.[5] The event had several component elements, including historical displays, musical performances and family entertainment such as firework displays, together with a major parade

---

4   The full list of 'stakeholders' (the term used by the committee) was as follows: 36th Ulster Division Memorial Association; Apprentice Boys of Derry; Confederation of Ulster Bands; Democratic Unionist Party; Grand Lodge of Ireland; Independent Loyal Orange Institution; Progressive Unionist Party; Ulster Volunteer Force Memorial Regimental Band Association; Somme Association; Traditional Unionist Voice; Ulster Bands Association; Ulster Defence Union 1893; Ulster Unionist Party.
5   See the statement issued through the Northern Ireland Community Relations Council (NICRC), 1 May 2012, available online at http://www.community–relations. org.uk/about-us/news/item/1023/decade-of-centenaries/ (accessed 28 January 2013). The NICRC website is a valuable resource for material relating to the decade of centenaries. For an expression of concern about the march's potential for trouble see the editorial in the *Belfast Telegraph*, 17 May 2012.

on Saturday 19 May that included approximately seventy bands and 10,000 marchers. Despite fears that the review in general, and the march in particular, might exacerbate communal tensions, in fact the two days passed off with no reports of major untoward incidents – an outcome that boded well for the much larger Covenant event four months later.

The decision to hold the Covenant parade and some of its details (notably the fact that it would terminate at Stormont) were made public in the April 2012 edition of the Orange Order journal, *The Orange Standard*.[6] The immediate build-up to the parade was over-shadowed, at least temporarily, by serious rioting in Belfast in late August and early September, following violations of directives from the parades commission relating to a loyalist parade outside St Patrick's Roman Catholic church on Donegall Street in Belfast on 25 August.[7] This led to a disagreement between the Orange Order and nationalist residents of the Carrick Hill area of the city, with the former refusing to meet representatives of the latter, preferring instead to deal directly with the clergy and parishioners of St Patrick's.[8] An attempt to mediate on the part of Presbyterian clergy having proved fruitless,[9] the parades commission, in its determination regarding the route of a feeder march for the main Covenant parade that sought to pass the church, imposed certain small restrictions on the plans submitted to it, in particular directing

---

6   For a summary see *The Belfast Newsletter*, 5 April 2012. It should also be noted that the parade was the culmination of a series of events that stretched over the preceding three weeks, which were initiated by an Orange Order parade in Enniskillen on Saturday 8 September – timed to commemorate the centenary of the visit by Edward Carson to the town that marked the start of the 'Carson trail'. See the statement on 5 September 2012 on the Orange Order website http://www. grandorangelodge.co.uk/news (accessed 28 January 2013).

7   For fears expressed that the Covenant parade might witness a repetition of such violence see *The Irish Times*, 4 September 2012.

8   The position of the two sides is discussed in the report on the matter in the *Belfast Telegraph*, 21 September 2012.

9   *Ibid.*, 22 September 2012.

a change in its return route and that hymns alone would be played as the parade passed St Patrick's.[10]

Perhaps as a consequence of pleas for peace from various quarters, perhaps as a consequence of appropriate policing and careful stewarding, perhaps as a consequence of self-restraint on the part of participants and perhaps because nationalists were aware that they had to play ball if *their* historic parades were to be likewise respected when the time came, the fears that attended the build-up to the parade proved unfounded.[11] The day in question (Saturday 29 September 2012) passed off, in the words of the official police statement, 'in relative peace and calm', with the hope expressed that the event would 'create a more positive platform for dealing with sensitive parades in 2013'.[12] Certainly it was an impressive feat of organisation, with estimates of 25,000–30,000 participants and an indeterminate number of onlookers along the length of the six-mile-route between Belfast city centre and Stormont. For once, it seems, the worst criticisms that could be levelled against a potentially contentious parade in Northern Ireland were expressed in the private grumblings of participants regarding the state of their blistered feet and the inadequate numbers of fast-food vans at their destination.[13]

In fact, not quite, for there were two flies in the ointment of the public reception afforded to the Covenant commemoration. Firstly, Ballymena Social Democratic and Labour Party (SDLP) councillor

---

10 The full ruling, dated 26 September, can be found at http://www.paradescommission.org/fs/files/det-2012-committee.pdf (accessed 28 January 2013).

11 Note, in particular, the joint appeal for calm by Peter Robinson, leader of the DUP, and Mike Nesbitt, leader of the UUP, as reported in *The Guardian*, 26 September 2012.

12 The full statement can be found at http://www.psni.police.uk/index/news-archive/news-2012/september-2012/pr_statement_at_conclusion_of_police_operation_on_29th_september_2012.htm (accessed 28 January 2013).

13 The sense of relief is captured in the title of a BBC report on the parade: 'Parade calm bodes well for Northern Ireland centenaries', available online at http://www.bbc.co.uk/news/uk-northern-ireland-19775759 (accessed 28 January 2013).

Declan O'Loan bucked the general trend of nationalist quietude regarding the parade, when he criticised it as not an appropriate way to mark the Covenant. His principal criticism was a familiar one: that the parade was an uncritical celebration of the Covenant rather than a measured appraisal of it, and one that wilfully overlooked the menace contained in its endorsement of the use of 'all means which may be found necessary' to defeat Home Rule – a phraseology in O'Loan's view that was the 'precursor to a period of shocking violence, division and separation in Ireland'. The significance of the point here is its place in O'Loan's wider censure of the commemoration process as a whole, or at least the Northern Ireland Executive's approach regarding same up to that point. He expressed the view that the failure to produce an agreed plan at Executive level (a state of affairs for which he blamed former DUP culture, arts and leisure minister Nelson McCausland) had produced an 'empty space' into which private organisations – presumably with agendas at odds with the public interest – had moved.[14] O'Loan's preferred approach was to rely on professional historians alone to convey an understanding of the past to the public – a suggestion that conveyed a fetching, if rather naive, belief in the capacity of such historians both to divest themselves and their work of all prejudice and bias, and to engage simultaneously the interest of all the citizens of Northern Ireland in an event for which few northern nationalists could be expected to show much enthusiasm.

In truth, there was little merit in his criticisms. As will be seen below there was, during the year, an abundance of opportunities for academic historians to express their views on the Covenant and the Home Rule crisis generally. Furthermore, whatever plans the Northern Ireland Executive might have agreed for a 'considered' appraisal

---

14   See O'Loan's interview in the *Ballymena Times*, 2 October 2012, and his letter to *The Irish Times*, 2 October 2012.

of the Covenant and the other events of the 1912–14 period, it was inevitable, and understandable, that unionists would have adopted a celebratory note towards events they regard as defining moments in *their* history. The day's proceedings, furthermore, were far from bombastic or triumphalist in character, at least by Northern Ireland's standards, but in the main were good-humoured – and, dare one say it, perhaps ever-so-slightly anticlimactical.

The second source of criticism was more unexpected. In the days immediately before the Covenant parade, the Methodist synod of Belfast issued a statement that expressed, amongst other sentiments, 'profound regret' at the fact that the Methodist Church in Ireland, in subscribing to the wording of the Covenant in 1912, implicitly suggested that God was on their side of the Home Rule divide and also endorsed the use of violence in support of that cause. The statement angered at least some within the broad unionist camp, who were no doubt annoyed that the 'common front' to the Covenant commemoration had been broken, and led a number of Methodists in the city to be openly critical of the synod.[15] The disagreement was, however, overshadowed by the various commemorative events that were scheduled during the week leading up to the Covenant parade, and its impact on that parade, and on the commemoration of the Covenant more generally, appears to have been slight.

In addition to these two principal gatherings, a brief mention should also be given to a wreath-laying ceremony at the statue of Edward Carson on the Stormont estate, performed by senior representatives of the Orange Order, accompanied by more than thirty unionist Members of the Legislative Assembly (MLAs), on Wednesday 26 September (that is, in the middle of the week-long series of events before the Covenant commemoration march). Their

---

15   See *The Belfast Newsletter*, 29 September 2012, for both extracts from the original statement, criticisms of same and the synod's response to those criticisms.

intention was to draw particular attention to the role played by Carson a century before – though this was scarcely necessary given the close scrutiny to which his actions as leader were subject during the year by a range of commentators, which is addressed in more detail below.[16]

These secular ceremonies had their counterpart in the religious field. In keeping with the active engagement of the Church of Ireland with the original mobilisation of Irish Anglicans against the third Home Rule bill, the Church of Ireland was likewise prominent in the commemoration of that mobilisation. Its engagement took two distinct, if interconnected, forms. The first involved the creation of a new liturgy to mark the centenary of the Covenant (but which could also be adapted to meet the needs of the successive anniversaries, including that of the 1916 Easter Rising). Details of the specially designed order of service were circulated to clergy in a letter jointly sent by Archbishops Harper of Armagh and Jackson of Dublin in January 2012, which stated that the church sought to mark the Covenant, and later events, 'in a manner that enhances understanding and helps build a shared future'.[17]

---

16   http://www.bbc.co.uk/news/uk-northern-ireland-19735337 (accessed 28 January 2013).

17   *The Belfast Newsletter*, 31 January 2012. Much the same tone was struck in the introduction to the liturgy, which reads thus: 'Brothers and sisters in Christ, at this time, one hundred years ago, half-a-million men and women signed a solemn declaration, a covenant rejecting the transfer of political power from Westminster to Dublin. Today we gather to recall a time of unprecedented change for the people of Ulster, of Ireland, of the United Kingdom and of Europe. In 1912 the prospects for social, political and economic catastrophe were evident, Europe eventually spiralling into a war of such costliness in terms of lost human life. National wealth and pride were such that these islands, in common with the rest of Europe, experienced a number of years of instability and transformation. Within Ireland, and especially in the Province of Ulster, the issue had its specific outcome in the work of establishing where political power should lie. This issue has continued to make significant demands on the society in this place; on the life and work of this city/town/parish, and so today, and in the coming years that chart the anniversaries of important milestones on the journey, we meet to mark in prayer, the points of both change and stability that form parts of this island's story. We do this in thanksgiving before God for those who have gone before us; in gratitude for the life we now possess, in all its

The second aspect of the church's engagement took the form of a number of commemorative services, some of which used this liturgy. Not surprisingly the most important coincided with, indeed marked the start of, the week-long series of events that culminated in the Covenant march of 29 September. It took place the Sunday before in St Anne's cathedral, Belfast, and was attended by the leaders of all the main Protestant denominations, the lord lieutenant of Northern Ireland, the mayor of Belfast and many leading and rank-and-file unionists, with a particular emphasis placed by the organisers on attracting families.[18] In his homily the dean of Belfast, Rev. John Mann, paid tribute to the Protestant generation of 1912, who, in his words, showed the determination 'to shape their own destiny', but he appealed in the modern era to and for a spirit of cross-community unity that, by dint of implication, was self-evidently lacking a century before.[19]

TEXTUAL
The spoken word
Those looking for enlightenment through the spoken word as to the issues at stake during the third Home Rule crisis, and its relevance to the present day, were not lacking in options during 2013. For those with the time and energy to attend full-scale academic conferences, there were at least three from which to choose, in addition to the proceedings held in University College Cork that form the basis for this book. First off the mark was Hertford College Oxford (in conjunction with the Faculty of History, University of Oxford, the Department of Humanities, University of Northumbria, and the

---

opportunities, in sorrow for the times when we have failed to imitate Christ as we should, mindful of those whose lives have been lost or blighted by physical violence or inner unrest of the soul and spirit, brought to the fore by conflict.' *Ibid.*
18   *Ibid.*, 22 September 2012.
19   *Belfast Telegraph*, 24 September 2012.

National Library of Ireland), which scheduled its 'The third Home Rule crisis: centenary perspectives' event on Friday 13 April 2012 (the nearest weekend date to the exact anniversary of the first reading of the bill, which took place on 11 April). Among the largely British-based academics who spoke at the gathering were Roy Foster, Lauren Arrington, Dan Jackson, Matthew Kelly, James McConnel and Senia Paseta, and they addressed topics as diverse as the rhetorical response to the bill, the role of Winston Churchill in 1912, and popular opposition to Home Rule in England, Scotland and Wales.[20] British-based academics were again prominent in the second conference, held in King's College London on 6–7 September, the line-up for which included Charles Townshend, Ian MacBride and Diane Urquhart as speakers.[21] Professor David Fitzpatrick reprised a talk delivered earlier in the year, at one of the biannual conferences organised by the Church of Ireland Historical Society, on the significant proportion of Ulster Protestants who did not sign the Covenant. A third conference (hosted by the Institute for British–Irish Studies, University College Dublin and the Irish Association for Cultural, Economic and Social Relations) slightly varied the format, with the inclusion of a number of non-academic speakers, including Michael McDowell and Lord Trimble of Lisnagarvey.[22] Interestingly this was the only such conference that took place in Northern Ireland during the year, being hosted by the Linen Hall library on Saturday 22 September.

In addition to these events, several series of lectures were also convened, all of which took place within Northern Ireland. The most important was organised by the Community Relations Council and took place on a weekly basis from mid-March to mid-May, being

20   See http://www.northumbria.ac.uk/static/5007/sasspdf/homeruleprogr for the full programme (accessed 28 January 2013).
21   The full programme is available online at http://sites.brunel.ac.uk/bais/events/events/the-ulster-covenant-1912-2012 (accessed 28 January 2013).
22   The full programme is available online at http://www.ucd.ie/ibis/filestore/Conference%20Programme.pdf (consulted 28 January 2013).

delivered by the cream of academics based in the area, including Éamon Phoenix, Keith Jeffery and Michael Laffan, who spoke twice.[23] A shorter series of talks, four in total, organised by the Public Record Office of Northern Ireland and focused primarily on the Covenant, was scheduled for September, to coincide with the anniversary of its signing.[24] The immediate build-up to the signing of the Covenant was also marked by the public library service for Northern Ireland, Libraries NI, with a concentrated series of lectures and presentations (over ten in total) in September.[25] A shorter run of lectures took place in November, in Newry Museum, to complement an exhibition there on the events of the revolutionary decade,[26] and relevant episodes of Jonathan Bardon's monumental 240-part Radio Ulster series 'A short history of Ulster' were broadcast at this time.[27]

Those more inclined to one-off lectures were also well catered for, with a large number of such events being organised across Northern Ireland during the year. In general these tended to be rather small affairs, frequently organised by local historical societies, the audience for which was, by and large, drawn from the immediate vicinity. There were, however, two significant exceptions, which occurred within a fortnight of each other in late March/early April, and were timed to

---

23   See *The Irish Times*, 23 March 2012, for a summary of Michael Laffan's paper 'Nationalism in Ireland 1900–1916: home rulers, separatists and Protestant nationalists', and *The Irish Times*, 10 March 2012, for Paul Bew's paper 'Two Irelands in conflict? 1912 Revisited'. The full set of lectures can be seen and heard online at http://www.community-relations.org.uk/marking-anniversaries/decade-of-centenaries-lecture-videos/ (accessed 28 January 2013).

24   For titles and speakers see http://www.proni.gov.uk/news_details.htm?newsRef=2143 (accessed 28 January 2013).

25   The full programme is available online as an image at http://www.ni-libraries.net/libraries/ballymena-library/?entryid3=17901 (accessed 28 January 2013).

26   For details of both the exhibition and lectures see http://newrytimes.com/2012/11/01/autumn-lecture-series-at-newry-museum/ (accessed 28 January 2013).

27   The episode that focused on the Covenant was aired, in timely fashion, on 27 September.

coincide (more or less) with the anniversary of the first reading of the third Home Rule bill. The first, and more important, was the 'Edward Carson lecture', entitled 'Reflections on Irish unionism', delivered by Peter Robinson to an invited audience in Iveagh House, the headquarters of the Department of Foreign Affairs in Dublin, on Thursday 29 March. This was, arguably, the single most significant set-piece speech delivered during the entire year, and in it the first minister for Northern Ireland argued for a revision of the received wisdom regarding Carson as an inflexible, 'conviction' politician, and proposed, instead, an interpretation that stressed his capacity for intellectual and political growth and willingness to change. Needless to say this 'historical' analysis was linked to an assessment of the more recent history of Northern Ireland and its contemporary politics. While there was no overt attempt in the lecture to lay claim to any Carsonite 'mantle', the title, timing and location of the talk inevitably conveyed an image of First Minister Robinson as Carson's latter-day heir.[28]

The second talk, or rather pair of talks, was delivered by Dermot Meleady and Frank Callanan SC on the exact centenary of the first reading of the bill, at a function in Waterford, bailiwick of John Redmond, Irish Party leader in 1912. The two spoke on different aspects of Redmond's leadership of the Home Rule party, with Meleady's talk covering the period from the reunification of the party through to the introduction of the third Home Rule bill and Callanan surveying his handling of the crisis of 1912–14. One of the principal arguments put forward by the latter was that Redmond was simply unlucky in facing a contrary turn of events that could not have been predicted and which produced difficulties that could not have been overcome and/or reconciled with the irreducible minimum of the standard Irish Party programme.[29]

---

28 The full speech is available online at http://cain.ulst.ac.uk/issues/politics/docs/dup/pr290312.htm (accessed 28 January 2013).
29 A revised version of the speech is available online at http://www.drb.ie/essays/

The printed word

Given that the onset of the decade of commemorations was widely flagged, it is a little surprising to note the relative dearth of new publications relating to the third Home Rule crisis during the 'publication cycle' relating to the same. Only one new full-scale monograph on the Home Rule crisis appeared during 2012 – Alan Parkinson's excellent *Friends in High Places: Ulster's resistance to Irish Home Rule, 1912–14*, in which exploration of the practical support afforded to the Ulster unionist campaign by elements of Britain's social and economic elite extended the historiographical boundary in a welcome direction. In addition there was a very thorough local study of these troubled years, Philip Orr's *New Perspectives: politics, religion and conflict in mid-Antrim, 1911–1914*, which, as good local history always does, shed as much light on the broader picture as on the parochial.[30] It had the added bonus of being linked to a very good website, hosted by the Braid Mid-Antrim Museum in Ballymena, with resources specially designed to aid teachers to engage with the subject.[31] Apart from that, however, there was almost nothing for the rest of the year, bar a new edition of a slight, and frankly partisan, account of the Covenant campaign as told from a unionist perspective,[32] and a curious melange of thoughts about the Covenant, the Easter Rising and the First World War Battle of the Somme from a variety of politicians, journalists and political activists north and south of the border.[33] That said, some very good work has appeared on the subject in the last two years,[34] and it may simply be that, scholarly

the-thing-that-never-was (accessed 28 January 2013).

30   P. Orr, *New Perspectives: politics, religion and conflict in mid-Antrim, 1911–1914* (Ballymena, 2012).

31   http://newperspectives.thebraid.com/ (accessed 28 January 2013).

32   G. Lucy, *The Ulster Covenant: an illustrated history of the 1912 home rule crisis* (second edition, Newtownards, 2012)

33   J. Collins (ed.), *Whose Past is it Anyway? The Ulster Covenant, the Easter Rising and the Battle of the Somme* (Dublin, 2012).

34   For example, see D. G. Boyce, 'Respectable rebels: Ulster Unionist resistance

journals excepted, publishers judged that, given the depressed state of the economy, the market could not sustain any more publications.

The fact that new books were in short supply did not, however, mean that those with an interest in reading about the issue of Home Rule were left short, as newspapers (and websites) devoted many column inches to the subject. Pride of place in this respect went to the two Belfast dailies, *The Belfast Newsletter* and *Belfast Telegraph*, both of which produced a series of high-quality articles throughout the year, which focused on the response in various localities within Ulster to the drama of the 1912–14 period.[35] Local papers, too, seized an obvious opportunity to promote a sense of local memory, with the *Ballymena Times*, *Londonderry Sentinel* and *Portadown Times* all producing copy geared towards the crisis.[36] South of the border *The Irish Times* provided its usual forum for letter-writers and also produced (in collaboration with the Department of Arts, Heritage and the Gaeltacht) a forty-page supplement on the crisis, which, if slightly disappointing in terms of content when compared to similar productions on previous occasions, was a useful resource, for schools in particular.

Virtual media also played an important role in facilitating both study and discussion of the crisis. As regards the former, a number of

---

to the third Home Rule Bill, 1912–14', in A. F. Parkinson and É. Phoenix (eds), *Conflicts in the North of Ireland, 1900–2000: flashpoints and fracture zones* (Dublin, 2010), pp. 28–39; É. Phoenix, 'Northern Nationalists in conflict: from the third Home Rule crisis to partition, 1900–21', in Parkinson and Phoenix, *Conflicts in the North of Ireland*, pp. 40–55; C. Reid, 'The Irish Party and the Volunteers: politics and the Home Rule Army, 1913–1916', in C. N. Dháibhéid and C. Reid (eds), *From Parnell to Paisley: constitutional and revolutionary politics in modern Ireland* (Dublin, 2010); and, best of all, A. Scholes, *The Church of Ireland and the Third Home Rule Bill* (Dublin, 2010).

35 For example, see the articles on the Enniskillen Horse, the sole cavalry unit within the Ulster Volunteer Force (UVF), in *The Belfast Newsletter*, 2 May 2012; on the east Tyrone UVF, *The Belfast Newsletter*, 9 October 2012; and on the City of Derry Regiment, *The Belfast Newsletter*, 11 December 2012.

36 The *Londonderry Sentinel* produced a special supplement on 19 September to mark the Covenant.

useful websites were created, or in some cases enhanced, with those provided by the BBC (http://www.bbc.co.uk/history/events/ulster_covenant) and the Public Record Office of Northern Ireland (http://www.proni.gov.uk/index/search_the_archives/ulster_covenant.htm) especially useful. In terms of discussion and analysis, sites such as politics.ie, thejournal.ie and sluggerotoole.com have provided forums for talented (and in some cases not-so-talented) commentators, who twenty years before would have lacked a public platform on which to air their views on the issues relating to the Home Rule crisis – and to have these instantly dissected.[37]

VISUAL
Exhibitions

The centenary commemoration of the third Home Rule crisis (both in and of itself, and as the opening event of the 'decade of centenaries') offered an abundance of opportunities for those who sought to convey the issues, thought and drama of the day in visual terms. The most popular sub-set within this category was the public exhibition, of which there were several during the year. It is difficult in such situations to suggest a hierarchy of significance of such events, not least because it is impossible to obtain comparable attendance figures, but the most important, in terms of commission and location at least, was probably the travelling exhibition created under the auspices of the Northern Ireland Office. This was unveiled at Westminster on Monday 12 March 2013, in the presence of An Taoiseach Enda Kenny and the-then secretary of state for Northern Ireland, Owen Patterson, and it remained there for a month before being moved to the National Library of Ireland in Dublin, before it took up final residence in Belfast.[38]

---

37 For one relevant discussion thread see http://www.politics.ie/forum/history/196541-100-years-ago-ulster-covenant-lights-fuse-conflict.html (accessed 28 January 2013).
38 Owen Patterson's speech on the occasion is available online at https://www.

The organisation of such exhibitions was not without controversy, however, and a senior member of the Orange Order, for one, publicly stated in May his belief that (to quote a newspaper report on his comments) 'some in the civic and political establishment' were deliberately trying to hinder efforts by the order to arrange an exhibition on the Covenant in one of the centres run by National Museums Northern Ireland. Dr David Hume, the order's director of services, stated during the course of a speech in Larne, 'In the balance of history we can see that mistakes were made on both sides. Now is the time to reflect on these so we do not repeat them and consign others to a repeat of earlier patterns.' He argued that this was impossible as 'the establishment [had] clearly decided to focus as little as possible on events such as the Covenant'.[39] It is difficult to give credence to such a view, however, given that a major exhibition, with the Covenant as a centrepiece, was at that very moment being organised by the Ulster Museum, before its opening on 21 September.[40]

Monuments, displays, re-enactments and walking tours

The erection of monuments is a classic device by which important events are commemorated, in Ireland and elsewhere, and 2012 was no exception in this regard – the only surprise being that only one such major monument was unveiled during the year. This was located in the centre of one of the traditional bastions of unionism, Portadown, with the ceremony itself taking place on Saturday 30 June and being performed by the granddaughter and great-grandson of Sir James Craig, Lord Craigavon.[41]

gov.uk/government/news/secretary-of-state-welcomes-an-taoiseach-to-exhibition-marking-the-centenary-of-the-third-home-rule-bill (accessed 28 January 2013). The event also saw a joint statement issued by Taoiseach Kenny and Prime Minister Cameron on the decade of commemoration as a whole.
39 *The Belfast Newsletter*, 25 May 2012.
40 *Ibid.*, 21 September 2012.
41 *Ibid.*, 3 July 2012.

Other, rather more transient, displays were also evident during the year, again originating exclusively from within the Protestant and unionist traditions. In July a controversy developed in Glengormley, when flags dedicated to the Ulster Volunteer Force (UVF) were publicly flown. While such emblems were defended on the basis that they commemorated the 'historic', Home Rule-era UVF rather than its latter-day incarnation, and were particularly dedicated to the memory of the original UVF who lost their lives in the First World War, there were protests from within the local, overwhelmingly Protestant, community and demands that the flags be taken down.[42] A number of Orange Lodges also commissioned new banners during the year, with some containing elements representing the events of the years 1912–14.[43]

Live-action re-enactments are also a traditional feature of many commemorative programmes; these took place during the year and, as with monuments and displays of flags, they occurred entirely within the context of unionist-organised events. The most significant was in Enniskillen at the beginning of September, to mark the anniversary of Sir Edward Carson's rallying cry in the town that saw the beginning of the 'Carson trail' back in 1912. Actors and Orangemen participated in the event, which organisers claimed was attended by 10,000 people.[44]

An increasingly popular form of open-air commemoration is the walking/study tour, and, again, these were available for interested parties. Two in particular deserve a mention. The first, which was oriented towards a unionist perspective of the events of 1912–14, focused on locations around the city of Belfast that were associated with the Covenant and took in sites such as the Ulster Reform

---

42   *Belfast Telegraph*, 3 July 2012.
43   For a report on the unveiling of one such banner, for Cairncastle Loyal Orange Lodge, see the *Larne Times*, 12 June 2012.
44   *The Belfast Newsletter*, 10 September 2012.

Club, First Presbyterian church and the Castle Court shopping centre (formerly the location of the Grand Central Hotel).[45] The second, which was a more cross-community affair, incorporated the evocatively titled 'Poppies and Lillies' residential tour and involved fifty community workers visiting sites associated with the Home Rule crisis, the First World War and the Easter Rising.[46]

Memorabilia

One other form of 'material commemoration' – which has been in existence in one form or another for centuries but which has become in recent years almost a fixture of the Irish calendar – should also be noted: the public auction of historic memorabilia. Demand for items dating back to the revolutionary decade has certainly been high in recent years (peaking in 2006, the ninetieth anniversary of both the Easter Rising and the Battle of the Somme), and even though the economic downturn after 2008 has dampened collectors' enthusiasm somewhat, it is no surprise that a number of auctions during the year contained items from the 1912–14 period. The auction houses Adam's, Mealy's and Whyte's all offered items for sale during the year, as did certain of their London equivalents. The most talked-about item was a very rare (possibly unique) copy of a poster dated 24 September 1913 proclaiming the creation of the Ulster Provisional Government, which was put up for sale at a Bonhams auctioneers' sale in London in June. Interestingly Jim Allister, leader of the Traditional Unionist Vote party, specifically raised the issue of the purchase of the poster with Minister of Culture, Arts and Leisure Carál Ni Chuilín, but at the time the Public Record Office of Northern Ireland denied that it had any plans for its purchase.[47] As events transpired the document

---

45   *Ibid.*, 5 March 2012.
46   *Belfast Telegraph*, 8 August 2012.
47   http://www.4ni.co.uk/northern_ireland_news.asp?id=144903 (accessed 28 January 2013).

was purchased by the state, by the Ulster Museum in fact, for £18,750, and was a centrepiece of its exhibition on the Home Rule crisis mentioned above. Perhaps surprisingly the price paid was below the lowest estimate for the sale and the damping down of expectations of a purchase by the state may simply have been a ruse to keep the bidding low.[48]

THE ARTS
Drama
One of the most welcome aspects of the commemoration process was the appearance of a number of new plays, whose subject matter (in whole or in part) focused on the events of a century before. While I am unqualified to offer an informed assessment of such theatre from an artistic perspective, the sudden proliferation of drama inspired by the Home Rule era is surely noteworthy as a significant phenomenon in its own right, irrespective of the ultimate place of any of the productions in the canon of Irish drama.

In some respects the most intriguing of these plays, certainly in terms of authorship, was *1912 – A Hundred Years On*. This was the product of collaboration between a Jesuit priest, Alan McGuckian, and Carrickfergus-based historian Philip Orr (author of one of the new historical works on the crisis referred to above).[49] The playwrights described their central theme thus: 'The challenge for the audience may be to try to understand more fully the motivations of their "forefathers" and "foremothers" but also the motivations of those with whom their ancestors quite possibly disagreed, in matters of

---

48   Details of the sale are available online at http://www.bbc.co.uk/news/uk-northern-ireland-18411365 (accessed 28 January 2013). Back in 2009 the National Museum of Northern Ireland had purchased two uniforms of Lord Carson for £42,000, again well below the lowest guide estimate; *The Irish Times*, Saturday 21 November 2009.
49   See above footnote 30.

faith and politics.'[50] Initially scheduled for a mere two-week run at ten different venues across Northern Ireland, the play proved sufficiently popular to warrant a further sixteen nights (many of which were sold out) in the autumn, including performances in some large, highly prestigious and unusual venues such as the Ulster Hall, Belfast City Hall and the National Museum in Dublin.[51]

White Star of the North, which debuted in Belfast's Lyric Theatre in March, was less ambitious in its historical scope, and more traditional in its framing, in that it focused on some of the main events of 1912–13 (the sinking of the *Titanic*, signing of the Covenant and formation of the Ulster Volunteer Force), and viewed them through the eyes of a small number of contemporaries (in this case, members of a Belfast Protestant family). While in the eyes of one local reviewer, Rosemary Jenkinson's text was too burdened with historical allusions 'to have seamless organic unity', and was overly influenced by a unionist perspective (although this was perhaps inevitable given the subject matter), nevertheless it was commended for its unexpected humour, 'imaginative stagecraft' and 'delicately crafted exchanges', and withal offered a 'poignant insight into the primal will to survive'.[52] Pádraig Coyle's *Home Rule*, which was commissioned by the Belfast Celtic Society, took as its subject matter the famous visit of Winston Churchill to Belfast in February 1912. Using the speech delivered by Churchill on that occasion as the basis for the exploration of a range of political, gender and other themes, the play was generally well received, and its opening

---

50   Quoted at http://sluggerotoole.com/2012/03/10/signing-up-to-the-covenant-an-alternative-vision-for-the-future/ (accessed 28 January 2013). For one very positive review see http://www.culturenorthernireland.org/article.aspx?art_id=4839 (accessed 28 January 2013).

51   See http://www.contemporarychristianity.net/joomla/index php?option=com_content&view=article&id=87&Itemid=137 for the autumn schedule (accessed 28 January 2013).

52   *The Belfast Newsletter*, 30 March 2012. For one negative review in the English press see *The Guardian*, 1 April 2012.

night was accompanied by a talk on the historical subject matter by Éamon Phoenix.[53]

Art, literature and music

The almost entirely neglected artistic dimension of the revolutionary decade in general, and the third Home Rule crisis in particular, was explored in some depth in a thoughtful and acclaimed art exhibition in Dublin's Hugh Lane gallery entitled 'Revolutionary states: home rule and modern Ireland'. Consisting, to a large extent, of portraits of prominent personalities from the era (including Edward Carson, John Redmond and Chief Secretary Augustine Birrell) taken from the gallery's own collection, the exhibits, including works by Sir John Lavery and Sir William Orpen, were complemented by an impressive series of explanatory lectures and an illuminating extended exhibition catalogue.[54]

I have not come across any new works of literature appearing in 2012 with the Home Rule crisis as their theme, but the centenary did, at least, provide the opportunity to revisit one of the authentic literary landmarks of the period, *The Red Hand of Ulster*, by Canon James Owen Hannay (aka George A. Birmingham), which was the subject of a specially commissioned programme on BBC Radio Ulster, broadcast in the week leading up to the Covenant march.[55]

Finally, reference should be made to the musical dimension of the commemoration. In addition to the large number of bands that accompanied street parades connected with the anniversaries during the year, one large set-piece indoor concert took place (along with a number of similar, smaller events), whose content understandably

---

53 *Derry Journal*, 6 September 2012.
54 See http://www.hughlane.ie/past/614-revolutionary-states-home-rule-and-modern-ireland (accessed 28 January 2013) for more details of the exhibition.
55 For details on the author and subject matter of the novel see *The Belfast Newsletter*, 22 September 2012.

reflected unionist sensibilities towards the period. The large concert was entitled 'Soul of a Nation' and was performed in the Ulster Hall on Wednesday 26 September, four days before the Covenant march. The main attraction was the east Belfast singer Lisa Williams, and the programme was completed with a number of pipe bands, along with poetry, drama and dance. A crowd of 900 was in attendance, and the event seems to have been an enjoyable one. A similar, albeit smaller, concert took place on New Year's Eve.

POLITICS

Given that the issues at the heart of the Home Rule crisis of 1912–14 – to name but a few: the relationship between the 'two communities', both north–south and within Northern Ireland itself; the question of Ireland's links to Britain; the threat of a recourse to violence to achieve political ends – had so many contemporary overtones, it is no surprise to find that a wide range of political views on that crisis were expressed during 2012, within Northern Ireland, across the island of Ireland and in Britain. It is equally unsurprising to note that, by and large, modern viewpoints tended to echo historic ones – so that latter-day unionists focused intensely, demonstratively and almost exclusively on 'their' heroes and 'their' story, while the nationalist dimension of the day received shorter shrift – a reflection of the virtual disappearance of the old Irish Party tradition that was, in turn, hastened by the third Home Rule crisis itself.

I shall briefly consider these viewpoints by focusing on the views expressed during formal discussions on the decade of commemorations, which took place during the year in the relevant deliberative assemblies (the Northern Ireland Assembly, Seanad Éireann and the House of Commons). The decorous conduct that is the norm in such venues inevitably means that neither the full diversity, nor intensity, of the political views held on the subject were captured by the official record of such debates, but it is believed they offer a sufficiently interesting sample of same to warrant the detailed discussion they receive here.

Westminster

Chronologically speaking, the first of the three chambers to discuss the matter was the House of Commons, on 21 March 2012, during the course of a meeting of the Northern Ireland Affairs Committee, which had been convened specifically to consider the issues arising from the decade of centenaries.[56] The meeting consisted in the main of the cross-examination of two expert witnesses from the Northern Ireland Office (NIO): Mary Madden, the deputy director of the 'Constitutional and political group', and Hugo Swire, MP, the minister of state – although, in fact, it was the latter who answered all of the questions as well as making the opening address. This address made it absolutely clear that a major concern of the British government with regard to the period 1912–23 was 'that these commemorations could be viewed by people across the divide in different ways, which could exacerbate the already tender relationships' evident in some areas – in other words, Her Majesty's government 'did not want … this decade to be hijacked by those who would seek to reinterpret history to suit their own narrow means'. Minister Swire did not expand on this point, nor identify which interpretations were considered objectionable by the government, although later on in his testimony, in response to a question from DUP MP David Simpson, he made it clear that it was dissident republicans whom the government had in mind when it spoke of those 'for whom it is just not in their interest for things to happen in the way we want them to happen'. Given the fragility of opinion within loyalism regarding Northern Ireland's peace 'settlement', it is debatable whether such an exclusive focus was

---

56 The full discussion is available online at http://www.publications.parliament. uk/pa/cm201012/cmselect/cmniaf/uc1906-i/uc190601.htm (accessed 28 January 2013).

entirely wise – a point that is discussed later. He laid great stress on the role of 'respected historians not politicians' as the 'monitors' of the various initiatives sponsored by the NIO and the British government more generally – although it is interesting in this respect that, at this time and in contrast to Dublin, London refused to go down the route of appointing a formal consultative committee, drawn from the historical profession, to advise government in such matters.[57]

This point was picked up by Oliver Colvile, Conservative MP for Plymouth, who enquired whether the British government contemplated 'producing any kind of guidance' regarding the running of commemorative events. The minister replied, very emphatically, in the negative. His reasoning was that 'anything that HMG says might not go down so well in various parts of the community who look on things in a different way'. The aim of the British and Irish governments, he continued, was to 'enshrine an architecture in which there can be a grown-up, sane discussion about what happened and what the effects were', rather than have government 'dictate' its interpretation of same. In response to a question along the same lines from Naomi Long (MP for Belfast East and deputy leader of the Alliance Party), he accepted that historians might not produce a consensus on any of the matters under discussion, but he was prepared to tolerate such a dissensus so long as it was 'argued in a rational and academic way'. Rather confusingly he subsequently went on to accept that there was little any government could do about any group 'hijacking history' or any particular event, but in such a scenario 'we can render irrelevant what they say and do by getting the consensus on what actually happened'.

---

57 Hugo Swire suggested that it was not the intention of the British government to appoint a team of historical advisors, although he did point out that the text of the exhibition on the Home Rule crisis that was opened at Westminster (see above) was sanctioned by, among others, Professor Paul Bew (Baron Bew) and Alistair Cooke (Baron Lexden).

When asked by Belfast-born Labour MP Kate Hoey for his view on the most appropriate way to commemorate the Ulster Covenant specifically, Swire's response was that the British government did 'not come to this with rigid views' – which is not surprising given that the coalition partners in Britain were on opposite sides of the debate a century before. His only requirement was that a debate regarding the Covenant should take place and that children had a right to learn about it 'in an unbiased way'.

Lady Sylvia Hermon, widow of Sir Jack Hermon (former chief constable of the Royal Ulster Constabulary), was, not surprisingly, particularly interested as to whether the views of the Police Service of Northern Ireland (PSNI) regarding the commemorations had been ascertained and what concerns, if any, the PSNI may have expressed. The minister's answer was that, while he could not put words into the mouth of Matt Baggott, chief constable of the PSNI, the latter's emphasis upon community policing meant that, heightened security fears notwithstanding, he was keen to ensure that the service was integrated into the community as far, and in as non-contentious a manner as possible.

The issue of whether the British education system could or should foster a knowledge of the events of the decade of centenaries in Ireland was raised by Kris Hopkins, a Conservative MP and former serving soldier with the British Army in Northern Ireland, who also quizzed the minister as to his views on the opportunities for enhanced Anglo-Irish understanding on foot of the Queen's state visit to Ireland. Mr Swire didn't give any response to the first question, but was entirely positive as to the benefits accruing from the state visit – 'extraordinary' being the term employed, with, for once, the superlative being entirely justified.

Reflecting the genial disposition of the membership committee itself, the session was conducted on an inquisitorial rather than adversarial basis and the discussion was good humoured, even, at times, light-hearted. Perhaps because of this, more problematic issues – such as the difficulties arising from the commemoration of the most contested events – were not explored in as much depth as they might, indeed should, have been. The overall impression created was of an administration committed to commemoration, not so much out of an interest in the innate significance of the events themselves as out of fear that the absence of state engagement would present an opportunity to (from a government viewpoint) irresponsible actors to peddle objectionable historical narratives. The ostensible aim was not to offer an uncontested 'official' history, but to utilise professional historians to convey the contested issues objectively and dispassionately. The advantages and drawbacks of such an approach are considered in more detail later.

Seanad Éireann

Three months later, on 7 June, it was the turn of Seanad Éireann to discuss the issues arising out of the decade of centenaries, to consider the programme of events with which the Irish government was involved and to offer suggestions as to how the state might most fruitfully revisit the controversies of the decade that gave rise to its creation.[58] The most significant part of the proceedings was the opening statement by Jimmy Deenihan, TD, minister for arts, heritage and the Gaeltacht, the department with general responsibility for the government's approach to the decade of commemoration. This was one of the few occasions during the year when Minister Deenihan had the opportunity to deliver a set-piece address on the matter, and he made the government's position clear from the outset. It is worth quoting from his speech at length:

---

58   The debate (which was conducted in two parts, over a period of about two hours) is available online at http://debates.oireachtas.ie/seanad/2012/06/07/00005. asp and http://debates.oireachtas.ie/seanad/2012/06/07/00007.asp (both accessed 28 January 2013).

On behalf of the Government, I have an absolute commitment to lead commemorations that are historically accurate, appropriate in tone and comprehensive in terms of the events that are commemorated and the perspectives that are offered on those events. I will place a premium on inclusion and public participation as I co-ordinate the development of a commemorative programme in a spirit of co-operation with political parties and community groups throughout Ireland. I welcome the interest and association of officeholders, institutions and the Irish abroad in building a programme that will acknowledge the sacrifices and celebrate the achievements of a revolutionary decade that, more than any other, shaped our modern world.

More specifically the minister referred to the work of two committees – the first an all-party Oireachtas one, consisting of political representatives, the second a panel of academic historians – both of which he anticipated would offer sage advice so as to ensure that the commemorations met the targets set out above. He noted that a number of events of various descriptions had already been organised by the Irish government, both on its own and in conjunction with interested parties within the state, such as local authorities, and without, including the Northern Ireland Assembly and the British government. He envisaged that the education system would 'have a key role' to play over the subsequent decade – although, in this context and probably wisely, he did not refer to the ongoing protests from numerous quarters at the proposal by his coalition counterpart, the minister for education and skills, Ruairí Quinn, to remove history from the list of compulsory subjects at Junior Certificate level – a point stressed by Senator Paul Bradford amongst others. He emphasised that the 1916 Rising would be 'at the centre' of the national programme, but added that other events and aspects of the period – such as the 1913 Lockout, the suffragette movement and the First World War – would not be neglected. On a more prosaic level he noted that, in spite of the 'special consideration on the appropriate marking of an important centenary anniversary' and in contrast to the sesquicentennial commemoration of the Famine in 1995, or the bicentenary of 1798 rebellion – when public finances were in better order – there was 'not yet a dedicated allocation from which support can be provided to applicants for commemorative initiatives', on the basis that 'the commemorative programme cannot be insulated from the necessary constraints on all public expenditure'.

In response to the minister's invitation to members of the house to 'come up with some good ideas' which could be added to the programme, a number of senators spoke at varying length, some more 'on topic' than others, with the discussion veering at times onto more peripheral matters (at least in this context) like the proposal by government to merge a number of cultural institutions (specifically the Irish Manuscripts Commission, the National Archives and the National Library) and the mooted abolition of the Seanad itself. With regard to the issue at the heart of the debate – that is, the general approach to the commemorative process – a constructive note was set early on by Senator Labhrás Ó Murchú, who suggested that the artistic, cultural and educational background of many of the prominent figures on the republican side in the 1916 Rising provided an ideal opportunity for the government to prioritise those aspects of the decade. He also placed great stress on the engagement of voluntary organisations with the process, including the Gaelic Athletic Association and the Gaelic League, but also others with less obvious historical dimensions to their remit (including Comhaltas Ceoltóirí Éireann and the Irish Countrywomen's Association). He made interesting observations on the crucial significance of language and the importance of replacing rhetoric that had become 'archaic and antiquated'. Speaking as an avowed nationalist (and one who, therefore, welcomed the minister's reference to the centrality of the Rising during the commemorative decade), his starting point was that to the extent to which commemoration inevitably implied some element of praise and/or celebration, then what was to be celebrated was not 'violence and division' but the 'generosity of spirit and sacrifice' that he perceived to be defining aspects of the period.

In a debate characterised by a very high degree of goodwill, a rare dissenting voice was that of Senator David Norris, who objected to Senator Ó Murchú's praise for the 1966 commemorations. In Senator Norris' eyes this had been a simple 'tribal celebration of bloodlust' from which anyone from a Church of Ireland or unionist background was excluded. It should be noted that, whatever may be the case about the latter, his remarks with regard to the former group are at odds with the record of engagement in the 1966 events of both the institutional Church of Ireland and individual members of the Irish Anglican community.

Understandably Senator Martin McAleese, husband of the former president, Mary McAleese, and prominent community and political actor in his own right, focused on the possible impact of the commemorations on the situation in Northern Ireland. Although half of his speech was dedicated to the fragile nature of the political situation in the six counties, without any particular reference to the forthcoming commemorations, when he did address the subject his tone was refreshingly upbeat. He sensed that the forthcoming decade 'offered a real opportunity to make further progress, provided we act with a full and true sense of inclusiveness, parity of esteem, generosity and above all, respect and sensitivity to the celebration of the centenary events of those whose traditions, heritage and ambitions we do not share'. He expressed no doubt that if 'this test' were passed, 'we will be on the cusp of a prolonged and sustainable peace on this island', where the 'two traditions' would still exist, but would do so in a spirit of peaceful mutual toleration and respect.

The need to commemorate the struggle for the enfranchisement of women was a point stressed by several speakers, including Senators

Catherine Noone and Ivana Bacik. Rather more curious was the suggestion by the latter that the commemoration of the 1916 Rising should not be 'too militaristic or a celebration of bloodshed' and that the role of pacifists, such as Louise Bennett and the Sheehy-Skeffingtons, needed to be celebrated, because the 'strong role of pacifists was part of events leading up to Easter 1916'. Quite how a state could properly commemorate a military rising by prioritising the role played by conscientious pacifists was not an issue explored in any great depth by the senator.

The debate threw up some interesting titbits, including a widespread acceptance on the part of those who addressed the subject of the desirability of inviting the leadership of the Orange Order to address the House (not coincidentally, two leading members of the Ulster Unionist Party, including the new leader Mike Nesbitt, were in the public gallery during the debate) and the historically ecumenical suggestion by Senator Paul Bradford (of Fine Gael) that the decade would be incomplete without the erection in Dublin of a public memorial to the memory of Éamon de Valera. The former took place in July 2012; at the time of writing there is no evident progress on the latter.

Northern Ireland Assembly

The third and final discussion took place in the Northern Ireland Assembly on 18 September 2012, that is, just before the start of the week-long programme of events, referred to above, that immediately preceded the centenary of the signing of the Covenant. In contrast to the previous cases, the deliberations in Stormont involved a formal debate (albeit one that only lasted an hour), which spoke to the following motion:

> That this Assembly recognises the signing of the Ulster covenant on 28 September 1912, in its centenary year, as an historic and significant

event in the history of Northern Ireland; notes the availability of all the digitised signatures of the covenant via the Public Record Office of Northern Ireland website; and affirms the importance of Ulster Unionists Lord Carson and Lord Craigavon and their legacy which remains in place today.[59]

Given this wording it is no surprise to find that it was moved by a unionist, Michael Copeland of the UUP, and received the active support of the DUP. What may be more surprising is that it garnered the passive acceptance (or at least the absence of active opposition) of Sinn Féin and the SDLP. In many respects the debate was more interesting than the two discussed above, partly because it was focused on historically specific events and personalities, and also because the very creation of Northern Ireland itself was organically linked both to the Home Rule crisis in general and to the particular sentiments embodied in the Covenant – thereby giving the exchanges added piquancy.

The opening speech by Michael Copeland covered a lot of ground and was perhaps more historically ecumenical than might have been expected. Fulsome in his praise of Edward Carson (if slightly less effusive with regard to James Craig) and keen to stress the politico-religious dimensions of the Covenant (which, he claimed, 'laid out not only the citizens' responsibility to God but, in a way in which only Ulster Presbyterians could, implied the responsibility of God to the citizens'), he was prepared to accept an organic link between the Ulster Volunteers and Irish Volunteers, and the illegality of the former in undertaking the Larne gun-running. His main focus was, however, the symbolism of the First World War, as expressed by three graves he came across in the military graveyard of Tyne Cot in Flanders.

---

59   The motion, and the ensuing debate, can be found at http://www.niassembly. gov.uk/Documents/Official-Reports/Plenary/2012-13/Plenary_180912.pdf (accessed 28 January 2013).

Located adjacent to one another, they contained the remains of three Irish soldiers from different regiments and, he reasonably inferred, different backgrounds: the first an Irish Guardsman and thus not necessarily either Catholic or Protestant; the next, a Royal Dublin Fusilier and thus quite probably a Catholic/nationalist; and the third, a member of the Royal Irish Rifles and almost certainly a Protestant/unionist. He observed:

> They lie together, embracing one another in death for eternity, to have given us the chance to make this island a better place for all of us and not to deny any aspect of our history but to look at it honestly and judge the sentiment as well as the actions.

A more strident tone was struck by Lord Morrow, of the Democratic Unionists, whose focus was less on the events preceding the creation of Northern Ireland than on the subsequent development of the two states on the island. In particular he was keen to stress what he saw as the stark contrast between the commitment to civil and religious liberties as expressed in the wording of the Covenant and in the statements of both Carson and Craig, and the sectarianism he saw as embedded in the structures of the southern state and the mindset of its political class. In truth his observations were based on a rather selective series of quotations and, to the credit of the speakers on the nationalist side, few were tempted to rise to the bait. Indeed Alex Maskey of Sinn Féin, who was the next speaker, may have been gently chiding Morrow by observing, at the start of his comments, that he did not think that any participant in the debate intended 'to do a historical accuracy fact-check'. His main concern was with the parades commemorating the Covenant that were then imminent, and he appealed to the organisers and participants to review the arrangements regarding same, which, as they stood, did not 'add anything to mutual understanding, greater respect or furtherance of reconciliation'. The need for inclusivity rather than exclusivity in the commemoration of historical events was his overriding concern, 'in order to make this a more fruitful decade that helps on the pathway towards reconciliation and a greater understanding amongst our communities'.

Interestingly Colum Eastwood, the young MLA from the SDLP, was keen to highlight one ironic consequence, for unionists, of what he saw as their excessive focus on the signing of the Covenant: the marginalisation of the tradition of *Irish* unionism. In his eyes, the real significance of 1912 lay in the fact that Ulster unionists chose 'to break with the tradition of Irish unionism' as well as with that of Irish nationalism, and in so doing, produced 'an unnatural and damaging division of Ireland's people'. He did not expect unionists to agree, but, at least, he hoped that they should seek to understand the perspective of nationalists on the issue.

The position of the Alliance Party on the motion (as expressed on this occasion by Trevor Lunn) was a little surprising, for he spoke rather more critically of the Covenant than did those in the nationalist camp. He mentioned that his party had discussed internally whether it 'should support a motion that gives praise to an organisation that threatened to take up arms against the legitimately elected Government of the day'. While it ultimately decided it would do so (on the rather questionable grounds that 'the times were different') he was equally critical of the legacy of both Carson and Craig, which included (*pace* Eastwood) not just the division of Ireland and the eclipse of the Irish unionist tradition, but also the 'break-up of Ulster' by virtue of the exclusion of Counties Cavan, Monaghan and Donegal. Further, and in contrast to the benign interpretation of the history of Northern Ireland since partition put forward by Lord Morrow, Lunn observed that for many years the government and administration of the area was conducted on a discriminatory basis that gave no cause for pride. He concluded by expressing the hope that in 2016 the assembly would be in a position to give all-party support to a similarly worded resolution regarding the Easter Rising, and the role played by Patrick Pearse and James Connolly.

The remainder of the contributions were more in keeping with the consensual contributions heard at the outset of the debate, with no dissenting voices expressed from any side of the chamber. The motion, as a consequence, passed without a division – a not inconsiderable achievement considering the rather partisan nature of its wording and the atmosphere within the assembly, which during 2012 was becoming increasingly fractious with each passing day.

Conclusion

On some levels the centenary commemoration of the early stages of the crisis over the third Home Rule bill could be deemed a great success. There was undeniably a wholehearted engagement with the process within the broad unionist community, with a wide variety of events, ranging from the impressively organised Covenant march of 29 September, with its mass participation, to lectures organised in intimate venues at village level. For their part, nationalists of all hues within Northern Ireland were less enthused about the year, but did little or nothing to obstruct the commemorative process, while the Irish and British governments and other agencies (such as the university sector in the islands) did their part to raise consciousness of a crisis that, for all its tumultuous significance in its day, had long since slipped off the popular historical radar in both jurisdictions. For anyone with the interest, leisure time and money to attend all the various events that were held during the year, the commemoration amounted to a once-in-a-lifetime opportunity to hear and read some of the best historians in the United Kingdom and Ireland talking in depth, at length, and over a short period of time, about a particular historical episode. Such an individual would have emerged at the end of the year with an enormously enhanced understanding of the crisis over the Home Rule bill.

Furthermore, and in contrast to the fears expressed in advance that the commemoration process might be 'hijacked' by those who sought to use them for political purposes (something, of course, all politicians, of all political descriptions, are wont to do), there was no obvious connection between the commemorative programme and political developments within Northern Ireland – at least, perhaps, until the very end of the year. Up until December 2012 the political scene in the area remained much as it had been for the previous two to three years, one marked by mutual suspicion tempered by political pragmatism within the Executive and by latent antipathies (occasionally flaring up into overt violence) in certain sectors of the broader community.

In that month, however, the political mood darkened – much to the dismay of those who may have hoped that the commemorative programme during the year might have served to bring the 'two communities' within Northern Ireland together by a process of shared reflection on their common history. Three developments in particular occurred, which together produced a marked polarisation of opinion within the six counties generally, and within unionism in particular, over and beyond that which had been seen for some years. The first, both chronologically speaking and in order of significance, arose from the decision of Belfast City Council, at its meeting on 3 December, to reduce the number of days on which the union flag would fly outside Belfast City Hall from 365 to 18 days a year. Eight days later the publication of the latest census results for Northern Ireland showed that for the first time the Protestant proportion of the population of Northern Ireland had fallen to less than half of the total (48 per cent), only 3 per cent ahead of those describing themselves as Catholic, the balance being made up of those who subscribed to other religions or none. The following day the de Silva enquiry into the death of the solicitor Pat Finucane in February 1989, the subsequent police enquiry into same, and allegations of complicity between British state agencies and loyalist paramilitaries, found in respect of this last point and in the words of Prime Minister David Cameron 'frankly shocking levels of collusion', amid many other damning conclusions.[60]

All of these events provoked anger and concern amongst the unionist community, for different, if similar, reasons. The 'flag' decision symbolised the continuation of a trend of declining commitment to the union that had been ongoing for some years; the census returns raised the prospect that a Catholic majority in Northern Ireland might occur sooner than most thought likely, and with it the possibility of a majority in favour of unification in the event of any referendum on the issue (even if polls seemed to suggest that a number of Catholics might oppose such a proposal); while the Finucane report represented the latest example of a worrying aspect of the post-Belfast Agreement political landscape, that is, an excessive focus on the crimes committed during the troubles by those who supported the union and a lack of will to investigate those perpetrated by those who opposed it.

For the purposes of this essay it is important to note that none of the controversies were linked in any direct way to the commemoration of the Home Rule crisis. But such has been the scale of the (at time of writing still ongoing) violence, and the extent of the crisis produced at a political level (with unionist–nationalist contact within the Executive dwindling to dangerously low levels), the events amounted to a worrying coda to the year. It may be possible to hypothesise some connection between the two – that the memory of the popular unionist mobilisation against the Home Rule bill in 1912–13, then so fresh in everyone's mind, persuaded some that something similar could be achieved in 2012–13 – although the suggestion must remain just that in the absence of more detailed investigation of the causes of the latter.

---

60 *House of Commons Debates*, 12 December 2012, col. 296, available at http://www.publications.parliament.uk/pa/cm201213/cmhansrd/cm121212/debtext/121212-0001.htm (accessed 28 January 2013).

At a more general level, however, two significant, and interrelated, questions/conclusions arise out of the commemoration of the third Home Rule crisis during 2012, with its characteristic focus on the 'cool' approach to commemoration, based primarily on the work of professional historians and with the role of public memory marginalised. The first is whether such an approach amounts to anything more than preaching to the converted, one that will interest that section of the population already historically literate, but with little to entice or engage the average citizen. The second regards the extent to which such an approach can ever satisfactorily recreate or convey to the average member of the public the subjective passions that gave rise to the original crisis. At present – and possibly at any time – it is difficult to give a positive answer to either question.

17

The third Home Rule bill in British history

Eugenio Biagini

The Amending Bill [for the temporary exclusion of Ulster from Home Rule] & the whole Irish business are of course put into the shade by the coming war.

Herbert H. Asquith to Venetia Stanley, 29 July 1914[1]

There is a paradox about the place of the 1912 Home Rule crisis in British history. On the one hand, it polarised opinion and brought the kingdom to the brink of civil war. On the other, twenty-first century observers struggle to understand why a bill that proposed a mild and conservative form of legislative devolution should have caused such violent responses. And it is not only our sceptical generation that takes this view: already in 1930 King George V, in a private conversation with his prime minister, J. Ramsay MacDonald, reportedly said: 'What fools we were ... not to have accepted Gladstone's Home Rule Bill. The Empire now would not have had the Irish Free State giving us so much trouble and pulling us to pieces.'[2] And in 1935 George

---

1   'Asquith to Venetia Stanley, 29 July 1914', in *H. H. Asquith Letters to Venetia Stanley*, selectors and eds M. and E. Brock (Oxford, 1982), p. 132.
2   Cited in H. C. G. Matthew, *Gladstone, 1875–1898* (Oxford, 1995), p. 184.

Dangerfield mused on how impenetrable 'the Imperialist mind' of the Edwardian age had become to the inter-war British public, who, far from perceiving Home Rule as a revolution, seemed to regard 'the Empire [as] ... so spiritual a structure that any large piece of it could break away with scarcely a groan'.[3]

It must be noted that incomprehensibility to later generations is a feature that the 1912 crisis shares with many other Edwardian reforms, which at the time were almost as divisive as Home Rule, but were quietly implemented after the First World War, becoming henceforth universally accepted and uncontroversial: these include women's suffrage, national insurance and the disestablishment of the church in Wales. Yet the 1912 Home Rule crisis is even more distant from the modern mindset than many of these. For example, women's rights remained a sensitive topic for the rest of the century and church issues excited occasional animosity, although intermittently, for decades to come – as was illustrated in 1928 by the revision of the Book of Common Prayer, in the 1990s by women's ordination in the Church of England and, recently, by the question of gay marriage. Even national insurance involved fiscal and financial problems that have continued to worry the public ever since. However, Irish Home Rule was already obsolete when implemented in 1920 and was immediately superseded and replaced for most of Ireland by a much more radical measure in 1921, as provided for by the Anglo-Irish Treaty, a settlement that in turn was overtaken by events within a generation, with the 1937 constitution of Éire/Ireland and the 1948 proclamation of the Republic of Ireland. As Dangerfield noted, by the 1930s even imperial devolution failed to excite any emotional response in the British public.

Incomprehensible to the inter-war generation, the third Home Rule crisis has also long been neglected by historians. This is not to say

---

3   G. Dangerfield, *The Strange Death of Liberal England* (London, 1936), p. 95; see also his *The Damnable Question: a study in Anglo-Irish relations* (London, 1976).

that *Irish* historians have missed the importance of the bill for their country – quite the opposite, as witnessed by the works of such scholars as Nicholas Mansergh, A. T. Q. Stewart, D. George Boyce, Paul Bew and many others.[4] But in England the 1912 crisis has not attracted anything like the academic attention and controversy generated by the first and the second Home Rule bills, which have been minutely dissected and examined by many of the leading twentieth-century historians, including John Morley, J. L. Hammond, John Vincent and Colin Matthew. Indeed, in the conversation quoted above, even King George V thought that the missed 'golden opportunity' had been the bill of 1886, not that of 1912, although he had been personally involved in negotiating the latter and not the former. Likewise, the Ulster crisis has been neglected by historians of Christianity, to the extent that even G. I. T. Machin, in his otherwise detailed and systematic *Politics and the Churches in Great Britain 1869–1921* (1987), pays no attention to the issue. Yet, there is no doubt that the 1912 crisis was not only constitutional, but also deeply religious, and polarised Protestant and Catholic opinion throughout the United Kingdom and the Empire, culminating in a series of confessional clashes including the one occasioned by the 1908 papal *Ne Temere* decree.[5]

The same neglect has affected the great leaders of the agitation which caused the crisis. Edward Carson, whose 1910–14 unionist crusades in Britain attracted crowds larger than those to which Gladstone had preached the Midlothian gospel in 1879, largely vanished

---

4   N. Mansergh, *Ireland in the Age of Reform and Revolution: a commentary on Anglo-Irish relations and on political forces in Ireland, 1840–1921* (London, 1940); A. T. Q. Stewart, *The Ulster Crisis 1912–1914* (London, 1967); N. Mansergh, *The Unresolved Question: the Anglo-Irish settlement and its undoing, 1912–72* (New Haven, 1991); P. Bew, *Ideology and the Irish Question: Ulster unionism and Irish nationalism, 1912–1916* (Oxford, 1998); D. G. Boyce and A. O'Day (eds), *The Ulster Crisis: 1885–1921* (Basingstoke, 2006); R. Fanning, *Fatal Path: British government and Irish revolution 1910–1922* (London, 2013).
5   A. F. Parkinson, *Friends in High Places: Ulster's resistance to Irish home rule, 1912–1914* (Belfast, 2012), pp. 90, 181.

from the British public record after the settling of the Northern Ireland boundary question in December 1925: for example, from 1926 to 1936 his name was mentioned only three times in *The Times* – two in passing references in readers' letters to the editor and once in a leading article commenting on his death.[6] Carson's religious views – which were so important at the time – still remain to be studied.[7] Moreover, the leader of the Tory Party – Andrew Bonar Law – has not found greater favour with the historian: his most recent biographer describes him as 'the least known' among 'those who reached the peak of British politics in the [twentieth] century'.[8] Even to a scholar of openly Conservative opinion, such as Robert Blake, Bonar Law appeared like a ghost shrouded in the mists of a remote age, separated from us by an emotional and political gap to the extent that, already in 1955, when Blake published his influential study, Bonar Law was described as 'the unknown Prime Minister'.[9]

For the general public the reasons for such an imagination gap – our inability to figure out why people were so upset by the 1912 bill – depend to an extent on the tragic events that characterised the immediate aftermath of the Ulster crisis. The latter was still going on when it was dwarfed by the unparalleled carnage of the First World War, in comparison with which even the Irish wars of 1919–23 were little more than 'troubles'. Drowned in a sea of blood, in Britain the memory of the third Home Rule bill was then buried under the rubble of the Great Slump of 1929–39, and wiped out by the Second World War, the Cold War and the demise of the British Empire. Indeed, Ireland as such, and Northern Ireland in particular, largely disappeared

---

6   W. O'Brien, 'George Wyndham and Irish reform', *The Times*, 10 May 1926; 'Lord Carson', *The Times*, 23 October 1935; I. Colvin, *The Times*, 4 December 1936.
7   Despite two important biographies: A. T. Q. Stewart, *Edward Carson* (Dublin, 1981), and A. Jackson, *Sir Edward Carson* (Dundalk, 1993).
8   R. J. Q. Adams, *Bonar Law* (London, 1999), flyleaf.
9   R. Blake, *The Unknown Prime Minister: the life and times of Andrew Bonar Law* (London, 1955).

from the radar of British consciousness during the period that extends from 1925 to 1968, until the outbreak of the troubles.

These factors, however, do not explain why professional historians and policy-makers have forgotten the first Ulster crisis. Even the reopening of the question of devolution from the 1970s – with Scotland and Wales demanding their own 'Home Rule' – failed to reawaken interest in the crisis of 1912. As D. George Boyce noted, the protagonists of the modern devolution debates have 'remained blissfully unaware of their illustrious, if unsuccessful, predecessors'.[10] This is partly because in the politics of the United Kingdom devolution has never been regarded as anything more than a 'crisis-management' option, to be used particularly in colonial contexts. Only the Liberals, at one end of the spectrum, and the Ulster unionists, at the other, have showed consistently any positive interest in the idea as an intrinsically desirable constitutional option.[11] Not much has changed in the years since the Northern Ireland peace process. On the one hand, Tony Blair, who oversaw the creation of devolved assemblies for both Scotland and Wales in 1997, displayed an astonishing ignorance of history, masked only by his pseudo post-Gladstonian rhetoric and association with Roy Jenkins. On the other, the leading contemporary historian of the union, Alvin Jackson, is an Ulsterman who holds the most prestigious history chair in Scotland, thus confirming the pattern which I mentioned above, that is, that Home Rule and the union do not excite *English* interest. His scholarship, moreover, provides one further illustration of a pattern already highlighted: for in his groundbreaking study *The Two Unions*, Jackson is surprisingly emotional about 1886 but does not study the 1912 crisis in any detail.[12]

---

10   D. G. Boyce, 'Federalism and the Irish question', in A. Bosco (ed.), *The Federal Idea*, (vol. 3) *The History of Federalism from the Enlightenment to 1945* (London, 1991), p. 137.

11   A. Jackson, *Home Rule: an Irish history 1800–2000* (2003), pp. 261, 311.

12   A. Jackson, *The Two Unions* (Oxford, 2012), p. 295.

Yet, it was not Gladstone, but Herbert H. Asquith, Winston Churchill, David Lloyd George and John Redmond who brought the Home Rule bill onto the statute book, and it was the 1912 bill, not those of 1886 and 1893, which nearly caused an army mutiny and civil war in the United Kingdom.

Here I shall try to explain some of the reasons for this case of prolonged collective historical amnesia. I shall first look at recent studies that have contributed to counterbalance the historiographical deficit. Then I shall explore what I call – borrowing Dangerfield's metaphor – the 'strange deaths' of political parties in this period, suggesting that this affected not only the Liberals, but also the Conservatives and Labour, at least in their Edwardian incarnations. I shall argue that such a high mortality rate was caused by a radical reorientation of British political priorities away from the issues that had been so dominant in 1912, and towards the 'modernity' of an allegedly secular and materialist world. Finally, I shall consider the extent to which the dramatic alternatives of 1912 – partition, rampant sectarianism or civil war – failed to excite the imagination of a later generation of historians despite these features becoming the norm in European and Middle Eastern politics, particularly from 1919 to 1945. Thereafter, public perceptions of ethnic and national problems underwent a further paradigm shift, with the rise of 'human rights', whose individualism was even more alien to the communitarian mindset of Edwardian Britain and Ireland.

Attempts to counterbalance the historiographical deficit

Until recently, with the exception of Mansergh's classic studies, the first of which was published in 1940, and a section in his more recent *The Irish Question* (1965), the most significant examination of the third Home Rule bill in British politics was the one written by a historian based in Australia and partly trained in Canada. Patricia Jalland's *The Liberals and Ireland: the Ulster question in British politics* was published in 1980. She adopted the then-fashionable view that, by focusing on Home Rule, the Liberal Party was engaging in an old-fashioned battle that would have been 'ripe for settlement' a generation before. As a consequence, she concluded: 'the Irish problem … demoralised the Liberal party at a critical time and contributed significantly to the party's decline … Home Rule highlighted Liberalism's difficulty in reconciling the "progressive" demands of the twentieth century electorate with the traditional commitments of Gladstonian Liberalism.'[13]

She was writing at a time when 'modern' politics was equated with 'class' and 'collectivist social reform', and anything to do with religion and 'status' was regarded as a relic of Victorianism, and therefore altogether irrelevant in the twentieth century.[14]

The balance began to be redressed by a new generation of scholars at the turn of the century. In 1997 Alvin Jackson published a provocative counterfactual on 'British Ireland: what if Home Rule had been enacted in 1912?'[15] Much of it, however – like much of the book he later published on the history of Home Rule – was about Ireland, not Britain. By contrast, G. K. Peatling's work, which was published in 2001, was entirely focused on the British perception of and response to Home Rule. Although his *British Opinion and Irish Self-government* covers the period 1865–1925, it focuses primarily on the 1912 crisis, and so does – as its title suggests – Dan Jackson's *Popular Opposition to Irish Home Rule in Edwardian Britain*, published in 2009.

Peatling shows how important Ireland was not only for the Gladstonian old guard, but especially for the *new* generation of Liberals. These included, among others, the social reformers L. T. Hobhouse

---

13   As cited in G. K. Peatling, *British Opinion and Irish Self-government, 1865–1925: from unionism to liberal commonwealth* (Dublin, 2001), p. 54.
14   P. F. Clarke, 'The electoral sociology of modern Britain', *History*, vol. 17 (1972), pp. 31–55.
15   A. Jackson, 'British Ireland: what if Home Rule has been enacted in 1912?' in N. Ferguson (ed.), *Virtual History: alternatives and counterfactuals* (London, 1997), pp. 175–227.

and Gilbert Murray – for whom the first Home Rule crisis had been 'a formative political experience'[16] – C. P. Scott of the *Manchester Guardian*, Henry Massingham, J. L. Hammond, the economist and analyst of imperialism J. A. Hobson, together with Henry Brailsford, Henry Nevinson and Arthur Ponsonby. Some of these became leading members or influences on the post-war Labour Party, within which they represented, together with George Lansbury and Arthur Henderson, the continuity between Gladstonian and Labour internationalism.[17] Whatever else the Liberal Party as a whole thought or did, its leading intellectuals and most promising figures felt that Home Rule in 1912 was an inevitable question about democracy, anti-jingoism and the defence of the constitution itself against the blackmail and violence of small groups and special interests. Hobson, for example 'had no doubts that the Ulster resistance was not bluff, but sedition, and should therefore be put down with all the resources of civilisation' – a view and a language deliberately reminiscent of Gladstone's attitude to the Land League in 1881.[18] If Hobson saw the Carsonites as terrorists, Massingham thought that they were nothing less than 'sickening', and deplored Ulster's 'arrogance ... ignorance ... [and] uncivilised and irreligious hatred'.[19] Peatling concludes that '[f]undamentally, the new Liberals were emotionally and ideologically committed to Home Rule for a united Ireland on Gladstonian lines'.[20]

In short, within the Liberal Party, Home Rule was the cause neither of the elderly and old-fashioned, nor primarily of the frontbenchers who were most immediately interested in the survival of the government, but of the young, the up-and-coming generation of radicals, who carried the flame of 'New Liberalism', social reform and

---

16   Peatling, *British Opinion and Irish Self-government*, p. 59.
17   See, in particular, P. Bridgen, *The Labour Party and the Politics of War and Peace 1900–1924* (Woodbridge, 2009).
18   As summarised by Peatling, *British Opinion and Irish Self-government*, p. 76.
19   *Ibid.*, p. 78.
20   *Ibid.*, p. 79.

democracy. Later, after the outbreak of revolution in 1916, they reacted most strongly against the policies adopted by London, criticising the way the Easter Rising had been put down and the execution of some of its leaders, as well as the murder of Francis Sheehy-Skeffington, a man who, in many ways, was an Irish New Liberal.[21] They also tried to avert the execution of Roger Casement, another who shared much ground with Liberal humanitarianism and anti-imperialism.[22] In 1919–21 they strongly criticised the British attempt to repress the revolution by means of terror and illegal military operations, which C. P. Scott's *Manchester Guardian* compared to the behaviour of the German forces in Belgium in 1914–15. This was a significant parallel at the time, for it was the Germans' 'methods of barbarism' that had contributed towards mobilising the public for the war in both Britain and Ireland, while later alleged Teutonic atrocities became the target of latter-day Gladstonian moral populism, when exposed by the Bryce commission.

Peatling's analysis of the unionist attitude is equally revealing. Again, the people most exercised by the Home Rule question were not phobic and foaming 'old fogies' from the shires, but forward-looking, radical Chamberlainites and Milnerites, who thought that the challenge of Home Rule was an opportunity for the Empire. Like the Liberal Unionists of 1886–93, they objected to parliamentary devolution only in so far as it was proposed as a special policy for Ireland, because it then acquired separatist implications. By contrast, they were prepared to consider it as part of a major scheme of imperial federation, which would not be about national independence, but about building closer imperial integration and interdependence.[23] Such Chamberlainites included men like Leo Amery but also Lionel Curtis and Philip Kerr, who served as Lloyd George's secretary in 1920. For them the Empire was about toleration, diversity and local

---

21 *Ibid.*, p. 83.
22 *Ibid.*, p. 84.
23 *Ibid.*, p. 132.

self-government, the answer to the madness of ethnic supremacism and militant imperialism that they saw spreading on the continent. Moreover, despite the Protestant militancy of most unionists, this group included Catholics, like the economist W. A. S. Hewins and Lord Lothian, who became a champion of federalism as a way of rebuilding Europe after the Second World War.[24]

While Peatling's study ends with 1925, Mo Moulton's new book is largely about the interwar period. *Ireland and the Irish in Inter-war England* (2014) is an important study, based on an impressive range of sources. It looks at the aftermath of the Rising in United Kingdom politics, society and culture, thus further exploring an area that has been much studied in recent years, for example in Ruán O'Donnell's collection of essays *The Impact of the 1916 Rising: among the nations* (2008) and Maurice Walsh's *The News from Ireland* (2011), and sheds new light on the legacies of the war for the way Irishness was perceived in interwar Britain. On the whole, Moulton confirms the importance and significance of the Home Rule question for the New Liberals and post-war humanitarians, as well as for the unionists, and, simultaneously, for the persistent fear of Irish immigration to England, where they formed a disaffected ethnicity associated with deep class tensions. This resulted, Moulton concludes, not in collective amnesia, but in the 'quarantining' of the British Irish, waiting for their full assimilation, as well as of the Ulster question. While the former were indeed successfully integrated, Northern Ireland became more and more 'alien' as it descended into violence from 1968.

One question that neither Peatling nor Moulton address is: how much did *ordinary* British people care about the Home Rule crisis in 1912–14? Generations of historians have taken a dismissive attitude to the whole matter as little more than a sideshow, with Ireland merely a pawn in the game of Westminster politics. The 'real' issues

---

24   *Ibid.*, pp. 115–16, 119.

were, we used to be told, social legislation, class and the rise of the Labour Party. In the process it was easy to forget the strength of the Conservatives and all that they stood for, including the union. Dan Jackson's book is a salutary reminder that the realities of popular politics before 1914 were more complex than one might think if one accepts the Whiggish mantras about modernity and the rise of Labour and class politics. His approach is boldly and healthily revisionist. His argument is that from the start of the third Home Rule bill crisis, there was, in Britain, considerable popular interest in the Irish issue. With a well-orchestrated agitation – ironically reminiscent of Gladstone's 'Midlothian' campaigns in the 1880s – the unionist leaders managed to turn such interest into a powerful movement, with the potential of affecting the result of the next general election, expected by 1915. Edward Carson was particularly prominent in this regard. His rhetoric and charisma – which hitherto historians have tended to regard as an Irish peculiarity – were amazingly effective in working the crowds of Liverpool and Glasgow into a feverish paroxysm, in my opinion comparable to the enthusiasm displayed by those at Italian and German meetings of the far right in the 1920s and 1930s.

This in itself is very interesting. Indeed, one of the areas in which Jackson's work will influence the scholarly debate is by encouraging a reappraisal of the political significance of the radical right. The latter has attracted considerable attention in recent years, but scholars have stressed its intellectual significance, rather than its populist potential and appeal. Jackson is now showing that, because of the Ulster question, radical-right ideas began to be widely canvassed and attracted a surprising degree of popular support. He adopts an eclectic method, borrowed as much from anthropology and sociology as from history. He argues that popular unionism in Britain developed a religious connotation most visibly in the mass meetings and processions addressed by Carson: these 'highly ritualised urban perambulations ... diverge from orthodox religious occasions only in the object venerated ... the Act of Union personified in a Loyal Irishman'.[25] The religious dimension was a function of a 'pan-British' version of nationalism, 'as collective reaffirmations of a type of British identity that felt increasingly under threat'.[26] Of course, this was compounded by the conflict over Home Rule, including a strong confessional dimension anyway, one that the evangelical revival of 1905–6 must have further strengthened in Britain as much as in Ireland.

While Jackson affirms the religious nature of much of the British unionist support for Ulster, it is not clear whether the mass demonstrations that he examines were anything more than self-contained and self-fulfilling expressions of popular involvement, and thus that the street theatre of 'Carsonism' was a noisy but ephemeral dimension of popular politics, or whether it influenced the whole nature of Conservatism and unionism. Whatever the case, Jackson's conclusion that the issue might have proved sufficiently important for the Unionists to win a general election, had Asquith dissolved parliament in 1914,[27] is in itself a reminder of the immense change brought about by the First World War in public attitudes to religion, sectarianism, the land question and Ireland in particular. For by 1918 and 1922, when elections were actually held, Ireland was no longer a significant factor, let alone a decisive one, and within a few years Carson, Bonar Law and the majority of the leaders of Edwardian unionism, as well as most of its programme, had been replaced by new men and different ideas.[28]

---

25 D. M. Jackson, *Popular Opposition to Home Rule in Edwardian Britain* (Liverpool, 2009), p. 6.

26 *Ibid.* See also D. Thackeray, *Conservatism for the Democratic Age: Conservative cultures and the challenge of mass politics in the early twentieth century* (Manchester, 2013).

27 Jackson, *Popular Opposition*, pp. 242–3.

28 The same applies to the Liberal strategy to counteract the unionist challenge, a strategy that focused on land reform: while this was very popular before the First World War, afterwards it suddenly became almost irrelevant: I. Packer, *Lloyd George, Liberalism and the Land. The land issue and party politics in England, 1906–1914* (London, 2001).

The strange deaths

This is the first and most dramatic of the 'strange deaths'. In order to understand the pathology that led to the early demise of such a healthy creature, British unionism, we must realise that, however enthusiastic and sincere its *popular* politics side was, the *leadership* of the movement consisted of a disenchanted and opportunist, if not cynical, group of executive politicians. Let us take Bonar Law. As the crisis unfurled, he was incredibly frank and candid about his motives in delaying a compromise solution involving partition. On 15 October 1913, in a memo of a private conversation with the prime minister, he noted that he had provided Asquith with three main reasons justifying 'how difficult such an arrangement [exclusion of the Ulster counties] would be [for his party]'. The first was a concern for the southern unionists, who would feel betrayed. The second was, revealingly:

> That the probable result of an agreement would be that the Welsh [Church disestablishment] Bill would go through under parliament act, and that, whatever may be the feeling of the party, it is my belief that a very much larger number of our members in the House of Commons would, if they had to choose, prefer Home Rule rather than disestablishment of the Church.

Apparently oblivious to the fact that this admission meant that – after all – the party did not really care much for either the southern unionists or Home Rule, or indeed the national interest, Bonar Law went on to say that his third and most important reason for resisting a compromise was:

> That if the question of Ulster were removed one of the strongest points in our favour in an Election would be gone and our chance of winning would … be diminished, and that also … there was still in our party a strong survival of the differences connected with the 'Die-Hard'

movement, and that if there was any suggestion that it would be regarded as a second climb down there would be much more danger of a split in the party than would be the case in ordinary times.[29]

So, for him, the Home Rule crisis had a primarily instrumental value, as one aspect of a strategy designed to corner the Liberal government, forcing it to choose between trying to impose Home Rule on Ulster at the cost of a civil war, or fighting a general election at a time when the government was unpopular.[30] In order to play this game Bonar Law was prepared to risk a major constitutional crisis, involving the army and the monarchy itself in a highly partisan manoeuvre, ostensibly justified by an appeal to the overarching importance of Ireland, which, as we have seen, was actually the least of his concerns. The most dangerous aspect of his strategy was the plan to hold up the annual Army Act in the Lords, in such a way as to release the forces from their duty to obey the government in 1913–15. It is amazing that he contemplated such an extreme step at a stage when a major European war was likely to break out at any time. It is revealing of the Conservative frame of mind that, as late as 1955, such an influential and highly regarded Tory historian as Lord Blake was prepared to defend Bonar Law to the extent that he presented the dragging of the monarchy into partisan conflict in 1914 as the fault of the prime minister whose party and coalition had won three elections in a row, rather than of the opposition leader who was prepared to encourage rebellion and civil war sooner than tolerate the implementation of a measure of parliamentary devolution.[31]

---

29 Blake, *The Unknown Prime Minister*, p. 161.
30 J. Smith, 'Bluff, blunder and brinkmanship: Andrew Bonar Law and the third Home Rule bill', *Historical Journal*, vol. 36 (1993), pp. 161–78.
31 Blake, *The Unknown Prime Minister*, pp. 161–72. When it comes to the army mutiny episode, however, he refers to the Tory machinations as 'reckless in the extreme ... an astonishing revelation of the extent to which the Irish problem had dazzled, almost blinded, the leading politicians of the Conservative party', p. 174.

However, as we have noted, it was not Home Rule as such that drove these men, but the prospect of Welsh disestablishment and – even worse – that of a fourth consecutive Liberal electoral victory, which might have sparked off the permanent minority status of the Tories, or even their disintegration. In short, it was the fear that democracy would at last bring about the end of the old order, as Lord Salisbury had anticipated as early as 1867 and dreaded for the rest of his career. He was not alone: throughout Europe, as a reaction to the rise of the democratic and socialist left, authoritarian conservatism was rearing its head under new and radical ideological garments, involving militarism and mass mobilisation. In the run up to the First World War, in Germany, Austria-Hungary and Italy anti-constitutional plots were continuously being hatched in court or military circles by elites who had reason to fear that only force – or a major European war – could stop the democratic rot from finally setting in. Even republican France experienced this form of culture war, particularly during the Dreyfus crisis in the 1890s.

Bonar Law represented the most vocal exponent of the United Kingdom version of this last-ditch struggle against democracy and desire for an aristocratic counter-revolution.[32] That the movement found its most explicit advocates in what Tom Villis has described as the intellectual and poetic reactionary avant-garde might be read as a sign that it was not politically serious.[33] We must remember, how-

---

32 W. Kaiser, 'The decline and rise of radicalism: political parties and reform in the twentieth century', in P. Catterall, W. Kaiser and U. Walton-Jordan (eds), *Reforming the Constitution: debates in twentieth-century Britain* (London, 2000), p. 57. On the subject see also G. R. Searle, 'The "Revolt of the right" in Edwardian England', in P. Kennedy and A. Nicholls (eds), *Nationalist and Racist Movements in Britain and Germany before 1914* (Basingstoke, 1981), pp. 21–39; A. Sykes, 'The Radical right and the crisis of Conservatism before World War One', *Historical Journal*, vol. 26, no. 3 (1983); F. Coetzee, *For Party or Country: nationalism and popular conservatism* (1990); A. Sykes 'Radical conservatism and the working classes in Edwardian England: the case of the Workers' Defence Union', *English Historical Review*, vol. 113, no. 454 (1998), pp. 1180–209.

33 T. Villis, *Reaction and the Avant-garde: the revolt against liberal democracy in early*

ever, that militant Conservatism secured as many votes as militant Liberalism in two consecutive general elections in 1910. Throughout this period the leaders of the party which secured over forty per cent of the popular vote were prepared to plot against the government with the help of Anglo-Irish generals such as Lord Roberts and Sir Henry Wilson. The Tories 'regarded it as quite compatible with his official duties to pass confidential information to the Leader of the Opposition, where such information might be of value in the struggle against Home Rule'.[34]

Throughout Europe as much as in Britain, the changes brought about by the First World War were astonishing. In most countries on the continent there was first a victory for democracy – with communist uprisings, the establishment of new republics, or election victories for centre-left coalitions – gradually followed by a conservative reaction from the 1920s. In Britain the most dramatic change was in the programme and vision of the Conservative and Unionist Party. As late as 1914 it was considering dragging the United Kingdom into anarchy for the sake of Ulster and union with Ireland, as well as 'more important' issues such as the institutional status of the church. By 1922, however, the same party, under much the same leaders, had accepted not only Welsh disestablishment and Home Rule for the six counties, but also the Anglo-Irish Treaty and a measure of devolution for India. Moreover, having campaigned for national service on the German model, in 1919 they proceeded to cut the military estimates and reduce the size of the army, which reverted to the old professional system. While the war and navy budgets were slashed, welfare expenditure increased sharply – funded by Lloyd George's income tax, not by tariff revenue – and women were given the parliamentary franchise. There was a brief attempt to revive the protectionist cause

twentieth-century Britain (London, 2006).
34   Blake, *The Unknown Prime Minister*, p. 179.

in 1923, but when the Conservatives came back to office in 1924 Baldwin made sure to have a free-trader and former New Liberal, Winston Churchill, in charge of the Treasury.

It is not that in the 1920s the pre-war issues did not matter any more, nor that the Conservatives had suddenly shed their anti-democratic and illiberal legacy in a mad rush to the centre. It is rather that the war had shifted politics so much to the left that democracy and even colonial devolution seemed to provide the only viable lines of defence against the new Bolshevist threat, the only plausible source of political legitimacy in the 'brave new world' of Lenin and Woodrow Wilson. Thus the Conservatives had no option but to adopt many of the policies which before the war had been distinctly Liberal. As Ian Cawood has recently noted, this gave a new lease of life to the 'Liberal Unionist' wing of the party, which now came to represent the party's future, despite the death of the cause that had brought it into existence in 1886.[35] In other words, as *Daily Telegraph* journalist Edward Pearce noted in 1999, 'what died with the Edwardian era was not liberalism, but the savage, unstable Toryism which saw revolution in reform, and in Ulster played godfather to armed revolt'.[36]

Dangerfield made a memorable case for the Liberal Party, and indeed for their whole worldview, being overwhelmed by successive waves of 'irrational' politics: trade union militancy in 1911–13; women's suffrage militancy, 1910–14; Ulster militant unionism, 1912–20; Irish militant nationalism, 1916–21; and state violence, protectionism and suppression of civil rights in wartime, 1914–18. All of these were of course unpleasant and unwelcome developments, difficult to reconcile with Liberal rationalism, which allegedly went to an early grave (the second 'strange death' considered in the present chapter). Yet it was its ideals and worldview that were triumphant

---

35 I. Cawood, *The Liberal Unionist Party: a history* (London, 2012).

36 E. Pearce, *Lines of Most Resistance: the Lords, the Tories and Ireland, 1886–1914* (London, 1999), quotation from flyleaf.

at the end of the war. What undermined the Liberals as a force in British elections was not intellectual collapse in the face of the brutal realities of the twentieth century, but internal party divisions, personality clashes and the plagiarism of their pre-war programme by both Labour and the Conservatives. From 1917 to 1922, moreover, the widespread obsession with the Bolshevist threat, and Lloyd George's idea that the 'Red menace' from Moscow required a new alignment in British politics and the formation of a wider and inclusive centre party, had particularly negative effects on the party's ability to fight elections. In 1919, as army tanks rolled into George Square in Glasgow and troops were deployed on Clydeside to fight the proletariat if the latter tried to storm the local equivalent of the Winter Palace, the debates on the 1912 Irish Home Rule bill looked remote and irrelevant.

In government circles, imperial federalism remained associated with Winston Churchill and Lloyd George.[37] It is perhaps significant that one was a former Conservative and an imperialist, the other a former Welsh nationalist. While this does not mean that the issue was necessarily marginal within the party, it is remarkable that other Liberal Home Rulers – particularly John Morley – dismissed the proposal, which was quietly dropped. It is also interesting that this debate – like the original 1886 Home Rule one – reflected the Canadian experience and the alleged advantages of a federal solution. The latter had been applied to South Africa in 1909, with considerable and lasting success. Over the next seventy-five years federalism was also applied to various other parts of the Empire/Commonwealth, as the latter underwent decolonisation. However, at no stage was there any serious debate about adopting federalism in the United Kingdom.

---

37 P. Jalland, 'United Kingdom devolution 1910–1914: political panacea or tactical diversion?', *English Historical Review*, vol. 94, no. 373 (1979), pp. 757–85; on federalism see also M. Wheatley, 'John Redmond and federalism in 1910', *Irish Historical Studies*, vol. 32, no. 127 (May 2001), pp. 343–64.

As Jalland concludes, the federalists remained a disparate and divided group.[38] The realisation that England was not interested in regional self-government and that devolution for Scotland and Wales would not simplify the Irish question, contributed to the shelving of the proposal. Even the rise of the Welsh and Scottish national parties – in 1925 and 1934 respectively – did nothing to change the situation.

In part this was because of the rise of a new parliamentary centralism, which gradually superseded the Victorian constitution and its powerful local authorities, particularly through the creation of the welfare state. Already by 1918 Lloyd George had become accustomed to parliamentary centralism, which was essential for the operation of wartime collectivism and the government's involvement in the running of the economy. The settlements of 1920–1 effectively excluded Irish business from the House of Commons and in this way eliminated the main reason for considering a federal arrangement.

There were two additional problems with the federal idea, as D. George Boyce has noted. One was that it treated the component parts of the United Kingdom as equal, while there was an obvious asymmetry between them: in terms of population, wealth and votes England mattered more than the other three countries put together.[39] The other problem was that, in the Empire as a whole, federation had lost much of its pre-war prestige: after Gallipoli and Vimy Ridge even the most loyal cubs of the British lion, like Australia and Canada, were eager to distance themselves from the metropole, to make sure that they would not be dragged into another European conflict by some blundering statesman in London.

This global rejection of imperial federation affected both historical memory and political instincts: significantly John Pinder of the Lothian Foundation concluded his 1991 study with a section enti-

---

38   Jalland, 'United Kingdom devolution 1910–1914', p. 785. See also P. Jalland, *The Liberals and Ireland: the Ulster question in British politics to 1914* (Brighton, 1980).
39   Boyce, 'Federalism and the Irish question', p. 135.

tled 'A rich heritage, briefly remembered and then forgotten'.[40] This does not mean that nobody was interested in such a legacy: on the contrary, men like Philip Kerr, Lionel Robbins, William Beveridge and many others contributed powerfully to its development in the interwar years, and later the Liberal Party remained the staunchest advocate of European integration, with its federalist implications. The Liberals were, however, never again able to secure a majority of the popular vote for their party. While attitudes to Europe were half-hearted and guided by short-term pragmatic concerns, the long-term significance of developments elsewhere – in the Commonwealth in particular, with the rise of federal India, Nigeria and South Africa – were ignored. As Pinder has concluded, at the end of the twentieth century 'Britain appear[ed] to be parochially unaware [of] how far the liberal constitutional principles that the British did so much to develop [were] becoming the world's political paradigm'.[41]

The third 'strange death': the myth that class struggle would change British politics

The Liberal Party had during that period [1886–1905] persisted in assuring the English people anxiously that it had no intention of doing anything for England (its object being to show its abhorrence of socialism) and that it cared for nothing but Home Rule in Ireland. Now as the English electors, being mostly worse off than the Irish, were anxious to have something done to alleviate their own wretched condition, they steadily voted for the Unionist Party (not because it was unionist, but because it cared more for England than for Ireland), except on one occasion in 1893, when the Liberals put all their Home Rule tracts on fire, and fought on a program [sic] of English Social reform,

---

40 J. Pinder, 'The federal idea and the British Liberal tradition', in Bosco, *The Federal Idea*, (vol. 3), p. 113.

41 *Ibid.*, p. 115.

known as the Newcastle Program [*sic*], drawn up by my friend and Fabian colleague, Mr Sidney Webb …[42]

This is how G. B. Shaw, an Irish Protestant socialist, conceptualised the difficulties of the Liberal Party at the turn of the century. Basically, Ireland did not matter, social reform did, and class politics was modern politics, which the Liberals wilfully neglected. Hence their decline and, by implication, the rise of Labour. Generations of historians – from Élie Halévy and G. D. H. Cole to Peter Clarke and Ross McKibbin and, as we have seen, Patricia Jalland – basically agreed, with Clarke contesting this view only in the sense that he argued that the Liberals had in fact updated their ideological arsenal by 1906 and were successfully fighting class politics by 1910.[43]

The problem with this view is that 'class politics' in the Marxist sense of the expression did *not* replace traditional forms of party alignment, and the Labour Party, though a spectacular success in the long run, took a long time to triumph, securing its first majority of the popular vote only in 1945.[44] The party that was most successful under universal suffrage was not Labour, but the Conservatives. While Labour did not rise, the Liberals did not collapse in 1918, contrary to what the 'franchise factor' theory of Matthew, McKibbin and Kay would lead us to expect.[45] Despite their quarrelling and discredited leaders, the Liberals held their ground successfully until

---

42 G. B. Shaw, 'Preface to the Home Rule edition', *John Bull's Other Island*, ed. D. H. Lawrence (London, 1984), p. 54.

43 P. F. Clarke, *Lancashire and the New Liberalism* (Cambridge, 1971) and *Liberals and Social Democrats* (Cambridge, 1978).

44 M. Pugh, *The Making of Modern British Politics 1867–1939* (Oxford, 1982).

45 H. C. G. Matthew, R. I. McKibbin and A. Kay, 'The franchise factor in the rise of the Labour party', *English Historical Review*, vol. 91, no. 361 (1976), pp. 723–52 and P. F. Clarke's reply, 'Liberals, Labour and the franchise', *English Historical Review*, vol. 92, no. 364 (1977), pp. 582–9. See also D. Tanner, 'The electoral system, the fourth Reform Act, and the rise of Labour', *Bulletin of the Institute of Historical Research*, vol. 56 (1983), pp. 205–19 and K. Laybourn, 'The rise of Labour and the decline of liberalism: the state of the debate', *History,* vol. 80 (1995), pp. 207–26.

1931, in 1923 securing nearly three times as many votes as in 1906. In short, there is no Liberal Party equivalent of the sudden collapse of the Irish Party in 1918.

Furthermore, it is interesting that in 1906–29 the Liberals, far from performing better when they espoused collectivist social reform, fared much worse, for example in the two elections of 1910. By contrast, they did well when they stuck to Gladstonian causes such as free trade, in particular in 1906 and 1923. In 1914 Lloyd George had reached the same conclusion and was preparing to fight the next general election on land reform, another Gladstonian issue, rather than further 'New Liberal' proposals.[46] This is not all, for Duncan Tanner has demonstrated that, to all intents and purposes, before 1918 the Labour Party was similar to the Liberals and competed for the same anti-Conservative share of the vote. Other scholars, working on specific regional case studies, have shown that this continued to be the case throughout the 1920s: for example, it was temperance and the nonconformist vote that was decisive for Labour taking off in Norfolk.[47] What mattered more than anything else was that the Conservatives adopted free trade and dropped their opposition to Home Rule for Ireland and the disestablishment of the church in Wales, issues that – had the Tories stuck to their long-cherished programme – would have renewed the progressive alliance by forcing Ramsay MacDonald to support the Liberals as he had done before the war.[48]

---

46   Packer, *Lloyd George, Liberalism and the Land*, pp. 76–177, *passim*.
47   B. Doyle, 'Urban Liberalism and the "Lost Generation": politics and middle-class culture in Norwich, 1900–1935,' *Historical Journal*, vol. 38, no. 3 (1995), pp. 617–34; M. Dawson, 'Liberalism in Devon & Cornwall, 1910–31: "the old-time religion"', *Historical Journal*, vol. 38, no. 2 (1995), pp. 405–23; M. Hart, 'The Liberals, the war and the franchise', *English Historical Review*, vol. 97, no. 385 (1982), pp. 820–32; and D. Tanner, *Political Change and the Labour Party, 1900–18* (Cambridge, 1990).
48   S. Evans, 'The Conservatives and the redefinition of unionism, 1912–21', *Twentieth-Century British History*, vol. 9, no. 1 (1998), pp. 1–27.

So, far from being irrelevant and marginal, as G. B. Shaw and many historians have argued, Ireland continued to be emotive and potentially explosive at the level of popular politics. Precisely because it was so important, it had to be settled and sidelined quickly if the Conservative and Labour parties were to unlock the situation that had made both of them so impotent and marginal before 1914 and, in the case of the Conservatives, increasingly aligned on anti-constitutional policies such as Ulster militancy. The latter did bring people out onto the streets, but its threat of violence was bound to alienate the city, business and the really 'conservative' part of public opinion. In 1924 the first Labour government adopted the same priorities, largely because it was concerned with its own electoral future, and this required an end to 'progressivism', even if it meant undermining radicalism for two generations.[49] Like Bonar Law in 1913–14 and Baldwin from 1922, in his approach to Irish affairs MacDonald was guided by an ambition to see Labour in power, replacing the Liberals as the alternative to the Conservatives as a party of government.[50] As Martin Pugh has written:

> After 1918 Labour found it easier to mobilise the Irish community because the Liberals had undermined their loyalty as a result of Asquith's heavy-handed response to the Easter Rebellion in 1916 and Lloyd George's use of the Black and Tans. In any case, the settlement of the Home Rule issue in 1920–1 largely removed the previous constraints on Labour voting. On the other hand, relations were not greatly helped by the 1924 Labour government which was rather too anxious to conform to the attitudes of its Conservative predecessors towards Ireland.[51]

---

49 Kaiser, 'The decline and rise of radicalism', pp. 57–63.
50 P. Canning, *British Policy towards Ireland 1921–1941* (Oxford, 1985), p. 100.
51 M. Pugh, *Speak for Britain!: a new history of the Labour Party* (London, 2010), p. 152.

In this respect at least, far from being an innovative force making a fresh start, Labour offered little more than a combination of old liberalism and new unionism, its claims favouring Irish unity and independence being mere rhetoric. Whatever the British people thought of the matter, in the interwar years Ireland was, more than ever before, a pawn in the Westminster political game.

The fashion of the age

G. K. Peatling has argued that – had it been implemented in 1912 – Home Rule 'might have produced a long-term settlement of the Irish question which … would have been more peaceable than the events of the next ten years'.[52] This is very plausible. But of course 'the events of the next ten years' included, crucially, the First World War, which made self-government inevitable not only in Ireland, but also everywhere else in Europe – from Bohemia to Latvia and from Estonia to Poland. Furthermore, local variations of the 'Ulster question' emerged everywhere, as self-government created new disgruntled minorities and irredentist aspirations of one sort or another. Together with self-government, 'partition' had become something like the new craze of Europe, often with devastating consequences.[53]

The solution to the Anglo-Irish conflict was due not only to Conservative and Labour eagerness to 'dish' the Liberals by accepting their principles, but also to the general triumph of belief in the right of self-determination after the war. Albeit ambiguously, and in a contradictory way, 'Wilsonism' and the Versailles conference created a sort of consensus that the consistent expression of political will by a majority of the electors in a specific area would be binding on

---

52   Peatling, *British Opinion and Irish Self-government*, pp. 80–1.
53   R. W. Seton-Watson, *Eastern Europe between the Wars, 1918–1941* (London, 1945), especially chapter 7, and M. Mazower, *Dark Continent: Europe's twentieth century* (London, 1998); T. K. Wilson, *Frontiers of Violence: conflict and identity in Ulster and Upper Silesia, 1918–1922* (Oxford, 2010).

existing governments and international opinion, and also would be sanctioned by the League of Nations. In the United Kingdom this was no novel principle: as early as 1886 such an idea had been an important part of the reasoning behind Gladstone's decision to offer Home Rule to Parnell in the aftermath of the landslide victory of the Irish Party in 1885, when it secured over eighty per cent of the Irish seats at Westminster. At the time this claim had been bitterly contested by the Conservatives and the Liberal Unionists, and only partly accepted by Liberal imperialists, including Asquith, because of the idea that constitutional legitimacy and imperial sovereignty could not be partitioned and that it was only the people of the United Kingdom as a whole who could sanction the end of the union. From this perspective, the 1912–17 debates represent an intermediate stage, during which the various parties – the government, the Irish nationalists and the Ulster unionists – negotiated a new understanding of constitutional legitimacy involving the view that, after all, sovereignty *was* divisible. Partition, and the establishment of two Home Rule governments instead of one, was the direction in which such debate was already clearly going in the summer of 1914, but even the victory of Sinn Féin in the 1918 general election failed to convince the coalition government of the separatist will of the south. However, 'Once the local government election of January 1920 confirmed the political dominance of Sinn Féin in nationalist Ireland, Lloyd George moved quietly to lay the foundation of a rapprochement with it.'[54]

By the same token, the equally resolute will of a majority of the north-eastern electors to stay within the United Kingdom was more compelling in 1920 than it had been in 1914, precisely because partition had become common democratic practice in Europe after the

---

54 B. Follis, *A State under Siege: the establishment of Northern Ireland 1920–1925* (Oxford, 1995), p. 188.

war. The creation of a distinct administration in Belfast represented the acceptance of such a will and an acknowledgement that Northern Ireland was different not only from the twenty-six counties, but also from the rest of the United Kingdom.

Throughout the nineteenth century Ireland had been the recipient of much British political and social engineering. The establishment of Northern Ireland in 1920 marked a further radical development in this direction. The province became a distinct political unit, with high levels of devolved executive and administrative authority, combined with continuing and increasing central government expenditure. Not only was this in itself unprecedented as a model of constitutional interaction between London and a component part of the United Kingdom, but also unparalleled within the British Empire and very different from colonial self-government as implemented in Canada, Australia, New Zealand and South Africa.

This came at a price, for the six counties included – and still do – a substantial nationalist minority: thus 'the price of Ulster Unionist self-determination was its denial to northern nationalists'.[55] As Bryan Follis has written:

> Granting self-government in Ireland was a means of facilitating Irish nationalist claims to self-determination, while the establishment of Northern Ireland was an attempt to meet Ulster unionist claims for self-determination outside of an Irish state. While the 1920 Act was not a source of the Irish problem, neither was it a solution, since partition could be no more than an exercise in conflict-management.[56]

More or less the same thing happened almost everywhere in Europe: partition was the only way of dealing with the fragmentation of

---

55 *Ibid.*
56 *Ibid.*, p. 191.

multi-ethnic states – the Habsburg, the Hohenzollern, the Romanov and the Ottoman empires. From Latvia to the Balkans, from Poland to Czechoslovakia, Austria and Yugoslavia, partition created new disgruntled minorities with a need for protection and civil rights. Everywhere, the solution to the local equivalent of the 'Irish question' created marginalised minorities. The new 'nation states' could not match pre-existing ethnic/cultural/religious divides, and the search for homogeneity led not only to the Balkanisation of the territories of former multi-ethnic empires, but also to population exchange on an unprecedented scale, wars, the assertion of German and eventually Soviet imperialism, and further fragmentation of the political map. Minorities ceased to be internal matters for individual states and became an international problem, closely linked to the preservation of peace – of which there was little in the 1920s.[57] The minorities' most vocal champions were the eastern European Germans, such as Paul Schiemann in the Baltic states. Schiemann advocated 'the transfer of freedom of conscience from the religious to the cultural realm': against an 'absolutist' nation state, that is, the modern state's claim to monopoly of citizens' allegiance.[58] In 1918, indeed, the Baltic states embraced the idea of non-territorial cultural autonomy and minorities became cultural corporations recognised by the state.[59] This involved a government policy that not only sanctioned the self-contained status of religious or secular groups, but provided public funding for their separate institutions, including schools and places of worship or meeting. For their part, the minorities thus recognised provided 'cradle-to-the-grave' support for their own communities,

---

57 R. Gerwarth and J. Horne (eds), *War in Peace: paramilitary violence in Europe after the Great War* (Oxford, 2012).

58 J. Hiden, *Defender of Minorities: Paul Schiemann, 1876–1944* (London, 2004), p. 132.

59 J. Hiden and D. Smith, 'Looking beyond the nation state: a Baltic vision for national minorities between the wars', *Journal of Contemporary History*, vol. 41, no. 3 (2006), pp. 387–99.

segmenting society into religious and secular blocs and subcultures. This amounted to something like 'segmented pluralism': societies were seemingly tolerant of minorities, while at the same time segregating them, according to a system that in the Netherlands and Belgium was known as 'pillarisation'.[60]

Conclusion

When considered within such a European post-imperial conceptual framework, Ireland's experience is far from 'peculiar'. In fact it exemplifies problems affecting many other regions and countries in post-1918 Europe, where the disintegration of multi-national empires created a kaleidoscopic and multi-layered reality, within which minorities struggled to come to terms with the expectations of newly created 'nation states'.

Yet, as Michael Laffan has noted, 'in contrast to those terms of the Versailles Treaty which concerned plebiscites and the demarcation of frontiers, the terms of the boundary commission proposed by the British were vague and ambiguous'.[61] The inhabitants of the disputed areas of Ulster were not consulted and even the Irish delegation abandoned the demand that they should be. Clearly a line was drawn prescribing the level at which the principle of 'self-determination' could be applied, and, in contrast to the debates of 1912–14, this now meant that there would be no opt-out clause at county level in Ulster.

This was a major concession to the northern unionists, though they claimed to be disappointed and betrayed. As Carson said in a speech in the Lords, 'I was only a puppet, and so was Ulster, and so was Ireland, in the political game that was to get the Conservative Party into power.'[62] This was true enough, but had no relevance to the outcome as far as Ulster and Ireland were concerned. A majority

---

60   C. de Voogd, *Histoire des Pays-Bas des origines à nos jours* (Paris, 2004).
61   M. Laffan, *The Partition of Ireland 1911–1925* (Dublin, 1983), p. 88.
62   *Ibid.*, p. 89.

of the population of some counties might well have preferred to be governed by Dublin rather than Belfast, while some in the south were desperate to escape the feared 'Rome rule' of a nationalist state. But, as in Czechoslovakia or Poland, partition had to be territorially workable and sustainable to prevent violence and achieve a viable political solution, and this involved disappointing some communities, including the Sudeten Germans, the Polish Masurians and the northern Irish nationalists.

In Ireland this outcome was facilitated by the fact that southern negotiators were more interested in trimming down the authority of the king within the Irish Free State than in winning national unity, while the British were primarily concerned about the fiscal and financial stability of both Irish states. As Churchill wrote to his wife Clementine in August 1922:

> The session closed peacefully with a quiet Irish debate. I think things may yet turn out well there. Extraordinary people! They are all paying their taxes. Revenue is up to the mark: cattle trade roaring. Record entries for the horse show. And civil war galore! All that they cd. desire.[63]

Like Gladstone in the 1880s, in the 1920s Churchill preferred financial rectitude and a reliable relationship with a semi-independent partner, however nationalist, than direct British control with its military and fiscal complications. Under the Treaty the Irish were going out of their way to meet his expectations and hope. Unfortunately, the 'happy ending' of the boundary dispute in 1925 – when, '[i]n return for promises for the Irish ministers not to meddle any longer in the internal affairs of Northern Ireland on behalf of the Catholic minority, Craig agreed that the determination of the Boundary Commission should remain a secret' – took even Churchill aback,

---

63   Letter of 4 August 1922, cited in Canning, *British Policy*, p. 29.

and he pleaded in vain for the two Irish governments to agree on a joint plan for future action.[64] William T. Cosgrave's unwillingness to subject his government's policy to domestic debate and radical nationalist criticism was further confirmed by his decision not to submit to the Dáil Éireann for approval the so-called Ultimate Financial Agreement between Britain and the Irish Free State. This was to result in a major dispute from 1932–8, when Éamon de Valera decided unilaterally to discontinue the payment of the land annuities.

Many aspects of what was supposed to constitute Ireland's 'exceptionalism' have started to look much more 'normal' since 1989, when the grand secular ideologies of the Cold War collapsed and more traditional values and passions resurfaced. In particular, it used to be believed that the challenges experienced by Ireland in the twentieth century – with religion hardening collective identities in the way that it did in the days of the Reformation – were unusual in the 'modern' world, allegedly shaped by materialist ideologies. Indeed, in the 1920s there were government officials whose confidence in the secularist certainties of the age were such that they could not admit exceptions, even for Northern Ireland. In particular, F. B. Bourdillon, the secretary of the Boundary Commission, and a man 'who had prior experience with the Upper Silesian Commission', and who 'made it clear beforehand that he did not regard religion ... to be of much, if any, importance, in regard to the delimitation of a boundary'.[65] He should have known better, given the extent to which ethnic violence in Upper Silesia was inspired by religious differences.[66] Sectarianism was central to much of the debate on minorities and national identity in central and eastern Europe throughout the period from 1915 to 1955, from the expulsion of Muslims and Christians from, respectively, Greece and Turkey, to the persecution of the Armenians,

---

64 *Ibid.*, p. 106.
65 *Ibid.*, p. 102.
66 Wilson, *Frontiers of Violence, passim.*

the minority legislation in Latvia and Estonia, and the campaign to Catholicise Masurian and German Poles and Protestant Czechs. Later, the Holocaust added a much more tragic dimension to the whole debate on ethnicity and national identity, but even the Cold War was not enough to quench the fire generated by the religious issue when mixed with national boundaries, as illustrated by Hubert Butler's campaigns on behalf of the Orthodox Christians in central and eastern Europe. Events in recent decades in the Balkans and elsewhere have made us think twice about the secularist assumptions of policy-makers and analysts like Bourdillon. Their teleological vision of modernity, national identity and secularism has been further undermined by Islamic and Christian revivals in the twenty-first century. Nowadays most scholars agree with Peter Berger that the crucial relationship is not between modernisation and secularisation, but between the latter and religious pluralism.[67]

That the problems of 1919 were long term and effectively insoluble within the parameters of 'self-determination' was already evident by 1945. Over the next seventy years the rise of the European Union created a multi-ethnic, multi-national system for the management of common economic interests and resources, but also, unwittingly, a facilitating mechanism for the fragmentation of the old 'nation states' such as Spain and Britain. How this process will develop depends on the outcome of the Scottish referendum and the reform or final collapse of the eurozone. One thing, however, is certain: the problems of identity and governance with which the people of 1912 struggled are still present and are likely to remain so for the foreseeable future.

---

67 P. Berger, 'Introduction: the cultural dynamics of globalization', in P. Berger and S. P. Huntington, *Many Globalizations: cultural diversity in the contemporary world* (Oxford, 2002), pp. 12–6.

Index

L

M